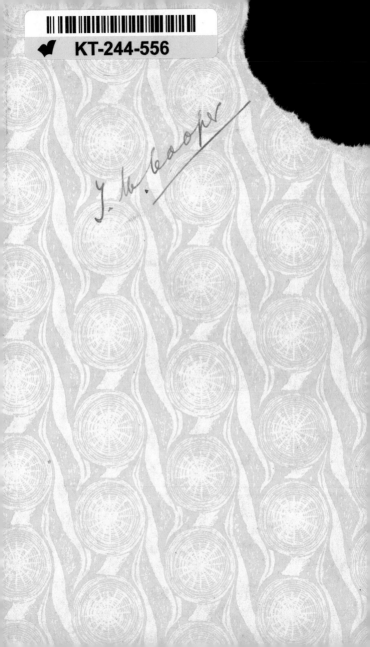

Everyman, I will go with thee, and be thy guide,
In thy most need to go by thy side.

This is No. 948 of Everyman's Library. A
list of authors and their works in this series
will be found at the end of this volume. The
publishers will be pleased to send freely to all
applicants a separate, annotated list of the
Library.

J. M. DENT & SONS LIMITED
10–13 BEDFORD STREET LONDON W.C.2

E. P. DUTTON & CO. INC.
286–302 FOURTH AVENUE
NEW YORK

EVERYMAN'S LIBRARY
EDITED BY ERNEST RHYS

ESSAYS & BELLES-LETTRES

STORIES, ESSAYS, & POEMS
BY HILAIRE BELLOC

HILAIRE BELLOC, born on 27th July 1870.
Educated at The Oratory School, Edgbaston.
After leaving school served as a driver in the
8th Regiment of French Artillery at Toul.
Matriculated at Balliol College, Oxford, in
January 1893 (Brackenbury History Scholar,
and 1st Class in Honour History Schools in
June 1895).

STORIES, ESSAYS, AND POEMS

HILAIRE BELLOC

LONDON: J. M. DENT & SONS LTD

INTRODUCTION

MR HILAIRE BELLOC is famous for many things — for his histories, for his poems, for his seafaring, for his landfaring, for his prodigious knowledge, for his prodigious conversation, for his epigrams, for his invective, for his passion for telephoning, for his wit, and for his Legend with a capital L, and for scores of other intellectual qualities, day-to-day exploits, and permanent achievements.

But in a short preface to an anthology of Mr Belloc's work, it is right to sweep aside the great mass of things for which he might be, has been, and will be, praised elsewhere, and to speak only of his qualities as a writer of English prose and a writer of English poetry. It is these two qualities which are commemorated in this volume and it is by these that his ultimate fame will be secured.

Let us consider his prose-writing first.

There are, I suppose, two ingredients which make or mar all prose in any language—the choice of words and the order in which those words are placed. And both these ingredients must have lucidity. They must be understood by the ordinary reader. There is nothing clever in using a complicated word; it merely implies the ownership of a big dictionary. There is nothing clever in the construction of a complicated sentence. It merely demonstrates the ownership of a muddled mind. The first thing to be said about Mr Belloc's prose is that every line is clear. I defy any one to produce a line of his the meaning of which is not completely obvious at the first glance. You may passionately disagree with what he says, you may stubbornly disbelieve what he says, but at least you know with certainty exactly what it is that he is saying.

This transparent clarity of Mr Belloc's is often ascribed to the French strain in his heredity, and it may be so. But there is nothing French in his other great quality — his amazing command of variation. French is essentially a language of conventionality, beautiful and limited, felicitous and almost stiff. Mr Belloc's English can best be compared to an orchestra —or perhaps to that delicious personage of our youth, 'the one-man band.' Many people can imitate—rather unsuccessfully—his reverberating thunder; many people have toyed with the idea that they can touch the light elegance of *The Path to Rome*; or that they can be thoughtfully and gaily romantic as in *The Four Men*; or deeply musical as in some of his revolutionary pages. But no one, so far as I know, has ever had the nerve to think he could play as Mr Belloc does on all the instruments of the great orchestra, or move with such certainty and ease from one instrument to another in the course of a single small piece.

This power of swift transition is one of Mr Belloc's secrets. He never lets the mental ear of the reader grow accustomed to one style or one note. As with his rhythms and his endless variations on the instruments between trumpets and flutes, so with his choice of words. The best-known quotations from Mr Belloc are the splendid and sonorous passages such as the last page of his *Danton* or his 'So perished the French Monarchy,' and very splendid they are. But almost as exciting, and certainly as moving, is his sudden and unexpected use of little words. Listen to this, for instance, from an article in the *Observer* on the death of G. K. Chesterton:

> Who shall determine whether a man does more by speaking or by writing, if in both he is lucid and illuminates all that he touches? Sometimes speech alone, and in a small circle, has had higher effect than any writing; sometimes the man who can reach the limits of excellence in writing has of speech no power at all. In Gilbert Chesterton the two were so welded that I sometimes think in reading printed sentences of his that I still hear his voice. It was a voice from which I learnt continually, from the first day I heard it until the last; acquiring from it discoveries, explanations, definitions which continue to increase my possessions.
> Nor does it cease. Nor will it cease.

There is a perfect felicity about that sequence of small words at the end which only a master could achieve.

But although Mr Belloc is the greatest living master of prose form in the language, it is as a poet that he touches the Pleiades. For when he writes as a poet his subject is the universal theme of poetry, and so is indissolubly joined to the magic of the words. Many poets have written badly about Love and some, like Swinburne, have written magnificently about Nothing or Zero or General Emptiness—whatever you like to call it. But none, since Shakespeare wrote his sonnets, have written about Love with such beauty and such passionate fire as Mr Belloc. His sonnets are burning with love, love of God and of women and of beauty, the triple universal theme of all true poetry. Who since Shakespeare could have written this?

> What are the names for Beauty? Who shall praise
> God's pledge he can fulfil His creatures' eyes?
> Or what strong words of what creative phrase
> Determine Beauty's title in the skies?
> But I will call you Beauty Personate,
> Ambassadorial Beauty, and again
> Beauty triumphant, Beauty in the Gate,
> Beauty salvation of the souls of men.

Or is there any verse in our poetry that is more moving in its simplicity than:

> And when your prayers complete the day,
>   Darling, your little tiny hands
> Were also made, I think, to pray
>   For men that lose their fairylands.

My one regret about this anthology is that for technical reasons it has not been possible to include in it the great poem *In Praise of Wine*. This is the climax of Mr Belloc's poetry. Indeed, it may be called the climax of Mr Belloc's life. For it is more than a poem. It is an affirmation of faith in all the things in which he has always believed and for which he has always fought. In eight pages of 'rhymed heroic couplets' he praises all that Latin civilization means to the world, Mediterranean sun and Orvieto wine and gaiety and the Catholic Faith and discipline and the invention of the arch, and then adds his final prayer, in which all that he has praised becomes personal to himself:

> When from the waste of such long labour done
> I too must leave the grape-ennobling sun
> And like the vineyard worker take my way
> Down the long shadows of declining day,
> Bend on the sombre plain my clouded sight
> And leave the mountain to the advancing night,
> Come to the term of all that was mine own
> With nothingness before me, and alone;

and then all that has become personal to himself is symbolized in the Last Sacrament:

> So, my Friend,
> Let not Your cup desert me in the end.
> But when the hour of mine adventure 's near,
> Just and benignant, let my youth appear

* A 948 A

Bearing a Chalice, open, golden, wide,
With benediction graven on its side.
So touch my dying lip: so bridge that deep:
So pledge my waking from the gift of sleep,
And, sacramental, raise me the Divine:
Strong brother in God and last companion, Wine.

Reputations rise and fall. Some who are accounted great in one century are very small beer in the next and vice versa, and the critics who acclaimed the one and trounced the other look correspondingly foolish. But I am not afraid to put it on record, in this page, that I hold Mr Hilaire Belloc to be the greatest master of English prose and poetry in our time.

1938.   A. G. MACDONELL.

The following is a list of the chief works of Hilaire Belloc with the date of their first appearance in volume form:

Verses and Sonnets, 1895; *The Bad Child's Book of Beasts*, 1896; *More Beasts for Worse Children*, 1897; *The Modern Traveller*, 1898; *A Moral Alphabet*, 1899; *Danton*, 1899; *Lambkin's Remains*, 1900; *Paris*, 1900; *Robespierre*, 1901; *The Path to Rome*, 1902; *Caliban's Guide to Letters*, 1903; *Avril*, 1904; *Mr Burden*, 1904; *The Old Road*, 1905; *Esto Perpetua*, 1906; *Hills and the Sea*, 1906; *The Historic Thames*, 1907; *Cautionary Tales*, 1907; *On Nothing*, 1908; *The Eye-Witness*, 1908; *Mr Clutterbuck's Election*, 1908; *The Pyrenees*, 1909; *On Everything*, 1909; *A Change in the Cabinet*, 1909; *Marie Antoinette*, 1910; *On Anything*, 1910; *Pongo and the Bull*, 1910; *Verses*, 1910; *The Great Enquiry*, 1910; *The Girondin*, 1911; *More Peers*, 1911; *The Party System* (with Mr C. Chesterton), 1911; *On Something*, 1911; *First and Last*, 1911; *The French Revolution*, 1911; *Warfare in England*, 1912; *The Four Men*, 1912; *The Green Overcoat*, 1912; *The Servile State*, 1912; *The River of London*, 1913; *This and That*, 1913; *The Stane Street*, 1913; *The Book of the Bayeux Tapestry*, 1913; *Continuation of Lingard's History*, 1914; *The European War, First Phase*, 1915; *The European War, Second Phase*, 1916; *The Last Days of the French Monarchy*, 1916; *The Free Press*, 1917; *The Principles of War*, 1918; *Europe and the Faith*, 1920; *The House of Commons and the Monarchy*, 1920; *The Jews*, 1922 (new and revised ed. 1937); *The Mercy of Allah*, 1922; *The Campaign of 1812 and the Retreat from Moscow*, 1923; *On*, 1923; *The Contrast*, 1923; *Economics for Helen*, 1924; *Sonnets and Verse*, 1924 (new and enlarged ed. 1938); *History of England*, vols. i and ii 1925, vol. iii 1928, vol. iv 1932; *The Cruise of the 'Nona,'* 1925; *Mr Petre*, 1925; *Miniatures of French History*, 1925; *The Emerald of Catherine the Great*, 1926; *A Companion to Mr Wells' 'History of the World,'* 1926; *The Haunted House*, 1927; *James II*, 1928; *Many Cities*, 1928; *But Soft, we are Observed*, 1928; *A Conversation with an Angel*, 1928; *How the Reformation Happened*, 1928; *Where are the Dead ?*, 1928; *Belinda*, 1928; *Short Talks with the Dead*, 1928; *Survivals and New Arrivals*, 1929; *Joan of Arc*, 1929; *The Missing Masterpiece*, 1929; *Richelieu*, 1929; *The Man who made Gold*, 1930; *Wolsey*, 1930; *New Cautionary Tales*, 1930; *Cromwell*, 1931; *Cranmer*, 1931; *A Conversation with a Cat*, 1931; *Six British Battles*, 1931; *The Postmaster-General*, 1932; *Napoleon*, 1932; *Essays of a Catholic*, 1932; *Charles I*, 1933; *The Tactics and Strategy of the Great Duke of Marlborough*, 1933; *William the Conqueror*, 1933; *Cromwell*, 1934; *A Short History of England*, 1934; *Milton*, 1935; *Sussex*, 1936; *The Battleground*, 1936; *The Hedge and the Horse*, 1936; *The Crusade*, 1937; *Characters of the Reformation*, 1937; *The Crisis of our Civilization*, 1937; *An Essay on the Nature of Contemporary England*, 1937; *Monarchy, a Study of Louis XIV*, 1938; *Return to the Baltic*, 1938.

CONTENTS

V. CRITICISM

VI. SONNETS AND VERSE

I. ESSAYS

THE MOWING OF A FIELD

THERE is a valley in South England remote from ambition and from fear, where the passage of strangers is rare and unperceived, and where the scent of the grass in summer is breathed only by those who are native to that unvisited land. The roads to the Channel do not traverse it; they choose upon either side easier passes over the range. One track alone leads up through it to the hills, and this is changeable: now green where men have little occasion to go, now a good road where it nears the homesteads and the barns. The woods grow steep above the slopes; they reach sometimes the very summit of the heights, or, when they cannot attain them, fill in and clothe the coombes. And, in between, along the floor of the valley, deep pastures and their silence are bordered by lawns of chalky grass and the small yew trees of the Downs.

The clouds that visit its sky reveal themselves beyond the one great rise, and sail, white and enormous, to the other, and sink beyond that other. But the plains above which they have travelled and the Weald to which they go, the people of the valley cannot see and hardly recall. The wind, when it reaches such fields, is no longer a gale from the salt, but fruitful and soft, an inland breeze; and those whose blood was nourished here feel in that wind the fruitfulness of our orchards and all the life that all things draw from the air.

In this place, when I was a boy, I pushed through a fringe of beeches that made a complete screen between me and the world, and I came to a glade called No Man's Land. I climbed beyond it, and I was surprised and glad, because from the ridge of that glade I saw the sea. To this place very lately I returned.

The many things that I recovered as I came up the countryside were not less charming than when a distant memory had enshrined them, but much more. Whatever veil is thrown by a longing recollection had not intensified nor even made more mysterious the beauty of that happy ground; not in my very dreams of morning had I, in exile, seen it more beloved or more rare. Much also that I had forgotten now returned to me as I approached—a group of elms, a little turn of the parson's wall, a small paddock beyond the graveyard close, cherished by one man, with a low wall of very old stone guarding it all round. And all these things fulfilled and amplified my delight, till even the good vision of the place, which I had kept so many years, left me and was replaced by its better reality. 'Here,' I said to myself, 'is a symbol of what some say is reserved for the soul: pleasure of a kind which cannot be imagined save in a moment when at last it is attained.'

When I came to my own gate and my own field, and had before me the house I knew, I looked around a little (though it was already evening), and I saw that the grass was standing as it should stand when it is ready for the scythe. For in this, as in everything that a man can do—of those things at least which are very old—there is an exact moment when they are done best. And it has been remarked of whatever rules us that it works blunderingly, seeing that the good things given to man are not given at the precise moment when they would have filled him with delight. But, whether this be true or false, we can choose the just turn of the seasons in everything we do of our own will, and especially in the making of hay. Many think that hay is best made when the grass is thickest; and so they delay until it is rank and in flower, and has already heavily pulled the ground. And there is another false reason for delay, which is wet weather. For very few will understand (though it comes year after year) that we have rain always in South England between the sickle and the scythe, or say just after the weeks of east wind are over. First we have a week of sudden warmth, as though the South had come to see us all; then we have the weeks of east and south-east wind; and then we have more or less of that rain of which I spoke, and which always astonishes the world. Now it is just before, or during, or at the very end of that rain—but not later—that grass should be cut for hay. True, upland grass, which is always thin, should be cut earlier than the grass in the bottoms and along the water meadows; but not even the latest, even in the wettest seasons, should be left (as it is) to flower and even to seed. For what we get when we store our grass is not a harvest of something ripe, but a thing just caught in its prime before maturity: as witness that our corn and straw are best yellow, but our hay is best green. So also Death should be represented with a scythe and Time with a sickle; for Time can take only what is ripe, but Death comes always too soon. In a word, then, it is always much easier to cut grass too late than too early; and I, under that evening and come back to these pleasant fields, looked at the grass and knew that it was time. June was in full advance, it was the beginning of that season when the night has already lost her foothold of the earth and hovers over it, never quite descending, but mixing sunset with the dawn.

Next morning, before it was yet broad day, I awoke, and thought of the mowing. The birds were already chattering in the trees beside my window, all except the nightingale, which had left and flown away to the Weald, where he sings all summer by day as well as by night in the oaks and the hazel spinneys, and especially along the little river Adur, one of the rivers of the Weald. The birds and the thought of the mowing had awakened me, and I went down the stairs and along the stone floors to where I could find a scythe; and when I took it from its nail, I remembered how, fourteen years ago, I had last gone out with my scythe, just so, into the fields at morning. In between that day and this were many things, cities and armies, and a confusion of books, mountains and the desert, and horrible great breadths of sea.

When I got out into the long grass the sun was not yet risen, but there were already many colours in the eastern sky, and I made haste to sharpen my scythe, so that I might get to the cutting before the dew should dry. Some say that it is best to wait till all the dew has risen, so as to get the grass quite dry from the very first. But, though it is an advantage to get the grass quite dry, yet it is not worth while to wait till the dew has risen. For, in the first place, you lose many hours of work (and those the coolest), and next—which is more important— you lose that great ease and thickness in cutting which comes of the dew. So I at once began to sharpen my scythe.

There is an art also in the sharpening of a scythe, and it is worth describing carefully. Your blade must be dry, and that is why you will see men rubbing the scythe-blade with grass before they whet it. Then also your rubber must be quite dry, and on this account it is a good thing to lay it on your coat and keep it there during all your day's mowing. The scythe you stand upright, with the blade pointing away from you, and you put your left hand firmly on the back of the blade, grasping it: then you pass the rubber first down one side of the blade-edge and then down the other, beginning near the handle and going on to the point and working quickly and hard. When you first do this you will, perhaps, cut your hand; but it is only at first that such an accident will happen to you.

To tell when the scythe is sharp enough this is the rule. First the stone clangs and grinds against the iron harshly; then it rings musically to one note; then, at last, it purrs as though the iron and stone were exactly suited. When you hear this, your scythe is sharp enough; and I, when I heard it that June dawn, with everything quite silent except the birds, let down the scythe and bent myself to mow.

When one does anything anew, after so many years, one fears very much for one's trick or habit. But all things once learnt are easily recoverable, and I very soon recovered the swing and power of the mower. Mowing well and mowing badly —or rather not mowing at all—are separated by very little; as is also true of writing verse, of playing the fiddle, and of dozens of other things, but of nothing more than of believing. For the bad or young or untaught mower without tradition, the mower Promethean, the mower original and contemptuous of the past, does all these things: He leaves great crescents of grass uncut. He digs the point of the scythe hard into the ground with a jerk. He loosens the handles and even the fastening of the blade. He twists the blade with his blunders, he blunts the blade, he chips it, dulls it, or breaks it clean off at the tip. If any one is standing by he cuts him in the ankle. He sweeps up into the air wildly, with nothing to resist his stroke. He drags up earth with the grass, which is like making the meadow bleed. But the good mower who does things just as they should be done and have been for a hundred thousand years, falls into none of these fooleries. He goes forward very steadily, his scythe-blade just barely missing the ground, every grass falling; the swish and rhythm of his mowing are always the same.

So great an art can only be learnt by continual practice; but this much is worth writing down, that, as in all good work, to know the thing with which you work is the core of the affair. Good verse is best written on good paper with an easy pen, not with a lump of coal on a whitewashed wall. The pen thinks for you; and so does the scythe mow for you if you treat it honourably and in a manner that makes it recognize its service. The manner is this. You must regard the scythe as a pendulum that swings, not as a knife that cuts. A good mower puts no more strength into his stroke than into his lifting. Again, stand up to your work. The bad mower, eager and full of pain, leans forward and tries to force the scythe through the grass. The good mower, serene and able, stands as nearly straight as the shape of the scythe will let him, and follows up every stroke closely, moving his left foot forward. Then also let every stroke get well away. Mowing is a thing of ample gestures, like drawing a cartoon. Then, again, get yourself into a mechanical and repetitive mood: be thinking of anything at all but your mowing, and be anxious only when there seems some interruption to the monotony of the sound. In this mowing should be like one's prayers—all of a sort and always the same, and so made that you can establish a monotony and work them, as it were, with half your mind: that happier half, the half that does not bother.

In this way, when I had recovered the art after so many years, I went forward over the field, cutting lane after lane through the grass, and bringing out its most secret essences with the sweep of the scythe until the air was full of odours. At the end of every lane I sharpened my scythe and looked back at the work done, and then carried my scythe down again upon my shoulder to begin another. So, long before the bell rang in the chapel above me—that is, long before six o'clock, which is the time for the *Angelus*—I had many swathes already lying in order parallel like soldiery; and the high grass yet standing, making a great contrast with the shaven part, looked dense and high. As it says in the *Ballad of Val-ès-Dunes*, where—

> The tall son of the Seven Winds
> Came riding out of Hither-hythe,

and his horse-hoofs (you will remember) trampled into the press and made a gap in it, and his sword (as you know)

> . . . was like a scythe
> In Arcus when the grass is high
> And all the swathes in order lie,
> And there's the bailiff standing by
> A-gathering of the tithe.

So I mowed all that morning, till the houses awoke in the valley, and from some of them rose a little fragrant smoke, and men began to be seen.

I stood still and rested on my scythe to watch the awakening of the village, when I saw coming up to my field a man whom I had known in older times, before I had left the Valley.

He was of that dark silent race upon which all the learned quarrel, but which, by whatever meaningless name it may be called—Iberian, or Celtic, or what you will—is the permanent root of all England, and makes England wealthy and preserves it everywhere, except perhaps in the Fens and in a part of Yorkshire. Everywhere else you will find it active and strong. These people are intensive: their thoughts and their labours turn inward. It is on account of their presence in these islands that our gardens are the richest in the world. They also love low rooms and ample fires and great warm slopes of thatch. They have, as I believe, an older acquaintance with the English air than any other of all the strains that make up England. They hunted in the Weald with stones, and camped in the pines of the green-sand. They lurked under the oaks of the upper rivers, and saw the legionaries go up, up the straight paved road from the sea. They helped the few pirates to destroy the towns, and mixed with those pirates and shared the spoils of the Roman villas, and were glad to see the captains and the priests destroyed. They remain; and no admixture of the Frisian pirates, or the Breton, or the Angevin and Norman conquerors, has very much affected their cunning eyes.

To this race, I say, belonged the man who now approached me. And he said to me, 'Mowing?' And I answered, 'Ar.' Then he also said 'Ar,' as in duty bound; for so we speak to each other in the Stenes of the Downs.

Next he told me that, as he had nothing to do, he would lend me a hand; and I thanked him warmly, or, as we say, 'kindly.' For it is a good custom of ours always to treat bargaining as though it were a courteous pastime; and though what he was after was money, and what I wanted was his labour at the least pay, yet we both played the comedy that we were free men, the one granting a grace and the other accepting it. For the dry bones of commerce, avarice and method and need, are odious to the Valley; and we cover them up with a pretty body of fiction and observances. Thus, when it comes to buying pigs, the buyer does not begin to decry the pig and the vendor to praise it, as is the custom with lesser men; but tradition makes them do business in this fashion:

First the buyer will go up to the seller when he sees him in his own steading, and, looking at the pig with admiration, the buyer will say that rain may or may not fall, or that we shall have snow or thunder, according to the time of year. Then the seller, looking critically at the pig, will agree that the weather is as his friend maintains. There is no haste at all; great leisure marks the dignity of their exchange. And the next step is, that the buyer says: 'That's a fine pig you have there, Mr ———'

(giving the seller's name). 'Ar, powerful fine pig.' Then the seller, saying also 'Mr' (for twin brothers rocked in one cradle give each other ceremonious observance here), the seller, I say, admits, as though with reluctance, the strength and beauty of the pig, and falls into deep thought. Then the buyer says, as though moved by a great desire, that he is ready to give so much for the pig, naming half the proper price, or a little less. Then the seller remains in silence for some moments; and at last begins to shake his head slowly, till he says: 'I don't be thinking of selling the pig, anyways.' He will also add that a party only Wednesday offered him so much for the pig—and he names about double the proper price. Thus all ritual is duly accomplished; and the solemn act is entered upon with reverence and in a spirit of truth. For when the buyer uses this phrase: 'I'll tell you what I *will* do,' and offers within half a crown of the pig's value, the seller replies that he can refuse him nothing, and names half a crown above its value; the difference is split, the pig is sold, and in the quiet soul of each runs the peace of something accomplished.

Thus do we buy a pig or land or labour or malt or lime, always with elaboration and set forms; and many a London man has paid double and more for his violence and his greedy haste and very unchivalrous higgling. As happened with the land at Underwaltham, which the mortgagees had begged and implored the estate to take at twelve hundred, and had privately offered to all the world at a thousand, but which a sharp direct man, of the kind that makes great fortunes, a man in a motor car, a man in a fur coat, a man of few words, bought for two thousand three hundred before my very eyes, protesting that they might take his offer or leave it; and all because he did not begin by praising the land.

Well then, this man I spoke of offered to help me, and he went to get his scythe. But I went into the house and brought out a gallon jar of small ale for him and for me; for the sun was now very warm, and small ale goes well with mowing. When we had drunk some of this ale in mugs called 'I see you,' we took each a swathe, he a little behind me because he was the better mower; and so for many hours we swung, one before the other, mowing and mowing at the tall grass of the field. And the sun rose to noon and we were still at our mowing; and we ate food, but only for a little while, and we took again to our mowing. And at last there was nothing left but a small square of grass, standing like a square of linesmen who keep their formation, tall and unbroken, with all the dead lying around them when a battle is over and done.

Then for some little time I rested after all those hours; and the man and I talked together, and a long way off we heard in another field the musical sharpening of a scythe.

The sunlight slanted powdered and mellow over the breadth of the valley; for day was nearing its end. I went to fetch rakes from the steading; and when I had come back the last of the grass had fallen, and all the field lay flat and smooth, with the very green short grass in lanes between the dead and yellow swathes.

These swathes we raked into cocks to keep them from the dew against our return at daybreak; and we made the cocks as tall and steep as we could, for in that shape they best keep off the dew, and it is easier also to spread them after the sun has risen. Then we raked up every straggling blade, till the whole field was a clean floor for the tedding and the carrying of the hay next morning. The grass we had mown was but a little over two acres; for that is all the pasture on my little tiny farm.

When we had done all this, there fell upon us the beneficent and deliberate evening; so that as we sat a little while together near the rakes, we saw the valley more solemn and dim around us, and all the trees and hedgerows quite still, and held by a complete silence. Then I paid my companion his wage, and bade him a good night, till we should meet in the same place before sunrise.

He went off with a slow and steady progress, as all our peasants do, making their walking a part of the easy but continual labour of their lives. But I sat on, watching the light creep around towards the north and change, and the waning moon coming up as though by stealth behind the woods of No Man's Land.

THE WING OF DALUA

TIME was, and that not so long ago, when the Two Men had revealed to them by their Genius a corner of Europe wherein they were promised more surprises and delights than in any other.

It was secretly made known to them that in this place there were no pictures, and that no one had praised its people, and further that no Saint had ever troubled it; and the rich and all their evils (so the two men were assured) had never known the place at all.

It was under the influence of such a message that they at once began walking at a great speed for the river which is called the River of Gold, and for the valleys of Andorra; and since it seemed that other men had dared to cross the Pyrenees and to see the Republic, and since it seemed also, according to books, records, and what not, that may have been truth or may have been lies, that common men so doing went always by one way, called the Way of Hospitalet, the Two Men determined to go by no such common path, but to march, all clothed with power, in a straight line, and to take the main range of the mountains just where they chose, and to come down upon the Andorrans unexpectedly and to deserve their admiration and perhaps their fear.

They chose, therefore, upon the map the valley of that torrent called the Aston, and before it was evening, but at an hour when the light of the sun was already very ripe and low, they stood under a great rock called Guie, which was all of bare limestone with façades as bare as the Yosemite, and almost as clean. They looked up at this great rock of Guie and made it the terminal of their attempt. I was one and my companion was the other: these were the two men who started out before a sunset in August to conquer the high Pyrenees. Before me was a very deep valley full of woods, and reaching higher and higher perpetually so that it reminded me of Hyperion; but as for my companion, it reminded him of nothing, for he said loudly that he had never seen any such things before and had never believed that summits of so astonishing a height were to be found on earth. Not even at night had he imagined such appalling upward and upward into the sky, and this he said though he had seen the Alps, of which it is true that when you are close to them they are very middling affairs; but not so the Pyrenees, which are not only great but also terrible, for they are haunted, as you shall hear. But before I begin to write of the spirits that inhabit the deserts of the Aston, I must first explain, for the sake of those who have not seen them, how the awful valleys of the Pyrenees are made.

All the high valleys of mountains go in steps, but those of the Pyrenees in a manner more regular even than those of the Sierra Nevada out in California, which the Pyrenees so greatly resemble. For the steps here are nearly always three in number between the plain and the main chain, and each is entered by a regular gate of rock. So it is in the valley of the Ariège, and so it is in that of the Aston, and so it is in every other valley until you get to the far end where live the cleanly but incomprehensible Basques. Each of these steps is perfectly level, somewhat oval in shape, a mile or two or sometimes five miles long, but not often a mile broad. Through each will run the river of the valley, and upon either side of it there will be rich pastures, and a high plain of this sort is called a *jasse*, the same as in California is called a 'flat': as 'Dutch Flat,' 'Poverty Flat,' and other famous flats.

First, then, will come a great gorge through which one marches up from the plain, and then at the head of it very often a waterfall of some kind, along the side of which one forces one's way up painfully through a narrow chasm of rock and finds above one the great green level of the first jasse with the mountains standing solemnly around it. And then when one has marched all along this level one will come to another gorge and another chasm, and when one has climbed over the barrier of rock and risen up another two thousand feet or so, one comes to a second jasse, smaller as a rule than the lower one; but so high are the mountains that all this climbing into the heart of them does not seem to have reduced their height at all. And then one marches along this second jasse and one comes to yet another gorge and climbs up just as one did the two others, through a chasm where there will be a little waterfall or a large one, and one finds at the top the smallest and most lonely of the jasses. This often has a lake in it. The mountains round it will usually be cliffs, forming sometimes a perfect ring, and so called cirques, or, by the Spaniards, cooking-pots; and as one stands on the level floor of one such last highest jasse and looks up at the summit of the cliffs, one knows that one is looking at the ridge of the main chain. Then it is one's business, if one desires to conquer the high Pyrenees, to find a sloping place up the cliffs to reach their summits and to go down into the further Spanish valleys. This is the order of the Pyrenean dale, and this was the order of that of the Aston.

Up the gorge then we went, my companion and I; the day fell as we marched, and there was a great moon out, filling the still air, when we came to the first chasm, and climbing through it saw before us, spread with a light mist over its pastures, the first jasse under the moonlight. And up we went, and up again, to the end of the second jasse, having before us the vast wall of the main range, and in our hearts a fear that there was something unblessed in the sight of it. For though neither I told it to my companion nor he to me, we had both begun to feel a fear which the shepherds of these mountains know very well. It was perhaps midnight or a little more when we made our camp, after looking in vain for a hut which may once have stood there, but now stood no longer. We lit a fire, but did not overcome the cold, which tormented us throughout the night, for the wind blew off the summits; and at last we woke from our half-sleep and spent the miserable hours in watching the Great Bear creeping round the pole, and in trying to feed the dying embers with damp fuel. And there it was that I discovered what I now make known to the world, namely, that gorse and holly will burn of themselves, even while they are yet rooted in the ground. So we sat sleepless and exhausted, and not without misgiving, for we had meant that night before camping to be right under the foot of the last cliffs, and we were yet many miles away. We were glad to see the river at last in the meadows show plainly under the growing light, the rocks turning red upon the skyline, and the extinction of the stars. As we so looked north and eastward the great rock of Guie stood up all its thousands of feet enormous against the rising of the sun.

We were very weary, and invigorated by nothing but the light, but, having that at least to strengthen us, we made at once for the main range, knowing very well that, once we were over it, it would be downhill all the way, and seeing upon our maps that there were houses and living men high in the further Andorran valley, which was not deserted like this vale of the Aston, but inhabited: full, that is, of Catalans, who would soon make us forget the inhuman loneliness of the heights, for by this time we were both convinced, though still neither of us said it to the other, that there was an evil brooding over all this place.

It was noon when, after many hours of broken marching and stumbling, which betrayed our weakness, we stood at last beside the tarn in which the last cliffs of the ridge are reflected, and here was a steep slope up which a man could scramble. We drank at the foot of it the last of our wine and ate the last of our bread, promising ourselves refreshment, light, and peace immediately upon the further side, and thus lightened of our provisions, and with more heart in us, we assaulted the final hill; but just at the summit, where there should have greeted us a great view over Spain, there lowered upon us the angry folds of a black cloud, and the first of the accidents that were set in order by some enemy to ruin us fell upon my companion and me.

For a storm broke, and that with such violence that we thought it would have shattered the bare hills, for an infernal thunder crashed from one precipice to another, and there flashed, now close to us, now vividly but far off, in the thickness of the cloud, great useless and blinding glares of lightning, and hailstones of great size fell about us also, leaping from the bare rocks like marbles. And when the rain fell it was just as though it had been from a hose, forced at one by a pressure instead of falling, and we two on that height were the sole objects of so much fury, until at last my companion cried out from the rock beneath which he was cowering, 'This is intolerable!' And I answered him, from the rock which barely covered me, 'It is not to be borne!' So in the midst of the storm we groped our way down into the valley beneath, and got below the cloud; and when we were there we thought we had saved the day, for surely we were upon the southern side of the hills, and in a very little while we should see the first roofs of the Andorrans.

For two doubtful hours we trudged down that higher valley, but there were no men, nor any trace of men except this, that here and there the semblance of a path appeared, especially where the valley fell rapidly from one stage to another over smooth rocks, which, in their least dangerous descent, showed by smooth scratches the passage of some lost animal. For the rest, nothing human nor the memory of it was there to comfort us, though in one place we found a group of cattle browsing alone without a master. There we sat down in our exhaustion and confessed at last what every hour had inwardly convinced us of with greater strength, that we were not our own masters, that there was trouble and fate all round us, that we did not know what valley this might be, and that the storm had been but the beginning of an unholy adventure. We had been snared into Fairyland.

We did not speak much together, for fear of lowering our hearts yet more by the confession one to the other of the things we knew to be true. We did not tell each other what reserve of courage remained to us, or of strength. We sat and looked at the peaks immeasurably above us, and at the veils of rain between them, and at the black background of the sky. Nor was there anything in the landscape which did not seem to us unearthly and forlorn.

It was, in a manner, more lonely than had been the very silence of the further slope: there was less to comfort and support the soul of a man; but with every step downward we were penetrated more and more with the presence of things not mortal and of influences to which any desolation is preferable. At one moment voices called to us from the water, at another we heard our names, but pronounced in a whisper so slight and so exact that the more certain we were of hearing them the less did we dare to admit the reality of what we had heard. In a third place we saw twice in succession, though we were still going forward, the same tree standing by the same stone: for neither tree nor stone was natural to the good world, but each had been put there by whatever was mocking us and drawing us on.

Already had we stumbled twice and thrice the distance that should have separated us from the first Andorran village, but we had seen nothing, not a wall, nor smoke from a fire, let alone the tower of a Christian church, or the houses of men. Nor did any length of the way now make us wonder more than we had already wondered, nor did we hope, however far we might proceed, that we should be saved unless some other influence could be found to save us from the unseen masters of this place. For by this time we had need of mutual comfort, and openly said it to one another—but in low tones—that the valley was Faëry. The river went on calling to us all the while. In places it was full of distant cheering, in others crowded with the laughter of a present multitude of tiny things, and always mocking us with innumerable tenuous voices. It grew to be evening. It was nearly two days since we had seen a man.

There stood in the broader and lower part of the valley to which we had now come, numerous rocks and boulders; for our deception some one of them or another would seem to be a man. I heard my companion call suddenly, as though to a stranger, and as he called I thought that he had indeed perceived the face of a human being, and I felt a sort of sudden health in me when I heard the tone of his voice; and when I looked up I also saw a man. We came towards him and he did not move. Close up beside his form we put out our hands: but what we touched was a rough and silent stone.

After that we spoke no more. We went on through the gathering twilight, determined to march downwards to the end, but knowing pretty well what the end would be. Once only did we again fall into the traps that were laid about us, when we went and knocked at the hillside where we thought we had seen a cottage and its oaken door, and after the mockery of that disappointment we would not be deceived again, nor make ourselves again the victims of the laughter that perpetually proceeded from the torrent.

The path led us onwards in a manner that was all one with the plot now woven round our feet. We could but follow the path, though we knew with what an evil purpose it was made: that it was as phantom as the rest. At one place it invited us to cross, upon two shaking pine trunks, the abyss of a cataract; in another it invited us to climb, in spite of our final weariness, a great barrier of rock that lay between an upper and a lower jasse. We continued upon it determinedly, with heads bent, barely hoping that perhaps at last we should emerge from this haunted ground, but the illusions which had first mocked us we resolutely refused. So much so, that where at one place there stood plainly before us in the gathering darkness a farmhouse with its trees and its close, its orchard and its garden gate, I said to my companion: 'All this place is cursed, and I will not go near.' And he applauded me, for he knew as well as I that if we had gone a few steps towards that orchard and that garden close, they would have turned into the bracken of the hillside, bare granite and unfruitful scree.

The main range, where it appeared in revelations behind us through the clouds, was far higher than mountains ever seem to waking men, and it stood quite sheer as might a precipice in a dream. The forests upon either side ran up until they were lost miles and miles above us in the storm.

Night fell and we still went onward, the one never daring to fall far behind the other, and once or twice in an hour calling to each other to make sure that another man was near; but this we did not continue, because as we went on each of us became aware under the midnight of the presence of a Third.

. . . . . .

There was a place where the path, now broad and plain, approached a sort of little sandy bay going down towards the stream, and there I saw, by a sudden glimpse of the moon through the clouds, a large cave standing wide. We went down to it in silence, we gathered brushwood, we lit a fire, and we lay down in the cave. But before we lay down I said to my companion: 'I have seen the moon—she is in the *north*. Into what place have we come?' He said to me in answer, 'Nothing here is earthly,' and after he had said this we both fell into a profound sleep in which we forgot not only cold, great hunger, and fatigue, but our own names and our very souls, and passed, as it were, into a deep bath of forgetfulness.

When we woke at the same moment, it was dawn.

We stood up in the clear and happy light and found that everything was changed. We poured water upon our faces and our hands, strode out a hundred yards and saw again the features of a man. He had a kind face of some age, and eyes such as are the eyes of mountaineers, which seem to have constantly contemplated distant horizons and wide plains beneath their homes. We heard as he came up the sound of a bell in a Christian church below, and we exchanged with him the salutations of living men. Then I said to him: 'What day is this?' He said 'Sunday,' and a sort of memory of our fear came on us, for we had lost a day.

Then I said to him: 'What river are we upon, and what valley is this?'

He answered: 'The river and the valley of the Aston.' And what he said was true, for as we rounded a corner we perceived right before us a barrier, that rock of Guie from which we had set out. We had come down again into France, and into the very dale by which we had begun our ascent.

But what that valley was which had led us from the summits round backward to our starting-place, forcing upon us the refusal of whatever powers protect this passage of the chain, I have never been able to tell. It is not upon the maps; by our description the peasants knew nothing of it. No book tells of it. No men except ourselves have seen it, and I am willing to believe that it is not of this world.

THE FIRST DAY'S MARCH

I very well remember the spring breaking ten years ago in Lorraine. I remember it better far than I shall ever remember another spring, because one of those petty summits of emotion that seem in boyhood like the peaks of the world was before me. We were going off to camp.

Since every man that fires guns or drives them in France— that is, some hundred thousand and more at any one time, and taking in reserves, half a million—must go to camp in his time, and that more than once, it seems monstrous that a boy should make so much of it; but then to a boy six months is a little lifetime, and for six months I had passed through that great annealing fire of drill which stamps and moulds the French people to-day, putting too much knowledge and bitterness into their eyes, but a great determination into their gestures and a trained tenacity into the methods of their thought.

To me also this fire seemed fiercer and more transforming because, until the day when they had marched me up to barracks in the dark and the rain with the batch of recruits, I had known nothing but the easy illusions and the comfort of an English village, and had had but journeys or short visits to teach me that enduring mystery of Europe, the French temper: whose aims and reticence, whose hidden enthusiasms, great range of effort, divisions, defeats, and resurrections must now remain the principal problem before my mind; for the few who had seen this sight know that the French mind is the pivot on which Europe turns.

I had come into the regiment faulty in my grammar and doubtful in accent, ignorant especially of those things which in every civilization are taken for granted but never explained in full; I was ignorant, therefore, of the key which alone can open that civilization to a stranger. Things irksome or a heavy burden to the young men of my age, born and brought up in the French air, were to me, brought up with Englishmen an Englishman, odious and bewildering. Orders that I but half comprehended; simple phrases that seemed charged with menace; boasting (a habit of which I knew little), coupled with a fierce and, as it were, expected courage that seemed ill suited to boasting—and certainly unknown outside this army; enormous powers of endurance in men whose stature my English training had taught me to despise; a habit of fighting with the fists, coupled with a curious contempt for the accident of individual superiority—all these things amazed me and put me into a topsy-turvy world where I was weeks in finding my feet.

But strangest of all, and (as I now especially believe) most pregnant with meaning for the future, was to find the inherited experience in me of so much teaching and careful habit— instinct of command, if you will—all that goes to make what we call in Western Europe a 'gentleman,' put at the orders and the occasional insult of a hierarchy of office, many of whose functionaries were peasants and artisans. Stripes on the arm, symbols, suddenly became of overwhelming value; what I had been made with so much care in an English public school was here thought nothing but a hindrance and an absurdity. This had seemed to me first a miracle, then a grievous injustice, then most unpractical, and at last, like one that sees the answer to a riddle, I saw (when I had long lost my manners and ceased to care for refinements) that the French were attempting, a generation before any others in the world, to establish an army that should be a mere army, and in which a living man counted only as one numbered man.

Whether that experiment will hold or not I cannot tell; it shocks the refinement of the whole west of Europe; it seems monstrous to the aristocratic organization of Germany; it jars in France also with the traditions of that decent elder class of whom so many still remain to guide the Republic, and in whose social philosophy the segregation of a 'directing class' has been hitherto a dogma. But soon I cared little whether that experiment was to succeed or no in its final effort, or whether the French were to perfect a democracy where wealth has one vast experience of its own artificiality, or to fail. The intellectual interest of such an experiment, when once I seized it, drove out every other feeling.

I became like a man who has thoroughly awaked from a long sleep and finds that in sleep he has been taken overseas. I merged into the great system whose wheels and grindings had at first astonished or disgusted me, and I found that they had made of me what they meant to make. I cared more for guns than for books; I now obeyed by instinct not men, but symbols of authority. No comfortable fallacy remained; it no longer seemed strange that my captain was a man promoted from the ranks; that one of my lieutenants was an Alsatian charity boy and the other a rich fellow mixed up with sugar-broking; that the sergeant of my piece should be a poor young noble, the wheeler of No. 5 a wealthy and very vulgar chemist's son, the man in the next bed ('my Ancient,' as they say in that service) a cook of some skill, and my bombardier a mild young farmer. I thought only in terms of the artillery: I could judge men from their aptitude alone, and in me, I suppose, were accomplished many things—one of Danton's dreams, one of St Just's prophecies, the fulfilment also of what a hundred brains had silently determined twenty years before when the staff gave up their swords outside Metz; the army and the kind of army of which Chanzy had said in the first breath of the armistice: 'A man who forgets it should be hanged, but a man who speaks of it before its time should be shot with the honours of his rank.'

All this had happened to me in especial in that melting-pot up in the eastern hills, and to thirty thousand others that year in their separate crucibles.

In the process things had passed which would seem to you incredible if I wrote them all down. I cared little in what vessel I ate, or whether I had to tear meat with my fingers. I could march in reserve more than twenty miles a day for day upon day. I knew all about my horses; I could sweep, wash, make a bed, clean kit, cook a little, tidy a stable, turn to entrenching for emplacement, take a place at lifting a gun or changing a wheel. I took change with a gunner, and could point well. And all this was not learnt save under a grinding pressure of authority and harshness, without which in one's whole life I suppose one would never properly have learnt a half of these things—at least, not to do them so readily, or in such unison, or on so definite a plan. But (what will seem astonishing to our critics and verbalists), with all this there increased the power, or perhaps it was but the desire, to express the greatest thoughts — newer and keener things. I began to understand De Vigny when he wrote: 'If a man despairs of becoming a poet, let him carry his pack and march in the ranks.'

Thus the great hills that border the Moselle, the distant frontier, the vast plain which is (they say) to be a battlefield, and which lay five hundred feet sheer below me; the far guns when they were practising at Metz, the awful strength of columns on the march moved me. The sky also grew more wonderful, and I noticed living things. The Middle Ages, of which till then I had had but troubling visions, rose up and took flesh in the old town, on the rare winter evenings when I had purchased the leisure to leave quarters by some excessive toil. A man could feel France going by.

It was at the end of these six months, when there was no more darkness at roll-call, and when the bitter cold (that had frozen us all winter) was half forgotten, that the spring brought me this excellent news, earlier than I had dared to expect it—the news that sounds to a recruit half as good as active service. We were going to march and go off right away westward over half a dozen horizons, till we could see the real thing at Châlons, and with this news the world seemed recreated.

Seven times that winter we had been mobilized; four times in the dead of the night, once at midday, once at evening, and once at dawn. Seven times we had started down the wide Metz road, hoping in some vague way that they would do something with us and give us at least some manœuvres, and seven times we had marched back to barracks to undo all that serious packing and to return to routine.

Once, for a week in February, the French and German Governments, or, more probably, two minor permanent officials, took it into their silly heads that there was some danger of war. We packed our campaign saddles every night and put them on the pegs behind the stalls; we had the emergency rations served out, and for two days in the middle of that time we had slept ready. But nothing came of it. Now at least we were off to play a little at the game whose theory we had learnt so wearily.

And the way I first knew it would easily fill a book if it were told as it should be, with every detail and its meaning unrolled and with every joy described: as it is, I must put it in ten lines. Garnon (a sergeant), three others, and I were sent out (one patrol out of fifty) to go round and see the reserve horses on the farms. That was delight enough, to have a vigorous windy morning with the clouds large and white and in a clear sky, and to mix with the first grain of the year, 'out of the loose box.'

We took the round they gave us along the base of the high hills, we got our papers signed at the different stables, we noted the hoofs of the horses and their numbers; a good woman, at a large farm gave us food of eggs and onions, and at noon we turned to get back to quarters for the grooming. Everything then was very well—to have ridden out alone without the second horse and with no horrible great pole to crush one's leg, and be free—though we missed it—of the clank of the guns.

We felt like gentlemen at ease, and were speaking grandly to each other, when I heard Garnon say to the senior of us a word that made things seem better still, for he pointed out to a long blue line beyond Domremy and overhanging the house of Joan of Arc, saying that the town lay there. 'What town?' said I to my Ancient; and my Ancient, instead of answering simply, took five minutes to explain to me how a recruit could not know that the round of the reserve horses came next before camp, and that this town away on the western ridge was the first halting-place upon the road. Then my mind filled with distances, and I was overjoyed, saving for this one thing, that I had but two francs and a few coppers left, and that I was not in reach of more.

When we had ridden in, saluted, and reported at the guard, we saw the guns drawn up in line at the end of the yard, and we went into grooming and ate and slept, hardly waiting for the morning and the long regimental call before the réveillé; the notes that always mean the high road for an army, and that are as old as Fontenoy.

. . . . . .

That next morning they woke us all before dawn—long before dawn. The sky was still keen, and there was not even a promise of morning in the air, nor the least faintness in the eastern stars. They twinkled right on the edges of the world over the far woods of Lorraine, beyond the hollow wherein lay the town; it was even cold like winter as we harnessed; and I remember the night air catching me in the face as I staggered from the harness-room, with my campaign saddle and the traces and the girths and the saddle cloth, and all the great weight that I had to put upon my horses.

We stood in the long stables all together, very hurriedly saddling and bridling and knotting up the traces behind. A few lanterns gave us an imperfect light. We hurried because it was a pride to be the first battery, and in the French service, rightly or wrongly, everything in the artillery is made for speed, and to speed everything is sacrificed. So we made ready in the stable and brought our horses out in order before the guns in the open square of quarters. The high plateau on which the barracks stood was touched with a last late frost, and the horses coming out of the warm stables bore the change ill, lifting their heads and stamping. A man could not leave the leaders for a moment, and, while the chains were hooked on, even my middle

horses were restive and had to be held.   My hands stiffened at
the reins, and I tried to soothe both my beasts, as the lantern
went up and down wherever the work was being done.   They
quieted when the light was taken round behind by the tumbrils,
where two men were tying on the great sack of oats exactly as
though we were going on campaign.

These two horses of mine were called Pacte and Basilique.
Basilique was saddled; a slow beast, full of strength and sympathy, but stupid and given to sudden fears.   Pacte was the
led horse, and had never heard guns.   It was prophesied that
when first I should have to hold him in camp when we were
practising he would break everything near him, and either kill
me or get me cells.   But I did not believe these prophecies,
having found my Ancient and all third-year men too often to
be liars, fond of frightening the younger recruits.   Meanwhile
Pacte stood in the sharp night, impatient, and shook his harness.
Everything had been quickly ordered.

We filed out of quarters, passed the lamp of the guard, and
saw huddled there the dozen or so that were left behind while
we were off to better things.   Then a drawn-out cry at the head
of the column was caught up all along its length, and we trotted;
the metal of shoes and wheel-rims rang upon the road, and I
felt as a man feels on a ship when it leaves harbour for great
discoveries.

We had climbed the steep bank above St Martin, and were
on the highest ridge of land dominating the plain, when the
sky first felt the approach of the sun.   Our backs were to the
east, but the horizon before us caught a reflection of the dawn;
the woods lost their mystery, and one found oneself marching
in a partly cultivated open space with a forest all around.   The
road ran straight for miles like an arrow, and stretched swarm-
ingly along it was the interminable line of guns.   But with the
full daylight, and after the sun had risen in a mist, they deployed
us out of column into a wide front on a great heath in the
forest, and we halted.   There we brewed coffee, not by batteries,
but gun by gun.

Warmed by this little meal, mere coffee without sugar or
milk, but with a hunk left over from yesterday's bread and
drawn stale from one's haversack (the armies of the Republic
and of Napoleon often fought all day upon such sustenance,
and even now, as you will see, the French do not really eat till
a march is over—and this may be a great advantage in warfare)
—warmed, I say, by this little meal, and very much refreshed

by the sun and the increasing merriment of morning, we heard the first trumpet-call and then the shouted order to mount.

We did not form one column again. We went off at intervals by batteries; and the reason of this was soon clear, for on getting to a place where four roads met, some took one and some took another, the object being to split up the unwieldy train of thirty-six guns, with all their wagons and forges, into a number of smaller groups, marching by ways more or less parallel towards the same goal; and my battery was left separate, and went at last along a lane that ran through pasture land in a valley.

The villages were already awake, and the mist was all but lifted from the meadows when we heard men singing in chorus in front of us some way off. These were the gunners that had left long before us and had gone on forward afoot. For in the French artillery it is a maxim (for all I know, common to all others—if other artilleries are wise) that you should weight your limber (and therefore your horses) with useful things alone; and as gunners are useful only to fire guns, they are not carried, save into action or when some great rapidity of movement is desired. I do, indeed, remember one case when it was thought necessary to send a group of batteries during the manœuvres right over from the left to the right of a very long position which our division was occupying on the crest of the Argonne. There was the greatest need for haste, and we packed the gunners on to the limber (there were no seats on the gun in the old type—there are now) and galloped all the way down the road, and put the guns in action with the horses still panting and exhausted by that extra weight carried at such a speed and for such a distance. But on the march, I say again, we send the gunners forward, and not only the gunners, but as you shall hear when we come to Commercy, a reserve of drivers also. We send them forward an hour or two before the guns start; we catch them up with the guns on the road; they file up to let us pass, and commonly salute us by way of formality and ceremony. Then they come into the town of the halt an hour or two after we have reached it.

So here in this silent and delightful valley, through which ran a river, which may have been the Meuse or may have been a tributary only, we caught up our gunners. Their song ceased, they were lined up along the road, and not till we were passed were they given a little halt and repose. But when we had gone past with a huge clattering and dust, the bombardier of my piece, who was a very kindly man, a young farmer, and who happened to be riding abreast of my horses, pointed them out to me behind us at a turning in the road. They were taking that five minutes' rest which the French have borrowed from the Germans, and which comes at the end of every hour on the march. They had thrown down their knapsacks and were lying flat taking their ease. I could not long look backwards, but a very little time after, when we had already gained nearly half a mile upon them, we again heard the noise of their singing, and knew that they had reshouldered their heavy packs. And this pack is the same in every unmounted branch of the service, and is the heaviest thing, I believe, that has been carried by infantry since the Romans.

It was not yet noon, and extremely hot for the time of year and for the coldness of the preceding night, when they halted us at a place where the road bent round in a curve and went down a little hollow. There we dismounted and cleaned things up a little before getting into the town, where we were to find what the French call an *étape*; that is, the town at which one halts at the end of one's march, and the word is also used for the length of a march itself. It is not in general orders to clean up in this way before coming in, and there were some commanders who were never more pleased than when they could bring their battery into town covered with dust and the horses steaming and the men haggard, for this they thought to be evidence of a workmanlike spirit. But our colonel had given very contrary orders, to the annoyance of our captain, a man risen from the ranks who loved the guns and hated finery.

Then we went at a walk, the two trumpets of the battery sounding the call which is known among French gunners as 'the eighty hunters,' because the words to it are, '*quatre-vingt, quatre-vingt, quatre-vingt, quatre-vingt, quatre-vingt, quatre-vingt, quatre-vingt, chasseurs*,' which words, by their metallic noise and monotony, exactly express the long call that announces the approach of guns. We went right through the town, the name of which is Commercy, and the boys looked at us with pride, not knowing how hateful they would find the service when once they were in for its grind and hopelessness. But then, for that matter, I did not know myself with what great pleasure I should look back upon it ten years after. Moreover, nobody knows beforehand whether he will like a thing or not; and there is the end of it.

We formed a park in the principal *place* of the town; there were appointed two sentinels to do duty until the arrival of the gunners who should relieve them and mount a proper guard, and then we were marched off to be shown our various quarters. For before a French regiment arrives at a town others have ridden forward and have marked in chalk upon the doors how many men and how many horses are to be quartered here or there, and my quarters were in a great barn with a very high roof; but my Ancient, upon whom I depended for advice, was quartered in a house, and I was therefore lonely.

We groomed our horses, ate our great midday meal, and were free for a couple of hours to wander about the place. It is a garrison, and, at that time, it was full of cavalry, with whom we fraternized; but the experiment was a trifle dangerous, for there is always a risk of a quarrel when regiments meet, as there is with two dogs, or two of any other kind of lively things.

Then came the evening, and very early, before it was dark, I was asleep in my clothes in some straw, very warm; but I was so lazy that I had not even taken off my belt or sword. And that was the end of the first day's marching.

THE GOOD WOMAN

UPON a hill that overlooks a western plain and is conspicuous at the approach of evening, there still stands a house of faded brick faced with cornerings of stone. It is quite empty, but yet not deserted. In each room some little furniture remains; all the pictures are upon the walls; the deep red damask of the panels is not faded, or if faded, shows no contrast of brighter patches, for nothing has been removed from the walls. Here it is possible to linger for many hours alone, and to watch the slope of the hill under the level light as the sun descends. Here passes a woman of such nobility that, though she is dead, the landscape and the vines are hers.

It was in September, during a silence of the air, that I first saw her as she moved among her possessions; she was smiling to herself as though at a memory, but her smile was so slight and so dignified, so genial, and yet so restrained, that you would have thought it part of everything around and married (as she was) to the land which was now her own. She wandered down the garden paths ruling the flowers upon either side, and receiving as she went autumn and the fruition of her fields; plenitude and completion surrounded her; the benediction of Almighty God must have been upon her, for she was the fulfilment of her world.

Three fountains played in that garden—two, next to the northern and the southern walls, were small and low; they rather flowed than rose. Two cones of marble received their fall, and over these they spread in an even sheet with little noise, making (as it were) a sheath of water which covered all the stone; but the third sprang into the air with delicate triumph, fine and high, satisfied, tenuous and exultant. This one tossed its summit into the light, and alone of the things in the garden, the plash of its waters recalled and suggested activity—though that in so discreet a way that it was to be heard rather than regarded. The birds flew far off in circles over the roofs of the town below us. Very soon they went to their rest.

The slow transfiguration of the light by which the air became full of colours and every outline merged into the evening, made of all I saw, as I came up towards her, a soft and united vision

27

wherein her advancing figure stood up central and gave a meaning to the whole. I will not swear that she did not as she came bestow as well as receive an influence of the sunset. It was said by the ancients that virtue is active, an agent, and has power to control created things; for, they said, it is in a direct relation with whatever orders and has ordained the general scheme. Such power, perhaps, resided in her hands. It would have awed me but hardly astonished if, as the twilight deepened, the inclination of the stems had obeyed her gesture and she had put the place to sleep.

As I came near I saw her plainly. Her face was young although she was so wise, but its youth had the aspect of a divine survival. Time adorned it.

Music survives. Whatever is eternal in the grace of simple airs or in the Christian innocence of Mozart was apparent, nay, had increased, in her features as the days in passing had added to them not only experience but also revelation and security. She was serene. The posture of her head was high, and her body, which was visibly informed by an immortal spirit, had in its carriage a large, a regal, an uplifted bearing which even now as I write of it, after so many years, turns common every other sight that has encountered me. This was the way in which I first saw her upon her own hillside at evening.

With every season I returned. And with every season she greeted my coming with a more generous and a more vivacious air. I think the years slipped off and did not add themselves upon her mind: the common doom of mortality escaped her until, perhaps, its sign was imposed upon her hair—for this at last was touched all through with that appearance or gleam which might be morning or which might be snow.

She was able to conjure all evil. Those desperate enemies of mankind which lie in siege of us all around grew feeble and were silent when she came. Nor has any other force than hers dared to enter the rooms where she had lived: it is her influence alone which inhabits them to-day. There is a vessel of copper, enamelled in green and gilded, which she gave with her own hands to a friend overseas. I have twice touched it in an evil hour.

Strength, sustenance, and a sacramental justice are permanent in such lives, and such lives also attain before their close to so general a survey of the world that their appreciations are at once accurate and universal.

On this account she did not fail in any human conversation,

nor was she ever for a moment less than herself; but always and throughout her moods her laughter was unexpected and full, her fear natural, her indignation glorious.

Above all, her charity extended like a breeze: it enveloped everything she knew. The sense of destiny faded from me as the warmth of that charity fell upon my soul; the foreknowledge of death retreated, as did every other unworthy panic.

She drew the objects of her friendship into something new; they breathed an air from another country, so that those whom she deigned to regard were, compared with other men, like the living compared with the dead; or, better still, they were like men awake while the rest were tortured by dreams and haunted of the unreal. Indeed, she had a word given to her which saved all the souls of her acquaintance.

It is not true that influence of this sort decays or passes into vaguer and vaguer depths of memory. It does not dissipate. It is not dissolved. It does not only spread and broaden: it also increases with the passage of time. The musicians bequeath their spirit, notably those who have loved delightful themes and easy melodies. The poets are read for ever; but those who resemble her do more, for they grow out upon the centuries —they themselves and not their arts continue. There is stuff in their legend. They are a tangible inheritance for the hurrying generations of men.

She was of this kind. She was certainly of this kind. She died upon this day [1] in the year 1892. In these lines I perpetuate her memory.

[1] 22 December.

HOME

THERE is a river called the Eure which runs between low hills often wooded, with a flat meadow floor in between. It so runs for many miles. The towns that are set upon it are for the most part small and rare, and though the river is well known by name, and though one of the chief cathedrals of Europe stands near its source, for the most part it is not visited by strangers.

In this valley one day as I was drawing a picture of the woods I found a wandering Englishman who was in the oddest way. He seemed by the slight bend at his knees and the leaning forward of his head to have no very great care how much further he might go. He was in the clothes of an English tourist, which looked odd in such a place, as, for that matter, they do any-where. He had upon his head a pork-pie hat which was of the same colour and texture as his clothes, a speckly brown. He carried a thick stick. He was a man over fifty years of age; his face was rather hollow and worn; his eyes were very simple and pale; he was bearded with a weak beard, and in his ex-pression there appeared a constrained but kindly weariness. This was the man who came up to me as I was drawing my picture. I had heard him scrambling in the undergrowth of the woods just behind me.

He came out and walked to me across the few yards of meadow. The haying was over, so he did the grass no harm. He came and stood near me, irresolutely, looking vaguely up and across the valley towards the further woods, and then gently towards what I was drawing. When he had so stood still and so looked for a moment he asked me in French the name of the great house whose roof showed above the more ordered trees beyond the river, where a park emerged from and mixed with the forest. I told him the name of the house, whereupon he shook his head and said that he had once more come to the wrong place.

I asked him what he meant, and he told me, sitting down slowly and carefully upon the grass, this adventure:

'First,' said he, 'are you always quite sure whether a thing is really there or not?'

'I am always quite sure,' said I; 'I am always positive.'

He sighed, and added: 'Could you understand how a man might feel that things were really there when they were not?'

'Only,' said I, 'in some very vivid dream, and even then I think a man knows pretty well inside his own mind that he is dreaming.' I said that it seemed to me rather like the question of the cunning of lunatics; most of them know at the bottom of their silly minds that they are cracked, as you may see by the way they plot and pretend.

'You are not sympathetic with me,' he said slowly, 'but I will nevertheless tell you what I want to tell you, for it will relieve me, and it will explain to you why I have again come into this valley.'

'Why do you say "again"?' said I.

'Because,' he answered gently, 'whenever my work gives me the opportunity I do the same thing. I go up the valley of the Seine by train from Dieppe; I get out at the station at which I got out on that day, and I walk across these low hills, hoping that I may strike just the path and just the mood—but I never do.'

'What path and what mood?' said I.

'I was telling you,' he answered patiently, 'only you were so brutal about reality.' And then he sighed. He put his stick across his knees as he sat there on the grass, held it with a hand on either side of his knees, and so sitting bunched up began his tale once more.

'It was ten years ago, and I was extremely tired, for you must know that I am a Government servant, and I find my work most wearisome. It was just this time of year that I took a week's holiday. I intended to take it in Paris, but I thought on my way, as the weather was so fine, that I would do something new and that I would walk a little way off the track. I had often wondered what country lay behind the low and steep hills on the right of the railway line.

'I had crossed the Channel by night,' he continued, a little sorry for himself, 'to save the expense. It was dawn when I reached Rouen, and there I very well remember drinking some coffee which I did not like, and eating some good bread which I did. I changed carriages at Rouen because the express did not stop at any of the little stations beyond. I took a slower train, which came immediately behind it, and stopped at most of the stations. I took my ticket rather at random for a little station between Pont de l'Arche and Mantes. I got out at that little station, and it was still early—only midway through the morning.

'I was in an odd mixture of fatigue and exhilaration: I had not slept and I would willingly have done so, but the freshness of the new day was upon me, and I have always had a very keen curiosity to see new sights and to know what lies behind the hills.

'The day was fine and already rather hot for June. I did not stop in the village near the station for more than half an hour, just the time to take some soup and a little wine; then I set out into the woods to cross over into this parallel valley. I knew that I should come to it and to the railway line that goes down it in a very few miles. I proposed when I came to that other railway line on the far side of the hills to walk quietly down it as nearly parallel to it as I could get, and at the first station to take the next train for Chartres, and then the next day to go from Chartres to Paris. That was my plan.

'The road up into the woods was one of those great French roads which sometimes frighten me and always weary me by their length and insistence: men seem to have taken so much trouble to make them, and they make me feel as though I had to take trouble myself; I avoid them when I walk. Therefore, so soon as this great road had struck the crest of the hills and was well into the woods (cutting through them like the trench of a fortification, with the tall trees on either side) I struck out into a ride which had been cut through them many years ago and was already half overgrown, and I went along this ride for several miles.

'It did not matter to me how I went, since my design was so simple and since any direction more or less westward would enable me to fulfil it, that is, to come down upon the valley of the Eure and to find the single railway line which leads to Chartres. The woods were very pleasant on that June noon, and once or twice I was inclined to linger in their shade and sleep an hour. But—note this clearly—I did not sleep. I remember every moment of the way, though I confess my fatigue oppressed me somewhat as the miles continued.

'At last by the steepness of a new descent I recognized that I had crossed the watershed and was coming down into the valley of this river. The ride had dwindled to a path, and I was wondering where the path would lead me when I noticed that it was getting more orderly: there were patches of sand, and here and there a man had cut and trimmed the edges of the way. Then it became more orderly still. It was all sanded, and there were artificial bushes here and there—I mean bushes not native to the forest—until at last I was aware that my ramble had taken me into someone's own land, and that I was in a private ground.

'I saw no great harm in this, for a traveller, if he explains himself, will usually be excused; moreover, I had to continue, for I knew no other way, and this path led me westward also. Only, whether because my trespassing worried me or because I felt my own dishevelment more acutely, the lack of sleep and the strain upon me increased as I pursued those last hundred yards, until I came out suddenly from behind a screen of rose bushes upon a large lawn, and at the end of it there was a French country house with a moat round it, such as they often have, and a stone bridge over the moat.

'The château was simple and very grand. The mouldings upon it pleased me, and it was full of peace. Upon the further side of the lawn, so that I could hear it but not see it, a fountain was playing into a basin. By the sound it was one of those high French fountains which the people who built such houses as these two hundred years ago delighted in. The plash of it was very soothing, but I was so tired and drooping that at one moment it sounded much further than at the next.

'There was an iron bench at the edge of the screen of roses, and hardly knowing what I did—for it was not the right thing to do in another person's place—I sat down on this bench, taking pleasure in the sight of the moat and the house with its noble roof, and the noise of the fountain. I think I should have gone to sleep there and at that moment — for I felt upon me worse than ever the strain of that long hot morning and that long night journey — had not a very curious thing happened.'

Here the man looked up at me oddly, as though to see whether I disbelieved him or not; but I did not disbelieve him.

I was not even very much interested, for I was trying to make the trees to look different one from the other, which is an extremely difficult thing: I had not succeeded and I was niggling away. He continued with more assurance:

'The thing that happened was this: a young girl came out of the house dressed in white, with a blue scarf over her head and crossed round her neck. I knew her face as well as possible: it was a face I had known all my youth and early manhood—but for the life of me I could not remember her name!'

'When one is very tired,' I said, 'that does happen to one: a name one knows as well as one's own escapes one. It is especially the effect of lack of sleep.'

'It is,' said he, sighing profoundly; 'but the oddness of my feeling it is impossible to describe, for there I was meeting the oldest and perhaps the dearest and certainly the most familiar of my friends, whom,' he added, hesitating a moment, 'I had not seen for many years. It was a very great pleasure . . . it was a sort of comfort and an ending. I forgot, the moment I saw her, why I had come over the hills, and all about how I meant to get to Chartres. . . . And now I must tell you,' added the man a little awkwardly, 'that my name is Peter.'

'No doubt,' said I gravely, for I could not see why he should not bear that name.

'My Christian name,' he continued hurriedly.

'Of course,' said I, as sympathetically as I could. He seemed relieved that I had not even smiled at it.

'Yes,' he went on rather quickly, 'Peter—my name is Peter. Well, this lady came up to me and said: "Why, Peter, we never thought you would come!" She did not seem very much astonished, but rather as though I had come earlier than she had expected. "I will get Philip," she said. "You remember Philip?" Here I had another little trouble with my memory: I did remember that there was a Philip, but I could not place him. That was odd, you know. As for her, oh, I knew *her* as well as the colour of the sky: it was her name that my brain missed, as it might have missed my own name or my mother's.

'Philip came out as she called him, and there was a familiarity between them that seemed natural to me at the time, but whether he was a brother or a lover or a husband, or what, I could not for the life of me remember.

'"You look tired," he said to me in a kind voice that I liked very much and remembered clearly. "I am," said I, "dog tired." "Come in with us," he said, "and we will give you some wine and water. When would you like to eat?" I said I would rather sleep than eat. He said that could easily be arranged.

'I strolled with them towards the house across that great lawn, hearing the noise of the fountain, now dimmer, now nearer; sometimes it seemed miles away and sometimes right in my ears. Whether it was their conversation or my familiarity with them or my fatigue, at any rate, as I crossed the

moat I could no longer recall anything save their presence.
I was not even troubled by the desire to recall anything; I was
full of a complete contentment, and this surging up of familiar
things, this surging up of it in a foreign place, without excuse
or possible connection or any explanation whatsoever, seemed
to me as natural as breathing.

'As I crossed the bridge I wholly forgot whence I came or
whither I was going, but I knew myself better than ever I
had known myself, and every detail of the place was familiar
to me.

'Here I had passed (I thought) many hours of my childhood and my boyhood and my early manhood also. I ceased
considering the names and the relation of Philip and the girl.

'They gave me cold meat and bread and excellent wine, and
water to mix with it, and as they continued to speak even the
last adumbrations of care fell off me altogether, and my spirit
seemed entirely released and free. My approaching sleep
beckoned to me like an easy entrance into Paradise. I should
wake from it quite simply into the perpetual enjoyment of
this place and its companionship. Oh, it was an absolute
repose!

'Philip took me to a little room on the ground floor fitted with
the exquisite care and the simplicity of the French: there was
a curtained bed, a thing I love. He lent me night clothes,
though it was broad day, because he said that if I undressed
and got into the bed I should be much more rested; they would
keep everything quiet at that end of the house, and the gentle
fall of the water into the moat outside would not disturb
me. I said on the contrary it would soothe me, and I
felt the benignity of the place possess me like a spell. Remember that I was very tired and had not slept for now thirty
hours.

'I remember handling the white counterpane and noting the
delicate French pattern upon it, and seeing at one corner the
little red silk coronet embroidered, which made me smile. I
remember putting my hand upon the cool linen of the pillow-
case and smoothing it; then I got into that bed and fell asleep.
It was broad noon, with the stillness that comes of a summer
noon upon the woods; the air was cool and delicious above the
water of the moat, and my windows were open to it.

'The last thing I heard as I dropped asleep was her voice
calling to Philip in the corridor. I could have told the very
place. I knew that corridor so well. We used to play there

when we were children. We used to play at travelling, and we used to invent the names of railway stations for the various doors. Remembering this and smiling at the memory, I fell at once into a blessed sleep.

'. . . I do not want to annoy you,' said the man apologetically, 'but I really had to tell you this story, and I hardly know how to tell you the end of it.'

'Go on,' said I hurriedly, for I had gone and made two trees one exactly like the other (which in nature was never seen) and I was annoyed with myself.

'Well,' said he, still hesitating and sighing with real sadness, 'when I woke up I was in a third-class carriage; the light was that of late afternoon, and a man had woken me by tapping my shoulder and telling me that the next station was Chartres. . . . That's all.'

He sighed again. He expected me to say something. So I did. I said without much originality: 'You must have dreamed it.'

'No,' said he, very considerably put out, 'that is the point! I didn't! I tell you I can remember exactly every stage from when I left the railway train in the Seine valley until I got into that bed.'

'It's all very odd,' said I.

'Yes,' said he, 'and so was my mood; but it was real enough. It was the second or third most real thing that has ever happened to me. I am quite certain that it happened to me.'

I remained silent, and rubbed out the top of one of my trees so as to invent a new top for it since I could not draw it as it was. Then, as he wanted me to say something more, I said: 'Well, you must have got into the train somehow.'

'Of course,' said he.

'Well, where did you get into the train?'

'I don't know.'

'Your ticket would have told you that.'

'I think I must have given it up to the man,' he answered doubtfully, 'the guard who told me that the next station was Chartres.'

'Well, it's all very mysterious,' I said.

'Yes,' he said, getting up rather weakly to go on again, 'it is.' And he sighed again. 'I come here every year. I hope,' he added a little wistfully, 'I hope, you see, that it may happen to me again . . . but it never does.'

'It will at last,' said I to comfort him.

And, will you believe it, that simple sentence made him in a moment radiantly happy; his face beamed, and he positively thanked me, thanked me warmly.

'You speak like one inspired,' he said. (I confess I did not feel like it at all.) 'I shall go much lighter on my way after that sentence of yours.'

He bade me good-bye with some ceremony and slouched off, with his eyes set towards the west and the more distant hills.

THE PLEASANT PLACE

A GENTLEMAN of my acquaintance came to me the other day for sympathy. . . . But first I must describe him.

He is a man of careful, not neat, dress: I would call it sober rather than neat. He is always clean-shaven and his scanty hair is kept short-cut. He is occupied in letters; he is, to put it bluntly, a literatoor; none the less he is possessed of scholarship and is a minor authority upon English pottery.

He is a very good writer of verse; he is not exactly a poet, but still, his verse is remarkable. Two of his pieces have been publicly praised by political peers and at least half a dozen of them have been praised in private by the ladies of that world. He is a man fifty-four years of age, and, if I may say so without betraying him, a little disappointed.

He came to me, I say, for sympathy. I was sitting in my study watching the pouring rain falling upon the already soaked and drenched and drowned clay lands of my county. The leafless trees (which are in our part of a low but thick sort) were standing against a dead grey sky with a sort of ghost of movement in it, when he came in, opened his umbrella carefully so that it might not drip, and left it in the stone-floored passage —which is, to be accurate, six hundred years old—kicked off his galoshes and begged my hospitality; also (let me say it for the third time) my sympathy.

He said he had suffered greatly and that he desired to tell me the whole tale. I was very willing and his tale was this:

It seems that my friend (according to his account) found himself recently in a country of a very delightful character.

This country lay up and heavenly upon a sort of table-land. One went up a road which led continually higher and higher through the ravines of the mountains, until, passing through a natural gate of rock, one saw before one a wide plain bounded upon the further side by the highest crests of the range. Through this upland plain ran a broad and noble river whose reaches he could see in glimpses for miles, and upon the further bank of it in a direction opposite that which the gate of rock regarded, was a very delightful city.

The walls of this city were old in their texture, venerable and majestic in their lines. Within their circumference could be discerned sacred buildings of a similar antiquity, but also modern and convenient houses of a kind which my friend had not come across before, but which were evidently suited to the genial, sunlit climate, as also to the habits of leisured men. Their roofs were flat, covered in places by awnings, in other places by tiled verandas, and these roofs were often disposed in the form of little gardens.

Trees were numerous in the city and showed their tops above the lower buildings, while the lines of their foliage indicated the direction of the streets.

My friend was passing down the road which led to this plain —and as it descended it took on an ampler and more majestic character—when he came upon a traveller who appeared to be walking in the direction of the town.

This traveller asked him courteously in the English tongue whether he were bound for the city. My friend was constrained to reply that he could not pretend to any definite plan, but certainly the prospect all round him was so pleasant and the aspect of the town so inviting, that he would rather visit the capital of this delightful land at once than linger in its outskirts.

'Come with me, then,' said the Traveller, 'and if I may make so bold upon so short an acquaintance, accept my hospitality. I have a good house upon the wall of the town and my rank among the citizens of it is that of a merchant—I am glad to say a prosperous one.'

He spoke without affectation and with so much kindness, that my friend was ravished to discover such a companion, and they proceeded in leisurely company over the few miles that separated them from their goal.

The road was now paved in every part with small square slabs, quite smooth and apparently constructed of some sort of marble. Upon either side there ran canalized in the shining stone a little stream of perfectly clear water. From time to time they would pass a lovely shrine or statue which the country people had adorned with garlands. As they approached the city they discovered a noble bridge in the manner, my friend believed, of the Italian Renaissance, with strong elliptical arches and built, like all the rest of the way, of marble, while the balustrade upon either side of it was so disposed in short symmetrical columns as to be particularly grateful to the eye. Over this bridge there went to and fro a great concourse of people, all smiling, eager, happy and busy, largely acquainted, apparently, each with the others, nodding, exchanging news, and in a word forming a most blessed company.

As they entered the city my friend's companion, who had talked of many things upon their way and had seemed to unite the most perfect courtesy and modesty with the widest knowledge, asked him whether there was any food or drink to which he was particularly attached.

'For,' said he, 'I make a point whenever I entertain a guest —and that,' he put in with a laugh, 'is, I am glad to say, a thing that happens frequently—I make a point, I say, of asking him what he really prefers. It makes such a difference!'

My friend began his reply with those conventional phrases to which we are all accustomed: 'That he would be only too happy to take whatever was set before him,' 'That the prospect of his hospitality was a sufficient guarantee of his satisfaction,' and so forth: but his host would take no denial.

'No, no!' said he. 'Do please say just what you prefer! It is so easy to arrange—if you only knew! . . . Come, I know the place better than you,' he added, smiling again; 'you have no conception of its resources. Pray tell me quite simply before we leave this street'—for they were now in a street of sumptuous and well-appointed shops—'exactly what shall be commissioned.'

Moved by I know not what freedom of expression, and expansive in a degree which he had never yet known, my friend smiled back and said: 'Well, to tell you the truth, some such meal as this would appeal to me: First two dozen green-bearded oysters of the Arcachon kind, opened upon the *deep* shell with all their juices preserved, and each exquisitely cleaned. These set upon pounded ice and served in that sort of dish which is contrived for *each* oyster to repose in its own little recess with a sort of side arrangement for the reception of the empty shells.'

His host nodded gravely, as one who takes in all that is said to him.

'Next,' said my friend, in an enthusiastic manner, 'real and good Russian caviare, cold but not frozen, and so touched with lemon—only just so touched—as to be perfect. With this I think a little of the wine called Barsac should be drunk, and that cooled to about thirty-eight degrees (Fahrenheit). After this a True Bouillon, and by a True Bouillon,' said my friend with earnestness, 'I mean a Bouillon that has long simmered in the pot and has been properly skimmed, and has been seasoned not only with the customary herbs but also with a suspicion of carrot and of onion, and a mere breath of tarragon.'

'Right!' said his host. 'Right!' nodding with real appreciation.

'And next,' said my friend, halting in the street to continue his list, 'I think there should be eggs.'

'Right,' said his host once more approvingly; 'and shall we say——'

'No,' interrupted my friend eagerly, 'let me speak. Eggs *sur le plat*, frizzled to the exact degree.'

'Just what I was about to suggest,' answered his delighted entertainer; 'and black pepper, I hope, ground large upon them in fresh granules from a proper wooden mill.'

'Yes! Yes!' said my friend, now lyric, 'and with *sea* salt in large crystals.'

On saying which both of them fell into a sort of ecstasy which my friend broke by adding:

'Something quite light to follow . . . preferably a sugar-cured Ham braised in white wine. Then, I think, spinach, not with the ham but after it; and that spinach cooked perfectly dry. We will conclude with some of the cheese called Brie. And for wine during all these latter courses we will drink the wine of Chinon: Chinon Grillé. What they call,' he added slyly, 'the *Fausse maigre*; for it is a wine thin at sight but full in the drinking of it.'

'Good! Excellent!' said his host, clapping his hands together once with a gesture of finality. 'And then after the lot you shall have coffee.'

'Yes, coffee roasted during the meal and ground immediately before its concoction. And for liqueur . . .'

My friend was suddenly taken with a little doubt. 'I dare not ask,' said he, 'for the liqueur called Aquebus? Once only did I taste it. A monk gave it me on Christmas Eve four years ago and I think it is not known.'

'Oh, ask for it by all means!' said his host. 'Why, we know it and love it in this place as though it were a member of the family!'

My friend could hardly believe his ears on hearing such things, and said nothing of cigars. But to his astonishment his host, putting his left hand on my friend's shoulder, looked him full in the face and said:

'And now shall *I* tell you about cigars?'

'I confess they were in my mind,' said my friend.

'Why then,' said his host with an expression of profound happiness, 'there is a cigar in this town which is full of flavour, black in colour, which does not bite the tongue, and which none the less satisfies whatever tobacco does satisfy in man. When you smoke it you really dream.'

'Why,' said my friend humbly, 'very well then, let us mention these cigars as the completion of our little feast.'

'Little *feast*, indeed!' said his host, 'why it is but a most humble meal. Anyhow, I am glad to have had from you a proper schedule of your pleasures of the table. In time to come when we know each other better, we will arrange other large and really satisfactory meals; but this will do very well for our initiatory lunch as it were.' And he laughed merrily.

'But have I not given you great trouble?' said my friend.

'How little you will easily perceive,' said his companion, 'for in this town we have but to order and all is at once promptly and intelligently done.' With that he turned into a small office where a commissary at once took down his order. 'And now,' said he emerging, 'let us be home.'

They went together down the turnings of a couple of broad streets lined with great private palaces and public temples until they came to a garden which had no boundaries to it but which was open, and apparently the property of the city. But the people who wandered here were at once so few, so discreet and so courteous, my friend could not discover whether they were (as their salutes seemed to indicate) the dependents of his host, or merely acquaintances who recognized him upon their way.

This garden, as they proceeded, became more private and more domestic; it led by narrowing paths through high, diversified trees, until, beyond the screen of a great beech hedge, he saw the house . . . and it was all that a house should be!

Its clear, well-set stone walls were in such perfect harmony with the climate and with the sky, its roof garden, from which a child was greeting them upon their approach, so unexpected and so suitable, its arched open gallery was of so august a sort, and yet the domestic ornaments of its colonnade so familiar, that nothing could be conceived more appropriate for the residence of man.

The mere passage into this Home out of the warm morning daylight into the inner domestic cool, was a benediction, and in the courtyard which they thus entered a lazy fountain leaped and babbled to itself in a manner that filled the heart with ease.

'I do not know,' said his host in a gentle whisper as they

crossed the courtyard, 'whether it is your custom to bathe before the morning meal or in the middle of the afternoon?'

'Why, sir,' said my friend, 'if I may tell the whole truth, I have no custom in the matter; but perhaps the middle of the afternoon would suit me best.'

'By all means,' said his host in a satisfied tone. 'And I think you have chosen wisely, for the meal you have ordered will very shortly be prepared. But, for your refreshment at least, one of my friends shall put you in order, cool your hands and forehead, see to your face and hair, put comfortable sandals upon your feet and give you a change of raiment.'

All of this was done. My friend's host did well to call the servant who attended upon his guest a 'friend,' for there was in this man's manner no trace of servility or of dependence, and yet an eager willingness for service coupled with a perfect reticence which was admirable to behold and feel.

When my friend had been thus refreshed he was conducted to a most exceptional little room. Four pictures were set in the walls of it, mosaics, they seemed—but he did not examine their medium closely. The room itself in its perfect lightness and harmony, with its view out through a large round arch upon the countryside beyond the walls (the old turrets of which made a framework for the view), exactly prepared him for the meal that was prepared.

While the oysters (delightful things!) were entering upon their tray and were being put upon the table, the host, taking my friend aside with an exquisite gesture of courteous privacy, led him through the window-arch on to a balcony without, and said, as they gazed upon the wall and the plain and the mountains beyond (and what a sight they were!):

'There is one thing, my dear sir, that I should like to say to you before you eat . . . it is rather a delicate matter. . . . You will not mind my being perfectly frank?'

'Speak on, speak on,' said my friend, who by this time would have confided any interests whatsoever into the hands of such a host.

'Well,' said that host, continuing a little carefully, 'it is this: as you can see we are very careful in this city to make men as happy as may be. We are happy ourselves, and we love to confer happiness upon others, strangers and travellers who honour us with their presence. But we find—I am very sorry to say we find . . . that is, we find from time to time that their *complete* happiness, no matter with what we may provide

them, is dashed by certain forms of anxiety, the chief of which
is anxiety with regard to their future receipts of money.'

My friend started.

'Nay,' said his host hastily, 'do not misunderstand me. I do
not mean that preoccupations of business are alone so alarming.
What I mean is that sometimes, yes, and I may say often
(horrible as it seems to us!), our guests are in an active pre-
occupation about the petty business of finance. Some few
have debts, it seems, in the wretched society from which they
come, and of which, frankly, I know nothing. Others, though
not indebted, feel insecure about the future. Others, though
wealthy, are oppressed by their responsibilities. Now,' he continued firmly, 'I must tell you once and for all that we have a
custom here upon which we take no denial: *no denial whatsoever*.
Every man who enters this city, who *honours* us by entering
this city, is made free of *that* sort of nonsense, thank God!'
And as he said this, my friend's host breathed a great sigh of
relief. 'It would be intolerable to us to think,' he continued,
'that our welcome and dear companions were suffering from such
a tawdry thing as money-worry in our presence. So the matter
is plainly this: whether you like it or whether you do not, the
sum of £10,000 is already set down to your credit in the public
bank of the city; whether you use it or not is your business; if
you do not it is our custom to melt down an equivalent sum of
gold and to cast it into the depths of the river, for we have of
this metal an unfailing supply, and I confess we do not find
it easy to understand the exaggerated value which other men
place upon it.'

'I do not know that I shall have occasion to use so magnificent a custom,' said my friend, with an extraordinary relief
in his heart, 'but I certainly thank you very kindly for its
intention, and I shall not hesitate to use any sum that may be
necessary for my continuing the great happiness which this
city appears to afford.'

'You have spoken well,' said his host, seizing both his hands,
'and your frankness compels me to another confession: We
have at our disposal a means of discovering exactly how any
one of our guests may stand: the responsibilities of the rich, the
indebtedness of the embarrassed, the anxiety of those whose
future may be precarious. May I tell you without discourtesy
that your own case is known to me and to two trustees, who are
public officials—absolutely reliable—and whom, for that matter
you will not meet.'

My friend must have looked incredulous, but his host continued firmly: 'It is so, we have settled your whole matter, I am glad to say, on terms that settle all your liabilities and leave a further £50,000 to your credit in the public bank. But the size of the sum is in this city really of no importance. You may demand whatever you will, and enjoy, I hope, a complete security during your habitation here. And that habitation, both the Town Council and the National Government beg you, through me, to extend to the whole of your life.'

. . . . . .

'Imagine,' said my friend, 'how I felt. . . . The oysters were now upon the table, and before them, ready for consumption, the caviare. The Barsac in its original bottle, cooled (need I say!) to exactly thirty-eight degrees, stood ready . . .'

At this point he stopped and gazed into the fire.

'But, my dear fellow,' said I, 'if you are coming to me for sympathy and simply succeed in making me hungry and cross . . .'

'No,' said my friend with a sob, 'you don't understand!' And he continued to gaze at the fire.

'Well, go *on*,' said I angrily.

'There isn't any *on*,' he said; 'I woke!'

We both looked into the fire together for perhaps three minutes before I spoke and said:

'Will you have some wine?'

'No thank you,' he answered sadly, 'not *that* wine.' Then he got up uneasily and moved for his umbrella and his galoshes, and the passage and the door. I thought he muttered: 'You might have helped me.'

'How could I help you?' I said savagely.

'Well,' he sighed, 'I thought you could . . . it was a bitter disappointment. Good night!' And he went out again into the rain and over the clay.

TALKING (AND SINGING) OF THE NORDIC MAN

I

Behold, my child, the Nordic man,
And be as like him as you can;
His legs are long, his mind is slow,
His hair is lank and made of tow.

II

And here we have the Alpine Race:
Oh! what a broad and brutal face!
His skin is of a dirty yellow.
He is a most unpleasant fellow.

III

The most degraded of them all
Mediterranean we call.
His hair is crisp, and even curls,
And he is saucy with the girls.

THIS translation is my own. I offer it with diffidence, for I recognize that it does not reproduce the deep organ tones of the original. But it gives the substance of that fine poem, and it is only with the substance—I mean that description of The Race which it conveys—that I have here to deal.

I heard so much about the Nordic Man in these last few months that I was moved to collect recently a great mass of information upon him and to co-ordinate it. Upon the Alpine Man and the Mediterranean Man I am not so erudite: nor is it indeed to any great purpose that I should be—for they are clearly inferior. But the Nordic Man is worth anybody's trouble; and here is what I have found out about him.

He is the Conqueror and the Adventurer. He is the Law-giver and the essentially Moral Man. He arranges the world as it should be arranged. He does everything for his own good and for the good of others. He is a Natural Leader. Even those who hate him, fear him; all respect him. The Alpine Man sits sullenly at his feet awaiting his orders; the Mediterranean Man flies in terror from his face.

But it is not enough to learn these general characters in the Nordic Man, pleasing though they are. No sound biologist could be content until he knew something intimate of his origin and habits; where he may be found, what he does, and how to tell him at sight.

This, then, is what I have found about the Nordic Man. I have space only for the most salient points, but I hope to complete the picture in detail when I shall have leisure to write my book on the species. It will be fully illustrated and will have a very complete Index.

The Nordic Man is born either in the West End of London or in a pleasant country house, standing in its own park-like grounds. That is the general rule; he is, however, sometimes born in a parsonage and rather more frequently in a Deanery or a Bishop's Palace, or a Canon's house in a Close. Some of this type have been born in North Oxford; but none (that I can discover) in the provincial manufacturing towns, and certainly none east of Charing Cross or south of the river.

The Nordic Man has a nurse to look after him while he is a baby, and she has another domestic at her service. He has a night and a day nursery, and he is full of amusing little tricks which endear him to his parents as he grows through babyhood to childhood.

Towards the age of ten or eleven, the Nordic Man goes to a preparatory school, the headmaster of which is greatly trusted by the Nordic Man's parents, especially by the Nordic Man's mother. He early learns to Play the Game, and is also grounded in the elements of Good Form, possibly the Classics and even, exceptionally, some modern tongue. He plays football and cricket; usually, but not always, he is taught to swim.

Thence the Nordic Man proceeds to what is called a Public School, where he stays till he is about eighteen. He then goes either to Oxford or Cambridge, or into the Army. He does not stay long in the Army; while from the University he proceeds either to a profession (such as the Bar, or writing advertisements) or to residence upon his estate. This last he can only do if his father dies early.

The Nordic Man lives in comfort and even luxury through manhood; he shoots, he hunts, he visits the South of France, he plays bridge. He hates the use of scent; he changes for dinner into a special kind of clothes every day. He is extremely particular about shaving, and he wears his hair cut short and even bald. The Nordic does not bother much about Religion, so when he approaches death he has to distract himself with some hobby, often that of his health. He dies of all sorts of things, but more and more of the cancer; after his death his sons, nephews, or cousins take up the role of the Nordic Man and perpetuate the long and happy chain.

Such is the life-story of the Nordic Man. I have only given it in its broadest lines, and have left out a great many sub-sections; but what I have said will be sufficient to indicate places in which he is to be surprised and the kind of things which you will there find him doing. As for his character, which lies at the root of all this great performance, that is less easily described, for one might as well attempt to describe a colour or a smell; but I can attempt some indications of it.

The Nordic Man dislikes all cruelty to animals, and is him-self kind to them in the following scale: first the dog, then the horse, then the cat, then birds, and so on till you get to insects, after which he stops caring. Microbes, oddly enough, he detests. He will treat them in the most callous manner.

In the matter of wine the Nordic Man is divided; you can-not predicate of him that he will drink it, or that if he drinks it he will know what it is. But in the matter of whisky you may safely say that it is his stand-by, save for a certain sub-section of him who dare not touch it. These stand apart and are savage to their fellows.

The Nordic Man is very reserved, save in the matter of speech-making. He hates to betray an emotion, but he hates still more the complete concealment of it. He has therefore established a number of conventions whereby it may be known when he is angry, pleased, or what not; but he has no convention for fear, for he is never afraid. This reminds me that the Nordic Man despises conflict with lethal weapons unless it be against the enemies of his country; but he delights in watching, and will sometimes himself practise, conflict conducted with stuffed gloves. As for fighting with his feet, he would not dream of it; nor does he ever bite.

The Nordic Man is generous and treats all men as his equals, especially those whom he feels to be somewhat inferior in rank and wealth. This is a very beautiful trait in the Nordic Man, and causes him to believe that he is everywhere beloved. On the other hand, the Nordic Man prefers to live with those richer than himself. The Nordic Man detests all ostentation in dress, and detests even more the wearing of cheap clothes. He loves it to be known that his clothes were costly. No Nordic Man wears a made-up tie.

The Nordic Man boasts that he is not addicted to the Arts,

and here he is quite right; but he is an excellent collector of work done by the inferior Mediterranean race, and is justly proud of the rare successes of his own people in this field. In the same way the Nordic Man will tell you with emphasis that he cannot write. Herein he tells the truth. Yet, oddly enough, he is convinced that no one has ever been able to write except Nordic Men; and this article of faith he applies particularly to True Poetry, which (he conceives) can only be inspired in his own tongue.

The Nordic Man does everything better than anybody else does it, and himself proclaims this truth unceasingly; but where he particularly shines is in the administration of justice. For he will condemn a man to imprisonment or death with greater rapidity than will the member of any other race. In giving judgment he is, unlike the rest of the human species, unmoved by any bias of class or blood, let alone of personal interest. On this account his services as a magistrate are sought far and wide throughout the world, and his life is never in danger save from disappointed suitors or those who have some imaginary grievance against him.

The Nordic Man is a great traveller. He climbs mountains; he faces with indifference tropical heat and arctic cold. He is a very fine fellow.

I must conclude by telling you all that I am not obtaining these details from any personal observations, as the part of the country in which I live has very few Nordic Men, and most of them are away during the greater part of the year staying either in the houses of other Nordic Men or in resorts of ritual pleasure upon the Continent. But I have had the whole thing described to me most carefully by a friend of mine who was for a long time himself a Nordic Man, until he had the misfortune to invest in British Dyes and crashed. He guarantees me the accuracy of his description.

.   .   .   .   .   .

Immediately after I had written those few words you have just read about the Nordic Man, I received a great quantity of letters from—I was about to write 'from all quarters of the world,' when I suddenly remembered that there would not be time for that, and that the lie would stick out—a great quantity of letters, I say, from all sorts of people. It shows at once how widely I am read, and what interest my handling of this great subject aroused.

Some of these letters are abusive, some laudatory, some critical; all three categories are to me sacred when the writers have the courage to give name and address, and I would not divulge to the public the confidences they contain. But I think I may be allowed to answer here such correspondents as refused to give name and address. They will serve as examples to show how little the true doctrine of the Nordic Man has, so far, penetrated the masses.

Of course it will soak through at last, as all great scientific truths do—such as the doctrine of Natural Selection and the peculiar properties of the stuff called Ether, not to speak of Magna Charta, which even the poorest scavenger in the street to-day reveres as the origin of his freedom.

But so far this new discovery of the Nordic Man has not spread as it should have done.

Thus the first of my correspondents (who signs 'Gallio' and gives no address but Brighton) is puzzled by the apparent aptitude of the Romans in their best period for administration and government, and even, in a primitive fashion, for war. He admits that all this may be much exaggerated, and from what he has seen of the Romans (he was down among them lately) he cannot believe all he hears of their ancestors. But still (he supposes) there must be a solid kernel of truth in it; for after all, the name 'Roman' was given to a great number of institutions —including the Empire itself—and he asks me—rather crudely —how this was possible if the Mediterranean race were as vile as our greatest authorities have discovered it to be? It is odd that the simple answer to this difficulty has not occurred to the writer. It is that those who governed the Empire, and led the armies, called 'Roman' were Nordic. This could be proved in several ways, but all of them might be open to objection save the unanswerable one that if these men had not been Nordic they could not have succeeded as they did. The Scipios, the Julian House, Hadrian—to cite at random—were manifestly and necessarily Nordic: for men do not act as they acted unless they are of pure-bred Nordic stock.

The same is true of other manifestations of intelligence and vigour in Mediterranean countries. Thus the Italians and even the Greeks have left a considerable body of remarkable literature both in prose and in verse, and in the case of Italy, we have even quite modern examples of literary excellence—at least, so I am assured by those who are acquainted with the idioms of the inferior races. But upon examination it will always be found that the authors, though using a base medium, were Nordic. The committee which we collectively call by the mythological term 'Homer,' and which drew up and passed certainly the *Iliad* and possibly the *Odyssey*, were clearly Nordic in composition. Catullus was as Nordic as he could be. The Nordic character of Aristotle is a commonplace. Dante was Nordic. So was Leopardi.

Take any outstanding Italian or other Mediterranean name and you will find upon close examination that the man to whom it is attached was of the Nordic type: Napoleon Buonaparte occurs at once to the mind.

Another correspondent has come upon the thing from a different angle. He knows enough of the great new discovery to understand the term 'cephalic index,' and he has had his own cephalic index taken by a cephalogian who practises in Ealing. He did so under the impression, of course, that he was of sound Nordic stock; but to his horror the measurements have come out an extreme form of Alpine! He asks me what he is to do about it? I can assure him (and though I do not claim to be an expert in Moronovitalogy I am fairly well up in my elements) that his anxiety is groundless. Though, of course, skull measurement is the basis of the three great divisions, yet if a man have Nordic qualities clearly apparent in his brith and culture, these easily predominate over what might be the natural tendencies of brachycephalic humanity. It would be a fine state of things, indeed, if we had to rule out of the Nordic excellence all those great men of the English past who, so far as we can judge from their portraits, had something flat-headed about them.

A third correspondent—who signs her letter 'Onyx'—is troubled about her children. There are five: three charming boys and two delightful girls. She has measured their heads with her husband's callipers (he is an architect in full employment) and she finds that her eldest and her youngest are quite unmistakably Mediterranean; her second eldest painfully Alpine, only her second youngest clearly Nordic; while the one in the middle, a boy (by name, she tells me, Ethelred), seems to be a strange mixture of all three.

I cannot reply personally to this correspondent, as she does not give an address; but I trust that these lines will meet her eye. I would have her note that in the first place the skulls of children are no index to the shape they will have when they fossilize in mature years; and next, that even if these varied types appear in her family, it is not remarkable, for all three types are present in England. Moreover, she may have travelled.

A fourth correspondent, a clergyman, I fancy, who signs 'Scholasticus,' writes me a long rigmarole (I cannot call it by any politer name), in which he calls the whole theory subversive of sound morals, and asks whether we are to believe that man 'created in the image of his Maker, and responsible to his Creator,' etc. etc. etc.

Really, to this kind of thing there is only one answer. Science does not clash with religion; it clashes with nothing except unreason and untruth. Science is simply organized knowledge, based upon experiment and accurate measurement over so wide a field as to be established with absolute certitude. Now Science clearly proves that these three races, the Nordic, the Alpine, and the Mediterranean, exist side by side in Europe, and affirms that the Nordic (to which all scientific men belong) possesses those qualities upon which alone men can pride themselves. Science demonstrates the defects and vices of the Alpine, and the baseness and degradation of the Mediterranean stock. If my reverend critic likes to knock his head against a stone wall, I cannot help it. But it seems to me an extraordinary thing to find any man possessed of enough education to write consecutively, opposing (at this time of day) established scientific truths in the name of hypothetical principles, the figments of imagination and vanity. His 'Creator,' 'image,' 'responsibility,' are all of them mere words; not one of them has been established by accurate and repeated measurement, nor have they one single experiment conducted under scientific conditions to support them; while on the other side we have the unanimous agreement of Meyerbath, Karsowitz, Brahmsohn, Farrago, Cent-Six, Blauwvenfeld, Tabouche, Smith of Milwaukee (Hamilcar Q. Smith—perhaps the greatest authority of all), van Houten and his famous relative Klotz—but why should I prolong the list? My objector will look in vain through all the distinguished ranks of modern science to find a single name supporting his ridiculous assumptions of a 'God,' 'Free Will,' and what not. All agree that our characters and actions proceed from a cephalic index, and all are agreed upon the relative values of the three main races of Europe.

PS.—To my correspondent 'Tiny,' who has also given no address, I must reply in this brief postscript. No, the facial angle, as measured from the point of the chin tangentially, the parietal curve of the forehead, and from the cusp of the left nostril to the base of the corresponding ear-lobe, is no longer the criterion of character. I thought I had made that plain. Thirty-five years ago, when I was a boy, all scientists were agreed that the facial angle was the one certain and only test of moral attitude and intellectual power; but that opinion is now universally abandoned, and the facial angle is replaced by the cephalic index.

So put that in your pipe and smoke it.

A CONVERSATION WITH A READER

PEOPLE whose books sell largely (mine do not, I am sorry to say—but perhaps some day they will) must often have had an experience which only came to me once in my life: that of talking familiarly with a member of the public who was reading one of my immortal works. But I cannot remember any one who has given the world an account of such an experience. I will take the opportunity of doing so here; for it still gives me perpetual pleasure and amusement.

It is now many years ago. I was travelling down from Birmingham to London on the Great Western Railway. I was in a third-class smoking carriage with one other person, whom I took (from his little black bag and his manner) to be a commercial traveller, but he may have been anything else, a publican or the Hangman. He had a good solid face, and rather a fine one; strong hands, and a quiet demeanour. It was in the early autumn and sunny weather—such weather prepared me to be contented with the world and any chance companion. My heart was already high, when it rose dizzily upon my catching the title of the book which my fellow-traveller had in his hand. It was one of my too numerous books of essays.

I thought to myself: 'This is fame; I am getting known. This man is a very good specimen of the average public. I love him; he is reading my book. Doubtless many hundreds up and down the great enchanted island are doing the same, some reading one book, some another. They will read and re-read these books until their covers are worn out, and then they will buy another copy. They will tell their friends. More and more copies will sell. The world has changed its complexion and my sun has risen at last.'

As these pleasing thoughts succeeded each other in my mind the man opposite me put down the volume with a sigh (or, to be more particular, chucked it down on the dirty cushion), looked up to me and said: 'Silly stuff that.'

I said, 'Yes,' and asked him how he came to read it.

He said, 'I dunno,' and looked calmly at nothing for a short space in silence.

Then he added: 'I was just looking over the bookstall and

the man recommended it to me. I think he must have taken it up by mistake for another book. Anyhow, it's a shilling wasted' (for in those days the cheap editions were at a shilling).

I asked him who the author was, and he again said dully: 'I dunno.' But he made a languid gesture, picked up the book again, looked at the back, pronounced my name wrongly, and then threw the book down again—and once more sighed.

'Funny thing,' he said, 'this idea of reading when one's travelling; but I have got so that I must read something—only I can't read *that* stuff.'

This time there was a note of bitterness in his complaint. I do not think he would have felt so strongly about it if he had found the poor little volume lying about; it was having spent a shilling on it that rankled.

I said: 'What's it all about?'

'I dunno,' he answered. 'Nothing that I can make out!'

He picked up the book again and looked at the title. 'It doesn't tell you on the outside. What they've printed there is just foolishness. There's no story I can make out. It's all cut up. Might be newspaper articles!'

All these words of his were painful ones. They were indeed newspaper articles which I, poor hack, had strung together, and put between covers for my living.

'Anyhow,' he went on, in the slightly more interested tone of a man who wants to begin a conversation, 'it beats me why people want to publish books like that!'

I said: 'It was probably done for money.' He repeated: 'Seems so; but there can't be much in it.' Then he said: 'Never heard of him before!' and looked out of the window sadly, and added: 'And don't want to hear of him again!'

I asked him who were his favourite authors. He mentioned several, to repeat whose names would, I suppose, be libel; one of them was a poet. It gave me pleasure to think that the man read verse, and I asked him what it was he liked about this poet. He suddenly became enthusiastic.

'It's splendid stuff,' he said; 'good ringing stuff! None of your little England about it!' and he recited the Poem called *Has made us what we are*.

'That's the stuff!' he said, and added 'to give 'em.' Then after a pause: 'It stirs the blood.' He was prepared to affirm that there was nothing the matter with old England so long as stuff like that could be written.

Then he started another kind of poem by the same man.

This time it was all about a dear little child. It was called *Sambo's Prayer*. When he had finished he sighed. Then he said with a kind of quizzical look, as though examining the depths of his heart: 'I wonder how it comes to 'em? It's genius, I suppose. You and I couldn't do that.' He shook his head: 'No, not for a handful of golden sovereigns we couldn't! It just comes to 'em.'

I asked him if he had ever met the Great Poet, but he said, 'Lord, no!' in tones of awe; as though such mighty accidents were not for mortal man.

The train was slowing up for Oxford, and the bagman or evangelist or commission agent, or whatever he was, got up, snapped his bag, and was evidently going to get out, when an Angel put a thought into my mind, and I did my Good Deed for the Day. I said: 'I really don't know whether you will think I am taking a liberty, but may I buy the book off you?' He said that this did not seem to be fair. I said: 'Well, the reason is I shall have nothing to read between this and London, and I am tired of doing geometry in my head.' 'Doing what?' he said. I said: 'Nothing; only reading passes the time, and I should really be glad of any book, even that book.' He rather hesitatingly accepted my offer; for he was an honest man, and he did not like the idea of my being a shilling out on such fearful rubbish. But he took the coin at last and the property changed hands.

No one else got in at Oxford. The train did not stop before Paddington (it was in the old days before the short cut through the Chilterns). I languidly opened the pages and my heart sank.

The man was quite right (I thought). It was a long time since I had seen those miserable essays, and now, as I turned from one to another, reading a sentence here and a phrase there, I was disgusted. What with affectation in one place and false rhetoric in another and slipshod construction in a third and a ghastly lack of interest in all, I wished from the depths of my soul that I had never made myself responsible for the thing at all. Then my misery was added to by the sudden recollection that it would be my duty, that very week, to gather together yet another sheaf of such chance articles and put them again between covers as I do here and now; for all life is a choice of two evils; and even a bad book to one's name is less dishonouring than a default in payment.

Soon the beauty of South England healed this wound and I applied the balm of landscape to my heart until the nasty suburbs had blotted out the view and my journey was done.

Never, from that day to this, have I ever *seen* any one anywhere reading any of my books. But if I do come on such a person again I shall certainly not examine him upon the effect of his reading.

THE COASTGUARD, OR THE BALM OF THE SALT

I HAVE just set down (and you, I hope, have read—since I wrote it for the strengthening of my fellow-men) an experience of mine with one of the readers of my books: a man in a train who treated what I had written with great contempt.

Now I have to relate a contrary experience. But I will not say that it happened to myself, for if I did that I should mislead. I will only swear to this, that it did happen to a penman of my own sort, that is, to a man who was not a best seller, and who ground out his livelihood in journalism and little known novels, and who loved the sea. So let *Jonah* be his name.

Well, this is what happened to Jonah; and, in reading it, let the great host of writers lift up their hearts and be comforted; it is, for them, a most encouraging story.

    .   .   .   .   .   .

The Sea that bounds South England has as many moods as any sea in the world, and one of its moods is that of calm vision like St Monica by the window at prayer.

When the Sea of South England is in this mood, it is very hard upon sailing men; especially if they have no horrible motor on board. For in this mood, there is no wind upon the sea; all lies asleep.

The sea was in such a mood two or three years ago, when this writing fellow, Mr Jonah, sat in his little boat cursing the saintly calm of the great waters. It was hot; it was about five o'clock in the afternoon; and save for the drift of the tide he had not made as many miles since noon as he had passed hours. Now and then a little cat's-paw would just dimple the silky water and then die out again. The big lug-sail which was her only canvas (for such breath as there was came aft, and it was no use setting the jib) hung like despair in the souls of evil men grown old. To the North, in the haze, and fairly close by, was England; that famous island. But in the way of a port or shelter, or place to leave the boat till the next free day (and writers never have much spare time for sailing), there was none for many miles.

He had hoped to get into a river mouth of his acquaintance

before evening: that hope he must now abandon. It was necessary for him to return to his disgusting labours with the pen, and he was anxious what he should do. With him was a younger companion; and when it was clear that things were hopeless, when the blazing sun had set in a sea of glass, and the long evening had begun, the unfortunate pedlar of prose and verse and rhetoric and tosh saw that there was nothing for it but to take to the oars. Before doing this he looked along the haze of the land through his binoculars and spotted a Coastguard Station. There he thought he would leave the craft for the night. His boat (it was the second and smaller of his fleet) was not too big to be hauled up above high-water mark, and there seemed no prospect of bad weather.

He could return to push her off again in a few days.

They bent to the oars, and before darkness had quite fallen the keel had gently slid up upon fine sand, and these two men, the nib driver and his younger companion, waded ashore with the warping rope, and on the end of it they bent a little kedge to hold her; for the tide had turned and the flood had begun.

They walked up to the Coastguard's house, and were received with due courtesy but without enthusiasm. The Coastguard undertook, however, to look after the boat for an agreed sum, and the column filler, this fellow Jonah, took a piece of paper to write down with his poor fountain pen his name and address, that he might give it to the Coastguardsman.

Then it was that the moment of miracle came!

The Coastguard bent his eyes upon the paper and was transfigured. His whole being was changed. His soul was illumined. His frame shook. When he spoke it was in a voice that seemed to hesitate in his throat with emotion—utterly different from that businesslike seaman's tone in which he had hitherto accepted payment for service.

'Can it be' (he said) 'that I am addressing the world-famous Mr Jonah? Not Mr Jonah the *writer*?—the *great* writer?' The phrase hawker was very much astonished by this form of address. He had never tasted fame, and least of all did he expect it from such a source in such a field. He remembered his sixth *Aeneid*: if good fortune is to come, it will come from a source whence one expects it least of all.

'Not Mr *Jonah*?' went on the Coastguard, in trembling tones, and reaching out his hand to steady himself upon the table, 'The *great* Mr Jonah? The *writer*? Never did I think that I should live to see this day.'

His eyes filled with tears, his voice trembled, and he was silent. But he gazed upon the eyes and nose of the hack with a wrapt, devout air, as upon the features of a God.

Praise is pleasant enough; at any rate, in its beginnings and before a man has had too much of it (for when he is getting plenty of it he will get plenty of hate as well). Fame is always an admirable thing to possess—though publicity is detestable.

The writer, thus finding (towards the close of a long and ill-spent life) Fame trumpeted to him from the lips of a sailor-man, was not displeased. He knew it was his turn to answer and he could think of nothing to say. He murmured the sort of words which he had been taught to murmur to rich women who pretended to have read his books, and who left them lying about uncut on the table when they knew he was to visit their houses. Then a good thought struck him, and he said: 'Would you like me to send you one of my books? I should think it a great honour.' This was a lie. He did really want to send the man a book, for he was grateful; but it was not true that he felt it to be a great honour. He would have felt it an honour if he had been dealing with a rich woman, but even then he would have worried about the expense.

For I must here digress to tell the reader, in case the reader is not a writer too (and I sincerely hope that she is not)—I must digress (I say) to tell the reader that literary men do not, as the cruel world imagines, get their books for nothing. *They have to buy their own books.* It is a very abominable custom, but so it stands.

He hoped, therefore, that the Coastguard would in his answer leave him the choice of the book, or (better still!) would name one of the cheap ones. But what did the Coastguardsman reply? Why, another thing, almost as astonishing as his first speech. He said:

'Oh, sir! I have them all!'

'What!' shouted the inky one. '*All* my sixty-nine books!'

'Well, sir, all that have anything to do with the Sea.'

At this the literary gentleman was struck dumb, for he had not found such faith in Israel.

He said: 'May I send you my ——,' and here he mentioned a book long dead, damned, and done for, but with plenty of the salt water about it; a book written in a very affected manner, and well deserving oblivion.

The Coastguard could hardly believe his ears.

'Oh, sir,' he said, 'if you will do that it will be the proudest moment of my life! And will you inscribe it for me?'

'I will indeed,' said the writer, courteously. So much flattery had turned him for the time being into a sort of Public Person, and he felt himself adopting the tone called 'What can I do for you?': as though he were a politician or a moneylender's tout. So true is it that well-being degrades the soul. 'I will indeed,' he said. And so he did.

It cost him five shillings, which he could ill afford. He inscribed the book to the Coastguardsman, and posted it.

Ever since then, when Mr *Jonah* considers the void and waste of a life spent in servitude to Apollo, the tyranny of the God, and his five gifts of Bitterness, Poverty, Contempt, Embarrassment and Drudgery—the gifts he has always given his favourites since he blinded old Homer and sent him about with a dog on a string through Asia, tapping with his stick upon the ground: ever since then, whenever Mr *Jonah* considers the intolerable waywardness of his Muse (she has not learned the elements of punctuality or of industry in all these forty years); ever since then, whenever he considers the vileness of his writer's trade, and the scorn in which men hold it among the living— he comforts himself with the assurance of some future fame, which must surely be very useful to a man after he is dead.

For he knows—does my friend Jonah—that the Coastguardsman will talk to other Coastguardsmen about his work, and that there will be established at last a sound school of good judges; Coastguardsmen, who will perpetuate his name, whatever the herd may fail to do.

A GUIDE TO BORING

I am distressed to note that in the interesting department of Boring (the Latin *Ars Taedica*) no outstanding work has been done upon the *active* side: the science and practice of Boring.

There has been plenty of writing upon the *passive* side, describing the horrors of being bored; and plenty of sound invective against the Bore; plenty of good description of his appearance and (what is more difficult) a few good descriptions of his approach and manner. But I can remember nothing at the moment describing the Art of Boredom: informing such of us (and I am one) as desire to inflict it upon our enemies. The book wants doing; and I would like to drop a few hints on it here.

In the first place, I will beg my readers to get out of their heads (if they have it lodged there) the idea that boring is not to be learnt and practised, because the bores he knows are commonly aimless. That is a great error. I admit that aimless men are often the best bores—the kind of men who would take the prizes in a National Bore Show. I will even admit that the King Bore is usually himself ignorant of his terrible powers. But for *deliberate* and *intentional* boring you must have a man of some ability to practise it well, as you must to practise any art well.

For Boring may properly be regarded as an art, and in connection with it I shall now enrich you by giving rules for its successful practice. With that object let me recite you the signs whereby you may discover that your efforts have effect.

The first sign is an attention in the eye of the bored person to something trivial other than yourself. If while you are talking to him his eye is directed to a person aiming a gun at him, that is not a sign of boredom. But if you see it directed to a little bird, or a passing cloud, that is a symptom, as the doctor said. Another symptom is occasional interjections which have nothing to do with what you are saying. A third, and very much stronger, symptom which should especially delight you as a proof of triumph is the bored one's breaking out into conversation with somebody else in the middle of your speech.

The choice of subject for boring is of not great consequence. Any subject can be made interesting, and therefore any subject can be made boring; but the method is all-important. And the first rule I would give in this matter is to speak in a sing-song, or at any rate with continuous repeated rhythm and accent. Those perfectly practised in the art can talk rapidly without punctuation and with no raising or lowering of the voice; but you rarely ever get this in its perfection except from politicians, though I have known others who were not bad at it. The chief master of the style, to my certain knowledge, never got into the House of Commons at all; he was only a candidate; but I walked miles to listen to him at his meetings for the sheer pleasure of seeing it done.

Another very useful tip is the bringing in of useless detail, and the branching of it out into a luxurious growth of irrelevance, and this works best of all when you are telling a story which is intended to please by its humour. Thus it is a very good plan to open with hesitation over a date: 'It was in July 1921—no, now I come to think of it, it must have been 1920, because—' (then tell them why it must have been 1920). 'No, now I think of it, it must have been 1921' (then tell them why it was '21)—'or was it 1922? Anyway, it was July, and the year doesn't matter; the whole point lies in the month.'

That is a capital beginning, especially the last words, which indicate to the bored one that you have deliberately wasted his time to no purpose.

A parallel method is to worry about a name which you have forgotten, and which is in no way material to your story.

A third tip, and a useful one, is the addition of all manner of local colour and descriptive touches. You must imitate as well as you can (it is not saying much!) the accent of the characters in your story, and you must begin a lot of sentences with 'It was one of those . . .' and then pile on the adjectives.

A further rule is to introduce digressions, especially of an aesthetic or moral sort. Stop in the middle of the thing and add to the agony by explaining that you don't mind a man's getting drunk, or that you do mind it, or that you have no objection to such a building as you are describing, or what not: for your private opinions in art and morals are the most exquisitely boring things in the world and you can't bring them in too much.

Again, remember that there are special ways of adding to the effect, of bringing out what may be called the high lights of boredom. Of these by far the finest is suddenly forgetting the end of your story, just as you are reaching it. It has an enormous effect. I knew one case where a man had a bottle thrown at him because he did this, and no handsomer proof of his success could have been given. The sharpest form of it is to lead your piece of boredom up to a question such as: 'And what do you think he answered?' and then you pause a minute and say: 'Damn it all! I ought to remember. . . . I 've almost got it! . . . You see, the whole point depends on getting the words exactly right. . . .' Then, after keeping them all in a little hell for thirty seconds, say, hopelessly, that you despair of getting it, and leave it at that.

The man who desires to shine as a bore, and uses this offensive weapon with *brio* and success, must also learn how to break down the defences. Those who have had to suffer high boredom, and who still have energy left in them, can put up a good fight; it is the duty of all bore-students to be ready for such opposition. Thus there is the defence of suddenly interrupting the borer and talking against him in a new and lively tone. For instance, if he begins: 'Do you know Rio? Well, once when I was in Rio . . .' the victim may suddenly disclose a nest of machine-guns, shouting: 'Rio! Bless you, yes! I know Rio!' then pouring out a spate of Rian recollections and thus mastering the enemy fire by a hose-play of words. There are only two ways of countering this. One is to complain openly that you are interrupted and insist on being allowed to go on with the torture. The other is to let the other man exhaust his ammunition and then riposte yourself with renewed energy.

A subtler form of defence, and a very effective one, was invented by a highly placed permanent official about thirty years ago. It consists in listening to the borer until he has made his point—or what he calls his point—just at that moment putting on an air of complete abstraction, and after that asking why he doesn't go on. To meet this form of defence it is no bad plan to begin the story all over again. That 'll teach him.

But the strongest defence—the one you have to fear most —is that of walking away. Most men who have studied the art of boring take this for a definite defeat. They need not. I know one man at a club from whom people used to walk away deliberately in the middle of his boring-exercise. He met the tactic by going after the quitter and catching hold of his coat, and quite half the time he was successful. But few men have such courage.

Lastly, let me urge on you two private recipes of my own. One is spells of silence in the intervals of boring—it's a paradoxical truth that they add vastly to the effect. They must not be so long as to let the victim take up a book, but just long enough to break his nerve. Watch his face, observe its gradual relaxation, and time yourself exactly for the renewal of the agony. The other is talking half incomprehensibly, mumbling, and the rest of it—then, when the boree impatiently asks you to repeat, do it still less clearly. It never fails.

But all these rules are, after all, mechanical. A man will never become a natural bore by the following of paper precepts any more than he will become a poet by book-learning; so perhaps I have written in vain.

A REMAINING CHRISTMAS

THE world is changing very fast, and neither exactly for the better or the worse, but for division. Our civilization is splitting more and more into two camps, and what was common to the whole of it is becoming restricted to the Christian, and soon will be restricted to the Catholic half.

That is why I have called this article 'A Remaining Christmas.' People ask themselves how much remains of this observance and of the feast and its customs. Now a concrete instance is more vivid and, in its own way, of more value than a general appreciation. So I will set down here exactly what Christmas still is in a certain house in England, how it is observed, and all the domestic rites accompanying it in their detail and warmth.

This house stands low down upon clay near a little river. It is quite cut off from the towns; no one has built near it. Every cottage for a mile and more is old, with here and there a modern addition. The church of the parish (which was lost of course three and a half centuries ago, under Elizabeth) is as old as the Crusades. It is of the twelfth century. The house of which I speak is in its oldest parts of the fourteenth century at least, and perhaps earlier, but there are modern additions. One wing of it was built seventy years ago at the south end of the house, another at the north end, twenty years ago. Yet the tradition is so strong that you would not tell from the outside, and hardly from the inside, which part is old and which part is new. For, indeed, the old part itself grew up gradually, and the eleven gables of the house show up against the sky as though they were of one age, though in truth they are of every age down along all these five hundred years and more.

The central upper room of the house is the chapel where Mass is said, and there one sees, uncovered by any wall of plaster or brick, the original structure of the house which is of vast oaken beams, the main supports and transverse pieces half a yard across, mortised strongly into each other centuries ago, and smoothed roughly with the adze. They are black with the years. The roof soars up like a high-pitched tent, and is supported by a whole fan of lesser curved oaken beams. There is but one window behind the altar. Indeed, the whole house is thus in its structure of the local and native oak, and the brick walls of it are only curtains built in between the wooden frame-work of that most ancient habitation.

Beneath the chapel is the dining-room, where there is a very large open hearth which can take huge logs and which is as old as anything in the place. Here wood only is burnt, and that wood oak.

Down this room there runs a very long oaken table as dark with age almost as the beams above it, and this table has a history. It came out of one of the Oxford colleges when the Puritans looted them three hundred years ago. It never got back to its original home. It passed from one family to another until at last it was purchased (in his youth and upon his marriage) by the man who now owns this house. Those who know about such things give its date as the beginning of the seventeenth century. It was made, then, while Shakespeare was still living, and while the faith of England still hung in the balance; for one cannot say that England was certain to lose her Catholicism finally till the first quarter of that century was passed. This table, roughly carved at the side, has been polished with wax since first it began to bear food for men, and now the surface shines like a slightly, very slightly, undulating sea in a calm. At night the brass candlesticks (for this house is lit with candles, as the proper light for men's eyes) are reflected in it as in still brown water; so are the vessels of glass and of silver and of pewter, and the flagons of wine. No cloth is ever spread to hide this venerable splendour, nor, let us hope, ever will be.

At one end of the house, where the largest of its many outer doors (there are several such) swings massively upon huge forged iron hinges, there is a hall, not very wide; its length is as great as the width of the house and its height very great for its width. Like the chapel, its roof soars up, steep and dark, so that from its floor (which is made of very great and heavy slabs of the local stone) one looks up to the roof-tree itself. This hall has another great wide hearth in it for the burning of oak, and there is an oaken staircase, very wide and of an easy slope, with an oaken balustrade and leading up to an open gallery above, whence you look down upon the piece. Above this gallery is a statue of Our Lady, carved in wood, uncoloured, and holding the Holy Child, and beneath her many shelves of books. This room is panelled, as are so many of the rooms of the house, but it has older panels than any of the others, and the great door of it opens on to the high road.

Now the way Christmas is kept in this house is this:

On Christmas Eve a great quantity of holly and of laurel is brought in from the garden and from the farm (for this house has a farm of a hundred acres attached to it and an oak wood of ten acres). This greenery is put up all over the house in every room just before it becomes dark on that day. Then there is brought into the hall a young pine tree, about twice the height of a man, to serve for a Christmas tree, and on this innumerable little candles are fixed, and presents for all the household and the guests and the children of the village.

It is at about five o'clock that these last come into the house, and at that hour in England, at that date, it has long been quite dark; so they come into a house all illuminated with the Christmas tree shining like a cluster of many stars seen through a glass.

The first thing done after the entry of these people from the village and their children (the children are in number about fifty—for this remote place keeps a good level through the generations and does not shrink or grow, but remains itself) is a common meal, where all eat and drink their fill in the offices. Then the children come in to the Christmas tree. They are each given a silver piece one by one, and one by one, their presents. After that they dance in the hall and sing songs, which have been handed down to them for I do not know how long. These songs are game-songs, and are sung to keep time with the various parts in each game, and the men and things and animals which you hear mentioned in these songs are all of that countryside. Indeed, the tradition of Christmas here is what it should be everywhere, knit into the very stuff of the place; so that I fancy the little children, when they think of Bethlehem, see it in their minds as though it were in the winter depth of England, which is as it should be.

These games and songs continue for as long as they will, and then they file out past the great fire in the hearth to a small piece adjoining where a crib has been set up with images of Our Lady and St Joseph and the Holy Child, the Shepherds, and what I will call, by your leave, the Holy Animals. And here, again, tradition is so strong in this house that these figures are never new-bought, but are as old as the oldest of the children of the family, now with children of their own. On this account, the donkey has lost one of its plaster ears, and the old ox which used to be all brown is now piebald, and of the shepherds, one actually has no head. But all that is lacking is imagined. There hangs from the roof of the crib over the Holy Child a tinsel star grown rather obscure after all these years, and much too large for the place. Before this crib the children (some of them Catholic and some Protestant, for the village is mixed) sing their carols; the one they know best is the one which begins: 'The First Good Joy that Mary had, it was the joy of One.' There are a half a dozen or so of these carols which the children here sing; and mixed with their voices is the voice of the miller (for this house has a great windmill attached to it). The miller is famous in these parts for his singing, having a very deep and loud voice which is his pride. When these carols are over, all disperse, except those who are living in the house, but the older ones are not allowed to go without more good drink for their viaticum, a sustenance for Christian men.

Then the people of the house, when they have dined, and their guests, with the priest who is to say Mass for them, sit up till near midnight. There is brought in a very large log of oak (you must be getting tired of oak by this time! But everything here is oaken, for the house is of the Weald). This log of oak is the Christmas or Yule log and the rule is that it must be too heavy for one man to lift; so two men come, bringing it in from outside, the master of the house and his servant. They cast it down upon the fire in the great hearth of the dining-room, and the superstition is that, if it burns all night and is found still smouldering in the morning, the home will be prosperous for the coming year.

With that they all go up to the chapel and there the three night Masses are said, one after the other, and those of the household take their Communion.

Next morning they sleep late, and the great Christmas dinner is at midday. It is a turkey; and a plum pudding, with holly in it and everything conventional, and therefore satisfactory, is done. Crackers are pulled, the brandy is lit and poured over the pudding till the holly crackles in the flame and the curtains are drawn a moment that the flames may be seen. This Christmas feast, so great that it may be said almost to fill the day, they may reprove who will; but for my part I applaud.

Now, you must not think that Christmas being over, the season and its glories are at an end, for in this house there is kept up the full custom of the Twelve Days, so that 'Twelfth Day,' the Epiphany, still has, to its inhabitants, its full and ancient meaning as it had when Shakespeare wrote. The green is kept in its place in every room, and not a leaf of it must be moved until Epiphany morning, but on the other hand not a leaf of it must remain in the house, nor the Christmas tree either, by Epiphany evening. It is all taken out and burnt in a special little coppice reserved for these good trees which have done their Christmas duty; and now, after so many years, you might almost call it a little forest, for each tree has lived, bearing witness to the holy vitality of unbroken ritual and inherited things.

In the midst of this season between Christmas and Twelfth Day comes the ceremony of the New Year, and this is how it is observed:

On New Year's Eve, at about a quarter to twelve o'clock at night, the master of the house and all that are with him go about from room to room opening every door and window, however cold the weather be, for thus, they say, the old year and its burdens can go out and leave everything new for hope and for the youth of the coming time.

This also is a superstition, and of the best. Those who observe it trust that it is as old as Europe, and with roots stretching back into forgotten times.

While this is going on the bells in the church hard by are ringing out the old year, and when all the windows and doors have thus been opened and left wide, all those in the house go outside, listening for the cessation of the chimes, which comes just before the turn of the year. There is an odd silence of a few minutes, and watches are consulted to make certain of the time (for this house detests wireless and has not even a telephone), and the way they know the moment of midnight is by the boom of a gun, which is fired at a town far off, but can always be heard.

At that sound the bells of the church clash out suddenly in new chords, the master of the house goes back into it with a piece of stone or earth from outside, all doors are shut, and the household, all of them, rich and poor, drink a glass of wine together to salute the New Year.

This, which I have just described, is not in a novel or in a play. It is real, and goes on as the ordinary habit of living men and women. I fear that set down thus in our terribly changing time it must sound very strange and, perhaps in places, grotesque, but to those who practise it, it is not only sacred, but normal, having in the whole of the complicated affair a sacramental quality and an effect of benediction: not to be despised.

Indeed, modern men, who lack such things, lack sustenance, and our fathers who founded all those ritual observances were very wise.

.   .   .   .

Man has a body as well as a soul, and the whole of man, soul and body, is nourished sanely by a multiplicity of observed traditional things. Moreover, there is this great quality in the unchanging practice of Holy Seasons, that it makes explicable, tolerable, and normal what is otherwise a shocking and intolerable and even in the fullest sense, abnormal thing. I mean, the mortality of immortal man.

Not only death (which shakes and rends all that is human in us, creating a monstrous separation and threatening the soul with isolation which destroys)—not only death, but that accompaniment of mortality which is a perpetual series of lesser deaths and is called change, are challenged, chained, and put in their place by unaltered and successive acts of seasonable regard for loss and dereliction and mutability. The threats of despair, remorse, necessary expiation, weariness almost beyond bearing, dull repetition of things apparently fruitless, unnecessary and without meaning, estrangement, the misunderstanding of mind by mind, forgetfulness, which is a false alarm, grief and repentance, which are true ones, but of a sad company, young men perished in battle before their parents had lost vigour in age, the perils of sickness in the body and even in the mind, anxiety, honour harassed, all the bitterness of living—become part of a large business which may lead to Beatitude. For they are all connected in the memory with holy day after holy day, year by year, binding the generations together; carrying on even in this world, as it were, the life of the dead and giving corporate substance, permanence and stability, without the symbol of which (at least) the vast increasing burden of life might at last conquer us and be no longer borne.

.   .   .   .   .   .

This house where such good things are done year by year has suffered all the things that every age has suffered. It has known the sudden separation of wife and husband, the sudden fall of young men under arms who will never more come home, the scattering of the living and their precarious return, the increase and the loss of fortune, all those terrors and all those lessenings and haltings and failures of hope which make up the life of man. But its Christmas binds it to its own past and promises its future; making the house an undying thing of which those subject to mortality within it are members, sharing in its continuous survival.

It is not wonderful that of such a house verse should be written. Many verses have been so written commemorating and praising this house. The last verse written of it I may quote here by way of ending:

> Stand thou for ever among human Houses,
> House of the Resurrection, House of Birth;
> House of the rooted hearts and long carouses,
> Stand, and be famous over all the Earth.

ON COMING TO AN END

OF all the simple actions in the world! Of all the simple actions in the world!

One would think it could be done with less effort than the heaving of a sigh. . . . Well—then, one would be wrong.

There is no case of Coming to an End but has about it something of an effort and a jerk, as though Nature abhorred it, and though it be true that some achieve a quiet and a perfect end to one thing or another (as, for instance, to Life), yet this achievement is not arrived at save through the utmost toil, and consequent upon the most persevering and exquisite art.

Now you can say that this may be true of sentient things but not of things inanimate. It is true even of things inanimate.

Look down some straight railway line for a vanishing point to the perspective: you will never find it. Or try to mark the moment when a small target becomes invisible. There is no gradation; a moment it was there, and you missed it—possibly because the Authorities were not going in for journalism that day, and had not chosen a dead calm with the light full on the canvas. A moment it was there and then, as you steamed on, it was gone. The same is true of a lark in the air. You see it and then you do not see it, you only hear its song. And the same is true of that song: you hear it and then suddenly you do not hear it. It is true of a human voice, which is familiar in your ear, living and inhabiting the rooms of your house. There comes a day when it ceases altogether—and how positive, how definite and hard is that Coming to an End.

It does not leave an echo behind it, but a sharp edge of emptiness, and very often as one sits beside the fire the memory of that voice suddenly returning gives to the silence about one a personal force, as it were, of obsession and of control. So much happens when even one of all our million voices Comes to an End.

It is necessary, it is august, and it is reasonable that the great story of our lives also should be accomplished and should reach a term: and yet there is something in that hidden duality of ours which makes the prospect of so natural a conclusion terrible,

and it is the better judgment of mankind and the mature
conclusion of civilizations in their age that there is not only
a conclusion here but something of an adventure also.   It may
be so.

Those who solace mankind and are the principal benefactors
of it, I mean the poets and the musicians, have attempted always
to ease the prospect of Coming to an End, whether it were the
Coming to an End of the things we love or of that daily habit
and conversation which is our life and is the atmosphere wherein
we loved them.   Indeed, this is a clear test whereby you may
distinguish the great artists from the mean hucksters and
charlatans, that the first approach and reveal what is dreadful
with calm and, as it were, with a purpose to use it for good,
while the vulgar catchpenny fellows must liven up their bad
dishes as with a cheap sauce of the horrible, caring nothing,
so that their shrieks sell, whether we are the better for them
or no.

The great poets, I say, bring us easily or grandly to the
gate: as in that *Ode to a Nightingale* where it is thought good
(in an immortal phrase) to pass painlessly at midnight, or, in
the glorious line which Ronsard uses, like a salute with the
sword, hailing 'la profitable mort.'

The noblest or the most perfect of English elegies leaves, as
a sort of savour after the reading of it, no terror at all nor
even too much regret, but the landscape of England at evening,
when the smoke of the cottages mixes with autumn vapours
among the elms; and even that gloomy modern *Ode to the West
Wind*, unfinished and touched with despair, though it will
speak of

> . . . that outer place forlorn
> Which, like an infinite grey sea, surrounds
> With everlasting calm the land of human sounds;

yet also returns to the sacramental earth of one's childhood
where it says:

> For now the Night completed tells her tale
> Of rest and dissolution: gathering round
> Her mist in such persuasion that the ground
>   Of Home consents to falter and grow pale.
>   And the stars are put out and the trees fail.
> Nor anything remains but that which drones
> Enormous through the dark. . . .

And again, in another place, where it prays that one may at
the last be fed with beauty

> . . . as the flowers are fed
> That fill their falling-time with generous breath:
> Let me attain a natural end of death,
> And on the mighty breast, as on a bed,
> Lay decently at last a drowsy head,
> Content to lapse in somnolence and fade
> In dreaming once again the dream of all things made.

The most careful philosophy, the most heavenly music, the best choice of poetic or prosaic phrase prepare men properly for man's perpetual loss of this and of that, and introduce us proudly to the similar and greater business of departure from them all, from whatever of them all remains at the close.

To be introduced, to be prepared, to be armoured, all these are excellent things, but there is a question no foresight can answer nor any comprehension resolve. It is right to gather upon that question the varied affections or perceptions of varying men.

I knew a man once in the Tourdenoise, a gloomy man, but very rich, who cared little for the things he knew. This man took no pleasure in his fruitful orchards and his carefully ploughed fields and his harvests. He took pleasure in pine trees; he was a man of groves and of the dark. For him that things should come to an end was but part of an universal rhythm; a part pleasing to the general harmony, and making in the music of the world about him a solemn and, oh, a conclusive chord. This man would study the sky at night and take from it a larger and a larger draught of infinitude, finding in this exercise not a mere satisfaction, but an object and goal for the mind; when he had so wandered for a while under the night he seemed, for the moment, to have reached the object of his being.

And I knew another man in the Weald who worked with his hands, and was always kind, and knew his trade well; he smiled when he talked of scythes, and he could thatch. He could fish also, and he knew about grafting, and about the seasons of plants, and birds, and the way of seed. He had a face full of weather, he fatigued his body, he watched his land. He would not talk much of mysteries, he would rather hum songs. He loved new friends and old. He had lived with one wife for fifty years, and he had five children, who were a policeman, a schoolmistress, a son at home, and two who were sailors. This man said that what a man did and the life in which he did it was like the farmwork upon a summer's day. He said one works a little and rests, and works a little again, and one drinks, and there is a perpetual talk with those about one. Then (he would say) the shadows lengthen at evening, the wind falls, the birds get back home. And as for ourselves, we are sleepy before it is dark.

Then also I knew a third man who lived in a town and was clerical and did no work, for he had money of his own. This man said that all we do and the time in which we do it is rather a night than a day. He said that when we came to an end we vanished, we and our works, but that we vanished into a broadening light.

Which of these three knew best the nature of man and of his works, and which knew best of what nature was the end?

Why so glum, my Lad, or my Lass (as the case may be), why so heavy at heart? Did you not know that you also must Come to an End?

Why, that woman of Étaples who sold such Southern wine for the dissipation of the Picardian Mist, her time is over and gone and the wine has been drunk long ago and the singers in her house have departed, and the wind of the sea moans in and fills their hall. The Lords who died in Roncesvalles have been dead these thousand years and more, and the loud song about them grew very faint and dwindled and is silent now: there is nothing at all remains.

It is certain that the hills decay and that rivers as the dusty years proceed run feebly and lose themselves at last in desert sands; and in its aeons the very firmament grows old. But evil also is perishable and bad men meet their judge. Be comforted.

Now of all endings, of all Comings to an End, none is so hesitating as the ending of a book which the Publisher will have so long and the writer so short: and the Public (God Bless the Public) will have whatever it is given.

Books, however much their lingering, books also must Come to an End. It is abhorrent to their nature as to the life of man. They must be sharply cut off. Let it be done at once and fixed as by a spell and the power of a Word; the word

FINIS

STORIES

BELINDA

I

WITHIN the parish, and adjoining the village, of Marlden, in a stately mansion known as The Towers, whose ample lawn sweeps down in smooth luxuriance to the pellucid waters of the River Avon, resided a gentleman respected throughout the County of Wiltshire as Sir Robert Montgomery; for such was, indeed, his name.

The baronet (for such was his rank) enjoyed the esteem of his equals, the respectful affection of his inferiors, and the devotion of an only daughter, an only child, upon whom her mother (long dead) had bestowed the pleasing name of Belinda.

That devotion the widowed father repaid with a particular and careful attention, the dignity of which could hardly veil his deep, his doting fondness. No expense was spared in providing Belinda's earliest years with a solid grounding in the rudiments of polite learning, while, as her girlhood blossomed into riper charms, a further selection of instructors drawn from both sexes perfected her in Italian, French, the art of painting in water-colours, every department of deportment, and the pianoforte.

Thus did Belinda Montgomery, as she entered her eighteenth year, unite every refinement of culture to beauty of an entrancing mould; a mind naturally apt and generous, trained to its fullest powers, informed a frame of surpassing grace, and the whole was inspired by a soul wherein had been firmly planted the precepts of our sublime religion.

To this last and awful matter the good vicar of the parish, the Reverend John Atkins, had applied himself with constant zeal. His living (of which Sir Robert was patron) did not so completely engross his time as to forbid him the hours required for the young lady's spiritual education: nor were the emoluments of such a task ungrateful to one whose humble needs were but narrowly met by the tithe and glebe of the parish.

Under such guidance Belinda grasped in turn the nature and attributes of her Creator, the scheme of the Atonement, the promise of a blessed Heaven, the menace of a dreadful Hell, the original institution of Episcopacy; and the errors of Rome upon the one hand, of Dissent upon the other. The Book of Common Prayer was her constant companion, and on the richly inlaid table of her private boudoir lay open, for daily consultation, the Holy Bible.

Can we marvel that under such auspices the radiant girl subjected to her sway whatever youths her careful parent permitted to approach her presence? The younger gentry of the county pledged with enthusiasm the Queen of Grace; their elders sighed that their own generation had known no sight like this. All were dazzled, all succumbed. The good discovered at once their supreme felicity in the influence of so much piety in such a setting, while the wicked were half converted and wholly abashed before so much virtue united to such ennobling beauty.

For, indeed, Belinda, at this her entry into life, was of a peerless loveliness. Her lustrous hair, of a delicate brown in hue, lay smoothly parted over a front of ivory. The perfect oval of her face 'twould need a Raphael to limn, a Petrarch to record. Her eyes, modest yet fearless, shone with the sunlit blue of our northern heavens; her lips, so refined in contour, albeit instinct with health, seemed ever at the point of smiling, but of smiling gravely: save when some fresh and innocent cause of laughter unbound her spirit. Her carriage was, perhaps, her final quality; for she seemed at once to glide, to float, to advance, to command—and yet to yield. Whether entering a room or leaving it, an equal measure of dignity would attend her action; and whether she sank to repose upon the soft divan or rose to sing some *morceau* of music, the world stood still to admire a presence as signal in the one posture as in the other.

Adjoining the Montgomery estate, lay the lands of a family also connected with Wiltshire, and famous for many generations among the gentry of that county.

Horatio Maltravers, the youthful occupant of these venerable acres, was the last descendant from a long line of squires, one of whom had acted as page to the Virgin Queen, another as equerry to the Third William, while yet another had served under the orders of General Whitelock in the capacity of ensign.

Halston House (for such was the name of the mansion) stood, a noble but sadly neglected pile, framed in tall elms and spreading oaks, whose antiquity in some way hinted at ruin. The very rooks, as they cawed at evening about its crumbling battlements, seemed to mourn the past glories of a family decayed, and the wild grass growing at random on the abandoned sward bore witness to the general decline.

The Towers of the Montgomerys, Halston of the Maltravers, lay each on the banks of this same river Avon, and the parks were so situate that a county road divided them; but on either side of that highway what a contrast! Sir Robert Montgomery's hedges, well trimmed and dense, proclaimed the careful wealth, the public sense, of their lord. Upon these, at the proper season of the year, a line of stout yeomen might be seen chastising with chopper and bill-hook the over-luxuriance of Nature, and reducing all to an exact design. Opposite, the hedges of Halston ran straggling and thin. Great gaps disfigured their alignment. Rank growths of bush, some already grown to stunted trees, sprang here and there untended; while an unsightly patching of stake, hurdle, and furze completed the disorder.

The passer-by upon his way to Bath, could not but exclaim (as he looked to the left): 'What decency! What exactitude!' Nor again (on turning to the right), could he restrain such expletives as 'Slipshod!' and even 'Disgusting!'

The fields told the same story; on the one hand sat plenitude upon a clean soil, where the tenacious dock, the invading thistle, and the insistent charlock were unknown; on the other was nothing but a starved and weedy misery. The north lodge of The Towers, a small but striking erection in the Gothic manner, was of newly-carven stone, roofed with careful slate and flanked by an ornamental paling; the south lodge of Halston could only be saved the title of hovel by some poor vestige of a former solidity. The cottages on either side of the turnpike proclaimed a similar opposition. From those of Sir Robert smiling faces looked out beneath new and deep thatch over charming groups of brilliant flowers, but from those of Horatio the wizened and anxious features of an uncertain peasantry watched with a sullen suspicion, while the roofs above them, gravely out of repair, matched the damp and blotchy walls of their unhappy tenements.

Yet was not the young owner of this anxious patrimony to blame for its deplorable appearance. Sir Robert himself, though his nearest neighbour, was the first to admit that Horatio was the victim of circumstances rather than of defect. His father, already impoverished by an unfortunate adventure in china clay, had married, late in life, an Irish lady of some charm but no appreciable dowry. She had died in giving birth to their only son, and the widower had passed some twenty years as a recluse, burying himself in a barren study of the Christian Fathers, and even of the Hebrew language.

His lawyer—and who shall blame him?—had taken full advantage of his client's unpractical disposition. Mortgage had followed mortgage, and compound interest had eaten deeply into the rent roll of Halston. When the aged scholar, not wholly conscious of his disaster, had died (some eighteen months before the opening of this tale), Horatio, then but twenty-three years of age and just returned from the University of Oxford, found himself dependent upon an income which, when all the charges of his dependants and reduced household were met, hardly exceeded £500 a year.

Upon this he maintained most narrowly the life to which he had been born. Only the most necessary repairs were undertaken by his legal advisers, who were also his creditors and the controllers of the estate. It was they who paid him quarterly his pittance of guineas, and with this he still contrived, by many a shift and device, and without hope of visiting town or of being active in any public service, to play a very modest part amongst his equals. He had his horse, his gun; some few friends who would visit his loneliness; and the pitying esteem, rather than the cordial regard, of his wealthier neighbours and their wives.

Yet was Horatio Maltravers at this moment well fitted to take up an ample role in the society of Wiltshire, had fortune proved less hard. He was above the middle height, well formed and vigorous, if somewhat too lithe in figure. His curled black hair sat admirably upon features pale and touched with melancholy, but noble and illumined by deep eyes of a dark intensity. His voice was low and full of feeling. Nor could his undeniable attractions be impeached of effeminacy—courteous and elaborate as was his ceremony, and easy and slow as was his gesture—for his mode of life was indeed manly.

He was quick and ready at every exercise native to his rank. His strength was equal to his agility. He was an excellent horseman, and untiring at every sport, whether to follow the fox, mounted, or to run on foot after the hare with a kind of dogs called beagles. He shot with accuracy from a fowling-piece, and (what is to every young man's advantage) was unerring with the pistolet at twenty paces. It is also to the credit of his father that, in spite of his strange, hermit way of life, he had had the boy trained in the art of fencing with the rapier, in which a French refugee, precariously settled in St Peter's Magna, and driven to Halston and back twice a week in a farmyard cart, had instructed him for a small fee. This same, a Monsieur de Chabrol, had also perfected him in the French language, which Horatio (though he concealed the talent with some shame) could speak with an excellent accent and an extensive vocabulary.

As may be imagined, Horatio in boyhood had constantly met, as playmate, the young heiress of The Towers. The children, each ignorant of sister or of brother, had formed, unknown to their elders, so warm a friendship as strikes root in later years. Horatio, a freshman at Christ Church College, Oxford, remembered his little companion of fourteen who would welcome him on his return for his first vacation, and was confused to discover that his visits were less warmly welcomed, his invitations to The Towers more rare. Belinda, in her fifteenth and sixteenth years, could not dismiss from her mind the permanent memory of her companion. She pictured him in his University life as something of a hero, knowing and doing things in a world greater than her own. Horatio, now come to manhood, kept the recollection of Belinda's voice as a furniture of his mind.

Upon Horatio's entering into his estate, Belinda was still in the schoolroom. Upon her return from London, after her presentation at Court, they met in the genteel life of the county, but upon dates far apart, and in the midst of crowds; save when, as courtesy demanded, Sir Robert would upon occasion ask his old neighbour's son to a meal. But he was then careful to seat at the table numerous other guests, nor was Horatio permitted too near an approach to the chief places of the board. If he might beg a dance of her in one house or another and exchange a word in the company of her relative and companion (Miss Hackman), it was his sole intercourse with one who had been, as it were, of his own blood in their childish years.

Less and less frequently did the young people meet. More and more formal grew their exchanges upon the rare occasions. Yet each retained certain playmate memories, and these, in one moment, the Inexorable Powers were to revive, to transfigure, and to inform with flame.

Winter had passed; the full trees were heavy with new leaves against the lingering sunsets of June, when Sir Robert Montgomery gave a Ball at his house, in order that Belinda might appear beneath her father's roof as the Queen of Wiltshire society. He was supported in this by a near female relative, a cousin, of austere and resolute presence, whose private means he had often supplemented, for whose worldly judgment he had a high regard, and whom he retained to accompany his daughter and advise him in his affairs.

Miss Hackman (as we have seen to be the lady's name) prepared the noble function in its every detail, and yet found time to suggest, to design, to command the ravishing *toilette* in which the débutante should conquer the admiration of all beholders. It was of a white and gauzy kind, relieved with large blue flowers of artificial construction; and while its ample but tenuous contours enhanced (if that were possible) the lure of her delightful carriage, its hue and cut proclaimed her charming innocence.

The movement of the crowded room, the hum of polite conversation, were halted to silence as the young Hostess appeared. That silence was succeeded by more eager words, till, at a signal from the band (which was conducted by M. Melchior himself), the music of the dance arose in sensuous grandeur and the partners were set for the 'Martagnaise.' In the third figure of this graceful though foreign measure, the gentlemen, as is well known, advance in rotation, and next, just touching with uplifted hands the fingers of an opposing number, step for a moment with each lady in order, until the file is exhausted and the manœuvre at an end. It is an occasion when those not partners in the dance yet greet for a moment, and when Beauty may be saluted (though not detained) by each admirer in turn.

Sir Henry Portly, a man of commanding contours, of excellent lineage, *distingué*, and but lately past his thirtieth year, had been selected for Belinda's partner. He was sensible of the honour conferred. His full but handsome face, dignified by small square whiskers, admitted a restrained emotion; nor was it mere pride in the envy of others that gave his somewhat ample frame a high bearing as he trod with long acquaintance the complicated postures of the first ritornelle. His *vis-à-vis* was a sufficient incitement to excellence, and as he *chasséed*, from left to right, from right to left, he replied with springing step to the more swan-like gestures of the lovely creature before him.

For the mere purpose of mutual configuration in the dance these two were well matched and contrasted; but there are other contrasts, other matchings. The third figure of the 'Martagnaise' was reached, with its light passing, one by one, of partner to new partner down the line. Charles Hawtry, Lord Henry Coat, gentle Mr Allen, in turn had made their bow and touched the uplifted hand, when, fourth, Horatio Maltravers passed before her in that maze of movement; the fingers of his hand upraised touched hers so delicately upraised in unison; his face met hers without design. She, leaning far back in just that posture which the latest mode demanded of this evolution, saw for one moment fully that dark, melancholy face—but in that same moment her hand, in the turn of the figure, had met some other hand.

The night advanced; the music, with its sedulous, its ceaseless charm, filled and overfilled the heart; and dance succeeding dance through the warm air, charged with swooning flowers, turned, in the minds of the young, that scene to a sort of dreaming. With the advent of the first grey light, the new day into which they dispersed under the silence of the dawn was of another world.

That night, in the long slumber which the eager exercise of youth both earns and enjoys, this mood of something other than all hitherto conceived still flooded the sleeping soul of Belinda. That night a vague but puissant call to nameless but divine adventures, to complete yet exalted satisfaction, echoed in dreams through the answering spirit of Horatio. Nor did the one, nor did the other know in either mood what summoned or what blessed. The influence so shed was general. No object, no person, appeared to either in their dreams. Rather was the whole creation filled with an ambient expectation of delight, with beatific air.

When, close on noon, the curtain of Belinda's couch was withdrawn by that one of her numerous attendants deputed for this task, she woke, indeed, to the day and place, yet these were changed as though now infused with wonder. At that same hour, in the poor dark room of ancient panelling where Horatio Maltravers arose once more to his decayed inheritance, it was into a novel scene that his young spirit entered, though every mark on the ruined woodwork, every outline of the trees without, had been his familiars from infancy.

So dreaming in full wakefulness, the girl, moved by what she thought a random, purposeless caprice, wandered under the high sun across the lawn, through the shrubbery and the iron gate, down the long park field and past the elms towards a dense wood of pines; there she proposed to rest awhile in the shade, and commune with a little brook which eddied clear under a plank thrown across its waters, and ran with a happy murmur to join the Avon near at hand. The stream formed part of the boundary which divided the Maltravers' from the Montgomerys' land, and though mere chance and whim had turned her feet towards that spot, some faint connection of name and person mixed with it.

Upon the further bank, in the neighbouring park from which the stream divided her, a sandy slope covered with high fern, led up by a narrow path between tall growths of bracken to a great grove which hid the old and ruinous house of Halston beyond. Thence, at that same hour, with high noon past and the more powerful sun distilling every savour from grass and leaf and earth, Horatio sauntered out, bound no whither, filled with the power of summer which grew to harvest all around, and still possessed by that strange mood of glamour and of change. The grove summoned him to its recesses; he received the influence of the great beeches and their shade as though the half darkness were alive. He came out into the further blinding light, and the sound of the stream below beckoned him insensibly down the path to the water between the wealths of fern.

She saw him as he came through the bracken, with active carriage, with uplifted face. It seemed to her that there was something there inspired; and her imagination put courage and adventure into his advance, as though he were setting out upon a quest. He turned a corner of the path to cross the rustic bridge, and was aware of one scarcely known yet deeply known, whose airy figure among the solemn pines arrested all his being. When he had approached and discovered her face, it was not the familiar feature of a friend, but Radiance personate. In him, for her, approached a god.

The moment was magical. It was as though some music had transformed the world.

Breast deep in fern, the small and laughing fauns, who love the awakening of life, hid tiptoe, sidling, peeping, benevolent; but in the heart of the high wood a Presence, shining in a shaft of light, triumphantly let fly the arrow from the bow.

.   .   .   .   .   .

They had passed through the high wood, side by side, saying but very little, not daring to touch each other's hands, when they saw before them, as they slowly paced, the figure of a woman.

She was standing by the fence of the open park field with the elms beyond, as though awaiting someone; as they approached her they discovered in her a strange majesty of mien which was the more intriguing from the simplicity of her garments. Indeed, by her dress she seemed to betray a belated attachment to the modes once fashionable at the Court of Bonaparte. For her gown was of one saffron piece, caught at the shoulder with one brooch of bronze, and zoned loosely at the breast. Nor was her head covered; but a noble diadem of hair, a tawny gold, crowned her low forehead and her level brows: her features had a repose at once regal and serene, but her eyes shone upon the pair with a sort of claim and (it might almost appear) of affection.

'Have you seen,' she said, addressing them first in a deep melodious voice and an accent hardly foreign, 'pray, have you seen my Boy as you came through the wood? He wandered there with a bow and arrows for his sport, and I expect his return.'

'We saw no one, Ma'am,' answered Horatio, with a respect which her carriage demanded. 'Shall we seek him for you?'

'Nay,' said the Lady, now turning upon Belinda a glance which was benignant and which nearly smiled; 'he will soon return, and I myself will saunter on to meet him there.'

With that she bowed very slightly and passed them. After a little advance they turned their heads discreetly to observe what way she took; but she had disappeared, and they thought that the neighbouring trees of the high wood must have hidden her from their sight.

'She must have been some stranger, lodging for a holiday in the village,' said Belinda. 'And come out a-strolling from near by. How pleasing, how arresting, was her demeanour! I shall hope to know her.'

'She may have been French or Italian, I think,' rejoined Horatio. 'Or an Englishwoman who has lived abroad; for I thought I perceived some touch of another manner in her speech.'

'It may be so,' answered Belinda, 'and I am glad we found her. My father indulgently permits the public to take their pleasure in the park, so long as they abstain from damaging the shrubs and fences, and are careful to shut after them the gates through which they pass.'

'It is consonant, indeed,' exclaimed Horatio, 'with his noble and generous nature, and had I the fortune to stand to him in any intimate relation, I should think myself fortunate to admire and revere more closely a character of such charity and wisdom.'

'You are right,' replied Belinda, with a grateful look. 'He has ever shown me from my first recollection a constant and devoted affection, a care for my every wish, which has inspired me with the most ardent and respectful devotion in return.'

'We have been set—you have been set—in happy places indeed,' said Horatio in a lowered voice. 'These scenes in which we have both grown up from childhood, these fertile vales, these clear brooks, these miles of forest, these rocky and abrupt but majestic hills, are one with that society which inhabits them, and with which they are now inextricably mingled in my heart.'

'Your words,' she answered in tones still more subdued, and thrilling with the fullness of her mood, 'express the inmost thoughts of my being. . . .'

Even as she spoke there were heard from a cupola of green copper above the stables the clear tones of a bell. Belinda, startled as from a profound and pleasant dream, said hurriedly: 'Ah! I must hasten my return! Yonder bell marks that hour when my father is accustomed to drink a glass of sherry wine with his steward (who is thus summoned), to give orders for his estate and to receive reports upon it daily. This business done, he is pleased to have me with him, alone. We arrange the order of the house, the entertainment of the morrow, the names and places of our guests; all which concluded, I play for him some favourite *morceau*. It is for me a sacred hour.'

'I will accompany you,' returned Horatio, 'no further than the iron gate at the entrance of the shrubbery. Permit me to remain, till then, at your side.'

The distance to be traversed was but a quarter of a mile. He strode with ease beside her somewhat accelerated steps. Each knew that on the morrow in the high noon the one and the other would be by the stream again. Neither looked at the other. Neither spoke. For such we are in youth—which is the heaven of our days. But when they came to the iron gate, and must part, she halted, turned, and lifted, or half lifted, her right hand from her side. He dared for one moment to touch it. They looked into each other's eyes, and the world was changed. He wheeled round, and was gone. In the cool shade of the arching greenery as she hurried towards the sunlit grass and the great house beyond, the air, her soul, was music, and all her being had entered beatitude.

III

Belinda hastily sought her father's study, where she found the Baronet standing at the central table, having before him a glass of brown sherry and three biscuits, of which refreshment it was his custom to partake at this hour of the day. Beside him stood Mr Carter, the steward, with whom he had been conferring upon the affairs of his estate. The latter he dismissed upon the entry of his daughter, who reminded him with a charming smile that it was time for the daily perusal of the household books and for taking his pleasure upon the ordering of dinner and the arrangement of guests.

Now that they were alone Sir Robert, looking upon her with some sadness and solemnity, motioned her to a *fauteuil*, into which the graceful creature sank with outward ease, but disturbed by an inward trepidation; for her father's gaze, as he stood there above her, had in it something at once so grave, so affectionate, and so mournful, as to warn her of a momentous communication.

He maintained this posture for a short while, still keeping fixed upon her his profound reflection, before which she cast her own eyes downwards, timorously awaiting his first words. Not until he had consumed his slight repast did he sigh heavily, and, sitting down beside her, take her hand with an affection and a sort of hesitation which deeply moved her.

'My dear,' he said, '(how dear you will never know, for it is not in the designs of Providence to communicate to children the devotion of their parents), I have to speak to you to-day upon a matter which will decide your whole life.'

Already Belinda trembled, for a deep instinct, young as she was, informed her that her father was approaching the subject of marriage.

The Baronet continued:

'You are my only child. You will inherit this place, my considerable fortune, and my name—for I propose that this shall, by some arrangement, be preserved. All is at my undisputed disposal, and all (need I say it?) will be yours, and

yours alone. I must tell you more. . . . I design that upon
your' (here was Belinda's trepidation almost openly apparent)
'. . . your . . . your departure from beneath my roof for the
house of another, a very substantial part of all my realizable
wealth shall accompany you as your dower. Moreover,' he
pursued in firmer tones, 'I have made, upon legal advice, such
arrangements as shall preserve these moneys for yourself or
whatever posterity' (Belinda blushed) 'it may please Heaven
to grant you. No one,' he added, with a rising voice, 'but
shall feel the honour and emolument of an alliance with the
Montgomerys of Marlden; but no one shall imagine that its
independent heritage is dissolved by marriage with his
own.'

Indeed, at the thought of such an indignity, the Squire's
manly voice was affected, and he paused, while Belinda, who
had recovered for the moment a full control of herself, awaited
his fateful words.

'I have made it a principle,' he continued, as he released her
hand, and rising, slowly paced the floor before her, 'I have
made it a principle never to coerce the young in matters of the
heart. Do not imagine,' and here he halted, the better to
emphasize his words, 'that I could for one instant dictate to
your inmost and most sacred feelings or even attempt to deflect
your choice by so much as a hair's breadth. But my knowledge
of the world, and,' here he cleared his throat, 'my paternal
position, make it incumbent upon me that I should at least
tender advice to one upon whom centre all my hopes, and whose
future welfare is my only concern. My dear,' and here he sat
down beside her again, and again took her hand, 'among the
multitude who naturally aspire to your alliance, you must have
noticed some few more attentive than the rest—perhaps some
one more devoted, more assiduous. His laudable ambition has
not escaped me; he is our neighbour: he has, like ourselves, an
honourable place in the county: his father was my friend. I am
his own elder friend, I hope, to this day. His worldly position
may not be quite equal to my own, but I value such things as
dust when I compare them with a chivalric temper, a manly
poise, and a manifest devotion to his intended course.'

The image of Horatio rose before Belinda's mind. She lifted
her eyes to Heaven with a happy sigh half formed, when her
incipient ecstasy was shattered by these awful words:

'I refer to Sir Henry Portly.'

At that name the young lady looked suddenly up in a startled,

dread, uncertain fashion—like one wakened from sleep by fire
—and cried aloud:

'Oh! My father! Oh! papa! Do not force upon me a man
whom my whole being rejects with an unspeakable loathing!
One whose very presence is repulsive! Whose person . . .'
she looked wildly about her, and immediately buried her head
in her hands.

Sir Robert halted in his stride. His features passed from an
expression of bewilderment to one of amazement, and at last
of stern reproof.

'Your words are strangely chosen,' he said at last, in cold
tones. 'They have an insane sound in my ears, Belinda.' (So
rarely did her devoted parent use her full name that its sound
appalled her.) 'You talk of this worthy, this excellent young
man in terms unfit for your lips, for our common position, and
for his own character; terms wholly unworthy of my simple
reference to his claims. Happily your extravagant outburst
is known to none save myself. . . . But,' he continued more
softly, 'my dear child, if indeed, for some extraordinary reason
you feel thus about a young and gallant neighbour of un-
exceptionable position, I shall be the last to press you. I will
leave time to paint his character in its proper light, and the
return of sober sense to aid your judgment. I certainly desire
you to consider the alliance—to consider it seriously. It would,
indeed, fulfil my wishes; but if another among those whom
I am so proud to call your admirers has moved you more nearly,
I would not disturb your ultimate decision. You have no lack
of choice; and when, of several, you shall tell me that you
prefer the prospect of this alliance or that, I will consider it
most tenderly—believe me!'

These words so encouraged the poor girl that she was moved
to stammer:

'It is not that. . . . It is not that! . . . My heart is plighted!'

'Your heart is plighted?' gasped the Baronet. 'Are these
terms in which a respectable female . . .'

He halted, choked in utterance.

Belinda, the unfortunate Belinda, could only whisper, as her
face sank into her hands:

'It is Horatio!'

There was a silence, during which Sir Robert stood like a
statue, with right foot advanced, left refused; his lips pressed
into a grim decision, his eyes staring. At last it broke.

'Horatio!' he thundered. 'Horatio Maltravers? A beggar's

brat, disreputably dragged up by a hermit? A pauper? A young wastrel? An out-at-elbows fellow, a scrap and rag-bag, a rotten Oxford coxcomb all curls and debts, a miserable futility whose . . .'

But his indignation was interrupted by a lamentable scream. Belinda had slipped from her seat and lay in a swoon upon the Aubusson carpet; her arms sank impotent beside her; her lovely face—as pale as death and with closed eyes—reclining upon the circle of ballooning skirts which enfolded her frame and decently covered her small and exquisitely modelled feet.

At such a sight the wretched father sprang back, transfixed with horror. He struck his forehead with his palm, stood for a moment speechless; then, leaping forward, pulled both bells on either side of the marble fireplace with frenzied violence, and rushing to the door, which he tore open, shouted:

'Dodgson! Carter! Mrs Hales! Joseph! Dorothy! Jane! Mary! Jackson! Henry! Emily! The boy! All the rest of you! Come quick! All of you! Miss Belinda . . . !'

The sound of hurrying feet filled the recesses of the mansion, a crowd of domestics gathered, Belinda's maid, Harrison, and Caroline, her private attendant, had the office of lifting the tender form towards the sofa, while the housekeeper advised the loosening of the young lady's garments, the burning of feathers under her nose, and even the respectful dashing of cold water over her face, an extreme remedy which happily needed not to be applied.

For Belinda languidly opened her beautiful eyes, and, to the unspeakable relief of her distracted parent, murmured some half-caught word just at the moment when Miss Hackman, who had entered later than the rest, and with dignified reserve had kept somewhat apart from the hubbub, prepared to take charge.

Sir Robert knelt at the sofa, fondling his daughter's hands and calling her by her tenderest names of childhood; once more she opened her eyes and wanly smiling at him, whispered: 'Dear papa!'; whereat tears filled the Baronet's eyes and a suppressed sob confused his utterance.

But here Miss Hackman gave orders that the menservants should take up the sofa as it was, bearing its divine burden, and carry it up bodily to Belinda's room, herself superintending the difficult task, and only returning when it was accomplished, and her cousin left in charge of the maid, to find Sir Robert seated at his desk with his head in his hands consumed by a grievous emotion.

'I beg you, Robert,' said that lady, not without *sécheresse,* 'to exaggerate in no way this trifling incident. All is well with the child. It was but a passing humour.'

'I fear . . .' began her cousin in reply—he was about to add 'that I was the cause of . . .' but he reconsidered his intention and was wisely silent.

'Such little passages are common enough in girls of Belinda's age,' continued the lady. 'I myself was never subject to them, as you know: *our* family is, I thank Heaven, exceptionally robust. But I have seen all this too often in others to make any affair of it. Believe me, by to-morrow she will be herself again, and within a week she will have forgotten all about it.'

'You are right, my dear Claudia,' answered Sir Robert, with affected cheerfulness. 'The truth is that nothing disturbs me save the fact that you and I must go to London by to-morrow's coach at the latest on the business of Lady Gordooly's legacy, which will not brook delay. We cannot be returned for a fortnight at the earliest. So long an absence gives me some slight anxiety. I am loath to leave the child in doubtful health, and alone with domestics.'

'Rest assured,' replied Miss Hackman, calmly. 'You have often heard me speak of my friendship and regard for an excellent gentlewoman (now in decayed circumstances) residing in Bath and by name Curll, for whom I have often done some small favour. She, I am sure, will be delighted to come here at no charge, sufficiently pleased to enjoy a change of air, an abundant board, and all the amenities of this ample establishment: not to speak of the gratitude she rightly feels towards myself. She can be summoned upon the instant. I will answer for her competence and devotion. She will take every care of Belinda till our return, and I shall even command the domestics to take her orders, so that our dear child may be relieved of such cares as household books and meals.'

'I am indeed obliged to you,' replied her cousin, with sincere good feeling. 'I admire your prompt and useful decision, and I thank you for it. She shall be warned this evening, if you will be good enough to couch the missive. A carriage shall fetch her early in the morning, and she shall be installed before our departure.'

Miss Hackman, full of her scheme, departed to her own boudoir in the north wing to compose the letter to her dependant. Her cousin took the opportunity of her absence to mount immediately to his daughter's room, where he was received with all the eagerness of affectionate regard by the reclining invalid.

Belinda had just refreshed her strength with a bowl of soup and a glass of port wine, brought with respectful deference by her particular attendant. The latter he dismissed, desiring a private conversation; the former he again took lovingly by the hand, as he seated himself on a chair at her side.

'My dear,' he said, after something of a pause. 'My darling child, the words I used caused in you a perturbation which I did not for a moment intend and which, believe me, I deplore. Your confidence was unexpected. Its purport took me by surprise.' Here he hesitated for some seconds, choosing his words.

'You must not think I am insensible to early affection' (and here he touched her hair) 'nor imagine that the passage of so many years has made me quite forget the natural effects of youth. . . . My whole, my only object, is your welfare. . . .' He paused again, desirous above all things, not to arouse her from her now calmer mood. Then, somewhat abruptly, he added: 'Your cousin and I—as you perhaps remember—must leave for London to-morrow afternoon by the coach. The business, which is of a financial nature and concerns our family, is peremptory. We can neither of us be excused.'

'Fear nothing, dearest papa,' answered Belinda, in a voice stronger than he had expected. 'My circulation is already restored. I shall be myself again before your return.'

'Yes, yes,' said the Baronet. 'I am sure of that. . . . Meanwhile, however, during the fortnight of our absence, I should, indeed, be anxious if I did not know that you were well cared for. . . . A friend of our cousin, a lady whose name you have heard and whom, perhaps, you have met, a Miss Curll of Bath, in whom she has complete confidence, shall be here to afford you companionship, and to relieve you from the petty affairs of the household during the next few days. She will in no way interfere with you, my dearest child, and her presence will greatly relieve me.'

'I am sure,' replied his daughter, 'that I shall like her very much, and your kindness is more, alas! than I deserve.' She sighed, and her father's eagerness to reassure and comfort her rose at that slight expression of her care.

'I have told you,' he said, 'that I know—I understand—the affections of youth. . . . I married late: you have a father too much advanced in years for your opening life. Your mother, who is now a saint in Heaven, you never knew. But I myself, long before your age, had among my companions one to whom the deepest of human feelings was far, far from unknown.'

He said no more, but in a little while, continued in a different voice:

'If—and can I doubt it?—this attachment is, for the moment, so strong in you, I will not——' she half rose, and would have spoken, eagerly, but he lifted his hand, 'I will not *wholly* forbid its expression. I am no tyrant . . . God knows! But I owe it to you who are innocent of the world and the effect of time, to make conditions. These conditions I have, in the main, delivered. You must agree with me—the future will show it —that they are wise and wholly for your good. I must make trial. I shall myself—this very night—send word to young Maltravers, telling him that if in a certain delay your mutual purpose still stands, I shall require of him, as a condition of my consent, that he enter a profession, though it be but that of a soldier; the purchase of a commission I could facilitate. I should prefer a career in which he may gain an honourable independence. I can by my influence secure him a minor post in Mr Aldwin's bank, where his capacity for regular work could be tested and his prospects, if he prove industrious, secured. When the required delay is exhausted, if his intentions prove firm under the ordeal, I must—I will—reluctantly, I confess— admit the prospect of such a union.'

'Oh, papa!' cried the enraptured girl, her face flushed with joy. 'You are too good. I long . . .'

He interrupted her.

'My dear,' he continued, 'the effects of time are stronger than your young heart can gauge. The trial may be too rude; your judgment of him fallible: my own more just. But if he show the manly purpose such an ordeal demands, and if you both, after a sufficient experience and attention, persist in your mutual purpose—why, I shall say that you have reached a well-considered conclusion, and that Horatio, by his *industry*, will merit my esteem, by his increasing *income* my respect.

'Meanwhile there is yet one more condition which is essential, and on which you shall not move me. You may correspond: you must not meet . . . as yet.'

'Alas! Alas!' cried Belinda, dissolving (to her father's alarm) into tears. 'I should have told you! I am a wicked, ungrateful child! . . . No later than to-morrow noon, by the stream

again, under the pine trees, Horatio and I were to find each
other, and I . . .'

'Do not be disturbed,' answered her father promptly. 'Even
had I not decided as I have, your health forbids. I shall send
a note to the boy myself to-night. I will tell him precisely how
my decision in this matter stands: as for to-morrow, I will say
that your indisposition confines you to the house. Later, when
we are gone, you are free to write to him, if you will, and he to
reply. But I repose my confidence in you that you will not
disappoint me, and that you will not meet him during my
brief absence.'

He embraced her fondly; she returned that embrace with
grateful and intense feeling. Her happiness had returned—for
was not such love as hers and Horatio's eternal?

IV

The Baronet went back to his study in a mixed mood, and
told the maid, who had waited upon the landing without, to
return to her mistress.

Seated at his desk, Sir Robert Montgomery took pen, wafer,
sand, and paper, heaved a deep sigh, and began to write as
follows:

'SIR,——'

Long did he ponder this word, considering all that lay beneath
so stern an opening; then, slowly, he crumpled the paper, threw
it into the basket, and began once more:

'MY DEAR HORATIO——'

Here he rested his chin upon his hand and raised his eyes to
the ceiling, in which attitude he remained, considering all that
lay beneath so affectionate, or at least, so familiar an address.
Still more slowly his right hand sought the sheet which once
again he crumpled into a ball, and hurled into the receptacle
at his side.

Then, abandoning further delay, he wrote rapidly and with
a fixed determination:

'MR MALTRAVERS,

'My daughter has communicated to me information which
I should have preferred to have been better prepared for.
I confess my surprise that you did not approach me before

paying her the addresses of which I now learn for the first time: upon the very eve of a necessary departure for London, where business will detain me for a fortnight or more. Upon my return, I will consider your claims: I shall not, I cannot, be indifferent to my daughter's feelings upon the one hand, nor, on the other, to my own opinion (after the experience of a long life) upon the imprudence of rash engagements. I shall beg of you to inform me upon your prospects—especially of a professional income—your approach to which shall not find me unsympathetic, but in the absence of which, I warn you, the prospect of such an alliance as you aspire to would be remote indeed. You have known each other from childhood; occasional correspondence is native to you both; I hesitate to forbid it in my absence, for its interruption would seem to both of you at once harsh and unfamiliar. But I strictly charge you that on no account are you, during that absence, to approach my house or make any appointment for meeting. My daughter has dutifully pledged me her word to the same effect, and, indeed, the state of her health is, for the moment, such that her medical adviser enjoins complete repose. Send no reply to this injunction. It would be useless, for I shall be gone before your answer could arrive. On my return, with which I will immediately acquaint you, I hope you will honour me with your presence at Marlden Towers, that we may discuss in full the matters I have put before you.'

The rapid pen here paused; he added—alas! he added—these fateful words:

'Whether her present mood shall endure is a matter for time to test: I am old enough to know that things which seem eternal at her age and yours may be a matter of weeks, or days, or even hours.'

With that he abruptly ceased, and signed:

'Your very obedient Servant to command,
'ROBERT MONTGOMERY.'

This message he folded with care, after his usual fashion, in three creases. And, not content with the informal wafer, he imposed upon red wax his seal, with the arms of the Marlden Montgomerys—or Mumries, as they were then called—granted under a patent of William and Mary: three dolphins gules, natant upon argent under a pale proper with the crest a pheasant branchee and the device: *Habet*.

He rang; he ordered the enclosure to be delivered at once by hand, with the message that the bearer did not await an answer. He turned to another and yet more difficult task.

With no hesitation on his form of address, but with far more deliberation in the construction of his phrases, he composed a letter which the reader shall now peruse:

'MY DEAR SIR HENRY,

'After the conversation you were good enough to accord me, but Tuesday last, upon the suit which you desired me to permit you to present to my daughter, I should be treating you ill indeed if I were to conceal from you a circumstance which has —in my view—modified that simple course which, as you know, I welcomed and approved. To be plain—and brief—I find upon the eve of my departure for London, that another—I need not fear to name him—the son of my late neighbour, "Hermit" Maltravers, a playmate of her earliest childhood, has made some impression upon Belinda's inclination. She and he were children together. I suspected nothing more than an old and warm friendship. For the moment they feel—or fancy they feel—a stronger tie.

'It is my duty to add that, if her decision prove fixed and permanent, I should deem it a fatal lack of judgment to oppose too prolonged a refusal.

'I am distressed. I am somewhat at a loss. I write to you in the knowledge that, during my absence (her health confines her to the house), a man of your honour will respect her indecision. I leave her under the care of a Miss Curll of Bath, an elderly gentlewoman in whom I have full confidence, and who will reside temporarily in my house. In a fortnight I shall be returned, and the whole matter shall be laid before you.

'It is possible, it is even probable, that this infatuation will pass, and that an alliance, *which you know I should have preferred*, may crown those wishes with the expression of which you honoured me but a few days since.

'I am,

'Your old and devoted friend,

'ROBERT MONTGOMERY.'

This last letter the Baronet dispatched as he had the first, immediately, and by hand; sending word at the same time that no answer could reach him until his return from London. The messenger, a well-mounted groom, rode through the darkness which had already fallen, towards that stately mansion, some seven miles distant, the ancestral home of the Portlys.

v

The Scene has changed.

We are now before those gloomy but impressive gates which are the castellated portals of the Portlys. For near three generations that family had inhabited the towering pile which Mr Portly of Cheapside, the grandfather of the reigning squire, had erected, his father amplified, and himself inherited at the early age of twenty-three; some eight years before the date of this narrative.

The mansion—known as Molcombe Abbey, from a ruined wall at the end of the kitchen garden, reputed to be a monastic relic—was in the Palladian order of architecture, but rising to no less than four stories and crowned by a tower of formidable dimensions, from which floated, when its owner was in residence, a flag bearing the Emblems of his Race.

The mounted messenger, approaching it through the evening, saw no more than the vast outline of this noble pile. The reader is more privileged. He may penetrate its massive walls and observe its occupant. Reclining at his ease upon an ancient canopied Dais of Tudor workmanship, the Master of the House mused over a vast fire of oaken logs, which illumined the panelled walls and fitfully revealed the soaring roof of his Hall.

He and his great inheritance seemed, in that setting, to lack nothing but the presence of some young *Châtelaine* worthy of the magnificent surroundings. Numerous suits of armour, panoplies of ancient weapons, many a dark canvas from the brush of more than one great master, adorned the walls. Rare porcelains and bronzes were dispersed in profusion, while a chandelier, saved from the sack of Chantilly, swung before a carved mantelpiece of the most elegant design.

From this splendid apartment a suite of not less gorgeous rooms could be perceived through the half-opened doors, the first in the manner of Louis Quinze, the next after the style put into fashion not so long ago by the Regent himself at the Pavilion; and beyond, again, a library, on the shelves of which were ranged the flights of genius, from the classic pages of Cicero and Virgil to the masterpieces of Scott and Alison. The whole combined to produce an effect of wealth and splendour which might have been envied by the highest in the land.

But this princely habitation was a deception to the visitor, a mockery to the embittered tenant of its glories. The apparent master of such treasures was in verity no more than a dependant; all was now abandoned as security to men of whose very names the ruined Henry Portly was uncertain, but who acted through Lawyer Fox, of Bath, himself a partner in the money-lending venture, and (so far as the only documents discovered to Sir Henry could show) the sole mortgagee of those vast estates and of that palatial residence, with all that it contained.

A personal allowance, not ungenerous, but galling and precarious, was secretly advanced to Sir Henry Portly, on condition that he should permanently reside upon the premises; for it was the conviction of the lenders that the maintenance of a certain pomp enhanced the value of their security. The wages of a considerable household were provided with equal secrecy by a monthly payment which this agent (or principal), Lawyer Fox, regularly made to the Baronet, after a full inspection of books, every farthing in which was closely examined and controlled. Little did the obsequious servants and tenants of Molcombe Abbey imagine, when the humble attorney paid his punctual monthly visit, that the roles were reversed: that the great gentleman inwardly trembled lest he should hear the fatal decision which might at any moment drive him from his roof, while the rusty solicitor exulted in an unlimited power over all around.

This lamentable situation had arisen from an action only too common upon the part of our gentry. Sir Henry's father had had the fatal imprudence to speculate on 'Change.

It was at the moment when the fate of Europe hung in the balance, when the Corsican adventurer had broken loose from Elba, and all England was in an agony of expectation to learn the event of the decisive action to be determined on the plains of Flanders.

The rumour spread by Herr Amschel—later and better known as the Baron de Rothschild—that the glory of Britain had set on the field of Waterloo, had led Sir Orlando (for such was his name) to sell three per cents upon account, in the hope of reaping an immense profit when all should be acquainted with the fatal truth. He had not allowed for the business acumen of the great banker. For Amschel-Rothschild had secretly procured the news of *victory* in advance of all, and had had the admirable foresight to spread accounts of *defeat* for the better preparation of the market.

It was upon these accounts that Sir Orlando had speculated in London, confident in the ruin of our cause. But within forty-eight hours it was known that the Iron Duke, despite the blunders of Blücher and the cowardice of the wretched foreigners under his command, had driven in headlong flight the insolent usurper from the field of Waterloo. The three per cents enjoyed an immediate and extraordinary rise in value, and the too sanguine expectant of future fortune was broken.

Sir Orlando was embarrassed beyond repair. Loan succeeded loan. The unfortunate gentleman sank into a premature grave under the burden of his misfortune, and his young heir, Henry, succeeded to the position I have described.

With each succeeding year Sir Henry's difficulty in meeting the interest grew greater, until at last nothing remained between him and foreclosure upon Molcombe Abbey save the delay in finding a sufficient offer of purchase by the mortgage holders. At this stage Sir Henry Portly's situation was—in his own judgment (and perhaps in theirs) — re-established by his approaching engagement to Belinda.

Her father's most hearty consent, her own feelings (which he fondly imagined would favour his suit!), he regarded as earnest of a certain alliance. The prospects of such a marriage he had described to Mr Fox in glowing colours: nor did the lawyer, upon making private inquiry, differ in his judgment upon the case.

After some interval (sufficient to render his young bride sensible of their common interests), Belinda's ample dowry, upon which her father had been both open and generous, would reduce the debt to manageable proportions; her inheritance (on which, moreover, an advance could be negotiated) would more than do the rest: and upon Sir Robert's demise—he was reputed to be of a gouty disposition, and his father had died in middle age—all would once more be stable and at ease in the combined estates of Molcombe Abbey and Marlden Towers.

Such was the line on which Sir Henry Portly's musings ran as he gazed that evening into the fire and erected dreams of an opulent future, when a manservant, clothed in the sumptuous green and mauve of the Portly livery, approached with a salver of massive silver in his hand, bearing a sealed *pli*, which he presented, with a low bow, to the master of the Abbey. It was Sir Robert's letter.

Sir Henry opened it—devoured its contents, grasped his peril in a flash, and immediately, with a rapidity worthy of a Caesar or a Duke of York, he had come to a decision.

With dreadful menaces against delay, he ordered his fleetest steed, Corsair, to be saddled in burning haste, and was galloping furiously down the Bath Road within ten minutes of receiving the fateful news. Alas! that such qualities of intelligence and will should be allied to so unscrupulous a morale: yet such is, indeed, too often the case!

Leaping from his foaming steed in the streets of Bath, at the door of the solicitor's office, he flung the bridle to a passing suppliant, hammered upon the door with his whip-handle, and was at once admitted.

He found Lawyer Fox seated at his desk, perusing, by the light of two candles, dusty documents tied in red tape, each of which doubtless stood for the ruin of the widow and the orphan.

With not a moment's delay the Baronet poured his tale into the ear of the attorney, whose sallow aquiline features, brilliant dark eye, compressed lip, and pointed chin, all marked his concentrated attention.

'There is not a moment to be lost,' cried Sir Henry, in conclusion. 'You know this woman Curll?'

'I do,' answered the Lawyer, in firm but quiet tones. He lifted his spare, black-clad figure from the chair, pulled open a high drawer marked with the letter 'C,' and drew from its recesses an endorsed file wherein were noted the occupation, age, character, and circumstances of that spinster. There were few, indeed, in all Bath and the surrounding district whom Mr Fox could not thus refer to and determine.

'Seek her at once!' the Baronet continued abruptly. 'It is your interest as much as mine.'

'More so,' interjected his creditor dryly.

'See to it that she shall be our agent!'

'Mine,' murmured Mr Fox.

'And that this wretched accident shall come to nothing. Quick! I repeat—there is not an hour to be lost! No one knows better how to act than you! I leave it in your hands.'

The attorney smiled in sinister fashion at the compliment, and taking an ample dark cloak which it was his custom to wrap about his form when engaged on his most secret errands, and a soft broad hat of the same sombre hue, which almost hid his features, he accompanied his client from the room to the street.

He chuckled to himself in mirthless irony as the younger man tossed a guinea to the poor wretch who had held his mount, and set off on his return to Molcombe. The lawyer hearkened a moment to the diminishing sound of the horse's hoofs as they receded in the distance, then, his powerful but evil mind charged with a plan of appalling wickedness, he hurried through the night towards the Crescent, where Miss Curll maintained her meagre *ménage*.

For now some hours that gentlewoman had received and ruminated upon the missive of her benefactress. Her neat but impoverished raiment, the embittered expression upon her pinched features, her very ringlets hanging scarce and grey upon either side of her gaunt face, betrayed her intimate emotion. She dared not neglect what was, indeed, a command, but she had noted with a sarcastic smile the absence of any mention of emolument, and she was considering that the brief morning hours before the arrival of the chaise from The Towers would not even give her the opportunity to find a tenant for her two poorly-furnished rooms during her absence. As is too frequently the case with deeds of benevolence, those of Miss Hackman had awakened no gratitude in the restricted breast of her dependant; and although but last Christmas she had received a gift of game and a bottle of Madeira from her superior and friend, she seemed to regard such munificence as less than her due.

She had already arrived at the conclusion to work upon Belinda's young and more impulsive nature, in order to obtain a handsome gratuity at their parting, when, with a sharp rap at the door, ushered in by the charity girl who was Miss Curll's sole attendant, Mr Fox appeared—presenting, in his dark cloak muffled about his mouth and caught over his extended arm, a figure mysterious and alarming.

He bowed upon his entry, took the chair presented him, thrust his sombrero into the folds of his black garment, and fixed his brilliant eyes upon the gentlewoman with a gaze the intensity of which disconcerted her and compelled her to cast her glance to the floor.

'Madam,' he said at length, 'I will be brief—and to the purpose. You are engaged to act as companion for some little time to Miss Montgomery at Marlden Towers.'

The unfortunate lady made a gesture as though to reply, when he interrupted her and continued:

'All is known to me. I approach you only for your own advantage—and, indeed, that of your employers.'

At the word 'employers' a faint flush, which did not escape her visitor, rose to this unfortunate lady's cheekbones. She repressed a protest and heard him out.

'This young lady—you may have heard it—or you may not —is pursued by the unwelcome attentions . . .'

'Whether they are unwelcome or no,' Miss Curll took courage to interrupt, 'it is not mine to judge. I am informed of the situation. I know the gentleman's name . . . I . . .'

'Madam—they must not meet.'

'Sir!' answered Miss Curll with some hauteur, 'I do not take orders from you! You forget yourself. . . . Moreover' (she added, as she noted a certain expression upon his lips), 'I may tell you that such a contingency does not arise. The young people are already pledged to such conduct as you advise. Indeed, my charge, Miss Montgomery, has promised her father that during his absence, there shall be no meeting between herself and young Mr Maltravers.'

'It is well,' answered Mr Fox briefly—and here he leant forward in an impressive manner and lowered his voice. 'But there is more. They are not to correspond.'

'Really, sir——' began Miss Curll, with rising tones, when she noticed that the hand of the lawyer had laid firmly upon the table, concealed or half-concealed, a banknote of an unknown denomination. Her colour came and went, she clasped her mittened hands, and nervously intertwined her fingers.

'They are permitted to correspond,' she almost whispered, 'at least, if I understand . . .'

'Madam,' broke in the Attorney, 'you have read wrong. It is to the interest of all—and of none more than of the young lady herself—that no letters should pass.'

With that he permitted so much of the note to be seen as disclosed the enormous sum of twenty-five pounds.

'Would you bribe me, sir?' cried Miss Curll, in haughty and louder tones.

'Such was my intention,' answered the lawyer cynically; 'if indeed,' he added hastily, 'any possibility of bribery were in question. . . . Come—I spoke in jest,' he continued, with a fixed and passionless expression. 'There is no idea of any such thing. Rather are we concerned to further interests which no one has more at heart than Sir Robert himself, and his cousin Miss Hackman. They will be grateful, believe me. I know all.'

'You bewilder me . . .' said Miss Curll, with hesitation. 'For whom do you speak?'

'For those who most desire Miss Montgomery's welfare. You *cannot*,' he added earnestly, 'act more for this poor young heiress's good, than by preventing a fatal course which all deplore. No one, in the end, will thank you more sincerely than her parent.'

'I know,' faltered Miss Curll, 'that you are in the secrets of the gentry in our neighbourhood as I am not . . . and . . . that you may well be speaking—I am sure you are speaking—with superior knowledge of the family and its affairs.'

'I am,' answered Lawyer Fox decidedly. 'Indeed, the matter is felt to be so urgent, that, on finding the mission fulfilled, a further seventy-five pounds will immediately be placed at your disposal, through my agency.'

Miss Curll was silent. The lawyer rose, leaving the twenty-five-pound note upon the table. Miss Curll rose also, but added not a word.

'Madam,' said the tempter, as he moved to the door, 'I leave it to your honour and to your solid sense—matured, if I may say so, by some experience of life—to discern and to effect the *true* interests of the young, wealthy, but infatuated female entrusted to your charge.'

With these words he was gone.

VI

Sir Robert, as he left for town, was delighted to observe the warmth with which his daughter received her companion, whom, indeed, she had not infrequently met in Bath when accompanying her cousin, Miss Hackman, upon errands of mercy. Her welcome argued success for his plans, and when, after warm embraces and benedictions, he fondly took his leave, he felt secure of her comfort until his return.

And, indeed, Miss Curll was assiduous in her attentions to her charge, immediately took over all household duties, and surprised the domestics by her lack of hesitation in the ordering of the household. Belinda accepted her solicitous advice on health and hours, and felt—after so many emotions—a sort of luxury in transferring the reins and relaxing into a complete vacuity from domestic cares.

But the more free was her mind from daily rounds, the more did the chief object of her thoughts return to her in a mixture of longing and delight. Soon (she mused) her ordeal would be at an end. Her dear papa would applaud her constancy—and meanwhile . . .

That same afternoon, a little before dinner, at about four o'clock, Miss Curll (who was standing at the window while

Belinda read a book, reclining at ease upon a canopy) observed a figure, not of the household, approaching at some distance down the fields from the direction of Halston.

She turned without haste to her charge.

'My dearest,' she said (she was already on such terms), 'you will excuse me, will you not? I shall take the air. I need it, and there is but a moment before we must dress for dinner, which I have postponed to the hour of five.'

She kissed the charming face, and, descending, strolled out towards the iron gates of the garden and on to the path through the park, as though careless of her steps.

The youth, whom she met half-way across the park field on the path to the wood saluted her awkwardly and would have passed. She stopped him with a smile, and asked him whither he was bound.

He told her that he bore a note from his master, Mr Horatio Maltravers, for Miss Montgomery, and that he had not been desired to await a reply.

'It is well,' answered Miss Curll graciously. 'I am glad to have met you; for Miss Montgomery is at this moment reposing, and I can convey this letter to her in due time, when she shall descend from her boudoir.' With that, in a genteel gesture which marked her early training, she withdrew the folded paper from the youth's hand, and smiling again with courteous confidence, placed it in her bosom. The lad, well pleased to be relieved of further duty, touched his forehead in rustic fashion and turned back the way he had come. Miss Curll slowly retraced her steps towards the mansion, humming in a somewhat worn but subdued voice one of those airs which Mr Moore, the Irishman, had rendered familiar to the nobility and gentry, and which is now widely known as *The Minstrel Boy*.

She regained her room. She opened a small casket of cedar wood, wherein her poor trinkets were kept. She was on the point of depositing therein the letter, unopened, when she paused, possessed by a desire which she was ashamed to admit even to her inmost soul, but weak enough to gratify.

It has been remarked by acute observers of the human species that the female is more prone to the vice of curiosity than the male. This impoverished gentlewoman was no exception to her sex. Her loneliness, her distant acquaintance with the wealthy, her soured memories of happier days, perhaps some faded phantasm of romance, conspired to tempt her.

If, as the Papists monstrously pretend, an angel were deputed guardian for each of us, to defend us from evils which our own resolute wills should suffice to contest, such an imaginary being would have wept to observe the struggle in the soul of Miss Curll and its lamentable catastrophe.

She gently forced open the sealed and folded sheet with every imaginable precaution; none the less was it slightly torn. At this accident she shrugged her shoulders imperceptibly under her Castilian shawl; she knew that it prevented any retreat or later subterfuge. She boldly opened the paper and was amused, interested, absorbed, to read these lines, penned in the bold and hasty hand of an impassioned lover:

'It is a word from your most honoured father which permits me to dare—to adventure—these words. I know not, in my perturbation, how to begin. I fear lest—once entered upon such a path—I cannot bring myself to end. The same indulgence which has granted me the supreme felicity of addressing you has informed me that we may not meet—for an eternity of days: at the earliest upon Sir Robert's return from the Metropolis. My agony is enhanced by his communication of its cause. What! You are suffering, and I may not be near you? You languish, and I may not fly to your side? I went this morning to the ferns, to the pines, to the streamlet —although I knew I should not find you there. Believe me, the woods were fragrant with your presence, and all the sunlit world was filled with you. I say no more: I dare not. But oh! if the sacred moment which has transformed my life be not a cheat and an illusion, grant me one written word to support me in my fixed attention for the blessed, the distant moment in which I shall hear your living voice again, and, with its first accent, enter Paradise. I dare not write more: with what a thirst I long for but the briefest phrase from the quill your hand has held you may not know. It will be the sole sustenance of Horatio: it is life to him who now, and for evermore, must offer his soul to your keeping.'

The letter was refolded: hidden in its receptacle, and locked away. Some trace of a cold tear rose to the eye of the unhappy woman who had thus betrayed her trust. She soon mastered this passing sentiment. She rose and moved towards Belinda's room.

Her charge was asleep as she noiselessly entered the apartment. She sat herself down at the window and, taking her wool and knitting-needles from the table where she had left them, occupied herself in the silent task until a delicate harmonious sigh revealed the awakening of her young companion.

'Miss Curll,' said Belinda, in a drowsy voice, 'is that you?' Then, fully awake, she added: 'I trust you enjoyed your stroll?'

'It was delightful, my dear,' replied the spinster with a pleasing glance. 'Silent communion with Nature is my chief joy; and I was pleased to discover that at such an hour I had the park to myself. No one stirred. I returned as I came, alone. The very leaves were at rest.'

Once more (but this time more deeply, and fully conscious) Belinda sighed. She rose from her couch, in spite of Miss Curll's remonstrance, and moved towards the window: there she stood pensive, watching the golden light in the west, her eyes unconsciously turning to the distant trees that hid the aged walls and crumbling turrets of the Maltravers.

Though but this one first day of separation was passing, she had hoped—she had dared to hope—that some sign would have come already from that house in all these long hours. She turned away and was silent.

'You are fatigued, my love,' said Miss Curll, implanting a kiss upon the pale brow. 'You shall dine in your room and early seek repose.'

'I will do so,' said Belinda resignedly. 'To-morrow I shall be completely recovered, believe me. To-night I must rest.'

.   .   .   .   .

With the next day an undimmed sun displayed the ancient groves and illumined the venerable precincts of Marlden Towers. Belinda, rising late, found herself, for the first time, unresponsive to the glorious sky. Her hours were passed in an increasing ill-ease to which she could give no name, while her desire to conceal it from her companion rendered it the more burdensome. It was not hers to let her thoughts dwell . . . yet dwell they would . . . on why . . . on whether. . . .

She told herself that two days were not a long delay upon such an occasion. That a letter or message from Horatio would come, must be patiently awaited. Next a hasty, passionate thought interrupted her melancholy—no sooner entertained than banished. With the fall of evening her feverish mind suggested to her the folly that her father might have overstated his indulgence in the account he had given her of his note to Horatio: that some harsh word of Sir Robert's might have abashed the younger man and rendered him silent: nay, that

Sir Robert might even have hinted against any correspondence, though he had himself assured her they were free to write.

She crushed the thought. It was followed by a miserable, unworthy dread lest even so short a separation should have changed Horatio's mind. This dread in turn yielded to what might in one less gifted, have verged on peevishness. At one moment it was with difficulty that she restrained her tears: at another her anger.

Darkness fell upon her unstable and feverish mood. A second night was passed in broken slumber.

The third day she was resolved to discover the cause—absence, neglect, illness . . . or chivalry?—the cause of that silence which had made her so to mourn.

She seated herself at her desk about midday, and, after making many a halt, many an inner consultation, she made bold to write as follows:

'I take my pen—with what hesitation you best will know; with what eagerness (Yes, let me write it!) you best will understand. Yet it is only to ask you, Horatio, for such news of yourself as you have so often given me during the many years of our neighbourhood—of our acquaintance. My father has written to you—he has told me so. He has informed you of my indisposition, which forbids me to walk abroad or to receive. It will soon be gone—indeed, with his return a fortnight hence I shall be free as ever. But, in the interval, he would not (he assured me) have me neglect to hear from you. I have feared a little lest some passing illness may have postponed your writing: if that be so, then send me word, that I may write again . . . but now . . . but now . . . I can write no more. You know what spirit moves my pen, as it signs my name for you,

'BELINDA.'

When she had read and re-read this simple letter—now dreading her daring, then emboldened by that inward flame—she took the step; she sealed it with her own ring; she summoned her maid.

Then, at a second thought, she determined to avoid anything that might by any misinterpretation seem clandestine, and boldly taking it to Miss Curll—for it was she who administered the household—begged her to see that a groom should at once bear the missive to Horatio.

'I will see to it without delay, my dear,' that lady assured her. 'But you must not leave your room without precautions —and so early! Remember,' she added archly, 'that I am your jailer and that your health is my great concern! Come, let me lead you back. I will return in a moment, and we will take our refection together in your apartments.'

Poor Belinda rewarded her with a sweet smile, and, after so trying an hour, lay down to rest, assured that a reply to her billet could not be long delayed.

Alas! My reader knows too well what the next action of the elderly companion could not fail to be! She hastened to her own room, locked the door, and with now eager, unhesitating fingers broke the seal, and perused those words which were meant for another, and for that other alone. This done, she put the letter hastily away in the casket, locked it, and returned to her ward. So true is it that one evil deed leads to another, and that what first our conscience will hardly permit we soon repeat with shameless ease!

.   .   .   .   .   .

Meanwhile, in the cobwebbed and decaying woodwork of his ancient hall, Horatio Maltravers feverishly paced, marvelling, as the hours dragged on and day succeeded day, how it was that no word had reached him from The Towers. Now he was in an agony of doubt lest that dear frame should be tortured by fever, now in wonder whether a letter might not have miscarried; at last, when full inquiry had assured him that the illness of his adored was slight and mending, that no letter had come to him from the neighbouring house, he nerved himself to write once more. His excuse was ample: five days had passed since his first message: five days without a word.

He wrote with a soul disturbed; he wrote unevenly, hesitating for expression, destroying *brouillon* after *brouillon* until at last he had composed these lines—these feverish lines:

'Belinda, if I have offended you in aught reveal it to me and I will make amends for life! If some ill rumour has reached you, which stains my honour in your eyes, briefly detail it to me and I will clear myself. If for any reason whatsoever you are prevented from sending notice of yourself, from letting me receive and worship the traces of your hand—oh! let me know it, and set at rest this tortured heart! But if you must still be obstinately silent, then believe, be sure, that I conclude my heaven to have been a brief illusion—your love (oh! my beloved)

never to have answered mine. Yet, even so, respond! respond!
I cannot be, I do not live, till I know even the worst: but oh!
at least reply!'

This message, sealed and (how tenderly!) directed, he entrusted
to the same messenger, then, relieved in some measure by such
a paroxysm of the soul, he retired to rest in his ancestral
chamber. In dreams he saw his appeal touched by divine
hands, and compassion entering those pure eyes which had in
them also the hidden flame of Heaven. It was but a dream;
that letter, like its fellows, was intercepted; one more missive
lay buried in the now crime-laden casket of Miss Curll.

Beyond those neighbouring elms, amid the well-appointed
recesses of Marlden Towers, in her own luxurious apartments
Belinda blushed and wept, self-tortured, as the days drew on.

Was it for this she had broken every rule of her condition and
sex, outraged the tradition of the Montgomerys, and lowered
herself to *originate* a correspondence with a *gentleman*? Was
she thus to be disdained, nay, ridiculed? Then (with the next
morn and after a troubled sleep) other counsels returned. It
was an error; an accident! He was absent! Ill perhaps!
And as this idea rose in her mind, her being stretched forth
through airy space to seek to console him.

Or again. . . . Or? . . . Or what dread explanation of his
silence?

It was no longer to be borne! She took once more in hand
that long goose quill of rosy tint, her soul's good instrument,
and, in the very moments when Horatio Maltravers was penning
her his piercing cry, Belinda Montgomery was inditing, through
blinding tears, this touching, this memorable appeal:

'Horatio, My Horatio,—I have abandoned all for you. I put
my very soul into these words. . . . Ah! Why have you given
me no sign? Why do I write? I know not what I write nor
how I write it. If you will not heed me, if you remain thus
obstinately turned away—why then I write no more nor,
indeed, exist. Forget, forgive the unfortunate Belinda.'

Such were the effects of passion and disappointment upon
the unhappy maid. Alas! that words so distraught (yet so
profoundly moving!) should have been lost in their turn. Within an hour they were locked away in the keeping of that
treasonable companion.

In Halston's venerable halls Horatio Maltravers woke from a
fevered sleep to one more unhappy, uncompanioned day. The
moments dragged like weeks; the morning half a year. He
could not endure the silence: he walked to the very edges of
his domain, still expecting against expectation some messenger
at last. He returned morose to his table. After a meal un-
tasted, wine barely sipped, he sat back silent in his chair and
alone, considering a great resolution. At last he rose, approached
his desk, took pen, ink, paper, sand, taper, wax, and seal, and
composed this terrible adieu:

'Belinda—I call you by your name: it is as though I spoke to
you, soul of my soul; for even to write your name is a benediction. Belinda, you remain deaf to my entreaty, dumb to
my poor request for one whispered word. You have thought
better of a foolish moment: and, indeed, what right had I to
envisage the escalade of heaven?

'Forgive, forget, the unfortunate Horatio.'

He sealed the folded sheet and, summoning a menial, bade it
be at once delivered at Marlden Towers. 'Saddle me Crusader!'
he cried (naming the stoutest in his poor stable). 'Bring me
saddle-bags: I will fill them myself. I ride to-night.'

The domestics of the shrunken household discussed in awed
and lowered voices their master's strange demeanour. As for
him, he put up but a small change of linen with a *rouleau* of one
hundred guineas (his sole reserve), left with his housekeeper a
short word announcing an absence of indefinite duration, and
in this feverish fashion, rode out into the night.

For such is youth! Irresponsible to itself and others, a cause
of ceaseless concern to age; but stirred with primeval fires.

'AL-RAFSAT,' OR THE KICK

IN the days of Abd-er-Rahman, who was among the wisest and
most glorious of the Commanders of the Faithful, there resided
in the City of Bagdad an elderly merchant of such enormous
wealth that his lightest expressions of opinion caused the
markets of the Euphrates to fluctuate in the most alarming
manner.

This merchant, whose name was Mahmoud, had a brother in
the middle ranks of Society, a surgeon by profession, and by
name El-Hakim. To this brother he had frequently expressed
a fixed determination to leave him no wealth of any kind. 'It is
my opinion,' he would say, 'that a man's first duty is to his own
children, and though I have no children myself, I must observe
the general rule.' He was fond of dilating upon this subject
whenever he came across his relative, and would discover from
time to time new and still better reasons for the resolution he
had arrived at. His brother received with great courtesy the
prospect held out to him by the wealthy merchant; but one
day, finding tedious the hundredth repetition of that person's
pious but somewhat wearisome resolve, said to him:

'Mahmoud, though it would be a mean and even an impious
thing to expect an inheritance from you to any of my seven
sons, yet perhaps you will allow these boys to receive from your
lips some hint as to the manner in which you have accumulated
that great wealth which you now so deservedly enjoy.'

'By all means,' said Mahmoud, who was ever ready to describe
his own talents and success. 'Send the little fellows round to
me to-morrow about the hour the public executions take place
before the Palace, for by that time I shall have breakfasted,
and shall be ready to receive them.'

The Surgeon, with profuse thanks, left his brother and conveyed the good news to the seven lads, who stood in order
before him with the respect for parents customary in the Orient,
each placed according to his size and running in gradation from
eight to sixteen years of age.

Upon the morrow, therefore, the Surgeon's seven sons, seated gravely upon crossed legs, formed a semicircle at the feet of their revered relative, who, when he had watched them humorously and in silence for some moments, puffing at his great pipe, opened his lips and spoke as follows:

'Your father has wondered, my dear nephews, in what way the fortune I enjoy has been acquired; for in his own honourable but far from lucrative walk of life, sums which are to me but daily trifles appear like the ransoms of kings. To you, his numerous family, it seems of especial advantage that the road to riches should be discovered. Now I will confess to you, my dear lads, that I am quite ignorant of any rule or plan whereby the perishable goods of this world may be rapidly accumulated in the hands of the Faithful. Nay, did any such rule exist, I am persuaded that by this time the knowledge of it would be so widely diffused as to embrace the whole human race. In which case,' he added, puffing meditatively at his pipe, 'all would cancel out and no result would be achieved; since a great fortune, as I need not inform young people of your sagacity, is hardly to be acquired save at the expense of others.

'But though I cannot give you those rules for which your father was seeking when he sent you hither, I can detail you the steps by which my present affluence was achieved; and each of you, according to his intelligence, will appreciate what sort of accidents may make for the increase of fortune. When you are possessed of this knowledge it will serve you through life for recreation and amusement, though I very much doubt its making you any richer. For it is not the method nor even the opportunity of intelligent acquisition which leads to great riches, but two other things combined: one, the unceasing appetite to snatch and hold from all and at every season; the other, that profound mystery, the Mercy of God.

'For Allah, in his inscrutable choice, frowns on some and smiles on others. The first he condemns to contempt, anxiety, duns, bills, Courts of law, sudden changes of residence and even dungeons; the second he gratifies with luxurious vehicles, delicious sherbet, and enormous houses, such as mine. His will be done.

'A dear friend of mine, one Moshé, was a receiver of stolen goods in Bosra, until God took him, now twenty years ago. He left two sons of equal intelligence and rapacity. The one, after numerous degradations, died of starvation in Armenia; the other, of no greater skill, is to-day governor of all Algeirah and rings the changes at will upon the public purse. *Mektub.*'

For a moment the ancient Captain of Industry paused with bent head in solemn meditation upon the designs of Heaven, then raising his features protested that he had too long delayed the story of his life, with which he would at once proceed.

.   .   .   .   .   .

'As a boy, my dear nephews,' began the kindly uncle, while his dutiful nephews regarded him with round eyes, 'I was shy, dirty, ignorant, lazy, and wilful. My parents and teachers had but to give me an order for me to conceive at once some plan of disobeying it. All forms of activity save those connected with dissipation were abhorrent to me. So far from reciting with other boys of my age in chorus and without fault the verses of the Koran, I grew up completely ignorant of that work, the most Solemn Name in which I to this day pronounce with an aspirate from an unfamiliarity with its aspect upon the written page. Yet I am glad to say that I never neglected my religious duties, that I prayed with fervour and regularity, and that I had a singular faith in the loving kindness of my God.

'I had already reached my seventeenth year when my father, who had carefully watched the trend of my nature and the use to which I had put my faculties, addressed me as follows:

' "Mahmoud, I wish you no ill. I have so far fed and clothed you because the Caliph (whom Allah preserve!) has caused those who neglect their younger offspring to be severely beaten upon the soles of their feet. It is now my intention to send you about your business. I propose'—and here my dear father pulled out a small purse—"to give you the smallest sum compatible with my own interests, so that if any harm befall you, the vigilant officers of the Crown cannot ascribe your disaster to my neglect. I request that you will walk in any direction you choose so only that it be in a straight line away from my doors. If, when this your patrimony is spent, you make away with yourself I shall hold you to blame; I shall be better pleased to hear that you have sold yourself into slavery or in some other way provided for your continued sustenance. But what I should like best would be never to hear of you again." With those words my father (your grandfather, dear boys), seizing me by the shoulders, turned my back to his doors and thrust me forth with a hearty kick the better to emphasize his meaning.

'Thus was I launched out in the dawn of manhood to try my adventures with the world.

'I discovered in my pouch as I set out along the streets of the city the sum of 100 dinars, with which my thoughtful parent had provided me under the legal compulsion which he so feelingly described. "With so large a capital," said I to myself, "I can exist for several days, indulge my favourite forms of dissipation, and when they are well spent it will be time enough to think of some experiment whereby to replace them."'

Here the eldest nephew said respectfully and with an inclination of the head: 'Pray, uncle, what is a dinar?'

'My dear lad,' replied the merchant with a merry laugh, 'I confess that to a man of my position a reply to your question is impossible. I could only tell you that it is a coin of considerable value to the impoverished, but to men like myself a denomination so inferior as to be indistinguishable from all other coins.'

Having so expressed himself the worthy merchant resumed the thread of his tale:

'I had, I say, started forward in high spirits to the sound of the coins jingling in my pouch, when my steps happened to take me to the water-side, where I found a ship about to sail for the Persian Gulf. "Here," said I to myself, "is an excellent opportunity for travelling and for seeing the world."

'The heat of the day was rising. No one was about but two watermen, who lay dozing upon the bank. I nimbly stepped aboard and hid myself behind one of the bales of goods with which the deck was packed. When the sun declined and work was resumed, the sailors tramped aboard, the sail was hoisted, and we started upon our journey.

'Befriended by the darkness of night I crept out quietly from my hiding-place and found a man watching over the prow, where he was deputed to try the depth of the water from time to time with a long pole. I affected an air of authority, and told him that the Captain had sent me forward to deliver his commands, which were that he should give me a flask of wine, some fruit, and a cake (for I guessed that like all sailors he had in his possession things both lawful and unlawful). These I told him I would take to my relative the Captain. He left me with the pole for a moment and soon returned with the provisions, with which I crept back to my hiding-place, and there heartily consumed them.

'During the whole of the next day I lay sleeping behind the bales of goods. With the fall of the second night I needed a second meal. I dared not repeat my first experiment, and lay musing till, hunger having sharpened my wits, I hit upon a plan with which surely Providence itself must have inspired a poor lonely lad thrown in his unaided weakness upon a cruel world.

'I bethought me that the watchman of either board would have some provision for the night. I remembered a sort of gangway between the high bales upon the main deck, which corridor led back far under the poop into the stern-sheets. It had been so designed for the convenience of stowing and un-loading, affording a passage for the workmen as they handled the cargo. I put these two things together in my mind (but to God be the glory) and formed of them a plan for immediate execution.

'I crept from my hiding-place and sauntered along the dark deck until I came upon the watchman, squatting by the rail, and contemplating the stars in the moonless sky. He had, as I had suspected, a platter the white of which I could just see glimmering against the deck beside him. I thought I also discerned a gourd of wine. I approached him as one of the crew (for they were chance strangers taken on at the wharf). We talked in low tones of the girls of Bagdad, of the police, of opportunities for theft, and of such other topics as are common to the poor, till, naturally, we came to wine. He cursed the poor quality of his own, in the gourd beside him. I, after some mystery, confided to him that I had a stock of excellent wine, and, as my friendship for him increased, I made a clean breast of it and told him it was in the stern-sheets, far under the poop deck along the narrow passage between the high bales. I offered to go with him and fetch it, allowing him, in his eager-ness, to go first. When he was well engaged in groping aft I turned, crept forward again silently and rapidly, picked up the loaf and cheese which I found on his platter, as also the gourd, and vanished into my hiding-hole.

'I ate my fill—though somewhat too hurriedly, and remarked how long a time my shipmate was spending at searching that empty place. As I heard him creeping back at last cursing violently in whispers, I was aware of faint dawn in the East, and determined that my cruise must end.

'We were already in the neighbourhood of the sea, as I dis-covered by tasting the water over the side in the darkness and discovering it to be brackish. I bethought me that my poor comrade had now an excellent reason for ferreting me out, that the Captain also would soon hear of me, and that, with daylight, I should certainly be visited with a bastinado or put into chains and sold. I therefore slipped over the side (for I was an excellent swimmer) and made for the shore. There I lay on a warm beach and watched through the reeds the great sail of the ship as it slipped down stream further and further away in the growing light.

'When the sun rose the vessel was out of sight, and looking about me I discovered a little village not far from the shore inhabited by simple fishermen, but containing several houses of some pretension, the residences of wealthy merchants who came here from Bosra in their moments of leisure to relax themselves from the catch-as-catch-can of commerce in that neighbouring city.

'My first action at the opening of the new day was to fall upon my knees and add to the ritual prayer a humble out-pouring of thanks for the benefits I had already received and a fervent appeal for guidance. That appeal was heard. I rose from my knees full of a new-found plan.

'To one of those wealthier houses which stood near the village I at once proceeded and sent in a message by a slave to its owner saying that my master, a wealthy dealer in carpets, solicited the custom of his lordship, and that if the great man would but accompany me to the quay I would there show him wares well worthy of his attention.

'It so happened (and here was Providence again at work) that this merchant had a passion for a particular sort of carpet which is solely made by the inhabitants of El Kzar, for they alone possess the secret, which they very zealously guard. The slave, therefore, brought me back the message that his master would not be at the pains of accompanying me unless such wares were present for his inspection. If my carpets were those of El Kzar he would willingly inspect them, but if they were of any other brand he was indifferent.

'And let this teach you, my dear nephews, how simple are the minds of the rich.

'I was willing enough that the carpets should be carpets of El Kzar, or, indeed, of any other place under heaven, for all were at my choice.

'I hastened, therefore, to send back a further message thae by a curious coincidence we had upon this occasion nothing else in stock but Kzaran carpets, and begged the slave to emphasizt this important point to his master.

'His reply was to twist his right hand, palm upwards, with

a strange smile. I pulled out my purse, showed him the shining dinars, and asked him whether he would rather have *one* now for his fee or *five* on the completion of the transaction. With glistening eyes—and even (as I thought) a pathetic gratitude —the slave leapt at the latter offer.

'And let this teach you, my dear nephews, how simple are the minds of the poor.

'He hastened off to deliver my message.

'Within a few moments the master of the house appeared in great haste, and all of a fever bade me lead him to the appointed spot.'

At this moment the merchant paused and with reverie and reminiscence in his eye remained silent for at least that space of time in which a dexterous pickpocket may gingerly withdraw a purse from the sleeve of a Holy Man. The second nephew thought the opportunity arrived to suggest a doubt which had been vexing his young mind. He said with an obeisance:

'Venerable uncle, we have listened to the beginnings of your career with admiration and respect, but we are more perplexed than ever to discover how such beginnings could have led to such an end. For you appear to us as yet only to have followed that path which leads to the torturers and the bow-strings.'

'Such,' replied his uncle, with a look of singular affection, 'is the general opinion entertained of all very wealthy men in the first step of their careers; but I hope that the sequel will teach you and your clever little brothers how wrongly informed are the vulgar.'

As the Merchant Mahmoud pronounced these words the Call to Prayer was heard from a neighbouring tower, and he hurriedly concluded:

'My dear nephews, we are called to prayer. I will cease here to speak and will continue to-morrow the story of Myself and Providence.'

Upon hearing these words his seven nephews rose together, and crossed their arms; following which gesture, with three deep bows performed as they walked backwards toward the curtains of the magnificent apartment, they left their uncle's presence.

·   ·   ·   ·   ·

'You will remember, my dear nephews,' said the Merchant Mahmoud when the lads were once more assembled in a half-circle before him with crossed legs and attentive countenances, 'that you left me hurrying with the collector of Kzaran carpets towards the quay where he should enjoy the sight of the merchandise. This merchant was reputed among the people of the place to be of a singularly cunning and secretive temperament, a character which (you may think it strange!) they admired as though it were the summit of human wisdom. I confess that I found him, in the matter of Kzaran carpets at least, very different from his reputation. A more garrulous old gentleman never trod this earth. He was in a perpetual stammer of excitement, and though I was careful to lead him by the most roundabout roads that he might have time to cool his ardour, the delay did but seem to increase it.

'"I implore you, sir," he said at last, as one who could no longer restrain some violent passion, "I implore you, pay no attention to others in this place who may have attempted to forestall me in the matter of your very valuable cargo. Your honour is, I know, sufficient in the matter. . . . I am confident you will give me a free market. Also, they know nothing of Kzaran carpets in these parts: they are mere buyers and sellers . . . and on what a margin! Let me tell you in your ear that while many men in this place carry on the appearance of riches, most are indebted to Parsees in the capital. I alone am in an independent position and' (here he whispered) 'I can well reward you *privately* and *in your own pocket* for any favour you may show me.'

'Seeing him so eager, I affected a certain hesitation and embarrassment, and at last confessed that I had been approached by a local merchant whose name I was forbidden to mention and who had very kindly sent me as a present by a slave the sum of 1,000 dinars. To this he had attached no conditions, but he had also, quite independently, sent word that he had himself orders for carpets which he was bound to fulfil. His profit (he had said), if I would give him a first choice, would be so considerable that he would be very ready to offer me a handsome commission on the completion of the bargain; quite apart from the 1,000 dinars which were but a little present from one man to another. "This thousand dinars," I added, "now in my possession, I have accepted. A present is a graceful act and can be taken with a clean conscience. But the *commission* is another matter. I must consider beyond everything the interests of my master. I shall not mention the offer made to me (for with all his confidence in me he is himself a business man and might misunderstand my position), but I shall think it my duty to give him no advice save to sell to the highest bidder."

'"It is I!" shouted the aged connoisseur eagerly, "it is I who will prove the highest bidder! Nay, my dear fellow, since such bargains are often concluded in private, would it not be better to tell your master forthwith that no possible competitor can stand against me in this place? Let him first discover the sum offered by my rival and I give you leave to suggest a sum larger by one-tenth, which shall decide his judgment. Meanwhile," he added, "two thousand dinars are but a small present for one in your position, and I shall willingly—joyfully—propose to give you that sum, not for a moment on account of the service which I am certain you design to do me, but purely as an expression of my esteem."

'His excitement had now so risen that I fear his judgment was lost. Already he saw before him in his mind's eye a pile of the noblest Kzaran carpets, all ready for the caravan. Already he saw a rival calmly acquiring them on the distant wharf, the witnesses placing their seals, the words of completion.

'He trembled as again he urged on me the little gift, the little personal gift, the trifling gift of two thousand dinars.

'"Sir," said I in reply, a little stiffly, "I am not accustomed to take secret commissions under any disguise. My duty is clear: if I cannot receive a firm offer superior to that already made me, and that backed with proof that you are indeed, as you say, the most solid man in the place—then I must close with my first client. If indeed I were certain of an immediate payment in a larger sum I would accept your proposal. But how can I know anything of this place? The thousand dinars of which I spoke are coined and in a wallet; I have them safe. With all the respect due to your age, I have no information upon your credit in this town. And I confess," I added in another tone, "that I *am* acquainted with your rival's position, which is perhaps more solid than you think. I confess I think it would be simpler and to the better interest of our house if I were to go straight to him now and have done with it."

'As I spoke thus the old man lost all reason. It was piteous to see one of his age and venerable hairs dancing and spluttering with excitement. He shook his fists in the air, he called to Heaven in shrill tones, he betrayed all the frenzy of the collector. He contrasted the mercantile motives of the unknown competitor with his own passion for Pure Art. He called Heaven to witness to the reality of his wealth, and at last in a sort of fury tore from his garments the jewels which ornamented them, thrust into my hand all the cash upon his person (it was in a leather bag, and amounted altogether to no more than five hundred dinars), added to this a brooch of gold, which he dragged from his scarf, and said that if this instalment were not a sufficient proof of his good faith and credit he knew not how to move me.

'I shrugged my shoulders and suggested that instead of making so violent a protestation and at such risk to his fortune he should go back soberly to his house and return with an instrument of credit and two witnesses (as the law demands), while I awaited him patiently at that spot. I, at least, was in no haste and would honourably abide his return. He was off at a speed which I should never have thought possible at his age.

'I waited until he had turned the corner of a distant hedge of prickly pears, and not until he was quite out of sight did I gather the jewels, the coins, and the precious ornaments which in his haste he had thrown at my feet, and very rapidly betake myself in the opposite direction.

'Never was the Mercy of Allah more evidently extended. The plain was naked outside the town, the river perhaps a mile distant; my plight, as it might appear, desperate. I pinned the gold brooch to my cloak, I distributed the jewels openly upon various parts of my person, and I proceeded at a smart pace over the open plain towards the river. It was with the greatest joy that I found upon its bank two fishermen about to set sail and proceed down stream to sea. Their presence inspired me with a plan for escape.

'I chatted negligently with them (still keeping one eye upon the distant house of my aged but excitable friend). At last with a light laugh I offered one of them a piece of gold, saying that I should be pleased to try the novel experience of a little cruise. The fisherman, who was quite unacquainted with so much wealth, and seemed somewhat awestruck, gave me some grand title or other, and promised me very good sport with the fish and a novel entertainment. But even as he and his companion pushed out from shore I turned in my seat on the deck and perceived in the plain a rising dust which betrayed the approach of the merchant with his witnesses and a company of his slaves.

'Suddenly changing my expression from one of pleased though wearied expectancy to one of acute alarm, I shouted to my new companions: "Push away for your lives and stretch your sail to its utmost! These are the Commissioners sent by the Caliph to re-assess and tax all fishing-boats upon a new valuation! Already had they seized three upon the beach when I left and found you here!"

'At these words the worthy fellows were inspired by a fear even greater than my own. They manfully pushed into the swiftest part of the current, and, though a smart breeze was blowing, hoisted every inch of the sail, so that the boat ran with her gunwale upon the very edge of the water and was indeed dangerously pressed. But I had the satisfaction of seeing the merchant and his retinue vainly descending the river-bank, at perhaps one-half our speed, calling down curses upon us, threatening with their fists, shouting their public titles of authority, their menaces of the law, and in every way confirming my excellent pair of fishermen in the story I had told them.

'It was a pleasant thing to loll on deck under the heat of the day, toying with the valuable ornaments I had so recently acquired and lazily watching my companions as they sweated at the halyards, or alternatively glancing along towards the shore at the little group of disappointed people which fell so rapidly behind us as we bowled down the tide. Soon their features were no longer plain, then their figures could scarcely be distinguished. The last impression conveyed to me was of some little very distant thing, stamping with impotent rage and shaking wild arms against the sky. I could not but deplore so grievous a lapse in dignity in one so venerable.

'When we were well away from the neighbourhood of the city I asked the fishermen whither they were bound; to which they answered that their business was only to cruise about outside and fish during the night, returning at dawn with their catch. "Would it not be better," I suggested, "seeing that these rapacious fellows will hang about for a day or so, to carry me to some town of your acquaintance along the coast where the reigning powers do not suffer from the tyranny of Bagdad? For my part I am free to travel where I will, and the prospect of a change pleases me. I shall be happy," said I, 'to reward the sacrifice of your catch with fifty dinars."

'At the prospect of much further wealth the fishermen were at once convinced: they sang in the lightness of their hearts, and for three days and three nights we sped down the Gulf, passing bleak mountains and deserted rocky promontories, until upon the fourth day we came to a town the like of which I had never seen.

'"Shall we land here?" said I.

'"No," said the fishermen, "for it is in a manner within the Caliph's dominions, and perhaps that accursed tax of which you spoke will be levied here also."

'"You know better than I," replied I thoughtfully, standing for a moment in affected perplexity. "Let me, however, land in your little boat. I have a passion for new places. I will come out to you again after the hour of the midday prayers, while you stand in the offing."

'To this arrangement they readily consented. I rowed to the land, and when I had reached the shore I was pleased to see my fearful hosts quite three miles out upon the hot and shimmering sea. Gazing at them, I hope with charity, and certainly with interest, I pushed the little boat adrift (for I had no reason to return to those poor people) and made my way inland. I disposed of my jewellery at prices neither low nor high with local merchants. I preserved the old fellow's golden brooch, which I imagined (for I am a trifle weak and superstitious) might bring me good fortune, and when all my transactions were accomplished I counted my total capital, and found myself in possession of no less than 1,500 dinars. The cold of the evening had come by the time my accounts were settled and the strings of my pouch were drawn. I set myself under an arbour where a delicious fountain played in the light of the setting sun, which shone over the waters of the sea, and drinking some local beverage the name of which I knew not, but the taste and effect of which were equally pleasing, I reflected upon my increase of fortune.

'"You left home, Mahmoud," said I to myself, "with one hundred dinars, of which your excellent and careful father deprived himself rather than see you face the world unarmed, or himself receive the bastinado. You have been gone from home a week; you are perhaps some eight hundred miles from your native city; your capital has been multiplied fifteen-fold, and so far you may look with an eager courage towards the further adventures of your life, for very clearly the Mercy of Allah is upon you."'

At this moment a nasal hooting from the neighbouring turret warned the company to turn their thoughts to heaven. The boys, who had sat fascinated by their uncle's recital, knew that the end of their entertainment had come. The third son of the

Surgeon was therefore impatient to exclaim (as he hurriedly did): 'But, dear uncle, though we see that a certain chance favoured you, and not only your native talents, yet we do not perceive how all this led to any main road to fortune.'

'My boy,' said the Merchant Mahmoud, pensively stroking his beard and gazing vacuously over the heads of the youngsters, 'I do not pretend to unfold you any such plan. Have I not told you that did such a plan exist all would be in possession of it? I am but retailing you in my humble fashion the steps by which one merchant in this city has been raised by the Infinite Goodness of the Merciful (His name be adored!) from poverty to riches. . . . But the call for prayer has already been heard and we must part. Upon this same day of next week, shortly after the last of the public executions has been bungled, you shall again come and hear me recite the next chapter of my varied career.'

GRIZZLEBEARD TELLS OF HIS FIRST LOVE

WHEN we had all four come in out of the rain into Mr Duke's parlour at the Bridge Inn, and when we had ordered beer and had begun to dry ourselves at the fire, the Sailor said: 'Come, Grizzlebeard, we promised to tell the stories of our first loves when we came to Arun; and as you are much the oldest of us do you begin.'

'With all my heart,' said Grizzlebeard, 'for, as you know, I am not one of those belated heretics who hold such things sacred, believing as I do that that only is sacred which attaches directly to the Faith. . . . Nevertheless . . . to remember that great time, and how securely I was held, and in what a port lay the vessel of my soul, I do feel upon me something that should silence a man. . . .'

'By what moorings were you held?' said I.

'By three,' he answered. 'Her eyelids, her voice, and her name.' Then after a little pause he went on:

'She was past her youth. Her twenty-fifth year was upon her. Her father and her mother were dead. She was of great wealth.

'She had one brother, who lived away in some great palace or other in the north, and one sister who was married far off in Italy. She herself had inherited an ancient house of stone set in her own valley, which was that of the river Brede, and most dear to her; for it was there that she had lived as a child, and there would she pass her womanhood.

'Into this house I was received, for she was much older than I, and when I first knew her I was not yet a man. Thither perpetually in the intervals of study I returned. Insensibly my visits grew most natural; I passed the gates which are the beginning of a full life, and constantly I found myself, in spite of a more active bearing and a now complete possession of my youth, alone in her companionship. Her many servants knew me as a part of their household: her grooms who first had taught me to ride, her keepers with whom I had first shot, her old nurse, a pensioner, who favoured this early friendship. The priest also called me by my name.

'We walked together in long avenues; the lawns of four

hundred years were a carpet for us. We paced her woods slowly together and often watched together in the frosty season of the year the early setting of the sun behind bare trees. At evening by her vast and regal fires we sat side by side, speaking in that light alone to each other of dead poets and of the wars and of things seen and of small domestic memories grown to be pictures clear and lovable.

'Then at last I knew what briar it was that had taken root within me.

'In her absence—during the long nights especially—there returned to me the drooping of her eyes: their slow and generous glances. Waking and far off from her, when I saw in some stranger that same rare lowering of the lids I was troubled.

'Her voice, because it was her very self, so moved me, that whenever I heard it upon my way to her doors, whenever I heard it speaking even in the distance no matter what things to another, I trembled.

'Her name, which was not Mary nor Catherine, but was as common and simple a name, was set above the world and was given power over my spirit. So that to hear it attached even to another or to see it written or printed on a page everything within me stirred, and it was as though a lamp had been lit suddenly in my soul. Then, indeed, I understood how truly there are special words of witchcraft and how they bind and loose material things.'

An enthusiasm came into Grizzlebeard's eyes, something at once brilliant and distant like the light which shines from the Owers miles out to sea. He opened his hand down on the table with a fine gesture of vigour, and cried out:

'But what a vision is that! What a spring of Nature even for the poor memory of a man! I mean the unrestricted converse with such a friend at the very launching of life! When we are still without laws and without cares, and yet already free from guardians, and in the full ownership of our own selves, to find a shrine which shall so sanctify our outset: to know, to accompany, and to adore!

'Do not ask me whether I contemplated this or that, union or marriage, or the mere continuance of what I knew, for I was up in a world where no such things are considered. There was no time. No future threatened me, no past could be remembered. I was high above all these things.

'By an accident of fortune I was called away, and in a distant town overseas had alien work put before me, and I mixed with working men. I faithfully curry-combed lean horses, and very carefully greased the axles of heavy wheels, till, after nineteen months, I could come home, and returning I made at once for the Valley.

'As I approached the house I was conscious of no change. The interval had vanished, and I was once again to see and to hear.

'The man that opened the door to me knew me well. I asked for her by her title and her name—for she was noble. He answered me, using her title but not her name. He told me that she would be home that evening late, and he gave me a note to read from her. The writing on that little square of paper renewed in me with a power I knew too well the magic of a sacred place to which I had deliberately returned. As I held it in my hand I breathed unsteadily, and I walked in a fever towards the great gates of iron; nor did I open the letter till I had taken refuge for the next few hours of evening in the inn of her village, where also I was known and had been loved by all in my boyhood.

'There, underneath a little lamp, alone and with food before me, I read the invitation from her hand.

'I learnt in it that she had married a man whose fame had long been familiar to me, a politician, a patriot, and a most capable manufacturer. She told me (for I had warned her of my landing) that they would be back at seven to pass two nights in this country house of theirs, and she begged me to be their guest, at least for that short time.

'A veil was torn right off the face of the world and my own spirit, and I saw reality all bare, original, evil and instinct with death. Nor would I eat and drink, but at last I cried out loud, mourning like a little child; and when I was rested of this I stood by the window and gazed out into the darkness until I had recovered my nature, and felt again that I was breathing common air.

'When spirits fall it is not as when bodies fall; they are not killed or broken; but I had fallen in those moments from an immeasurable height, and the rest of my way so long as I might live was to be passed under the burden to which we all are doomed. Then strong, and at last (at such a price) mature, I noted the hour and went towards the doors through which she had entered perhaps an hour ago in the company of the man with whose name she had mingled her own.'

Myself. 'What did he manufacture?'

Grizzlebeard. 'Rectified lard; and so well, let me tell you, that no one could compete with him.' Then he resumed: 'I entered and was received. Her voice gave me again for a moment some echoes of the Divine: they faded; and meanwhile her face, her person, with every moment took on before me a less pleasing form.

'I have been assured by many who knew us both that what I saw was far from novel. To me it was as strange as earth-quake. Her skin, I could now see, though in the main of a sallow sort, was mottled with patches of dead-white (for she disdained all artifice). Her teeth were various; I am no judge whether they were false or true. Her eyes suffered from some affection which kept them half closed; her voice was set at a pitch which was not musical; her gestures were sometimes vulgar; her conversation was inane. I thought in the next quarter of an hour that I had never heard so many things quoted from the newspapers in so short a time.

'But we chatted together merrily enough all three until she went to bed. Then I sat up for some hours talking with the jolly master of the house of politics and of lard. For I had found in my travels and in my new acquaintance with men that every man is most willing and most able to speak of his own trade. And let me tell you that this man had everything in him which can make a good citizen and a worthy and useful member of the State. His intelligence was clear and stable, his range of knowledge sufficient, his temper equable, and his heart so warm that one could not but desire him the best of fates. I have not met him for many years, but I saw in the last honours list that he had purchased a title. I still count him for an older friend.

'Next morning at a hearty breakfast I grew to like him better than ever, and I could see in the healthy light of a new day what excellent qualities resided even in the wife whom he had chosen. The work to which my poverty (for then I was poor) compelled me, called me by an early train to town, and since that morning I have lived my life.

'But that first woman still sits upon her throne. Not even in death, I think, shall I lose her.'

'Grizzlebeard, Grizzlebeard,' said I, 'these things are from Satan! Children and honest marriage should long ago have broken the spell.'

'I am not married,' said he, 'neither have I any children.'

'Then loves here and there should have restored you to yourself.'

He shook his head and answered: 'It was not for lack of them, great or small. There have been hundreds . . . but let us say no more! There was some foreigner who put it well when he said: "Things do not come at all, or if they come, they come not at that moment when they would have given us the fullness of delight."'

There remained in his pewter a little less than half the beer it had held. He gazed at it and noted also at his side, by the fire, a deal box full of sand, such as we use in my county for sanding of the floor.

Steadily, and with design, he poured out all the beer upon the sand, and put down his pewter with a ring.

The beer did not defile the sand. It was soaked in cleanly, and an excellent aroma rose from it over the room. But beer, as beer, beer meant for men, good beer and nourishing, beer fulfilling the Cervisian Functions, beer drinkable, beer satisfying, beer meet-to-be-consumed: that beer it could never be again.

Then Grizzlebeard said: 'You see what I have done. I did it chiefly for a sacrifice, since we should always forgo some part of every pleasure, offering it up to the Presiders over all pleausre and pouring it out in a seeming waste before the gods to show that we honour them duly. But I did it also for a symbol of what befalls the chief experience in the life of every man.'

There was a long silence when Grizzlebeard had done. From where I sat I could look through the window and see the line of the Downs, and the great beech woods, and birds swinging in the rainy air; and I remembered one pair of men and women, and another and another, and then I fell to thinking of a man whom I had known in a foreign place, who at once loved and hated—a thing to me incomprehensible. But he was southern. Then I heard the silence broken by the Poet, who was saying to the Sailor:

'Now it is your turn.'

THE GIRONDIN

I

IN WHICH AN OLD GENTLEMAN SHOWS THE WAY TO AN OLD LADY

THE regiment marched day upon day, a long train of straggling horses in the late summer weather; the new recruits were drilled evening after evening in the market-squares of the little towns.

Twice, at Loches and at Blois, there were desertions; and in the early mornings, after summary courts, firing platoons and the shooting of men.

At Blois, also, a few more recruits came in, too late, one would have thought, to be used—but in those days everything was used. The remounts were dragged from the stables of peasants, by force and under order of the Government, as they went along, not without squabbles, nor, once or twice, without bloodshed.

They reached Orleans, and stayed for forty-eight hours in the cavalry barracks of the town. The dull place was even fuller of rumour than had been Poitiers; the breath of Paris was upon it, and the colonel was anxious to be away, for even in that short delay he lost ten men, and he dared not recover them as he might have done further down country. They left Orleans before dawn for Châteauneuf, a short day, and one undertaken only to get away from the constriction of the populace and the Clubs and the turmoil of a great town that ruined the order of the regiment. But at Châteauneuf the rumour spread among the men that the march would now be direct for the frontier, and even in the little villages of the valley the news from the frontier had come: the armies of the kings were over the frontier; the invaders were on the soil of the Nation —and Verdun had fallen.

Soldiers are not concerned with news; but in the minds of soldiers, even though they be soldiers but recently civilian, every soldierly place and stronghold has a meaning. For armies have a sort of consciousness running through them; the chance words of officers overheard by their servants, the politicians of the barrack-room discussing affairs, a mere vague comprehension

of the map—all this inhabits the mind of the men whose trade
it is to go forward by the great roads to battle, and whose
nourishment is the open air.

Verdun had fallen; and the little town and the hussars that
had just ridden in were abuzz with the news.

Late that night, when, with half a dozen of the sergeants
who had midnight leave, Boutroux sat, wearied to death, in a
tiny inn, he heard opinion on fire. The men from the street
mixed with the soldiery, and one man urged another on to
violence. As he so sat—it was past ten o'clock, and he was
about to sacrifice his leave and sleep—a man came in from
quarters with an order. The regiment was pressed to march,
and the sergeants were sent for.

They rose, grumbling; they found in quarters the lights and
the movement of a disturbed evening and of sudden commands.
A captain, tall, and cloaked against the night, stood at the gate
of the guard checking a paper in his hand which one of the men
on guard lit from a lantern held above it. He murmured names
and the business of each to his non-commissioned officers; one
after another saluted and went off about the thing he was
bidden to do. The captain's pencil zigzagged down the sheet,
scratching out this, adding that. He came to the name Perrin.

'Sergeant Perrin,' he said.

Boutroux saluted.

'I think you are trustworthy?'

'I hope so,' said Boutroux.

'My lad,' said the captain in a totally different tone—as he
looked up under the lantern light, Boutroux saw the face of
one long broken to the service—'when you have been in the
career as long as I have, you will learn never to answer a
superior.'

The refrain sounded familiar, and Boutroux saluted again.

'Sergeant Perrin,' continued the captain, falling again into
the kindly and simple tone of a man who is ordering something very difficult, 'you will get five horses from a house which
is marked suspect.' He fumbled a little with his paper, peered
at it closely with his keen eyes, and added: 'The Spinster de La
Roche. Dismiss!'

Then it was that Boutroux wished one were allowed to ask
questions in the service; but he knew better by now, and with
the ridiculous stiff movement which the service requires, he
turned sharply round and walked away. The captain called
after him:

'You will take five men.'

He turned round stiffly again from about thirty yards away, saluted, and said: 'Yes, my Captain.'

He went back to the barrack-room, took five men at random; one of them had been his equal as a recruit in the first days of the march and pretended to familiarity with him; he silenced the man, made the five fall in with this old comrade as a sort of corporal to embrigade them, and marched out of quarters into the night.

The street was empty; there were no lights; he had no conception of where the Spinster de La Roche might live, still less did he know how he would be received.

'The service,' thought Boutroux, 'makes of men naturally polite a very nasty set of beings.'

He knocked at a door at random; there was no answer. He bade the men force it, and it was forced. From the top of the rude stair within came first a grumble as of a man half awake; there was the clicking of a tinder-box being struck; at last a light glimmered, and an old man of surprising energy put his head over a landing above and cursed them for a cartload of devils, asking whether he lived in a free country or not, and whether it was thus that a citizen should be disturbed at midnight, and who was safe when such things could be. To whom Boutroux called up sharply:

'You are required to give us direction to the house of the Spinster de La Roche, and, if necessary, to lead us there.'

'If necessary, to lead you there!' snarled the old man in his nightgown, holding the candle high above his head. 'If necessary, to lead you there! I'll lead you to hell first!'

'No,' said Boutroux, 'you will do that just afterwards.'

For a moment it seemed that the old man would give trouble: he was on the point of turning from them, and Boutroux foresaw questions in quarters and a very bad time next morning. But the citizen thought better of it. He reappeared with peasant trousers slipped over his legs, a rough coat upon his shoulders, still wearing his nightgown by way of a shirt, and his absurd cotton nightcap by way of a hat, and so came down.

'You can find it for yourself,' he grumbled, 'if you will follow my instructions—the woman's known enough in all conscience!' Then he chuckled.

'If your instructions are clear, Citizen,' said Boutroux, 'you need not come.'

The old man was a little mollified by that. He was weak

upon the grades of an army; he did not understand the stripes.

'Captain,' he said more humbly—and the private soldier leading the others grinned—'I am willing enough to come, but you understand one lives in the same town, and though the lady's reputation . . .'

'Oh, yes, I understand,' said Boutroux; 'but where is it?'

'I'll come with you,' sighed the old fellow. He fetched a ramshackle lantern, wasting an intolerable time about it, and came hobbling back with it. 'Now,' he said, 'let us go out. It is not half a mile.'

They left the town; they passed along a sandy lane through a little wood to the north of it; they came to a high wall, pierced by a green wooden door; the door was moss-grown and dilapidated.

'The Château is through there,' said the old man.

'The Château!' said Boutroux.

'She is a person of consequence,' said the old man. 'I have no quarrels; I am no politician; I live and let live. She is a person of consequence . . . of the rest I say nothing. And let me tell you, from what I know of the old cat, she dislikes to be disturbed, and her doors are always locked.'

'Doors give way so easily,' said Boutroux, 'and it's always work for the locksmith.' He beckoned two men forward. Their shoulders took the old green door: it did not open, but the rotten wood of it broke, and they forced their way through into a venerable and dilapidated garden. A grass-grown path, once gravelled, was before them; the lantern light shone high into the thick foliage of ancient trees.

'I need not go further, Major?' said the old man anxiously.

'Up to the house!' said Boutroux grimly, 'up to the house! You must remember we are strangers here and need an introduction.'

The old man went up to Boutroux's side and spoke in a low voice, that he might not be overheard by the men.

'You will be kind to me,' he whispered, 'Colonel? After all, we have to live and let live: it is a small town.'

'Come along, Citizen,' said Boutroux, 'come along!'—and the old man came along.

In fifty yards they were at the moat of the old great place. It stood awfully tall and sombre in the night, like a huge square tower with its high slate roofs, solemn chimneys of two hundred years among the stars; the big doors were shut fast, but a light glimmered within, and through the glass above the entry they could see the reflection of that light upon a carved and ancient ceiling. Outside these closed doors swung a great bell. They would not have found its chain in the darkness, but the old man showed them where to find it. Boutroux pulled it, and its loud clangour rang through the park and the trees, and woke echoes within the old house itself. There was a shuffling of feet within, and (how it reminded him of home!) a little square wicket, grated, pierced in the door, was opened cautiously. They were asked their business.

Boutroux gave it. 'The hussars,' he said. 'We are sent on requisition.'

A quavering woman's voice answered: 'I have orders to admit no one.'

'Tell your mistress,' said Boutroux, with his eye to the little iron opening, and seeing within a small, thin, trembling woman, white-haired and capped in the manner of the district, 'tell your mistress that we are here to do no harm—but there is urgent business from the Army.'

She bade him wait. She kept them waiting there a good quarter of an hour, and when she came back, said as pompously as her thin cracked voice would allow:

'My lady will receive you.'

'Give her my best regards,' said Boutroux, 'and bid her have no fear at all. It is the business of the Nation.'

The great doors were opened, creaking; the light from within poured upon the park.

The old man said anxiously, whispering again: 'Need I stay?'

'No, Citizen,' said Boutroux, 'you are free of these things.'

'You will not give my name to her? She has many friends —too many!' said the man anxiously.

'I would, of course, betray your name if I knew it,' said Boutroux doubtfully; 'but I do not know it. However, I will guess at it.'

The old man eyed him misunderstandingly, and made off. He had no love for the politics of his time, and as he went back through the darkness to his disturbed repose, he loved them less than ever.

'The world,' said he to himself, 'is coming to an end . . . so it was foretold . . . so it was foretold. Old Stephen's niece, whom he forced to be a nun in Orleans, foretold it. . . . She was right, it is the end of the world!' And so muttering, he went back homewards.

II

IN WHICH AN OLD LADY SHOWS THE WAY TO
A YOUNG GENTLEMAN

Boutroux entered the hall out of the night with his five men. He heard behind him a joke that did not please him, and he turned round sharply.

'*Fixe!*' he shouted.

They shuffled into a sort of line; he bade them put up their arms and take their places upon the oak bench with its fine carved end, that ran along the stone wall.

'If anything goes amiss to-night, I shall make it the worse for you,' he said; and as he said it, he looked at the man who had presumed upon his ancient comradeship, and the man was afraid.

As he turned round from saying this, he saw coming towards him the mistress of the place, and he heard a very pleasant, gentle, somewhat ironical voice saying to him:

'To what do I owe your visit, Lieutenant?'

'The number of ranks,' thought Boutroux, 'through which a man may pass in time of revolution and of war is infinite! . . . Madame,' he answered her aloud, 'it is a very small matter. Five horses were requisitioned, and they have not come.'

'They were requisitioned, Lieutenant,' said the lady, speaking like fine metal, like silver tempered to steel, 'a month ago. I have since held them ready; no one has asked for them . . . and now you come for them at midnight and in arms!'

Boutroux, standing straight, with his sword in its scabbard, respectfully held and low, as might be that of a gentleman with some message to give, took her in. He remembered the term 'suspect' in his orders, and he watched her well.

She was not tall nor large in body, and yet she was not frail; there was something of self-possession, if not in her soul, at least in her carriage, and a pretty dignity of movement. She was dressed all in black, with white lace at her throat and her wrists; her hands, he thought as he watched her, were singularly small and strong. They were clasped before her. Her hair was grey, with touches of a whiter grey in it; it was her own hair. Her face still wore that light ironic smile, and her eyes were very pleasing: they were black, and they had in them, as she watched him, an expression which provoked him not a little to know more of her.

'Madame, I have no written order,' said Boutroux, seriously moved. 'I intend no discourtesy—but the Army is in urgent need. If I had a written order it would be easier.'

'There is no need for that, Lieutenant,' she answered in a lower tone, and with a charming submission. 'The Army may do what it wills.'

'But I will give you the receipt and the claim, and all that you may ask for verification,' continued Boutroux eagerly. 'I really regret, I very greatly regret . . .'

'You need not regret, Lieutenant,' she said. 'We must all do our duty. And now let me tell you . . . But wait a moment: I will call a man.'

She left the hall; her light steps sounded fainter and fainter as she traversed the house to her offices. She came back with one of her grooms, low-browed, solemn, and resentful.

'Louis,' she said, 'you will accompany these gentlemen: they have come for West Wind, Pericles, Queen, Furtive, and Basilisk.'

The groom touched his head. 'Basilisk can't go out, my lady,' he said.

'Why not?' she asked.

'He's lame, my lady,' said the groom.

'Is it bad, Louis? Does it prevent his working?'

'Yes, my lady,' said the man more stubbornly than ever.

'Why, all the better,' said she cheerfully, this unexpected lady of the night. 'I could wish they all had such a complaint. I could wish they had each but three legs apiece,' and she smiled at Boutroux, who gravely and slightly smiled in return. 'Horses which are needed by the Nation, Lieutenant, are at the disposal of the Nation: and these are the five that were requisitioned, name for name. I regret that one of them should be lame.'

'Madame,' answered Boutroux solemnly, 'I have had stiff legs in the saddle myself, but I have not been excused from marching.'

'Louis,' said the lady, turning to the groom, 'take these gentlemen with you.' She pointed to the five soldiers. 'Do you requisition saddles also, Lieutenant?'

'Well, Madame,' said Boutroux, 'it is not in my orders, but I confess that horses without saddles, though the easier to ride, are impossible for the service. There is this and that and the rest . . .'

'But you cannot expect me to have campaign saddles?' she said.

'Madame,' he said, 'no doubt we shall find them when we join the main body.'

'No doubt,' she said, 'no doubt. . . . Come, Louis, take these gentlemen away!'

The groom, with the worst of wills, led off the lumpish soldiers.

'And you, sir,' she said, turning to Boutroux, 'pray come in and take wine; it will not be a short business, only two of the horses are in the stable here. Two others are at the farm at the end of the park, and one will have to be caught. He is out at grass.'

'I am at your orders, Madame,' said Boutroux.

She led him through two great *pièces* where tapestry hung, and of which the floors were of uneven chestnut, glazed to a polish by many generations of coming and going. In one of these, which was her dining-room, she picked up a flask of wine and a glass for him. She stooped to find bread in a sideboard: it was too low for her, and she went down upon one knee.

Said Boutroux to himself: 'What queens one finds upon the march!'

She brought out the bread and the flask; he took them from her.

'Really, Madame,' he said, 'I cannot allow . . .'

'Oh, be silent!' said the lady lightly. 'We know the Army here!' And then she added: 'Lieutenant—Verdun has fallen!'

'Yes,' said Boutroux, to whom that news was of no great weight at such a moment.

They went together into a little room through the door, a room with a tall ebony bookcase in it, a little marble chimney-piece, and the conventional sham gold clock of the time, with a looking-glass behind it. The little room was full of the scent of late roses, of which a glorious group stood in a jar upon her table. Upon that table also there was a book laid open, as though she had but just left reading it. He did not see the title of the book, and he wondered what it might be. Two candles stood upon that table, still and unflickering in the dark summer air. Their light shone on a terrace without.

'The night is warm, Lieutenant; we will take this wine for

you, and this bread, outside and put them upon a little iron table that is there, and sit there until your men have returned.'

Boutroux was willing enough. She followed him out to the terrace, and as she followed him she blew the candles out.

That small enclosed park was fragrant in the August night— it was secluded. One might dream in it, in such a night, that there were no such things as grooming and marching and arms.

There came from time to time a country noise from the distant village, the sharp bark of a dog, or the lowing of a beast in a stable: the faintest and most distant of those sounds could be heard through the clear summer air; and above them, shining through warm heaven, was a wilderness of stars.

'Lieutenant,' said the lady, 'are you for the frontier?'

'Yes, Madame,' he said, 'and all the regiment.'

For a few moments she kept silence, and then she said: 'I envy you, Lieutenant.'

'It is plain truth, Madame,' he said, 'that people told me your house was suspect; but I do assure you, by my lack of a beard, that I will keep faith with anything you say, for I am neither with one set of the dogs nor with the other.'

She laughed gently in the darkness.

'When you are my age, Lieutenant,' she said, 'you will be more certain of that than ever, and you will only take sides in the things to which your heart moves you. . . . No, the house is not suspect . . . but I regret the better times.' She drew her shoulders together; he could just see the movement: he thought she was cold, in spite of the warmth of the hour, or that she felt the dampness of the moat. He went in without her bidding, fumbled in the dark room, and at last brought out through the open window a shawl that he had noticed cast across the arm of a chair; he put it round her, not hastily.

'I have heard,' thought Boutroux to himself, as he lingered upon this gesture, 'that a woman is not a woman until she is forty: now this lady is certainly a woman.'

She thanked him, and she said: 'Lieutenant . . .? When do you march?'

'I do not know, Madame: too soon, whatever the hour may be.'

'But to-morrow?' she said.

'Yes, certainly, Madame, and more probably this very night.'

'You soldiers never sleep,' she replied to him, in such a tone of pity that he was moved again.

'But when we sleep, Madame, we sleep sound.'

'Yes,' she said, 'you sleep sound.'

He wondered what the Army was to her, and why she spoke
so of the Army. She went on: 'Lieutenant, will you do me
a favour?'

'Madame,' said Boutroux with singular alertness, 'I will do
you any favour that is within my power, and most of those
that are not.'

'You have spoken as a man of the trade should,' she answered
nobly. 'Do you know, Lieutenant, we women who stay behind
love men who will do what is asked of them by the Nation
. . . or by any other dame.'

'Aye, Madame,' he said, 'and we soldiers love to be asked
it. . . .'

She asked what he did not expect.

'Why then, Lieutenant, tell me, I pray you, while those
clodhoppers are stealing my cattle, tell me how you came to
be in the service, and to be marching thus. Had you ever the
King's commission?'

His eyes were used to the darkness, the haunting light of the
summer stars glimmered upon the gracious curves of her grey
and silvering hair, but her eyes were quite in shadow. Her
face was turned towards him, and he could imagine many
things.

'I will tell you the truth,' he said gravely, pausing a little
before he answered; 'I never held a commission of the King's.'

'Then why are you here?' she said. 'Was it the invasion
that stirred you?'

'No, Madame,' said Boutroux more gravely still, 'not even
the invasion, though I trust I should have done my duty.
Shall I tell you the whole story?'

'Why,' she said, with a little laugh, 'that is just what I have
asked you to do.'

Boutroux let his head fall back in the darkness, and stared
up at the great stars.

'I am by birth,' he said slowly, and thinking at large, 'I am
by birth the son of a lawyer in Paris, a Judge of the High
Court. My father was, and is, the kindest and tenderest of
fathers. He designed me in marriage — it was before the
troubles, Madame; it was before these worries that I hate, and
do not understand—he designed me in marriage for a young
lady against whom I have nothing to say. She had every grace
and quality and charm, and a dowry, as I was given to believe,
of three hundred thousand livres.'

'It is a large sum,' said the lady gently.

'It is a large sum, Madame,' agreed Boutroux, shrugging his shoulders, 'but it was destined never to be mine.'

'Indeed! Pray tell me more, for I am interested.'

'It is a simple story, Madame.' He drew a deep breath, which is a kind of inspiration, and continued:

'The lady who brought me up, you must know, was neither a nurse nor a governess, but something between the two. With her daughter I played as a sister, and we grew up together.'

'Boy,' said the lady here, 'I see what is coming.'

'Ah, Madame,' said Boutroux, 'then you are far wiser than I. . . . She died.'

'She died?' said the lady, surprised.

'Yes,' said Boutroux, leaning forward, and holding his scabbard between his knees, and letting his voice sink profoundly, 'she died: a purer, nobler, more . . .'

'Yes, yes,' said the lady. (Far off at the end of the little park lights were coming, and time was short.) 'I understand,' she ended rapidly.

'You understand, Madame,' said Boutroux with a sob.

'And so you are here?'

'And so I am here!' said Boutroux simply.

'Did you enlist, since you say you have not the King's commission?'

'I enlisted, Madame; I enlisted at St Denis at the cavalry depot. I was in the ranks for two years.'

The lady leaned towards him, and consented to put a hand for one moment upon his hand. Boutroux was willing; no movement of his condemned the gesture. The lights from the end of the park were approaching, and they could just begin to hear the loud banter of the five soldiers quizzing the groom.

'Men do not often rise as you have risen,' she said. 'Tell me before we part how you obtained your grade.'

'It is a curious story, Madame. An old gentleman whose name I did not know, but who had evidently great authority, was for promoting me with an indecent rapidity. I had already been named a sergeant for some weeks, when he urged me successively up the ranks of lieutenant, captain, major, and even colonel.'

'It is incredible!' said the lady, staring at him with wide eyes.

'Yes, Madame, incredible and, as I thought at the time, ill-judged, and even ignorant; but so it was. I paid but little attention to his patronage; I did not believe that he had any real power. What gave me my commission, and that to which I owe my lieutenancy, was the very generous act of a woman.'

'Really, Lieutenant,' said the lady, 'women seem to have played a part in your life!'

'Ah, Madame,' said Boutroux solemnly, 'I never knew how much until to-night.'

'And so,' went on the lady, a little too rapidly, 'it is to a woman that you owe your title of lieutenant, you very young man?'

'It is, Madame,' said Boutroux.

'Did she know you well?'

'No, Madame, nor I her; but for a brief moment upon a summer night I loved her well enough.'

'What power had she to give you such advancement?'

'Nothing, Madame, but her word; yet her words were of a sort and spoken in a tone which I will long remember.'

The horses moving up the drive, their pace upon the stones of it, the men leading them, and the grumbling of the groom, were now close at hand. She rose unwillingly.

They went into the darkened room together, and as she passed before him through the open windows she said, in the lowest of voices but one as clearly heard as a summons: 'We are in no haste to join the others.' It was some little time before either spoke again. When that silence broke, she broke it first in a changed voice, still holding him in the darkness.

'You march before dawn?' she asked.

'Madame,' he said, standing before her in the night, 'I have told you: we go when we are ordered, and I believe that the orders will come by daybreak or before.'

'Well,' she said, catching at her words, 'I shall ask from you a receipt . . . and a due note. . . . I can give you nothing more in exchange.'

She lit the candles again in that little room; he seemed to remember a room which he had known, not for a few moments, but for some days. She wrote in a delicate and clear hand the note of the horses' names, the description which she had afforded of them to the officials, and she put the paper before him to sign. He signed it. Neither had looked at the other's eyes. She sanded the ink and dried it: she folded the paper with his signature upon it, and put it into her bosom.

'And now,' she said, 'Lieutenant, Lieutenant, I can give you nothing more!'

'Why, Madame,' said he, 'your good wishes.'

'Well, you have had more than that,' she whispered, and Boutroux followed her into the hall. . . . Before the great door of it were the five horses and the men, and the groom standing sullen; they had waited too long.

Boutroux once outside her door, and standing at a horse's head, turned to the lady of the house as she stood with the light upon her, watching him go. 'Have I your leave to mount?' he said.

'All my leave to all you will,' she answered.

'Then,' said Boutroux to the groom, 'which horse did you say was lame?'

But the groom muttered: 'I take no orders from you.'

One of his men said, 'This one, Sergeant,' leading up a brown mare of no capacity. Boutroux took the stirrup iron in his right hand, and measured the stirrup leather against his left arm. 'It is my length,' he said, and he mounted. With the first movement of his mount he thought: 'No more lame than I —less!' He drew his sword and saluted as he left that house, then he sheathed it again.

'Louis,' said the lady—it was the last time he heard her voice—'show the lieutenant to the great gate and bid them open it. Lead the lieutenant!' she added sharply.

'Sergeant!' muttered the groom to himself.

The doors shut again upon her, and the little troop went up to the great stone pillars and the wrought-iron gate, where a light in the lodge was already awaiting them, and some figure was moving in the darkness to open.

Riding behind his men Boutroux could not forbear to look over his shoulder; he saw, or thought he saw, near a light upon the first story the head, and the inclination of the body, and the gesture with which an hour's acquaintance had too much accustomed him. But he turned and went through the gate, and he said to the groom as he did so:

'When they press you for the wars, my man, try to be under my command; and if I am colonel by that time—for my promotion is rapid—I will see that you have an easy time—in prison.'

The man answered him with a fine curse, and they parted.

THE 'ARK-ROYALL'

27TH JULY (OR, AS WE SHOULD SAY, 7TH AUGUST) 1588

The *Ark-Royall* was, during the struggle with the Armada, the flagship of the English Lord Admiral, a landsman, one of the Howards, a family recently grown very powerful through the wealth taken from the Church.

THE Straits of Dover, when one approaches them from the east, are like the mouth of a great river, nor do they ever bear that aspect more than at sunset, when, if one is in mid-stream and the day has been clear, one sees quite close upon either hand, not ten miles off each way, the highlands of either shore, those highlands branching outwards till they are lost on the horizon as might be lost the spreading highlands of an estuary.

If the stream be at the ebb the illusion is enhanced, for one sees the pouring out of the flood in the way that a river should go; it is then not difficult to forget the North Sea behind one, and to imagine, as one drifts down the mid-channel towards the colour in the west, that one is still embraced by the land, and that one is only just now setting out to sea. The sun broadens into a long belt of haze before it touches the horizon, and the light of it catches either line of cliffs. It seems a very peaceful sea.

July 27th 1588 was of this kind. The sun was setting beyond the shoals of the Varne and all the great roundell of Spanish ships were clustered in a group from Grisnez eastward, coming up very slowly against the tide; they sailed above an easy holding-ground not far from the French land. The huge bulk of transports, high forward and astern, cast long shadows upon the calm; it was the merest breath of wind that carried the Armada on, or rather, just held it against the strong coastwise stream. When the last of them and the slowest had passed outside the shoals that cluster under the steep of Grisnez the rattling of chains began through the clear and silent air; there were signals both with bugle and with bunting, a gun was fired, and the wide fleet dropped anchor in fifteen fathom and rode, every ship with its bows upstream and every high poop in the blaze of the sunset. It was Saturday evening. All week long they had crawled and beaten up the Channel, and all week long the little English craft with their much heavier artillery had stood the recoil of their own great guns and had peppered the enemy from well out of range; and one ship the Spaniards had lost by collision so that she lagged and Drake caught her, full of gold, and another a traitor had fired, and this also, or the charred hulk of it, had been towed into an English harbour.

The Lord Admiral of England all that week had followed in the *Ark-Royall*. He had followed them by day and by night; all the hours a man can see to fire he ordered the intermittent cannonade, and now upon this calm evening, with the northerly breeze gone westward and dying down, he and his men came up between the Spaniards and the sun. They also cast anchor just out of range, and from beyond the Straits from round the North Foreland came thirty more from London and joined the line.

It was soon dark. Long before midnight the craft began to swing, the smaller English vessels coming quickly round to the bubbling of the flood tide as it swirled round Grisnez, the larger Spanish transports catching the stream more slowly, but at last turned also east and west to the change of the sea, and with the turn of the tide the wind rose, though at first but little, and blew steadily out of the west and south in a gentle and constant manner, and the sky clouded. The beacon upon Dover cliff flickered far off to the west and the northward; one could see bonfires or the glare of them against the sky of the Weald, and there were more lights than usual passing up and down the English shore. Upon the French, the tall Pharos of Calais alone shone over the marshy flats. Grisnez was a huge lump against the darkness. But all the surface of the sea was dotted with the lamps of the fleets and the broken water was full of glints and reflections.

In Dunkirk, a very few miles up the shore, waited that army which, if in any manner it could have crossed the day's march of salt water, would have raised the Catholic north of England, occupied the indifferent south, and held London—to the complete reversal of the fate of Europe. Further still up coast, at Nieuport, was their reserve. It was midnight and past midnight; the Sunday morning had begun, and the wind, chopping a little northward and uncertain, but in general a little south of west, blew in gusts that soon joined to half a gale. The sea rose, and along the line of the sand and under the dark steep beyond, the long white line of breakers was very clear through the darkness.

Aboard the *Ark-Royall* the Lord Admiral Howard, the landsman, took counsel and did as he was told. They took eight ships of the worst, cleared them and stuffed them with all manner of burnable and missile things, they put in barrels of pitch and of powder, great stones and round shot, beams of dry wood and slack cordage. They warped them round in the difficulty and tossing of that weather till they pointed up stream, and they set square sails on each that the wind should catch them, so that with the gale and the flood tide together they might bear down upon the Spanish Fleet. These derelicts were held by warps from the stern, and the sails so set strained the warps too powerfully until the signal was given. Then, with great dispatch, the last men left aboard touched fire to matches in twenty places upon one or the other, and tumbled over the side. The strands that held them were cut, and as the first flames leapt from their decks they careened before the wind against the Armada. It was about two o'clock in the morning.

From the *Ark-Royall*, at the head of the English line, was a sight not seen again in history. The conflagration burnt up enormous, clear and high, blazing first from the sterns of the fireships and showing the square sails brilliant red against the night. The gale blew the flames before it in broad sheets, and one could hear the roaring of them even against the wind. Down weather that floating town of Spanish galleys shone out as the dreadful light came near; the tumbling and foaming sea in a circle all around was conspicuous in the strong glare, and the shape of every wave was marked clearly for a cable's length around.

The Armada awoke. Among the thousands who crowded the decks, impeding the haste of the sailors as they ran to let the anchors go, were many who remembered that same awful sight upon the Scheldt three years before, when the fireships had driven against Parma's boom. There was no time for the slow work of the capstans; men took axes and hacked at the cables forward; the canvas was run up as might be in such a medley, and the monstrous hulks paid round in a very varied manner, confused and hampering one another as their headsails, with the sheets hard aweather, caught the gale. Not a few, on whom too much had been set or too hastily, careened a moment dangerously to leeward, then recovered; there were

shouts everywhere and a babel of orders; men running with
fenders to hang over the sides, as one big wall of wood or another surged up too near in the darkness; at last all were turned
and free, and the herd of them went driving before the south-
west wind along that perilous shore. The men on the *Ark-
Royall* and the Lord Admiral, watching from the height of the
rail, cursed to see no fireship get home. The set of the seas and
the slant of the wind drove one after another upon the flat
stretches of the beach, and there they burnt out, bumping
higher and higher as the tide rose along the flats, and to their
burning was added dull explosions as the fire reached their
powder. But the Spanish fleet was gone.

The *Ark-Royall* also weighed anchor and all her sisters with
her to take up that long chase again. It seemed that the
attempt had failed—but with the weather that was to be and
the port of embarkation passed, the invasion could never come;
this island had been certainly saved before the stormy morning
broke beyond the marshes of the lowlands.

· · · · · ·

There was lightning all over heaven before it was day, and
the raging water was a little tamed by cataracts of rain. The
light grew dully through the furious weather, the Spanish line
was scattered twenty miles thwart of the Flanders shore; their
leading ships could see the opening of Ostend, their laggards
were still far west of Nieuport and near their panic of the night.
Off Gravelines the long-range artillery of the English caught
them. In spite of the gale each fleet rallied to the sound of the
cannon, and all that Sunday long the guns answered each other
without a pause, but the English had the range and the weather,
and the gigantic Spanish fabrics, leaning away from the blast,
shot short or high, while the English broadsides, leaning downward and toward the mark, poured in an accurate fire; those
smaller vessels also turned well and quickly even in such a sea,
making of themselves a changing target, but having fixed targets
before them in the lumbering masses of their opponents. The
success of their gunnery lent them hardihood, and the more
daring would sweep quite close to the Spanish sides and sheer
off again; so was Drake's ship chiefly struck. Had he chosen
he might have avoided any such offence and have done his
work at full range and in safety, but he was warm to it, and
the dancing manœuvre pleased him. He was hulled forty
times, but he swam.

When the night fell this running business had got off the mouth of the Scheldt. The wind backed a little and blew stronger, but no longer toward the land; the great Armada ran northward before it into the midst of a widening sea, and so up and away, and an end to the great concern.

But the men of the *Ark-Royall* (which had commanded all that success) did not know its greatness, and the Lord Admiral, back in port from putting the enemy past the Firth, was fearful of their return, and wrote to Walsingham: 'Sir,—Sure bind, sure find. A kingdom is a great wager. Sir, you know security is dangerous.'

He might have spared his ink; the thing was done.

THE APPRENTICE

29TH JANUARY (OR, AS WE SHOULD SAY,
10TH FEBRUARY) 1649

Charles I was executed on this day, upon a scaffold outside the second window on the north of Whitehall Banqueting Hall, at four in the afternoon.

MEN were well into the working week; it was a Tuesday and apprentices were under the hard eyes of their masters throughout the City of London and in the rarer business places that elbowed the great palaces along the Strand. The sky was overcast and the air distastefully cold, nor did anything in the landscape seem colder than the dark band of the river under those colourless and lifeless January clouds.

Whether it were an illusion or a reality, one could have sworn that there was a sort of silence over the houses and on the families of the people; one could have sworn that men spoke in lower tones than was their custom, and that the streets were emptier. The trial and the sentence of the king had put all that great concourse of men into the very presence of Death.

The day wore on; the noise of the workmen could be heard at the scaffold by Whitehall; one hour was guessed at and then another; rumours and flat assertions were busy everywhere, especially among the young, and an apprentice to a harness-maker in the Water Lane, near Essex House, knew not what to believe. But he was determined to choose his moment and to slip away lest he should miss so great a sight. The tyranny of the army kept all the city in doubt all day long, and allowed no news; none the less, from before noon there had begun a little gathering of people in Whitehall, round the scaffold at which men were still giving the last strokes of the hammer. Somewhat after noon a horseshoe of cavalry assembled in their long cloaks and curious tall civilian hats; they stood ranked, with swords drawn, all round the platform. Their horses shifted uneasily in the cold.

The harness-maker's apprentice found his opportunity; his master was called to the door for an order from Arundel House, and the lad left his bench quickly, just as he was, without hat or coat, in the bitter weather, and darting through the side door ran down through the Water Gate and down its steps to the river. The tide was at the flood and his master's boat lay moored. He cast her off and pulled rapidly up the line of gardens, backing water when he came to the public stairs just beyond Whitehall. Here he quickly tied the painter and ran up breathless to Whitehall Gate, fearing he might have missed his great expectation. He was in ample time.

It was perhaps half-past three o'clock when he got through the gate and found himself in the press of people. Far off to the left, among the soldiery that lined the avenue from the park to the Mall, and so to St James's, a continuous roll of drums burdened the still air.

The crowd was not very large, but it filled the space from the gate to the scaffold and a little beyond, save where it was pressed outward by the ring of cavalry. It did not overflow into the wide spaces of the park, though these lay open to Whitehall, nor did it run up towards Charing Cross beyond the Banqueting Hall.

The apprentice was not so tall as the men about him; he strained and elbowed a little to see, and he was sworn at. He could make out the low scaffold, a large platform all draped in black, with iron staples, and a railing round it; it covered the last three blank windows of Whitehall, running from the central casement until it met the brick house at the north end of the stonework; there the brickwork beneath one of the windows had been taken out so as to give access through it from the floor within to the scaffold on the same level without; and whispers round told the apprentice, though he did not know how much to trust them, that it was through this hasty egress that the king would appear. Upon the scaffold itself stood a group of men, two of them masked, and one of the masked ones, of great stature and strong, leant upon the axe with his arm crossed upon the haft of it. A little block, barely raised above the floor of the platform, he could only see by leaping on tiptoe, catching it by glimpses between the heads of his neighbours or the shoulders of the cavalry guard; but he noticed in those glimpses how very low it was, and saw, ominous upon it, two staples driven as though to contain the struggler. Before it, so that one kneeling would have his face toward the palace and away from the crowd, was a broad footstool covered with red velvet, and making a startling patch upon all that expanse of black baize.

It was cold waiting; the motionless twigs of the small bare trees in the park made it seem colder still. The three-quarters struck in the new clock behind him upon Whitehall Gate, but as yet no one had appeared.

In a few moments, however, there was a movement in the crowd, heads turning to the right, and a corresponding backing of the mounted men to contain the first beginnings of a rush, for the commanders of the army feared, while they despised, the popular majority of London; and the wealthy merchants, the allies of the army, had not joined this common lot. This turning of faces towards the great blank stone wall of the palace was caused by a sound of many footsteps within. The only window not masked with stone, the middle window, was that upon which their gaze universally turned. They saw, passing it very rapidly, a group of men within; they were walking very sharply along the floor (which was here raised above the level of the window itself and cut the lower panes of it); they were hurrying towards the northern end of the great Banqueting Hall. It was but a moment's vision, and again they appeared in the open air through the broken brickwork at the far end of the stone façade.

For a moment the apprentice saw clearly the tall king, his face grown old, his pointed beard left full, his long features not moved. The great cloak that covered him, with the Great Star of the Garter upon the left shoulder, he drew off quickly and let fall into the hands of Herbert. He wore no hat; he stepped forward with precision towards the group of executioners, and a little murmur ran through the crowd.

The old bishop, moving his limbs with difficulty, but suppliant and attendant upon his friend, stood by in an agony. He helped the king to pull off his inner coat until he stood conspicuous in the sky-blue vest beneath it, and round his neck a ribbon and one ornament upon it, a George carved in onyx. This also he removed and gave to the bishop, while he took from his hands a little white silken cap and fixed it firmly upon his long and beautiful hair. From beneath the sky-blue of his garment, at the neck and at the wrists, appeared frills of exquisite linen and the adornment of lace. He stood for a few moments praying, then turned and spoke as though he were addressing them all. But the apprentice, though he held his breath, and strained to hear, as did all others about him, could catch no separate word, but only the general sound of the king's voice speaking. The movement of the horses, the occasional striking of a hoof upon the setts of the street, the distance, covered that voice. Next, Charles was saying something to the masked man, and a moment later he was kneeling upon the footstool. The apprentice saw him turn a moment and spread his arms out as an example of what he next should do; he bent him toward the block—it was too low; he lay at full length, and the crowd lifted and craned to see him in this posture.

The four heavy strokes of the hour struck and boomed in the silence. The hands of the lying figure were stretched out again, this time as a final signal, and right up in the air above them all the axe swung, white against the grey sky, flashed and fell.

In a moment the group upon the scaffold had closed round, a cloth was thrown, the body was raised, and among the hands stretched out to it were the eager and enfeebled hands of the bishop, trembling and still grasping the George.

A long moan or wail, very strange and dreadful, not very loud, rose from the people now that their tension was slackened by the accomplishment of the deed. And at once from the north and from the south, with such ceremony as is used to the conquered, the cavalry charged right through, hacking and dispersing these Londoners and driving them every way.

.   .   .   .   .   .

The apprentice dodged and ran, his head full of the tragedy and bewildered, his body in active fear of the horses that pursued flying packets of the crowd down the alley-ways of the offices and palace buildings.

He went off by a circuitous way to find, not his master's house after such an escapade, but his mother's, where she lived beyond St Martin's.

The dusk did not long tarry; as it gathered and turned to night small flakes of snow began to fall and lie upon the frozen ground.

DROUET'S RIDE

21ST JUNE 1791

Louis XVI and Marie Antoinette, King and Queen of France, attempting to fly from Paris in the midst of the Revolution, were intercepted just as they reached safety by one Drouet, who galloped near midnight by a short cut to the town of Varennes through the forest and roused the populace.

It was already dark. The longest day of the year had been cloudy, and though at sunset a lurid shaft of red had shone from under the edges of the cloud, the sky soon covered again and one could see no stars. In the main room of the town house of Ste Menehould a number of men were talking all at once, as is the French habit, and accomplishing things with an incredible rapidity. Outside the public square was filling, and though the mob as yet did not clamour, the noise from it was rising; in one place a man was struggling with a soldier, calling him a German, and the soldier was crying that it was false and that he was a Frenchman from Burgundy. In the ugly steeple which one could see squat against the night the bells rang continuously and furiously, and twice a pistol shot was heard in the darkness. All were now convinced that the carriage which had left them not an hour ago had contained the king. But with every one volunteering at once to do this and to do that it was not until Drouet spoke with decision that the pursuit was determined on.

Drouet was by nature a silent man; tall, and with a face like a hawk. He had long, clean legs, suitable for riding on a horse; he had the roll of the cavalry, for he had served in that arm. He went down to his stables and saddled the two horses by lantern-light, and so went riding out with his companion. The crowd gathered round him; as he came to the limit of the town he got free of them, and immediately broke into a gallop down the Clermont road. They listened to the distant beat of the hoofs, expecting the trot or the walk when he took the rise into Argonne, but they did not hear it. Even in its utmost faintness, and before the noise of the ride was lost in the distance, it was still a gallopade and a rhythmical pounding through the night.

Over the crest of the hill and down into the steep and muddy ravine where the mountain village of Islettes, dirty and clumped, squats by the brookside, they galloped on, waking for one moment the villagers as they passed with the furious clatter of iron from the heavy hoofs of the posting horses; and again, after they had passed, there was heard that distant fading of the gallopade, for the long flat rise before them did not check their course. But just as they approached its summit in a place where the great trees of Argonne line the road upon the right, and upon the left are separated from it by nothing but a narrow strip of mead (where to-day the railway runs), there mixed with the noise of the hoof-beats beneath them the noise of a distant hail. They drew rein, and very soon tall riding figures loomed up in the night upon the skyline of the hill-top before them, and when they hailed again Drouet recognized his own grooms. The groups mingled, and to the panting of the two strained beasts, the occasional pawing of the tired post-horses of the others, the story of the coach was rapidly told. It was on two miles ahead, rolling rapidly to Neuville, and so to Varennes. It was bewildering news, for all Ste Menehould had thought that the king's flight was to Metz. And in a moment the active mind that lay behind the close-set eyes of Drouet seized the tactics of that night upon which depended the fate of the Capetian monarchy, and of all Europe too. The coach had doubled. Its start upon him was too great to be caught up by following the road; they would be at Varennes, and screened by a belt of soldiery, before he could ride them down. He must—it was his one opportunity—plunge across the base of that triangle and head the fugitives; but this short cut lay not even over fields or common, it lay through the immense forest of Argonne and the high tangled ridge of the hill. He had, across such country, not an hour before him, and more than eleven miles to cover. He leapt the ditch, he crossed the meadow, he took the thick of the trees on his left, and urged his mount by a direct threading of the undergrowth, until he came to the summit whence proceeds the long line of the hills. For that short mile only was the sound of the hoof-beats hushed and time lost in necessity of walking his horse. At the summit an alley opened before him; he struck spurs and galloped furiously down again.

He was so native to Champagne that he knew what none but the countryfolk knew, and what indeed no historian has dis-covered, that an old track lay along the summit of the hill, open through the dense growth of trees, dry from its situation on the ridge, with here and there a fallen trunk or a hummock of ground to imperil one, but still a road of a kind. It is of immense antiquity; the Gauls have used it, and the Romans, but the forest has grown up round its southern end; it comes up blindly against the undergrowth and leads nowhere. It had had no purpose in the history of the nation during all that thousand years in which the great edifice of the French monarchy had risen to the benefit of mankind; and now this deserted and haunted lane in the wood was the instrument by which that monarchy was destroyed.

Down it and down it, mile after mile, the horses thundered. The night wore on, and from the distant steeples of the villages in the plain between the half-hour struck; a couple of miles away down on the plain, and parallel to Drouet's riding, ran the straight high road, and on it, still rolling ahead, but gained on with every bound of the cavalryman's horses, went the berline and the destiny of the Bourbons.

The riders came to a place where years before murder had been done, and where a great white stone had been set by the peasantry, who dread the powers of evil that haunt such spots. This stone was Drouet's mark, for here there branches from the ridgeway a narrow and foul path which leads downwards on to the Varennes road, and strikes that road just as it issues from the forest and at the gate of the little town. By this way alone can a man on horseback get from the high ridgeway down to the plain, unless indeed he is to go all the way round and strike the main road through the pass which lies a mile or two ahead. This turning alone could accomplish Drouet's purpose, and even so the issue was very near. The hardest pace might fail to head the berline, and he might have ruined his mount and clattered into Varennes too late. They galloped and they galloped on, till the woods suddenly ceased upon either side. They heard beneath them the setts of the high road, and immediately saw before them such lights as still shone from the higher windows of Valmy. The clock was striking the hour. Drouet dismounted: wisely, for in the tortuous streets of the little place and with the business before him he was freer on foot than in the saddle.

The whole place was silent. One would have said that no one watched. The sluggish river slipping between the piles of the bridge was the only sound. He ran breathlessly up the High Street. Between him and the archway that crossed clean over it up the hill there was not a human being nor light, save at one door, from which light streamed, and in which a group of men were talking—politics of course, for it was a tavern; but of the coach, of soldiers, even of the horses for the change, not a sign. He thought for a moment that he had failed. He dashed into the tavern and asked if a berline had rolled by. The stolid people of these hills looked at him rather stupidly, wondering what he meant. But he was known, and they answered him. Nothing had been heard, nothing had been seen. Then Drouet for the first time in that night of thundering hoofs and riding saw the conclusion of his plan. He told them that in the coach was the king. Such time as it took, not to convince them, but to get the mere fact into their heads, was wasted: but soon they had understood or believed: they rose, they scattered, one man to raise the militia, another to find the mayor, a third to arm himself. As for Drouet, he went out into the air of the street, could see nothing at first for the glare of the light, waited a moment till his eyes should be accustomed to the darkness, then rapidly breasted the hill, keeping close upon the houses. And suddenly before he quite knew it, there was the berline right on him, a huge mass of leather and of packages and of humanity within and without, girding on its brakes and sliding down the stone of the street. His work was done, and the doom of the monarchy was accomplished.

THE DEATH OF MR BURDEN

MR BURDEN stood at the counter where little rails of shining brass were reflected in the polished wood. He looked for some immediate obedience; but his aspect at this moment was not such that his wealth or station could be seen.

Mr Burden stood at the counter with both his hands upon it, waiting till someone should notice that he was there. Such duties were reluctantly undertaken by the youngest of a company, and there approached him at length a young clerk with pale and curly hair, watery blue eyes, and of a frank, uncivil manner, as though his heart were in the right place but very small.

Mr Burden said to him:

'I want to see Mr Abbott.'

With easy negligence the young clerk shoved across the counter a form on which was printed:

> Name of applicant ....
> Nature of business.........................

Mr Burden looked at this form a moment, and then lifting his head:

'Give him my name,' he said.

'What *is* yer name.'

'Burden . . . Mr Burden. Tell Mr Abbott Mr Burden is here, and wishes most particularly to see him.

The young clerk sauntered off with a careless ease, and Mr Burden stood waiting at the counter. His face was very pale, his manner unsteady. Beyond, in little pens of glass, ill-paid men, working at books, peeped furtively; some smiled, others looked round to catch a neighbour's eye. Mr Burden was oblivious of it all.

The young clerk returned and said, as a servant in livery speaks to a tradesman in none:

'Mr Abbott can't see you.'

Patches of colour lit up in Mr Burden's face; but, before he spoke or moved, a little dry, grey man who had served his master faithfully for twenty years, and to whom Mr Burden was as familiar as the City streets, had seen what was passing and had come forward. He pushed aside the very foolish youth, and said in a low, respectful voice:

'You had much better wait a little, Mr Burden, sir; you had indeed.'

Mr Burden shook his head slowly. He took up an office pen and wrote a few lines upon a memorandum sheet. He folded it and put Mr Abbott's name outside. . . . 'Take him that,' he said, 'I must see him.'

What he had written I do not know; but I am assured that the address was almost illegible, so violently did his hand tremble.

The little grey man went off in some fear. He was not long away. When he came back, he bore in his hand the same note, unopened. 'I am very sorry, Mr Burden, sir,' he said, most anxiously . . . 'indeed, if you will let me . . .'

Mr Burden took the note from him and tore it into twenty pieces methodically and strongly, and scattered them upon the floor, casting them deliberately down like seed to grow up into some remorseful harvest. Then, the little grey man watching him anxiously as he went, he passed through the monumental doors into the street.

It was with a most unnatural energy that he pushed through the crowds on the pavement. His emotion forced a spasm of life through the worn channels of his brain; he walked rapidly, his head bent down, till he came to Broad Street and the offices of the M'Korio. The giant saw him as he passed up the great stairs and saluted him, but Mr Burden noticed nothing. He went on at once to that principal room, where he knew that a meeting of the Board was to be held, and into this room he strode, full of purpose, but checked a moment by the presence of others as he entered.

He saw by the window the little group which, as he thought, had ruined his peace for ever, and, among them, he saw Cosmo. He saw Cosmo standing as a friend of theirs should stand, talking with them familiarly.

They were four: Cosmo and Mr Barnett, Lord Benthorpe and Mr Harbury: their minds at ease on that quiet and sunlit afternoon, fresh with the activity of the City, ready for the action of life.

To each of them great fortune promised: and to Mr Barnett, who was already very wealthy, more than fortune—true political power, a thing to him worth all the effort of a life. They stood there at the window, these four men, making not only their own success, but the success of England, and building up yet another new people overseas. There was a natural buoyancy in all their attitudes; the hard work had been done, and only the last stone remained to be raised. Then the one would have recovered his honour, another have solved his indebtedness, another have found himself secure for the first time in permanent wealth, another in retirement and leisure, and strong over men.

They knew, indeed, what fantasies and little meticulous rules had haunted this fifth man that had entered. They knew their Mr Burden by this time; especially Cosmo, his son, foresaw what effort had still to be gone through. But they had no doubt of success, for a man thus sensitive is also weak and very yielding to persuasion: nay, as he entered, that weakness of his was apparent, in the hesitation of his step and the uncertain glance which he cast upon them.

Cosmo hung back a little, for he revered his father. The three others came forward with effusion; Lord Benthorpe with perhaps rather more restraint than the rest; and Mr Barnett, taking it upon himself to be spokesman, said:

'My dear Mr Burden!' and he took Mr Burden's hand in his right hand and put his left hand over it and held it fast, to show a real friendship; and then he pulled up to the table a great chair of dignity, and asked Mr Burden to be seated in it. Mr Burden said: 'Thank ye': he sat down slowly, as would a man that bore a heavy sack upon his shoulders, and the rest sat down around the table.

After a little silence, Cosmo asked his father whether his train had been punctual. Mr Burden answered oddly. He said in a manner, which (alas!) still savoured of pomposity:

'Gentlemen . . .' Then he coughed and was silent.

Mr Barnett, who all his life had possessed the art of managing men, smiled a ready, but not convincing smile, and said:

'Eh, Mr Burten? Yes?'

Mr Burden, with a troubled look and with eyebrows drawn together and upwards, looked round at them, avoiding the eyes of each, and gazed to his right at the window, as might a man who had the direction of a battle, but who knew nothing of war, and who saw the closing in of lines—and fate, and dread, and ending coming forward upon him out of the smoke and clamour.

He turned his head slowly round; he shifted his feet nervously, and he began again:

'Gentlemen . . . I have been thinking . . . that there are some things . . . I don't say many . . . but still there are some things which might be settled without hurting us and without hurting any one else, and . . . Of course I understand the position fully.' He tried to smile and failed. 'I am a man of the world, gentlemen; I understand the position fully . . . I know it may be a little sacrifice . . . I think you will all agree with me it should be settled.'

Mr Barnett, who all his life had possessed the art of managing men, cleared his throat, and spoke rapidly in a confident tone: his hands were clasped before him upon the table, his short creative thumbs were pressed together. He said:

'I think we exactly know what it is in Mr Burten's mind? It does Mr Burten to his honour. Mr Burten is alluding herein, Lord Bent'orpe' (for Mr Barnett always addressed Lord Benthorpe upon such occasions—and Lord Benthorpe bowed very slightly, as men do who owe nothing and can give much), 'Mr Burten is alluding, Lord Bent'orpe, I say, to our policy with regard to Mr Âppott herein. Mr Burten, it does you much to your honour.'

Lord Benthorpe, whose ignorance of all these things was that of a sincere and honourable gentleman, bowed again to Mr Burden: it was a very slight bow, even more slight than that accorded to Mr Barnett; and I am sorry to say that, immediately afterwards, he had the lack of tact to remark: 'I am sure that any such small matter as Mr Burden wishes can be arranged.'

Mr Barnett betrayed considerable irritation.

'With all respect due,' he said—in spite of his accent, he had a great command of English idiom—'with all respect due, and ready, Lord Bent'orpe, and with every desire I have to spare——' here he hesitated a moment, and Mr Harbury, to whom English was a familiar language, murmured, 'susceptibilities'—'susceptibilities,' continued Mr Barnett, still pondering on all the syllables, 'we have other interests herein than alone our own to consider. We have the interests also of the shareholders surely to consider. I think one will agree with me? Ah?'

He lay back a little in his chair, and looked round at his three companions, and then a little rapidly to his left at Mr Burden: Mr Burden was silent, and Mr Barnett went on:

'We have, I say also, the shareholder-interest to consider. If we had ourselves alone to safeguard so, we should be understanding Mr Âppott's position; indeed, I am very sure. Büt' (and here Mr Barnett lowered his voice in a manner which would have been impressive even to a larger audience, and wagged his head gloomily): 'Büt have we choice I fear . . .?'

He looked sadly a moment at the middle of the table, with an expression not unlike that of an animal about to be sacrificed, then throwing up his hands with the palms outwards, said in a sudden return of native feeling:

'Ach! God! He hass not come in! He hass not come in! It is right on his own head, I say.'

It was not often that Mr Barnett allowed a sudden revulsion of feeling to awaken in him the exclamations of his youth, but he felt strongly upon Mr Abbott's action; he thought it stupid; he thought it unbusinesslike. He thought it dangerous to the M'Korio Delta Development Co. He thought it, from what he knew of the English, un-English, and, during the few seconds of that angry phrase, a native phrase had returned to him, strongly borne upon a gust of natural passion.

Cosmo tentatively intervened:

'Perhaps, father, you could go and see Mr Abbot again?' Mr Burden, hearing the voice of his son, and being thereby suddenly reminded of his home and of many years, looked up with an awful pain in his eyes.

'No,' he said.

Then there was another awkward silence, which Lor Benthorpe did not much relieve by saying twice the words, 'I hope . . . I hope,' and looking round with an uncertain smile.

Mr Harbury broke in, with the air of a man whose thought has matured; he leant his chin upon his left hand, and looked steadily at Mr Burden.

'Mr Burden, I think you will admit that Mr Abbott should have come in. If he does not come in, we are absolutely bound to oppose him with all our force. You see that as well as I do. You cannot justly complain if we destroy that which attempts to destroy us. You cannot justly complain if you refuse to persuade him further, and refuse also to help us in our self-defence against him. There is no possible third course.'

All this was said fixedly and clearly, as Mr Harbury had long learnt to say the thing that should dominate a weak man's mind; but Mr Burden was so ill as to be perverse and irrational; and the anger that makes men drunk was rising up in him again.

He cried much louder than he had meant: 'I have said all I have to say.'

His anger filled and impelled him; he kept control of his

body to some extent, but no longer of his mind; and he continued still loudly, without reason, and forgetting his determination to be cold:

'I will not be a party to any intrigue against my friend!'

Now such are the limits of human nature, and such is its feebleness, that even men like Mr Barnett (who had known all his life how to manage men) can lose their steadfast poise in a sharp moment of wrath. He looked round smartly, he put his face somewhat too suddenly forward, as towards an opponent, and thrust into Mr Burden's already kindled fires the fuel of an insult.

Those two deep sunken lines which marked the financier's heavy cheeks like furrows and drew down the lowering corners of his mouth, were contracted into a kind of intense sneer: and he said, without opening his teeth:

'You will party be to your pocket whatever!'

Then Mr Burden, power bubbling up within him in spite of his age, in spite of his illness, and filled, in spite of his wealth, with a desire for freedom, cried out at him:

'Take care, Barnett, you 're going a little too far, just a little too far . . . I wouldn't have that . . . not for worlds!'

Mr Burden's breath came very quickly, and he had his lips as closely pressed together as any had yet seen them, and his head was full with the blood of his anger. But there was anger in Mr Barnett also, though of another race and kind and climate; and he said with a full sneer, where only half a sneer had been before:

'What can you do? So?'

I repeat, for the twentieth time, that Mr Barnett's knowledge of men had never failed him. He must not be judged on this exceptional case, nor condemned because he underestimated the follies that men like Mr Burden can commit, when their state of mind is such as was then Mr Burden's state of mind. For, a passion like a fighting passion possessed Mr Burden, and rioted through his aged and enfeebled body, forcing its organs beyond their power, and straining the material framework of his life. In that passion he had forgotten decent conduct; he had forgotten investments and all that investments should mean to a just and reasonable man. He repeated without moving:

'What can I do?' He said it two or three times in a low voice. He remembered a furious letter to the Press which he had not posted: he remembered his fear lest the Press should refuse to print it. He remembered his sufferings as the syndicate was preparing, he remembered his yielding, and what that yielding had cost him in the soul. He remembered above all Mr Abbott, Charles Abbott, his friend—and, remembering these things, he lost all control.

He snatched up his hat from the ground, and thrust it far back upon his head at random: he sprang upright: he held his chair tilted back with one hand; with the other he grasped his umbrella in a kind of swagger, tip to ground, as though it had been the scabbard of a sword. He seemed vigorous, or perhaps distraught: intoxicated with the words that rose in him.

Mr Harbury, whose judgment I will always trust in such matters, and who was once not unacquainted with the management of the stage, has told me that never in his life, not even in the Levant, had he seen so dramatic a passage of anger as was that of this old Englishman in the toils: all his respectable English dress was at random; his sober English gestures became those of a man who fights or labours; and it is a detail worthy of notice, that the bone stud at his throat broke as he started up, and that his collar went flying loose at random. He shouted at them:

'What can I do? Oh, I can do a great deal, I can! You, Barnett, and you, Harbury, and all of you! All!'

Perhaps he actually felt the presence of a crowd: the massed forces of this new world surging against him; he spoke as though to numbers.

'I can smash it! I can smash you, and your precious shareholders . . . and, and the Duke . . . and the whole thing! I can go and say why I went! Eh? Oh! good Lord! and I shall print it. . . . If they won't print it in your cursed papers, I 'll placard it; I 'll cover the town with it; I 'll put your names up high—all your names—your names that you hide, and the names that you have had and lost . . . swindlers and thieves and scum!'

And, after that outburst, he recovered himself a moment, and stood away from them, breathing too hard, while Mr Harbury looked down, and Mr Barnett smiled a drawn smile of hatred that would not betray fear.

Lord Benthorpe, a soldier in his youth, was very genuinely afraid; he was afraid of something indefinable, of catastrophe . . . he did not understand these things.

There passed through Mr Burden's mind a spasm of calm

which he mistook for self-control; he fumbled at his collar
trying to straighten it, he put on a civic dignity, and stood up
stiffly, and turned to his son and said:

'Come with me, Cosmo.'

Cosmo, whom this wild scene had distressed beyond bearing,
looked down nervously at the table, shuffled the papers before
him, and murmured almost inaudibly:

'Don't make a fool of yourself, father.'

Then Mr Burden, stooping forward hurriedly, went out.

There was a full three minutes of silence, during which
Mr Barnett's face looked like the face of one of those old and
monstrous things, enormous, dug from Assyrian sands, while
Mr Harbury coughed twice, and sidled his eyes uncertainly,
and Lord Benthorpe twiddled his fingers upon his trembling
knees.

Then Cosmo, still in confusion, desiring to see whether indeed
he would ruin them all and desiring to be rid of the atmosphere
of anger, got up and went out after his father.

.   .   .   .   .   .

In the street another beam of those few which support the
structure of human life crashed within him; the old man's brief
draft of energy ran out and was lost utterly.

The mechanical action continued; he could pass through the
crowds with whom he had mixed for fifty years, but he felt a
growing tension of the brain and some such abandonment of
grasp and power, as men feel who are drowning, and who lose
their consciousness just before they drown.

A few steps behind him followed Cosmo, his son. Interests,
more momentous than the life of one man, made it imperative
to Cosmo that the M'Korio should not be betrayed. There
was just time for his father to give notice of disclaimer; there
was ample time to visit some one of those newspapers that continued in spite of loss and a deserved unpopularity to attack
our great scheme of Empire. The exchange was shut. There
was time to ruin everything before the morning. Nor could
Cosmo know what his father suffered: he followed in the interests
of the M'Korio, and, happily, his father did not know that he
followed.

There are duties of many kinds; and Cosmo was doing one
of these many duties as best he knew.

He saw his father pass the statue of Mr Peabody, philan-
thropist, cross Cornhill, and King William Street, and make for

the Cannon Street terminus; but Cosmo was a man to do his duty, when he did it, thoroughly: it is a habit to which he owes the great position he now enjoys.[1] He did not lose sight of Mr Burden until he had seen him actually enter the gates of the railway station; then only did he turn away, with heaven knows how much relief, and plan such recreation as was legitimately his after the strain of the last few hours. He sent first a telegram to Mr Barnett to reassure him, and then cast off all business and went west, to spend the evening with such companions as he had previously engaged.

But Mr Burden, bowing under the increasing weight of his malady, hesitated as he went up to take his ticket. He had forgotten, and was at a loss in everything. He did not remember his season ticket; and, when he stood before the little window, an impatient crowd gathered behind him, cursing at his delay. He had forgotten even the name of the station for his home. The trained clerk was quick enough to meet the difficulty. He took the gold piece that the old merchant had put down, and gave him in exchange such a third-class ticket as would carry him to the very extremities of the suburban zone. Mr Burden looked at the unfamiliar name upon the pasteboard and moved slowly on to the platform; a considerable volley from the long queue whom he had just released followed his shambling figure; till a wit at the head of it restored the public humour by giving him very publicly the title of Methuselah. Mr Burden, wandering vaguely towards the train, did not so much as hear.

On the platform the porters knew him, and, in spite of the colour of his ticket, opened for him a first-class carriage; one, with the ready courtesy of his kind, helped him to his place, then, turning, tapped his forehead and jerked his thumb over his shoulder with a leer; for Mr Burden was evidently very ill indeed.

In the train he sat, relieved by some repose, and conscious (in a blurred way) that an old man in the corner of a railway carriage was safer from insult and observation, than wandering on a platform, a thing for gibes.

He sat dully, his brows contracting now and then. The names of the stations pleased him, because they were familiar. He tried to remember their order, or at least the name of such as he had not yet reached; but he could not. He was puzzled,

[1] Honorary LL.D. of Dublin: trustee of Holy Souls Hospital, P.G.M. of the A.G.O., and major in the volunteers.

and looked round at his fellow-passengers, as though for help. They glanced at him above their papers, and saw that he was ill. They feared for the decencies. One, more refined than the rest, bolted out at the next stopping-place. The others defended themselves with silence, reading steadily behind the bulwark of the evening papers.

The old man turned to the window beside them, and watched the stations and the people as the train went on. He saw the news upon the placards, flaring under the flaring lights. He recited the headlines slowly to himself. They were associated dimly, he knew not why, with anxiety; they distressed him.

Then there was a little darkness and a rumble, and he heard the name of Norwood. He recognized it at once, and got out, and stood irresolutely at the gate. The collector took the ticket out of his hand, and smiled. Mr Burden looked at him fixedly, wondering at his smile, and felt for a moment an angry wave of emotion. He took this man also for one of his enemies.

But a muddled feeling of pleasant association came after. He took him foolishly for a friend, and smiled and nodded in reply. Then, by pure instinct, such as animals have, he found the way towards his home.

He came up that familiar road, his head reeling, and a bond, as though of iron, oppressing it within; and, as he walked, he suffered some dull ache continually. His slow steps jarred him; and now and then those pulsating throbs that are Death's artillery preparing his attack, hammered at the walls of his being.

He kept to one line of the pavement to make more sure; and once he thought: 'Perhaps I am drunk.' For it flashed twice on him that he was something different from himself; and he mixed with a night forty years gone, when he had drunk a whole bottle of some kind of wine. He heard again his father's anger; and it seemed to him, in a fantastic way, that he was about to meet that anger now—after all those years.

The functions of humanity were breaking down in him: memory, connection, harmony. Oh, poor Mr Burden! He had not known what was meant by the preachers when they preached; he had not known what was before him when they talked of the Soul. Mr Burden had called it immortal in his recited creed, and very right had he been in so calling it, and he was to prove it right in astounding trials, but in so doing quite to pass beyond the meaning of his words or theirs.

He came up that familiar road: he saw the gates of his own house—they both stood white in the evening. Habit (or ritual), the mistress of men sane, the good nurse of the last hours, carried him stumbling beyond the first gate. He passed the lodge, and, stumbling still, he reached the steps at his door. Here the old man would have sat down, as beggars do, to rest, had not habit still sustained and preserved his manhood: for never in his life had he done so strange a thing as to sit upon the doorsteps of a house.

It was his house, and he was master of it. He felt in his pocket for a key, and found one. He tried the door with it; but the key was too large. Many thoughts at once confused him, for he was troubled by Pain and Mortality: Pain and Mortality wrestled with his failing manhood, to mount, to ride, to conquer. But they were not in the saddle yet. He was determined to open his own door. He fancied many things at once. That his door had changed, or the key. Of his home and himself he was still sure; but his key and his door had already entered that world where all things common change and mingle, and where some other things, less known, emerge quite fixed for ever. Of his home and himself, he was still sure. His key and his door were already passing; himself and his home were, alas! to follow.

As he grated at the door, a faithful servant of his, a woman of the name of Kate Hatteras, heard him, and ran and opened. He would have told her the miracle of the door and of the key, but Pain—now grown into the whole of himself and wrestling hard, a power that knew its aims—Pain constrained him. He groaned, and his servant supported him deftly with her laborious and dutiful arm, and there flashed between them that good bond of long acquaintance, and Charity came into this house and visited its dying master—the first of the last angels. And, after Charity, there came those three great spirits, whose Hebrew names I never knew, but which are called in our language the Design, and the Mercy, and the Justice, of God.

Charity and the old servant helped him up the stair, soothing him; he would have still spoken of the key and of the door; he smiled with smiles that were those of a child or of a man in extreme old age. Then his pain returned, and he groaned; for the pain was in the head, where is the citadel of a man besieged. His keep was taken.

Once, during that last little pilgrimage, upon a landing, he stopped, and tried to speak some senile syllables. He wished to thank his companion courteously. No one else had been directly good to him and to his dissolving humanity in all these terrible hours; but, in the midst of his attempt, the key returned to him.

He mixed the mention of it into his speech, frowned a little, and stopped.

'Come, sir,' said that admirable woman, 'come along; you'll be better, sir.   Don't you take on; now don't 'ee'; for she had been born away from towns, and her duty, her service, her honour, her hard work, and her kind of English, were all one thing.

So he took comfort, in spite of his pain, and her help was his support; nor had he any other friend, from that moment until he died.

Mr Burden was put to bed, not only by this servant, but by another named Elizabeth, and by the knife-and-boot boy too, whose daily task was indeed accomplished before nine, but who commonly remained against orders till eleven, that he might enjoy communion with his kind.   And all these three, Kate Hatteras, Elizabeth, and the knife-boy, were awed in the presence of this good man, whom God had made and preserved, and was now taking back from them, and from Upper Norwood, and from England.

The burden and the grotesque of their task wreathed up into the sublime; they felt like travellers over whom a mist is lifted until they see, startled, the majesty of great hills before them. Their souls were raised by the sharp apparent nearness of those awful gates, through which it was their high destiny also to pass at last.   They saw revealed for another (they themselves had caught the revelation) the things which each of us is born to see, each at his own time, upon his dreadful day.

Kate Hatteras, resolute and exact, left the boy to watch, called a messenger by telephone, sent him to a nursing home near by, and, finding a cab, directed it to fetch, not this or that celebrity, but a doctor of the place in whom she had some confidence.   Within an hour, she had in the house a nurse of some age and experience, but insufficiently refreshed with sleep; there came next all manner of appliances, and soon after, the young doctor, nervous and smiling rhythmically, who went up to the room and gave Death a long particular name.

But Death could have no need of definition here.   He was present with his most ancient titles, dominant upon a throne, ordering that infinite vast wherein the narrow walls of one poor human habitation were not seen, so tenuous were they.   His armies at a summons filled the place all round: He was in his court and power.

The servants were bidden by Kate Hatteras to go and sleep. The doctor wrote some useless thing, and left it for the morning.

It was past midnight.   Kate Hatteras lay down in the dressing-room near by, where, some few days before, the consultation had been held; she lay down dressed, and slept, and dreamt of a lonely shore where twilight stretched out endlessly along dull sands by a silent sea.   But next door, in his bed (and above him some text or other in a frame) lay Mr Burden, her good master, in the agony of that last steep beyond which, they say, is an horizon.

He muttered incoherently, with pauses of silence between, and the nurse, though lacking sleep, yet thought it her duty to watch.   The September night was chilly; a fire was lit.   She sat rigid and staring at the fire, till, in a longer spell of silence, her head drooped; and she living, her living body in spite of her will, fell unconscious into repose.   But round the dying man were other companions.

Now this, now that, out of the long past was with him; persons and things all trivial.   He spoke twice of an order—then he would bid a clerk write something . . . to whom?   He forgot the name . . . he forgot the name.   He complained of his memory; then he sighed a little, and was still.

In a moment he turned, and began his muttering again.   To many friends, long dead, he spoke of the key and of his honour, and of . . . of . . . he sought for a name that would fit at once a traitor and a lost friend, something evil in the world—some spirit or other.   Perhaps a son.   The effort strained him; he groaned again and was silent.   One fixed and harassing per-plexity recurred.   There was something being done against his will at home; some quarrel of judgment: the children surely —or was it a servant?   His wife was there by the bedside, renewing some ancient domestic difference . . . but there! he was willing to yield.   Anything, anything to cool the press of fever that was gaining upon the turmoil within him: yet he wished her nearer to him and understanding more, for he was very ill; and he kept on whispering: 'As you will, my dear, as you will.'   Then, almost aloud: 'Don't go! . . . don't go with-out settling it, my heart!'   But she was gone.

Mr Burden opened his eyes; he knew that he was awake: he saw the ceiling plainly, and the stucco pattern of it, above the dull light of the falling fire.   His wife, the real picture of her, rushed into his mind; he knew that she had gone that very moment, shutting the door and leaving him.   He could not move, for something had snapped, and all was changing: he felt himself utterly alone.

Loneliness caught him suddenly, overwhelming him; wave upon wave of increasing vastness, the boundaries leaping, more and more remote, immeasurably outwards with every slackening pulse at the temples. Then it was dark; and the Infinite wherein he sank was filled with that primeval Fear which has no name among living men: for the moment of his passage had come.

> Sanctus Fortis, Sanctus Deus,
> De profundis oro Te.
> Miserere, Judex meus,
> Mortis in discrimine.

Mr Burden's head jerked a little to the right, his jaw fell, his hands twitched and grew rigid. Mr Burden was dead.

. . . . . .

The dirty light grew in the east of the world, and lit without hope the labour and despair of the city; the masts and spars of the ships a long way off in the docks showed delicate and true. There was a little streak of murky rose which faded, and, without, one cameo noise and then another led on to the life of a new day. A bird among the black branches of the ruined smoky trees, a footfall in the road outside; a few more moments and the sound of wheels. It was Cosmo coming home.

His subdued, but rather husky voice, as he paid the driver, was carried on the rare morning: he dropped a coin to the pavement and it rang. Even the shaking key in the lock could be heard, though he turned it softly. He was careful for his father's repose, as he had always been when he came home after a night of pleasure with his equals. He pulled off his boots, not without many blunders, and went up the stairs noiseless, holding the banisters well. He reached his room above, and lay down at once to sleep, half dressed, the sleep he needed.

An hour later, when it was broad day, the nurse in the room with the dead man snored fitfully, stirred, and awoke. She started suddenly, as she looked round, at what was in the bed. Then her long experience composed her, she did what she had to do, and went into the next room, not liking to be alone. Kate Hatteras woke at her touch; and they watched together and only when they saw that the time had come did they rouse the household. The fires were lit for breakfast to be cooked, and someone called Cosmo and told him what had fallen in the night.

. . . . . .

Two days after, with reasonable pomp, they restored the body to the earth, in that part of the cemetery at Norwood where lay the vault he had purchased: just beyond the sections consecrated to the Roman Catholics and the Jews. Already, for some fifty-three hours, his spirit had returned to God who gave it.

Thus did they bury Emmanuel Burden, a dealer in hardware; and his son inherited his wealth.

I have no fears for him at the Judgment Seat. He had borne with affection for more than twenty years the common trials of domestic life. He had brought up three children to maturity. He had dissipated nothing of his health or patrimony; he had increased his fortune by sober and by honest means, and with it in some part the wealth of the country which he adored. He had voted consistently as he thought best for the interests of Britain, supporting Mr Gladstone's Administrations until the fatal year of 1885, and, since that date, concerning himself for the success of the Unionist or Conservative candidate. But Mr Burden is dead, and I do not quite see who there is to take his place.

Honest Englishman and good man—I wish I could have written of him in nobler terms.

MRS MARKHAM ON THE POLICE

TOMMY. It's a long time, dear Mamma, since you gave us some of that valuable information with which you supplement the instruction of our governess, Miss Pooke.

MRS MARKHAM. Yes, my dear Tommy, but the gap has been unavoidable, for I've been attending the Gallery of the House of——

MARY. Oh, Mamma, you promised us that you would not talk politics any more, and you promised dear Papa that you would not say a word about the Samue——

MRS MARKHAM. [*Sharply.*] Don't let me hear that word again, Mary! Papa has forbidden it to be mentioned in the house! He said only the other day that it was like *Ta-ra-ra-boom-di-ay*.

TOMMY. What is *Ta-ra-ra-boom-di-ay*, Mamma?

MRS MARKHAM. My dear, it was once a patriotic song, but you would not understand it, because you are still only a little boy.

MARY. I remember it, Mamma. Uncle Billy used to sing it. He used to come in singing it late at night after we had gone to bed, when I was quite a little girl.

MRS MARKHAM. [*Icily.*] Very possibly, my dear. Your father's brother William will often hum a song after it has ceased to be popular.

TOMMY. What does 'popular' mean, Mamma?

MRS MARKHAM. 'Popular,' my dear Tommy, signifies of, or belonging to the populace; widely spread among the populace generally accepted.

MARY. Then I suppose, Mamma, that policemen are popular?

MRS MARKHAM. No, my dear, not altogether in that sense. You see policemen are put over us for our good, and we do not always like what is put over us for our good. Nevertheless, if we know that it is for our good we should always accept it.

TOMMY. Do you accept policemen, Mamma?

MRS MARKHAM. Yes, certainly, and so does your Papa. And what is more, we should be ready to give aid to the police when they are in difficulties, for you must remember that we do not give arms to our policemen as people do upon the Continent, but they are plain citizens like ourselves. So if they need aid we ought to go to their help.

172

MARY. Who made the police, Mamma?

MRS MARKHAM. God made the police in the first place, but, of course, in a sense, man has made the police; that is, they could not have helmets and big thick blue coats and belts and truncheons and india-rubber shoes, unless man lent his active co-operation to the inscrutable designs of Providence.

TOMMY. I think I understand, Mamma. Active co-operation is what we use when we ask for grace——

MRS MARKHAM. No, my dear, you are confusing two things, but you are too young to understand. Anyhow, the police are put there to see that bad men do not do any harm to good people, and also to see that our houses are securely locked up at night. They also have to give evidence before magistrates of wicked deeds which they come across.

MARY. I know they look after our houses, Mamma, because only the other night a policeman showed Papa where our house was, and Papa was very grateful to him and gave him half a sovereign. Sarah told me so.

MRS MARKHAM. Did she, indeed!

TOMMY. Yes, and Sarah also told me that the policeman who comes and has dinner downstairs knew all about our house and all the other houses, and he told her——

MRS MARKHAM. [Severely.] That will do, Tommy. Well as I was saying, the police look after us and see that we can sleep comfortably in our beds, and prevent wicked men from attacking good men; so we ought to be very grateful to them, for if it were not for the police we should be in continual danger.

MARY. Why are all policemen so fat, Mamma?

MRS MARKHAM. They are not all very fat. You are deceived by their clothes.

TOMMY. But they have fat faces, have they not, Mamma?

MRS MARKHAM. That is because they are only chosen from healthy people. Only a healthy man could lead the life which policemen have to lead. There was once a great poet who wrote a song about it which begins: 'A policeman's life is not a happy one.'

MARY. But it is a happy one, Mamma, is it not, if he does his duty? You have often told us we shall all be happy if we do our duty, and policemen are always doing it.

MRS MARKHAM. [Reverently.] Yes, in that sense, my dear, a policeman's life is indeed a happy one, and he will have a crown of glory; but I mean that while he is of the Church Militant

and still upon this earth his life is not very happy, or at any
rate, he often finds himself in positions of great danger. For
instance, it is only the other day that a policeman was walking
down a vulgar street, whistling to himself, when three or
four wicked men came and knocked him down and jumped
upon him and left him for dead, so he had to be taken to
a hospital.

MARY. Oh dear, Mamma! I do hope they were caught and well
punished!

MRS MARKHAM. Well, my dear, I am afraid they did not catch
the actual men who did it, but I am glad to tell you that some
other men of the same sort were arrested instead. They
were punished, and if the injured policeman dies they will all
be hanged.

TOMMY. That is very satisfactory, Mamma, and do you know I
almost hope he does die so that these other men may be
hanged. What are their names?

MRS MARKHAM. Do you mean the names of the four men who
jumped upon the policeman?

TOMMY. No, Mamma, for of course we do not know those names.
Did you not tell us that they were not caught? I was only
asking for the names of the other four men who are to be
hanged instead of them just to show that policemen must be
treated respectfully.

MRS MARKHAM. Quite right, my dear Tommy; but I cannot give
you the names of those other four men.

MARY. But if the policeman does not die they will not be hanged,
will they, Mamma?

MRS MARKHAM. No, I am afraid they will not; but at any rate
they will be condemned to a long term of penal servitude.

TOMMY. Do policemen marry, Mamma?

MRS MARKHAM. Yes, my dear, sometimes, and they have little
children.

MARY. Do their little children grow up to be policemen?

MRS MARKHAM. No, my dear, not necessarily.

TOMMY. What do we call the wife of a policeman, Mamma?

MRS MARKHAM. She has no distinctive title, my dear, any more
than the wife of a Bishop. She is simply called Mrs So-and-so
after her husband's name.

TOMMY. She must live a very anxious life, the wife of a policeman, with all these wicked people about; especially as you
tell me, Mamma, that in this country we do not give the
police arms.

MRS MARKHAM. No, my dear, we do not give them arms because
we think this would be cruel and unjust. But we let them
have a thick stick called a truncheon, with which they can hit
people upon the head as hard as ever they like, to make them
obey.

MARY. Does this truncheon hurt, Mamma?

MRS MARKHAM. I have no personal experience of it, my dear
Mary, but I do not think it can hurt very much, or I am sure
they would not be allowed to use it. It hurts just enough to
make people obey, and no more.

TOMMY. What do they do, Mamma, when, after the policemen
have hit and hit and hit with their truncheons, and yet people
will not obey?

MRS MARKHAM. Such a case, my dear Tommy, very rarely
occurs. There was, indeed, one case which was very
grave.

MARY. [*Eagerly.*] Do tell us about it, Mamma!

MRS MARKHAM. I will. Houndsditch was infested at that time
with no less than two desperadoes. I am glad to say they
were not English, but Lithuanian in religion; and though the
police were only too willing to hit them on the head with their
truncheons it was impossible to get at them; for they *would*
shoot off revolvers, so that it was really dangerous for the
police to go near.

MARY. Did they succeed in getting away, dear Mamma?

MRS MARKHAM. I never heard, my dear, what happened to these
wicked men, but, anyhow, they never reappeared. Some say
that one of them was burnt alive when the police set fire to
the house.

TOMMY. I am very glad to hear this, Mamma. But I suppose
this does not often happen?

MRS MARKHAM. No, my dear. It has never happened before,
and I hope it will never happen again.

MARY. Have you anything more to tell us about the police,
Mamma?

MRS MARKHAM. My dears, I could tell you many things about
them. They protect the little birds that seek their food in
the street, and very often they begin to cry when they see
poor old men and women trying to cross through the heavy
traffic; and though thousands and thousands of them take
oaths in police courts during the year they always tell the
truth. But I think you have heard quite enough for one
evening.

TOMMY. Thank you, Mamma, though I am sorry you have stopped talking of the police, because it makes me think about what papa was saying about the Suffragettes years ago.

MRS MARKHAM. Yes, my dear Tommy; the police had, indeed, among other arduous duties, to be slapped in the face by Suffragettes and to smile all the time, but I will tell you more about them some other time.

III. HISTORY

THE CONVERSATION OF THE KING
(1245–50)

St Louis, the king, loved quiet speech, meeting the speech of others. He loved rallying and conversed with all as though with peers. Pomp wearied him, even where it was necessary for the dignity of so great a state. Those jests which complete a question and leave no more to be said he was amused to hear. Also he himself observed men with very great wisdom, often silently; and his eyes, which were a little weary even in youth from too much questioning of himself and of the world, and from too much business of fighting of every kind within and without, were always luminous and often smiled. His body, which was spare, exercised by continual chivalry and by the weight of arms, but a little wasted by solicitude, by mortification, and by occasional disease, suited his gesture and the holy irony with which he salted life.

All those, or nearly all, who came about the king—men themselves, for the most part, much grosser in temper or much less subtle in observation—felt this play of his intelligence upon theirs, and when he was dead remembered it most vividly. Nor were the words of St Louis and his manner things very conscious. They surrounded his personality like an air, impossible to define, easy to taste. They were a perfume. Some who thus received his influence wrote down a little clumsily what they remembered, and the things they wrote down, after so many catastrophes and such vast changes in Europe, stand to-day quite neat and clear. So that when you read of St Louis it is like looking out of a little window, unglazed, in a tower, and seeing through it, framed in the stones of the wall, a well-ordered, sunlit landscape, particular, vivid, and defined; full of small brilliant things, exact in outline.

One day in that good thirteenth century, when all was new, amid the new white buildings, upon the new ordered roads, when even the grass was new (for it was Pentecost), the king, Louis the Saint, was in Corbeil with eighty of his knights and certain others of his train. And when he had eaten the morning meal (which was at nine o'clock, for that was their hour), he went down to the field below the chapel to speak at the door with Count John of Brittany, and with him was the Seneschal of Champagne and others, younger and older men.   And as the groups stood there at the door in the spring sunlight, treading the spring grass, mown smooth, Robert of Cerbon (the same that founded the great college of Sorbonne, so that his name stands everywhere to-day for learning) took the young seneschal's coat and pulled him by it towards the king.   And the seneschal said:

'What would you with me, Master Robert?'

Robert said:

'I wish to ask you this: If the king were to sit himself down in this field, and you were to sit down without leave on the same bench, and higher than he, would you not be to blame?'

'Yes,' said the seneschal, 'I should.'

'Then,' said Robert, 'you are to blame now.   For even now you are far more nobly clad than the king, for your coat is of many colours, and embroidered nobly with green, and the king does not go so clothed.'

Louis, hearing this dispute, smiled at them but did not speak. And the seneschal answered sharply:

'Master Robert, saving your grace, I am not to blame at all, though I do dress in 'broidery and in green.   For this cloak was left to me by my father and my mother, who were noble.   But you are to blame.   For you are the son of a serf, and your mother was a serf as well, and you have given up the clothes that were left you by your father and your mother, and you are dressed in rich woollens much grander than the king's.'

And the seneschal, growing livelier still, took Robert of Cerbon's coat, and took the hem of the king's coat, and held them up side by side, and said triumphantly:

'There! See if I do not speak the truth. Look how much grander is the stuff you wear than the stuff that clothes the king.'

Then King Louis spoke, and first he put his hand upon the sward and sat him down at the gate of the chapel, and said to his sons, who were there, young men:

'Come, sit down beside me on the grass that we may hear each other the plainer.'

And they answered:

'Sire, we would not dare.'

Then he said to the seneschal:

'Seneschal, do you sit so.'

And so did the seneschal. He sat so close that their two cloaks touched.

Then said St Louis to his sons:

'You have done very wrong in that you did not obey at once, you, my sons.'

And then he said to the seneschal:

'You did wrong to speak thus to Master Robert, and when I saw how shamed you made him, I at once knew that it was my business to defend him; and as to dress, this is my counsel: you all of you should dress well and decently, in order that your women may love you more, and that your household may respect you; for the wise man says that we ought to dress ourselves and to arm ourselves in such a manner that neither shall the good men of this world blame us for extravagance nor the young blades for meanness.'

And upon another time, when they were sailing upon the sea, it being night, the ship was struck violently and lay over, and the storm rose so that it was thought she could not live. Then St Louis, understanding that death was at hand, went as he was, half-clad, to where the Blessed Sacrament was kept, and there expected death.

But when the storm as suddenly abated, and the morning was come, and the danger was passed, he asked by what name that wind was called which had nearly wrecked the King of France and all his people. To which the master mariner answered that this wind was no great wind, not one of the major winds of the world, not one of the cardinal winds, but a little side wind that hardly had a name, though some called it the little Gerbin wind.

When St Louis heard this, he said to one of those about him:

'See how great is God, and how He shows us His power. Since one of His little unimportant winds, which hardly has a name, all but destroyed the King of France, his children, and his wife, and all his household, in peril of the sea.'

St Louis, the king, loved also to tell this tale:

There was a master in divinity, one who had disputed for the Faith, and he came to Bishop William of Paris in great distress, and said that he was full of doubt, and that his heart would not bend to believe in the Sacrament of the Altar, and that this mood, sent by the Enemy, pressed him sore.

To whom Bishop William answered:

'And does this please you?'

To which the argufier answered vehemently:

'Not at all! I am tormented thereby!'

'Sir,' said the bishop again, 'would you be pleased that these new doubts should conquer?'

'I would rather,' said the poor man, 'that my limbs should be torn from my body.'

'Why, then,' said Bishop William, 'I will give you a parable. You know that the King of France wars now with the King of England, and that on the front of this war stands the castle of Rochelle, which is in the country of Poitiers. Now, if the king had given you Rochelle to guard, upon the edges of the war where the fighting is, but to me the hill of Laon, peaceably in the heart of his kingdom, which would he honour most—to whom would he give the greater reward?'

'To the man,' said the doubter, 'who held Rochelle.'

'Well, then,' said Bishop William, 'let me tell you that my heart is not even like the hill of Laon, but rather like the little hill of Montlhéri, near Paris, with its tower, for I have never doubted at all. So where God gives me in reward one measure, He will give you four.'

St Louis said that one should never speak ill of any man, and those who listened closely to his talk never remembered his speaking ill of any man; on which account also he would never so much as mention the name of the Devil.

Also one day, when he was in Cyprus, on Crusade, he said to a companion that put water into his wine:

'Why do you put water into your wine?'

Then that companion, who was a young man, answered:

'For two reasons. First, because the physicians have warned me to do so; and secondly, because I do not wish to get drunk.'

To which St Louis answered:

'You do well. For if you do not learn this custom in youth you will not practise it in age, and if in age you drink your wine unmixed, you will, without doubt, be drunk every evening of your life; which is a horrible thing to see in a valiant man.'

And thinking of this, he said again:

'Would you be honoured in this world, and then have Paradise?'

And the young man said 'Yes.'

Then the king said:

'This is the rule: Neither say nor do what you would fear that all men should know.'

And another time the king said to this young man, when they were on Crusade in the East:

'Tell me which you would rather be—a leper, or in mortal sin.'

And the young man, who was afraid to lie to the king, answered:

'I would much rather have committed thirty or forty mortal sins than be a leper.'

And the king did not answer him; but the next day he said to the young man:

'Come here and sit at my feet.' Which the young man did, and then St Louis said: 'You spoke yesterday like a wild man in a hurry, for all ills of the body are cured in a little time, when a man dies; but if your soul is tarnished, and you cannot be certain that God has pardoned you, that evil will last for ever as long as God sits in Paradise.'

And then he asked the young man suddenly whether he ever washed the feet of poor men on Maundy Thursday, and the the young man answered:

'Sire, far be it from me to wash the feet of poor men! No! Never will I do this thing!'

And the king said to him:

'You are wrong again—thinking yourself too grand to do what God did for our enlightenment. Now I pray you for the love of God and for the love of me, get yourself into the habit of washing poor men's feet.'

For this king loved all kinds of men, whatsoever kind God had made and Himself loved.

On which account also he would give castles to guard to men that had no claim on him, if they had renown in good deeds. And he would have at his table men of any birth for the same reason. And so seated once at his table he said to a companion:

'Tell me the reasons that a "loyal gentleman" is so good a thing to be called.'

Then they all began disputing and defining, and at the end the king said, giving no reasons and turning to Robert of Cerbon, the same whom he had defended for dressing well:

'Master Robert, this is what I think upon the matter: I desire to be called by men a "loyal gentleman," but much more to know that I am one. And if you would leave me that, you might take all the rest; for that title is so great a thing, and so good a thing, that merely to name it fills my mouth.'

Two historical problems are of prime importance to our race. To understand them sufficiently is to understand ourselves. To misapprehend them is to misapprehend our own nature: what made our culture and what threatens to destroy it.

The first of these problems is the conversion of the Roman Empire to Catholicism. 'How came the Pagan world to be baptized? What made Christendom?' The second is the disaster of the sixteenth century. 'How came Christendom to suffer shipwreck? What made the Reformation?'

It is the second of these questions which I here approach.

Neither can be completely answered; for these vast spiritual changes come of powers outside our experience: Heaven and Hell are at work. But an adequate answer may be given, sufficient to make the great event comprehensible. Its main lines may be so presented that they fall into a right perspective, and we can say: 'I now see how the thing happened. The human motives, at least, though their spiritual roots remain hidden, are clear and appear in their right order of importance. The surrounding circumstances in which they worked explain the results. The picture is rational and, within its limits, true.'

Now such an explanation of the affair is not presented to the modern mind by its accepted historians. The relation as given does not make sense: or only seems to do so if the reader is ignorant of the Catholic Church.

For the matter with which any story of the Reformation deals is the Catholic Church. The world upon which the Reformation fell, and which it in part destroyed, was the creation of the Catholic Church acting as a leaven for fifteen hundred, as a world-wide authority for a thousand years. The Reformation was an attack on that institution; its fruit, called Protestantism, is a negative product of that institution: the principle of unity in that fruit is reaction against that institution: therefore is full knowledge of the institution essential to knowledge of the conflict. Yet the general histories upon which opinion has been mainly nourished missed the very stuff with which they were dealing, because they proceeded from authors who had no intimacy with the Catholic Church: who did not know 'what it was all about.'

It is not a question of sympathy or dislike. A man may truly relate a battle whether he applaud or deplore its issue. But he cannot relate it truly if he does not know the ground. A man writing three centuries hence of Victorian England might love or hate its village life, but if he shall be all at sea on the gentry and their villages he will be writing equally bad history in praise or in blame of them. Whether he supports or denounces the despotism of the squires he will be worthless as an historian because the Victorian squires were not despots.

The two sources from which such historians have in the main proceeded are the academies of Protestant culture in the North, of anti-clerical in the South: each (in very different ways) out of touch with their material. Any brief list of half a dozen names at random are enough to establish that truth: Michelet, Thierry, Ranke, Carlyle, Macaulay. Because neither set of writers knows the material with which he is dealing, the Reformation seems to each a simple process with no problem to be solved. It is the man really acquainted with Catholicism who finds the difficulty of understanding the Reformation so great, its riddle so nearly insoluble. Just as a man penetrated with the high Pagan culture can hardly conceive its transfiguration into the Christian Empire at the approach of the Dark Ages, so a man conscious of what was (in part) destroyed at the Reformation is staggered by the mere possibility of such destruction: he knows what was lost; the facile historian of the Protestant sort on the one hand, of the anti-clerical on the other, does not.

To the first, the man of Protestant culture, the process leading to the Reformation seems obvious. From a variety of causes, knowledge vastly expanded at the close of the Middle Ages. Geographical discoveries followed each other rapidly and on a new scale of greatness; a true idea was acquired of the earth and heavens; arts improved; at the same time antiquity was rediscovered; original manuscripts were closely examined; a science of history began. The period is known as 'The Renaissance,' the 'New Birth' of Europe. Under such an influence the myths of a thousand uncritical years were exposed and dissolved. The institutions founded on these myths (the Papacy, the Mass, reliance on imagined influences of shrine and relic) were sapped, and with them crumbled all the society they informed.

Since men could not be expected to shed at once the religious influence of ten centuries, certain fragments of irrational mood survived, but they were increasingly rationalized. The Eucharist was retained as a form, but adversely discussed and more and more explained away. The Incarnation followed the same road, until the awful figure of a God Apparent faded into that of a mild young man at a loss. The successive liberations of the mind from illusion left man more and more himself: as by a successive stripping of veils. The old Catholic vesture was, indeed, retained by some of the more cultivated: but this retention was due either to their cowardice, their interest, or their routine, and the continued practice of superstitions in large societies was due to their racial inferiority, worked on by persecuting governments which forbade inquiry.

Among the higher types, when all the alien, infused Catholicism had dissolved, the Essential Fellow appeared, the Complete Man: who turned out to be in the Germanies an East Elbe Prussian, in England a well-to-do Englishman, but in the United States a citizen of the United States.

The results to which such history would lead were soon reached. The great national figures of the Middle, the Dark, and even the Pagan Ages became, as it were, Nature's Protestants. They may not have realized it fully at the time; but, at the core, Arthur, Penda, Offa, Arminius (more properly Hermann), Theodoric, Alfred, Otto, Edward I were of that material. History was 'read backwards' with a vengeance; and the Reformation could present no problem because it was but the final and necessary emergence of what had always been present below the surface in the noble ancestry of the writer.

Of *what* the thing they had lost might be, these historians knew nothing; and there is one major test among a thousand which can be unfailingly applied. To a man acquainted with the Catholic Church and the society it produces, nothing is clearer than that the plays of Shakespeare were written *by* a man plainly Catholic in habit of mind and *for* audiences in the same Catholic mood. Yet so simple and obvious a truth sounds absurd in the ears of men who attempt to write of the Reformation without knowing what the Catholic Church may be.

Now Shakespeare, be it remembered, came late. He came at a time when such historians talk of England as strongly anti-Catholic. He published his first poems well after the Armada. He is not so much Elizabethan as Jacobean. *Hamlet*, indeed, was written just before Elizabeth died. But *King Lear* is of the year of the Gunpowder Plot, and the great finale, *The Tempest*, later still.

Our historians, then, who make of Catholicism a thing unsuited to their race, and shed after Henry's breach with Rome, are ignorant of their subject-matter.

But the difficulty of explaining the Reformation, the problem it involves, is hardly better grasped by the historian of the second type, the sceptical or atheist historian, writing from within the nations of Catholic culture, notably the French or Italian.

To these men Catholicism seems a phase of thought present among their ancestry, natural to their blood, creative in its day, but now exposed as demonstrably false. It lamely survives to-day—principally in women—through a mere adhesion to traditional and homely things. It is also supported politically (but without conviction) by those who act from affection for the past, from a fear of disorder, or from mere interest. Its life, however, has departed. The Church is a corpse.

This kind of historical writer does not conceive of the past in terms of the present; he does not 'read history backwards,' nor is he necessarily warped by hatred. Some, indeed, of his sort are spoiled by a spirit of mere antagonism, but the greater part—on account of their early memories, of their friendships, of the Catholic air about them, and of unbroken social traditions from the past—have, for at least some portion or another of the Catholic scheme, a real affection (much what a grown-up man would feel for the mixture of strong emotions with illusions in his boyhood).

To them the Protestantism produced by the Reformation is ridiculous and intellectually contemptible—far lower than the Catholic past—and they despise the Protestant culture of to-day. Yet that the united Catholic scheme of Europe should have broken up in the sixteenth century seems to them inevitable; its loss they regard as an advantage to mankind, though they smile at the odd (now ending) interval of Bible worship and the rest. Though, then, such Continental 'anti-clericals' are far better fitted to deal with European historical problems than writers of Protestant culture (who are out of the main stream), yet they also find the problem of the Reformation easily solved —only because they do not know in what terms it should be stated.

That they are indeed thus unable to state the problem is apparent under a number of tests, of which these may be considered:

They are not only bewildered and exasperated by the recrudescence of Catholicism to-day but they give wrong explanations for it: they call it a fad, an hypocrisy, a decadent fashion, though the character of the new recruits is glaringly at variance with such bad judgment. The verse and prose, the attitude in war, the triumphant irony, the sacrifices of those returning to the faith to-day in the countries of Catholic culture, are manifestly the product of a mood not only sincere but strong, not only strong but lucid, not only lucid but well-armed; and it is in this last point that the anti-clerical historian most shows his lack of touch with reality, for it is *intellectually* that those whom he wildly calls 'Neo-Catholics' (their Catholicism being one with St Bernard's or St Augustine's) are proving his superiors.

Again, this sort of anti-clerical writer did, and does, not follow the true historical order of events—and that is a capital weakness in men of his trade. He imagined a false sequence. He saw the non-Catholic writers of the seventeenth century— and especially those on the anti-Catholic side of Europe—as the originators of popular government, the first to state clearly the metaphor of contract in society or the principles of communal authority. He did not know that they derived from the great Suarez. He imagined the new science of the Renaissance as the root of a later scepticism. He did not see the strong presence of scepticism *before* the advance of knowledge in the field of physical science, nor appreciate the significance of a Faith especially lively among the chief discoverers in that field.

Again (another grave weakness in his trade), he did not read the key-points: he despised and neglected those writings which would have explained to him the formation of that very culture from which he proceeded. Your anti-clerical historian of the nineteenth century had not read a line of St Thomas; he was ignorant of the fundamental debates permanently necessary to all philosophy, and never so vigorous as in the medieval schools. He missed the essential conflict of Nominalism with Realism. He knew not how all morals (property, authority, the diverse forms of government) had been analysed to exhaustion by those whom he left aside as unworthy of his attention. To take but one minor instance—a most illuminating one—he thought he could rely on the *Provinciales* of Pascal as the last word in a certain debate. He had never seen one page of Escobar's questions in the original. What is worse, he did not know that Pascal was under the same disability.

This sort of anti-clerical writer, then, explained the Reformation easily because he explained it wrongly. He saw it as a necessary phase in the general exodus of our race from darkness into light: a phase confused and full of contradiction, ridiculous superstitions, and savage fanaticism, but suffering all these inevitably as part of a great revolution which was to end in a stable and happy society.

But he was all wrong. The vision of progress was in his mind alone, not in the real world. The Reformation did not continue a direct Renaissance tendency towards larger things; it deflected that tendency. It did not introduce the arts; it cramped and thwarted them. Its last effects have not led to a society happy or stable; they have led to the society we see around us to-day.

These older schools, which found the great upheaval as inevitable as it was easily explicable, have lately lost much of their weight. The puzzle of the Reformation is presenting itself with added force to-day—in our generation, which has seen the last traces of Protestant dogma—not ethics—disappear: save perhaps from some backwaters, such as Dayton, in Tennessee.

Our generation lives in a world where Catholicism is the sole surviving positive force; where there surrounds that force a wide belt not Catholic, but in varying degrees of sympathy with Catholicism, while outside and beyond is a wreckage of philosophies inclining to despair.

It is to the Catholic, or at least to the man who knows what Catholicism is (that is, to the man in the very heart of European tradition), to the man who knows fully *what* it was that was abandoned, to the man who can feel the profound void and the quality of the loss involved by the Reformation, that its full problem appears.

He knows the balance, the satisfaction, the fullness of that which was rejected. How on earth came it ever to be rejected for such grotesque and petty aberrations as the various sects indulged in on its disappearance? Why was manifest good allowed to perish?

One who finds Greek sculpture dull, simple stuff will see no problem in its degradation and destruction in the failure of the Empire. But a man who knows what Greek sculpture is has a very different problem before him. *He* must try to understand how a thing so manifestly excellent, satisfactory to our civilized sense, ennobling, could have been left aside.

The Catholic can easily understand how there should arise an indifference towards Catholic practice, or even a reaction of hatred against official Catholic action and individual Catholic authorities; but what remains for him a problem still unsolved is how that which was the very nature of Europe, and surely necessary to the European mind; that in which it had been nurtured and which was intimately itself—so that European and Catholic meant the same thing and so that 'civilization,' 'Occidental,' 'Catholic' all meant the same thing—should have its own *being* utterly rooted out of it in certain regions, and an original, stable character, happy because it was in tune with itself, transformed into a new, uneasy and unhappy thing, which yet preferred to remain so transformed. *That* is the problem; *that* is the difficulty.

It hardly ever happens to the individual to-day. A person arriving at maturity in Catholic surroundings may grow hostile to authority or (more frequently) indifferent in practice; but he will hardly ever develop a general distaste for all the Catholic atmosphere and social tradition, still less an active hatred of them. Such an exceptional case would be like a loss of memory, or one of those strange phenomena which pathologists now and then discover in neurotic subjects.

Yet exactly that thing did happen to great groups of Europeans from three to four centuries ago, and what we must try, in part at least, to explain is how so astonishing a revolution and loss of personality was made possible: and in many places actually achieved and made permanent.

That is the problem. That is the question for which we have to try to find an answer.

I have said that no complete answer can be given, but at least the right sequence of political causes and their right proportion may be presented in a sketch of that fatal century, and that is what I shall attempt in what follows.

I shall begin by describing how, as the last of so many perils, united Christendom was growing unstable during the three generations between the Black Death and the early sixteenth century, that is, between 1350 and 1500.

I shall come next to the sudden flood of revolt in the German states and cities after 1517, and its spread elsewhere: a thing made possible by the constitution of Germany and especially by the invasion of the Turks.

Next, I shall present that strange fatality, the political accident whereby England, hitherto the least affected of all Christian provinces, was, under no popular pressure and without the will or knowledge of the policy's own author, turned face about to join the new alien movement. The dissolution of the monasteries in 1536-40, an act not connected in its author's mind with doctrine, proved the indirect cause of all that came after.

Then follows the mighty effect of Calvin, whose book, character, and organization provided form and substance for Protestantism, and gave it personal being: for Calvin's mind was a portent and became the power directing the storm.

Under his effect the opposing forces prepare—1547-9 to 1559—for conflict throughout the West.

A universal battle, of which France is the main field, rages undecided from 1559 to 1572, covering all the West—Netherlands, England, Scotland—until at the end of this, its first phase of active conflict, the final positions begin to appear: England and Scotland, the Northern Netherlands maintained in separation; France permanently divided, but the dynasty and the bulk of the nation rallying to the traditions of Europe.

The second phase of the great conflict—1572 to the end of the century—is but a confirmation of these new religious frontiers. The battle has ended in a draw, which leaves Europe permanently divided upon the lines it has since preserved.

There is a belated attempt, indeed, in the next century—1618-48—made by the Emperor to recover the many states and cities of Germany for unity and to establish his own authority and the ancient religion over all. It ends, through the genius of Richelieu, the conductor of French policy, in a failure. Germany remains divided, but not before the struggle (the Thirty Years War) has ruined German wealth and population for a century.

After that date (the peace of Westphalia in 1648) the main struggle is at an end throughout Europe, and the effects of the Reformation are established. The republic of Christendom is dissolved.

RICHELIEU AND BISMARCK

WERE Plutarch to return he would find no better modern subject for a parallel of lives than those of Richelieu and Bismarck.

Each born in the nobility of his realm, each at some distance from its highest ranks, each rose to be the chief in title.

Each served a dynasty, and each died leaving his crowned master at the very summit of power.

Each constructed and consolidated a realm, and each triumphed through a combination of diplomatic, political, and military qualities.

Each left, as the immediate fruit of his genius, a great succeeding epoch: Richelieu, the 'Siècle' of Louis XIV which directly inherited from his labours: Bismarck, that Prussian hegemony over Europe, and that rapid expansion in wealth and numbers of his 'Reich,' which expansion was the salient political fact in Europe over almost as great a stretch of time as the glory of Louis XIV. For the 'Grand Siècle,' beginning about 1660, is in full decline by 1710, that is in fifty years; it faded out before sixty had passed. Bismarck's Prussian hegemony over Europe is apparent in 1866, fully established in 1871, and endures to near the end of the Great War in 1918.

But there is a significance in the juxtaposition of these two men far deeper than the resemblance of their careers. For, as I have said, the one founded what the other completed. There is a succession between them, and the link of common agency in a mighty effect which the first had not foreseen nor the second directly designed, but to which both acted, the one as an originator, the other as a concluder, under the direction of powers far above human purpose. That mighty effect was the twofold thing we have been watching: the emergence of Nationalism as a chief motive for action in men and the consequent or accompanying reduction of the Catholic culture to the defensive under the supremacy of anti-Catholic and mainly Protestant forces.

The united and organized French state, given as a model by Richelieu to the world, was followed by the complete moral unification of England through the extirpation of a Catholic religious minority therein and of the Stuart dynasty protecting it. This twin example of French and English Nationalism slowly affected all Europe. The new Russian state of Peter the Great derived from that example. The idea of Nationalism became familiar, though not yet of effect, in the divided Germany and Italy of the eighteenth century. Prussia became almost as much a nation as a system. The Scandinavian victories left a similar heritage for Sweden. With the French Revolution that idea took fire and became the religion around us to-day, and, as an effect of it all, the mid-nineteenth century is full of 'nations struggling to be free' in regions where such a conception had hitherto meant nothing. The modern Italy was formed. Hungary asserted itself. The long-established partition of Poland did but emphasize the Polish demand.

At last comes Bismarck, who with unique dexterity uses the new ideal of nationalism to strengthen what would seem its very antithesis, the Prussian Crown and the domination of Berlin over the lesser units of the Northern and Central German peoples.

He creates an artificial nation so successfully that we had come to call it 'Germany' within thirty years of his death, although its very principle is the denial of German unity and the exclusion from that 'Germany' of whatever among Germans could outweigh the power of the Hohenzollerns. He relies upon this new Religion of Nationalism to inspire, give unity and life to, what began as a mechanical and artificial arrangement. He amply succeeds; and the next generation will die gladly for their new 'Reich,' indifferent to the body of Germanism external to it. At the same time, by his treatment of the French after his victories over them, by his increased harshness to the conquered Poles, he inflames Nationalism to the east and to the west of his new frontiers.

In the concomitant reduction of Catholic influence the same process is apparent. Richelieu by his toleration of the wealthy and numerous Huguenot body renders familiar to the French mind the conception of religious division within the state and the continual adverse discussion of its established worship: hence the growth of the sceptics, the strength of their propaganda, the rise of the anti-clerical spirit, until the official dominance of the Catholic hierarchy in France and its privileges become an anomaly. The Revolution resolves the problem with violence. Acute moral division within the remaining Catholic culture of Europe becomes everywhere the rule, and Nationalism reinforces the quarrel. France after her defeats in 1870, the new Italy risen on the abandonment of the Papacy, foster the decline of the Church, its morals and spirit. Meanwhile, eighteenth-century Britain, having extirpated Catholicism within her own boundaries, reduces Catholic Ireland to servitude; Holland is confirmed as a permanent power keeping under its rule a large Catholic minority. Turn where you will in Europe, when this process was in full power during the nineteenth century, you find everywhere in the Catholic provinces profound moral dissension, in the non-Catholic the rule of supremacy of hostile powers over Catholic minorities; never the reverse.[1]

Bismarck put the crown upon the edifice. He divided the Catholic forces of the Germans, swept into his net so much of the Catholic body as would cripple the rest without being large enough to endanger the moral mastery of their opponents. To the historical ideas and general culture of Protestant Prussia that Catholic minority in Bismarck's new arrangement gradually conformed, so that now the Reich, with a third of its people Catholic, counts as a Protestant power; the name 'German' has come to connote such a power, and the fact that one-half of German-speaking families are of the old religion is lost, in effect, upon the modern world.

The political subjection of Catholicism which Richelieu had unwittingly begun was by Bismarck confirmed: immediately in Germany and indirectly throughout Europe, until the tide was turned by the Great War.

Thus may we mark the way in which the work of these two men followed and completed the one the other. The parallelism and the succession are apparent.

But the contrast also must be noted; the contrast in character and the contrast in the respective advantages and disadvantages which aided and hindered them.

In physical appearance that contrast is glaring. No two figures are more opposed than the square, full-blooded, blunt face of the one, the pointed chin and finely cut, pale features of the other; the subtle fire and readiness to restrain or spring which Richelieu's face conveys, the deceptive mask of brute simplicity which covers Bismarck's. The bodies are in similar opposition. It is the Ox and the Leopard.

---

[1] A belated example of this system, probably the last we shall witness, was the precarious erection of the 'Six Counties' in Ireland. There, by careful calculation, a Catholic minority was cut off and left subservient to alien rule; this Catholic minority, withdrawn from the support of its fellows in the rest of Ireland, was made as large as possible compatibly with the maintenance of its subjection and impotence.

In the one, Bismarck, the supple spirit is hidden under an external directness and rough assertion which are not all put on, but derive, in part, from the blood of East Elbe squires. In the other a spirit as supple is expressed in every restrained gesture and in slight movements and glances of an exquisite delicacy. It may be said that the one could be likened to strong ale, the other to a rare brandy. They were so to the taste, superficially, but in effect, in the nourishment of a political plan, both were like a profound and rich wine. There appears in the one no visible reserve at all; in the other all seems reserve. But, in truth, each was exercising with full power all the interior discipline required to achieve his full effect.

The advantages in common to both were many. There was for both the continued support of a royal master whom each so devotedly served. There was the incompetence of that master (a negative quality very valuable to his servant). There was also the recognition by that master of his own incompetence (a positive quality more valuable still). Both enjoyed good fortune at critical moments, but Bismarck more than Richelieu. For Richelieu created his own success in every crisis—as for instance, on the famous 'Day of Dupes,' or again at Casale; while Bismarck had sheer luck time after time. Thus Bismarck was able to use Bavaria at will because the King of Bavaria was mad, and Bismarck had, without having to manœuvre for it, the neutrality of Britain; while Richelieu could count on no neutrality he had not himself engendered, and all his allies were on the alert for their own ends.

Both possessed an incomparable secret service which each had to create. Both had ample resources, though these could only be obtained by Richelieu at the expense of difficult and excessive taxation. Each stood in a geographical situation central for his time. For the France of Richelieu stood between the Empire and Spain in an age when there was no Russia. The Prussia of Bismarck stood between the then mighty Russian power and the West. Each was aided by the increase of mechanical invention and science during his period of action.

Both had the service of good subordinates, but Richelieu had here far greater fortune than Bismarck. For Richelieu had ready to hand a whole group of competent and devoted men like Charnacé, and, above all, the invaluable inspiration of Joseph du Tremblay, while Bismarck had no lieutenant worthy of his great task. Both managed to preserve their loyalty and service unbroken through all the useful years of life: years which Bismarck had the misfortune to outlive.

Of common disadvantages there were many. Both had to deal with jealousies at Court, though these in Richelieu's day formed a far more powerful obstacle than in the nineteenth century.

Both had to meet severe domestic opposition, both were hampered by religious and political differences in the area they intended to consolidate.

Both were condemned to considerable periods of apprenticeship and delay.

In other disadvantages they differed. Bismarck had the high advantage of physical health—at least, in all the active part of his career, while Richelieu was an invalid suffering more and more as the years drew on. Bismarck was secure on one frontier and could make reliance on Russia the corner-stone of his building. Richelieu was secure on none, but spent his life repelling and overcoming a ring of hostile forces.

Richelieu had to create from nothing, and against fierce opposition, the naval and military instruments of his policy; and each was doubtful in quality. Bismarck needed no navy and had inherited a superb instrument of war in the Prussian army, with traditions of two centuries behind it. To this great gift of fortune he owed those two dazzling campaigns against Austria and France, which established his power, as by magic, in four short years.

But while Bismarck had over Richelieu the very great advantage of immediate, overwhelming military success (with all the moral prestige it gives, and all the material power) he had one very bad handicap from which the Cardinal was free: he had to work under a secret divorce between his real and his ostensible aim.

Richelieu was impeded by no such spiritual chasm in his road. He openly desired the unity of his country, the strength of its central government, the attainment of its natural frontiers, the toleration of its religious divisions, the suppression, however, of a religious 'State within the State.'

In the details of Richelieu's diplomacy there was, of course, as there is in the details of all diplomacy, a great measure of insincerity. In order to overreach his opponents he had continually to be pretending to desire this or that when he was really desiring something else. He had continually to be presenting to allies their supposed advantage when really he was following the advantage of his own people. He had, as have all such, to master enmity, foreign and domestic, by strategy as well as by force.

But all that sort of duplicity is an essential in any handling of men by methods other than direct authority. It remains true that, on the large lines, Richelieu could afford to be sincere, Bismarck could not; and to be compelled to insincerity in the large lines of your action is a heavy burden, a large tax upon energy. Bismarck had to appeal to the strong German desire for racial unity when all the while his whole effort was aimed at the destruction of that unity for the aggrandizement of one section over the rest, and for the service of Prussia alone. Again, from the fact that his military instrument was essential to him, Bismarck, upon what was perhaps the most important point in the whole of his policy, allowed himself to be overruled. Richelieu was never overruled.

Bismarck was overruled in the matter of Metz.

He had proposed to draw the new frontiers, after the victories of 1870, so as to include whatever was (much as it detested Prussia) German-speaking (and in social life and custom German) upon the eastern frontiers of Napoleon III's Empire. He would have taken all Alsace, but of Lorraine only the German-speaking portion. He would have left Metz unannexed, and still attached to the French culture of which it forms a part. For Metz in 1871 was as French as Canterbury is English. Its architecture, its social custom, its civic language (allowing, of course, for the fact that many German-speaking people from a few miles away would come into the town) were all French; and indeed, there is no more striking example (within my experience at least) of the power of the modern state, with its crushing machinery of universal compulsory education, than the transformation of Metz into a German-speaking town. I have myself seen the process going on decade by decade during my own lifetime, and it has been of absorbing interest. For here you now have a population transformed in fifty years. Metz is to-day in the main German-speaking and reading its papers in the German tongue, yet inheriting social traditions wholly French and living in houses and worshipping in churches as French in spirit and design as those of Amiens and Beauvais.

Well, it was the fact that Bismarck allowed his wisdom to be overruled by the folly of the generals which ultimately led to the German disasters after his death. For though the proposition may be vehemently denied, I cannot but judge (for my part) that if Metz had been left French and the Prussian annexation in Lorraine had been confined to the purely German-speaking districts, time would have consolidated these with the rest of the Reich; and this, even when we have allowed for the incapacity of the Prussian official to govern. For he suffers, as do most good administrators, from a singular insuccess in ruling; for ruling is based upon persuasion but administration upon mechanical order.

Now in nothing of such importance was Richelieu ever overruled. He was not overruled, for instance, in the matter of Catalonia. It is due to him that French Catalonia has its maritime frontier at the Pyrenees and the broad Cerdagne. He would not give rein to the dangerous jingoism which wished to stretch beyond the mountains, and it was through his influence that, long after his death, the Treaty of the Pyrenees established natural defensible frontiers for France.

He was not overruled in the matter of the left bank of the Rhine. He suffered sharply in taking the decision to restrain French influence there, and to restrict it to the frontiers of his choosing. He did not so decide until after consultation with Père Joseph, and perhaps at the suggestion of that other; but he was not overruled by that other.

He was not overruled in the matter of Gustavus Adolphus. He did not get all that he wanted, nor had he previously been able to get all he wanted, for he could not get the Swedish captain (any more than he had previously been able to get the Danish king) to work with the Catholic League. He had to take second or third best; but he had not to suffer the imposition of another will.

With that word 'will' I am led to one last consideration upon these problems, which is not only curious but important to their comprehension. I have said that Bismarck's fatal decision in the case of Metz was due to his being overruled by the Army. Was there not behind that submission some defect of the will?

I think there was. Among the many and sometimes violent contrasts between these two strangely parallel lives, you find a contrast in moral texture which extends to the region of the will. Bismarck's will had not that incisive, rapier quality, that quality of highly tempered steel—flexible, unbreakable, of mortal effect, decisive, a sword—which had Richelieu's. Bismarck's will had rather the quality of a crowbar, sometimes to be used as a bludgeon. In the government of self, Bismarck's will broke down from time to time, as Richelieu's never did: and, after all, the government of self is the supreme test of will. Bismarck quarrelled, often foolishly, in private matters: under rebuff he was even peevish. I am not suggesting that his will was not strong: it was very strong; and the metaphor I have used of the crowbar and the bludgeon does not suggest weakness. But it lacked temper. Of Richelieu I think you may say that his was the most highly tempered will in modern history.

But on another side of character Bismarck seems to have had the advantage. I hope I shall not be called paradoxical if I say that in the mere use of the *intelligence* he would seem to be somewhat the superior of Richelieu.

Richelieu's judgments upon men and situations were excellent, his political maxims were wise. He admirably adapted himself to his needs. But I cannot help observing, in sayings of his which are authentic, and even now and then in deeds, a certain narrowness of thought—perhaps the inevitable result of so much concentration. With Bismarck, when the intelligence alone is at work, you are watching an instrument of somewhat more general power.

I come to a last consideration in my comparison of these two: the permanence of the structure built by each.

The permanence of his achievement is perhaps an unjust test of greatness in a man; but inevitably we ephemeral creatures born to an immortal destiny turn to permanence as a measure of success. We can but ask, 'Has the work lasted?' The boundaries of Diocletian define ecclesiastical dioceses and civil provinces to this day. The existing calendar is a testimony to Caesar. The commandments of Mohammed are still obeyed from the Atlantic to the China seas—and we judge by such things.

It might be said of both men that at first sight their achievement was not of lasting quality. The absolute monarchy which Richelieu erected crashed, to all appearance, in less than one hundred and fifty years, and the supremacy of the Hohenzollerns over the new state which Bismarck called into existence was destroyed in less than sixty.

But these failures are only apparent. The real work of both men has proved far more enduring. How long that of Bismarck may survive we cannot tell, but it is fair to say that after it had stood firm through the better part of a lifetime its essentials have (so far) survived the mortal ordeal of the Great War. Bismarck's Reich may well prove to have taken root strong enough for indefinite duration. I will discuss this in a moment.

The Hohenzollerns have disappeared, perhaps permanently, but the Reich remains. And its specific character, its essential (which is the subordination of a large Catholic minority to a government centred in Anti-Catholic Berlin) is as apparent to-day as it was fifty years ago.

In the same way the achievement of Richelieu was the consolidated unity of the French people, and not even the destruction of the Capetian monarchy has, as yet, appreciably affected that result. It is not time, therefore, to say that the work of either of these great men has been undone.

But there are present in the achievement of each certain forces which, if they continue uninterrupted and increase in power, will destroy either or both creations.

In the case of Bismarck's creation, the destructive act would be the union of the German race. Even a loose federation would be sufficient to undo Bismarck's work. The inclusion of the Germans of the Middle Danube and of those of the Alps into the same federal system as has hitherto been confined to the Germans of the Rhine, the Upper Danube, and the Northern plains, would be the dissolution of Bismarck's achievement. It would restore the old balance which he destroyed; it would restore the German Catholic culture; it would create at least three centres of energy, upon the Danube, upon the Rhine, and in the Northern plains, instead of leaving all dependent, as at present, on one pole in Berlin. It would probably reawaken that age-long instinct of the German people for separate local systems and for a sort of tribal diversity. But that union of the Germans has not happened yet and it may not happen at all.

As for Richelieu's achievement, what would destroy it would be a pushing of the religious quarrel among the French to such a limit that either the sentiment of national unity should disappear, or the Catholic culture itself should perish from the land. To-day such an extreme seems impossible, but there are already apparent the symptoms of some such possible catastrophe. We have in these last few years seen the hatred of the Catholic Church among its organized enemies in France preferred to the financial and political security of the country. We have seen it nearly ruin the attachment of Alsace and destroy in a brief ten years the enthusiasm of the recovered province for its old comrades. We have seen the financial stability of the country grievously endangered by men who are chiefly concerned with the suppression of the religious orders because they know that the religious orders are the strongest force for preserving and protecting the Catholic faith; and daily we can perceive compulsory state instruction in the schools eradicating from the mind of the French masses the roots of the Catholic culture. Now with the loss of that culture France will cease to be what, historically, we have known. The effects are already beginning to show in French architecture—which is growing repulsive—and in French prose—which is growing turgid. Such ulcers point to causes deeply affecting the whole body of society.

It would be a strange Nemesis, in the case of either Bismarck or Richelieu, if such a fate should fall upon their work. It would be a piece of historic irony of the first class, for it would be the destruction of a man's edifice by his own instruments of construction. What was Bismarck's chief moral instrument in erecting his 'Reich'? Why, of course, the cry of 'German Unity.' And yet the one thing most perilous for his work would be the restoration of a real German unity.

What was Richelieu's guiding principle in the attainment of an indivisible France? It was the permission of deep religious cleavage in the French nation as the price to be paid for preserving that political union by which, as he thought, the national soul could be alone (and sufficiently) preserved.

In the one case as in the other, what may undo all the builder did is the very moral force he originally relied on.

So much for the edifice which each genius erected in his own society: the Reich and United France. Both still stand. Will it be the same with their European effect, the political subjection of Catholicism? It may be doubted. The Great War released Ireland and Poland. It has produced a strong Italy. It has increased the difficulties of industrial Capitalism and correspondingly helped the peasant. It has had another effect of the highest import. It has set up the strength of the United States over against Europe. Now, in reaction against pressure, Europe will tend to rally to its own ancient traditions.

Meanwhile, in what governs all, in the things of the mind, Catholicism visibly expands its power, and what were once the fixed doctrines of its chief opponents, notably the Calvinist, are in dissolution.

MARSTON MOOR

Marston Moor was the action which established Cromwell, and of described actions in which great captains have taken part, Marston Moor is one of those which best illustrate the mixture of talent and good fortune which make up a complete reputation. That reputation, once established, of itself strengthens a man, he does better for being suspected of invincibility. There is thus nearly always in the career of any great captain a moment after which all changes with him. Before that moment he was known to have such and such capacity, which might be disputed or criticized: after that moment his fame — sure to be exaggerated — is fixed, he is indispensable, and the army begins, in spirit if not by definite appointment to regard him as the one leader.

So it was with Cromwell at Marston Moor. It was so because he retrieved what had become in a very short interval of fighting more than a desperate—rather a wholly ruined—situation; something approaching a rout. The situation was not only retrieved but completely reversed; an action which had already become as to more than three-quarters of it a breakdown of the Parliamentary forces, was turned in something over half an hour into a total defeat of the Royalists. And that turning was due to, and coincident with, a victorious movement which Cromwell led on his own extreme end of the field. Had he been one of other successful leaders in a general victory such as the superiority of the numbers of his side would have warranted, Marston Moor would never have had this effect upon his career: it was the vivid contrast between what he did and the failure of all the rest that served him. We shall see how much in this was due to the advantage of numbers and to the aid of others: but the decisive act was his own.

The battle of Marston Moor was in itself so confused that no one present there could have told you properly what happened. In the accounts which have come down to us the confusion has, of course, got a great deal worse. One eye-witness gives us the right for the left, sometimes writing in terms of the Parliamentary and sometimes of the Royalist line of battle. The various Parliamentary commanders gave, as was common form, their various

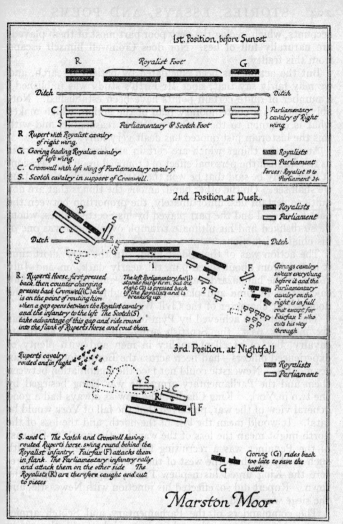

1st. Position, before Sunset

R   *Royalist Foot*   G

Ditch   Ditch

C   *Parliamentary*
S   *Parliamentary & Scotch Foot*   *cavalry of Right wing*

R   Rupert with Royalist cavalry of right wing.
G   Goring leading Royalist cavalry of left wing.
C   Cromwell with left wing of Parliamentary cavalry.
S   Scotch cavalry in support of Cromwell.

▨ *Royalists*
▢ *Parliament*

forces: Royalist 19 to Parliament 24.

2nd. Position, at Dusk.

▨ *Royalists*
▢ *Parliament*

Ditch   Ditch

R   Rupert's Horse, first pressed back, then counter charging presses back Cromwell (C) and is on the point of routing him when a gap opens between the Royalist cavalry and the infantry to the left. The Scotch (S) take advantage of this gap and ride round into the flank of Rupert's Horse and rout them.

The left Parliamentary foot (1) stands fairly firm, but the right (2) is pressed back by the Royalists and is breaking up.

Goring's cavalry sweeps everything before it and the Parliamentary cavalry on the right is in full rout except for Fairfax F who cuts his way through

3rd. Position, at Nightfall

Rupert's cavalry routed and in flight

▨ *Royalists*
▢ *Parliament*

S. and C.   The Scotch and Cromwell having routed Rupert's horse, swing round behind the Royalist infantry. Fairfax (F) attacks them in flank. The Parliamentary infantry rally and attack them on the other side. The Royalists (R) are therefore caught and cut to pieces.

Goring (G) rides back too late to save the battle

Marston Moor

From 'Cromwell' by permission of Cassell & Co. Ltd

accounts, which, seeing the very poor part most of them played, are naturally full of lies. Nor does Cromwell himself escape from this frailty.

But the action has been elucidated by patient research, and we may fairly say that, since Mr Firth's study was published,[1] a number of quite certain points have been established. Notably, there is a contemporary plan of the action, which makes what is common to the various accounts reasonable, and with this the historian just quoted has dealt very fully.

Among the things which are certain are those which permit us to establish the personal effect of Cromwell upon the decision. It may fairly be said that he won the battle, and why this is true we shall see. On the other hand, among the things that are not quite so certain lies, unfortunately, the proportion between the part he played and the part played by his Scottish allies, whom he so disliked and his ultimate triumph over whom was one of his chief satisfactions.

The action was of the oddest kind. In the very short time it lasted (from about seven p.m. till nearly dark, on 2nd July 1644), in the haphazard way in which it began, in the lack of all calculation of time and place, it thoroughly conforms to the nondescript character of the Civil War as a whole.

The great plan achieved by Pym had been accomplished this six months past, the Scottish army—ill-mounted as to its cavalry, but of excellent quality in men and with plenty of experienced officers—had been across the Border for more than six months. Newcastle could not face the combination between them and the Parliamentary army; he was being besieged by the two in York. King Charles, who now as always had a good general view of the war, perceived that the fall of York would be fatal. It would mean the loss of the north, and the loss of the north might mean the loss of the war, for the north to the east of the Pennines was a recruiting field and a source of wealth such as the north to the west of the Pennines was not. Therefore the King urged his nephew Prince Rupert to relieve the town. Rupert did so, effected his junction with Newcastle, and the siege was raised.

The commanders of the Parliamentary and Scotch armies proposed to retire southward and stand between the newly joined Royalist forces and all that area controlled from London which was vital to them. They were still in superior numbers to Rupert and Newcastle combined. There was some discussion

[1] *English Historical Review*, New Series, vol. xiv.

between the latter as to whether the enemy should be attacked as he retired, and made to stand, or be allowed to go. Rupert's advice prevailed, and the whole Royalist command, save a fraction left for garrison in York, filed out westward to the open space of Marston Moor, the centre of which was five miles from the town. The allied Revolutionary armies, Scotch and English, were marching away southwards towards Tadcaster when the news came that the Royalists were close upon them and harrying the baggage and the rear. Cromwell himself was with the rearguard.

It was necessary, therefore, for the Parliamentary leaders to accept battle, lest they should be caught by the enemy in column of route. They retraced their steps, and formed in line of battle on the slopes which look northward towards Marston Moor, over the lane between Long Marston and Tockwith. Opposite them, seeing the battle was challenged, Rupert and Newcastle drew up their troops on the knoll to the north of that lane. The opposing forces were in number probably about 19,000 on the Royalist, 24,000 on the Parliamentary side. On both sides the usual formation was adopted, the infantry in the centre, the cavalry on either wing. On the Royalist side, facing southward and drawn up upon the Moor itself, Rupert at the head of the Royalist cavalry, and with him Byron at the head of the Irish troops, were upon the extreme right or west. On the Parliamentary side the cavalry of the corresponding wing, that is, the left of the Parliamentarians, was under the command of Cromwell. As the retirement of one force and the acceptation of battle by the other had taken a considerable time, it was afternoon before the lines were being ordered, and late afternoon before the formation was complete. The Parliamentary forces and their Scotch allies stood in fields of rye on a slope facing northward and overlooking the Royalists.

Cromwell there upon the left opposite Rupert had a superiority over his immediate opponents in face of him which should be noted: that superiority was due to the presence of a considerable Scottish contingent, nearly one-third of the total mounted force at that point. The actual number of sabres present, English and Scottish, under Cromwell's command as head of the mounted forces on this left wing of the Parliamentarians, over against Rupert, can of course only be a matter of conjecture, because we do not know the difference between the 'paper strength' and the actual strength. There were seventy troops, of which twenty-two were Scottish. With full complement this would mean 4,200 sabres, of whom just over 1,300 would be Scottish—very nearly one-third. But we are certain, of course, that the full complement was not present with either force; for it is always so in war, after long trials such as are involved in a siege and lengthy marches. The Scottish contingent has even been put as low as 600 sabres; it was probably something between that and a thousand. It was commanded by David Leslie. They were excellent soldiers, but ill-mounted on small and insufficient horses. Cromwell's men, five-sevenths of the total, were heavily armed, still carrying the cuirass, which was gradually eliminated in the course of the war—it was Cromwell's clinging to this form of defensive armour which had caused Rupert to give him the nickname of 'Ironsides,' after the old Anglo-Saxon Prince of history, and, as we know, the title spread gradually until it was attached to the Parliamentary cavalry in general; it has been changed by modern writers into a sort of laudatory epithet.

The cavalry thus under Cromwell's command upon the left Parliamentary wing was certainly greatly superior to the cavalry of the Royalist command. How much superior we do not know; the total superiority of the Parliamentary forces and the Scottish combined was to their opponents roughly as twenty-five to nineteen, possibly as twenty-five to eighteen. The numerical preponderance of the revolutionary cavalry over the constitutional Royalist cavalry was not so high; but here on the western side of the battle where Rupert stood on the right of the Royalist line and Cromwell on the left of his, facing Rupert, there was a considerable preponderance, because this wing had been specially strengthened.

Between the two forces lay a ditch. It was not so difficult an obstacle as at the other, eastern, end, but it did have this effect—it would interrupt the movement of cavalry and make either side hesitate to take the first step. For there could be no properly ordered charge over such an obstruction.

Although the two forces were thus drawn up for battle it seemed unlikely that the struggle would begin so late in the day, and more probable that it would be joined at the first dawn of the next morning. It was after four o'clock before the two lines were fully formed, and five before a desultory cannonade of no effect was over. There was still some daylight left, as the date was Tuesday, the 2nd of July, but still it was very late to begin an action. Neither side would risk the disadvantage of attempting an advance across the ditch.

The afternoon wore on till nearly seven without motion[1] along these two opposing columns of men, a mile in length. It would seem, though we are not absolutely certain of it, that the determination to attack came first from the Parliamentary side. It is possible that the initiative lay with Cromwell, but unlikely, for his position was still subordinate; the left, of which he formed a part, was under Manchester, and we may be certain that if his had been the deciding voice or act it would later, after the victory, have been plentifully advertised. At any rate, the whole Parliamentary line did attack at that very late hour. And what happened in the succeeding thirty minutes was roughly this:

I say 'roughly,' because the accounts are so confused and the result so extraordinary that it is impossible to present a clear plan. The Royalist left had a complete success against the Parliamentary right, their horse here under Goring scattered and pursued their opponents, turned on the flank of the abandoned infantry, and the mass of the Parliamentary body broke and fled. The Royalist infantry in this part of the field and the centre, the kernel of which was the very fine body of Newcastle's own tenants and followers, conspicuous in their rough white coats of undyed wool, pressed forward triumphantly. On the right and the right centre of the Parliamentary line the battle was lost for the revolution. Just about sunset there was a disorganized mass of men flying down the Tadcaster road with one part of Goring's cavalry sabring in pursuit, and the rest wheeling round to attack such units as had tried to stand. Among these certain isolated Scottish were conspicuous; but the Parliamentary foot went to pieces.

The battle seemed so obviously lost even while the sun was setting that the three commanders, the elder Fairfax, Manchester, and Lord Leven, fled (as the classical phrase goes) 'in all directions.' Each had determined that the defeat was final. The younger Fairfax—a strange episode in this mere turmoil—cut his way through to the back of the advancing Royalists, with what results we shall see.

Meanwhile, in that very brief last hour of the sinking sun and advancing night, what happened on the Parliamentary left and the Royalist right—that is on the west of the line—was strange, and at variance with the fortunes of the rest. Cromwell's cuirassed mounted men had crossed the ditch and attacked the first line of Rupert's command; the Irish cavalry under Byron.

[1] Save for a short desultory cannonade of no effect.

In the first shock against this first line Cromwell's men had the best of it, but Rupert, who like Newcastle had little expected an attack at such an hour, was immediately in the saddle and on the spot, and the counter-attack by his second line was successful. It threw Cromwell and his cuirassiers in spite of their superiority of numbers back towards the ditch. In the mêlée Oliver himself was slightly wounded, in the neck it would seem, and the pressure of Rupert's energy and his men, though in slightly inferior numbers, bid fair to do here upon the west of the battle (the Royalist right) what was being done upon the Royalist left. Had he succeeded Marston Moor would have been a complete decision for the King. It would have been the beginning of the end of the war—in his favour.

The account of such a hurly-burly, even were it possible to get one from an unbiased witness suffering neither from vanity nor excitement, would be confused enough—we can only see it as the success of the Royalist counter-charge, with the leader of the Parliamentary cavalry, Cromwell himself, out of action for the moment.

Now note carefully what certainly followed. In this successful counter-attack of Rupert's and the pushing back by force of Cromwell's cuirassiers, a gap had opened between the Royalist horse and the Royalist foot to the east (or left) of them. It was not the wounded and occupied Cromwell who saw the opportunity, it was David Leslie. His some hundred sabres were directed at once from the reserve and rear of Cromwell's body where they had stood, right into this gap, and appeared upon the flank of Rupert's so far victorious cavalry. And it was this which decided the issue.

The Scottish mounts were bad, as I have said, and the Scottish force was acting alone, for their English allies were already very nearly in rout; but they had the advantage of coming suddenly upon a flank, and the fierceness of their onslaught did the trick. The pressure upon Cromwell's immediate command was relieved, Rupert's began to lose order, the English Parliamentary horse rallied and pressed forward, the Royalist horse—now attacked in front as well as in flank—began to break. With the dusk still gathering they broke altogether and were driven in disordered masses towards Wilstrop Wood, some six furlongs to the north, half a mile behind their original line.

Reading of how that gap was pierced by Leslie, of how through such advantage the whole line was turned and a decision attained, the mind reverts, not without sadness, to the Battle of the Marne.

It is comparing small things with great, but the mournful parallel is there. During the Marne also, in a front of not one mile but over a hundred, a gap opened; and on the Marne also it opened between the extreme right wing of the enemy and the mass of his troops. Through that gap also the line might have been turned, and the security of our civilization saved. But there were none present to take advantage: those who should have done at that place what Leslie did were from ten to twenty miles away.

There remained with the Scottish and with Leslie the feeling that they had done the whole thing—that naturally became their tradition. Cromwell himself must have been detained, if only to have his wound dressed, but he was now once again at the head of the pursuit and ordering his men before the light should fail altogether.

Then it was, with Rupert's men in flight, with the Parliamentary infantry which had stood just beyond the Scottish horse to the east still in good formation and standing up well to the Royalist infantry in front of them—though with all the rest of the Parliamentary line gone to pieces—that Cromwell executed his manœuvre.

It was, so far as we know, the first time he used it; like all great commanders who have discovered a method of their own, he was to repeat it. He reined up his men, left a detachment to follow the flying and defeated Royalist horse, and with those whom he had checked and kept with him he wheeled round to the right. Part of his men were thus on the flank of the Royalist foot in their immediate neighbourhood, and the rest were extended eastwards behind the whole Royalist line as they rapidly advanced in the gathering darkness.

The successful Royalist centre, Newcastle's men, hitherto pressing forward victoriously against the revolutionary foot in front of them, hitherto cheered by seeing the complete breakdown of the Revolutionary horse to the east, with Goring thundering in pursuit of them, suddenly found themselves attacked from the rear. Their comrades of the foot upon the right flank, to the west of them, were already in confusion through the repeated Parliamentary charge of Cromwell's men —and still the rapidly advancing line of his horse drew eastward, until all the Royalist centre, but a few minutes ago certain of victory, found themselves surrounded. Those whom they were driving back in defeat would rally; the rear ranks of the Royalist centre had to turn to receive the shock of this new unexpected assault from the north—the whole shape of the battle had changed. Cromwell riding eastward with his bandaged neck found in the gloaming the younger Fairfax, his face open with a wound—the man who had cut his way through from the rout of the rest of the Parliamentary cavalry. Such horse as he had with him joined with Cromwell's own forces. The enclosed and now doomed—so recently confident and victorious—Royalist foot, centre and left, were trapped and at the mercy of the foot and horse from the south, from the east, from the north and the outflanking movement now begun from the west as well.

Then was seen one of the few sublime passages of these wars, the death and sacrifice of Newcastle's men. The white coats would not surrender to the rebels nor ask for quarter: their fate certain, they preferred to meet it. At the end of the slaughter forty were left alive to find their way off through the darkness: no more.

Men hardly knew what had happened. It was full dark under the showery clouds: there was no moon: the battle—and for that matter though men could not tell it yet, the war also—was won.

How many were killed we cannot certainly tell: the account on the Parliamentary side that they lost only 300 is ridiculous and need not be entertained. The Royalists can hardly have lost less than 4,000; 1,500 officers and men were prisoners; 10,000 stands of arms were piled, 130 barrels of powder and all the twenty-five guns of the King; and of the colours sheaves upon sheaves.

It was not till the next day, the Wednesday, that the fugitive Parliamentary Generals returned; and by that time the dead had been stripped and plundered by the Puritan soldiery. On the day after, the 4th of July, Cromwell set off on a pursuit of Rupert and his remaining 6,000 men, whom he had kept sufficiently in hand to save them from their pursuers: the pursuit therefore failed. The little garrison in York stood out for another eleven days under Glenham; it got good terms, capitulating with the right to march out with the whole garrison intact for the King. Manchester's soldiers who were to escort the retirement of these men plundered them. It is to be remembered that by the time they had reached Cromwell to the west, in his futile pursuit of Rupert, they were better treated.

Oliver Cromwell through this day of Marston Moor became fully famous. His name was now first among the soldiers. Had he been but one in a general victory, as he might well have been seeing the superiority of the forces upon the Revolutionary side, he would not have attained so rapidly and so immediately the reputation due to his high talent. Fortune had favoured him greatly, in that he was thus conspicuous in succeeding where the rest had failed and marked him out in contrast, the hero of the day. Fortune had favoured him also most conspicuously in lending him the Scotch (whom he despised and disliked) just at the moment when his fate lay in the balance. But it would be a great error to belittle Cromwell by too much emphasis upon these advantages. But for him—his eye, his will, his clarity of perception, his flash of decision—the dreadful harvest of that day would never have been reaped.

Remember once again the famous epigram of Foch, which cannot be too often repeated: 'It was not a Carthaginian Army which crossed the Alps, it was Hannibal.' So one may say of Marston Moor. 'It was not the well-disciplined English horse, saved by the Scottish charge, which won the battle, nor was it propitious fortune: it was Oliver Cromwell.'

THE DEATH OF DANTON

IN the night the armed police came round to the Passage du Commerce; one part of the patrol grounded their muskets and halted at the exits of the street, the other entered the house.

Desmoulins heard the butts falling together on the flagstones, and the little clink of metal which announces soldiery; he turned to his wife, and said: 'They have come to arrest me.' And she held to him till she fainted and was carried away. Danton, in his study alone, met the arrest without words. There is hardly a step in the tragedy that follows which is not marked by his comment, always just, sometimes violent; but the actual falling of the blow led to no word. Words were weapons with him, and he was not one to strike before he had put up his guard.

They were taken to the Luxembourg, very close by, a little up the hill. We have the story of how Danton came with his ample, firm presence into the hall of the prison, and met, almost the first of his fellow-prisoners, Thomas Paine. The author of *The Rights of Man* stepped up to him, doubtless to address him in bad French.[1] Danton forestalled him in the English of which he was a fair master.

'Mr Paine,' he said, 'you have had the happiness of pleading in your country a cause which I shall no longer plead in mine.' He remembered Paine's sane and moderate view on the occasion of the king's trial, and he envied one whose private freedom had remained untrammelled with the bonds of office; who had never been forced to a 2nd of June, nor had to keep to an intimate conversation his fears for the Girondins. Then he added that if they sent him to the scaffold he would go gaily. And he did. There was the Frenchman contrasted with his English friend.

Beaulieu, who heard him, tells us that he also turned to the prisoners about him and said: 'Gentlemen, I had hoped to have you out of this, and here I am myself; I can see no issue.'

So the prisoners came in, anxiously watched by reactionaries, to whom, as to many of our modern scribblers, one leader of the

[1] Paine's ignorance of French was such that his speech on Louis's exile was translated for him.

Revolution is as good as another—Lacroix, Westermann (the strong soldier with his huge frame overtopping even Danton's), and Desmoulins. As they passed to their separate cells, for it was determined to prevent their communication, a little spirit of the old evil [1] used the powerful venom of aristocracy, the unanswerable repartee of rank, and looking Lacroix up and down, said: 'I could make a fine coachman of that fellow.' He and his like would have ruined France for the sake of turning those words into action.

Till the dawn of the 11th Germinal broke, they were kept in their separate rooms. But the place was not built for a prison. Lacroix and Danton in neighbouring rooms could talk by raising their voices, and we have of their conversation this fragment. Lacroix said: 'Had I ever dreamt of this I could have forestalled it.' And Danton's reply, with just that point of fatalism which had forbidden him to be ambitious, answered: 'I knew it'; he had known it all that night.

There was a force stronger than love—private and public fear. It is a folly to ridicule, or even to misunderstand that fear. The possessions, the families of many, the newly-acquired dignity of all, above everything, the new nation had been jeopardized how many times by a popular idol turned untrue. The songs of 1790 were all for Louis, many praised Bailly; what a place once had Lafayette! Who had a word to say against Dumouriez eighteen months before? The victories had just begun—barely enough to make men hesitate about the Terror. The 'Vieux Cordelier' had led, not followed opinion, as it was just that the great centre of energy should lead and not follow the time. And, men would say, how do we know why he has been arrested, or at whose voice? How can we tell where the sure compass of right, our Robespierre, stands in the matter? and so forth. Nothing then was done; but Paris very nearly moved.

There were thus two gathering forces; one vague and large, one small but ordered, and on the result of their shock hung the life of Danton—may one say (knowing the future) the life of the Republic?

Now the struggle with Europe had taught the Committee a principal lesson. Perhaps one should add that the exuberant fighting power of the nation and of the age had forced the Committee to a certain method, apparent in the armies, in the measures, in the speeches: it was the method of detecting at

[1] La Roche du Maine.

once the weakest spot in the opposing line, and of abandoning everything for the purpose of concentrating all its strength and charging home. So their descendants to-day in their new army practise the marvellous massing of artillery which you may watch at autumn in the manœuvres.

What was the opposing line? A vague ill-ordered crowd— Paris; the undisciplined Convention, lacking leaders, ignorant of party rule. Where was its weakness? In the want of initiative, in the fact that, till someone spoke, no one could be sure of the strength of the corporate feeling. Also, on account of the public doubt, during that time men were grains of dust; but the dust was like powder, and speech was always the spark which permitted the affinities of that powder to meet in fierce unity and power. A sudden blow had to be struck and the fire stamped out before it had gathered power; this is how the check was given.

In the morning of the 12th Germinal the Convention met, and each man looked at his neighbour, and then, as though afraid, let his eyes wander to see if others thought as he did. At last one man dared to speak. It was Legendre the butcher; [1] he vacillated later before a mixture of deceit in others and of doubt in himself, but it should be remembered to his honour that he nearly saved the Revolution by an honest word. 'Let Danton be heard at the bar of the Convention,' was his frank demand; common-sense enough, but it fatally opened his guard, and gave an opportunity to the thrusts most dangerous in the year II—an accusation of desiring privilege, and an accusation of weakening that government which was visibly saving the state on the frontiers.

Tallien was President that day, and he gave the reply to Robespierre. Now Robespierre was no good fencer. The supreme feint, the final disarming of opinion, was left to an abler man. He had gone home from the Committee to Duplay's house in the early morning; a monomaniac hardly needing sleep, he reappeared at the early meeting of the Convention. But, poor debater as he was, he could take advantage of so easy

[1] Levasseur tells us that Delmas spoke first, and that his remarks took the form of a definite motion for the appearance of the Committees to account for their action. Legendre is mentioned here because he alone is agreed upon by all the eye-witnesses (and by the *Moniteur*) as being the principal defender of Danton. We must not underestimate his courage; it was he who with a very small force shut the club of the Jacobins on the night of the 9th Thermidor, and so turned the flank of the Robespierrian faction.

an opportunity. In a speech which was twice applauded, he asserted that Legendre had demanded a privilege. He struck the note which above all others dominated those minds. 'Are we here to defend principles or men? Give the right of speech to Danton, and you give rein to an extraordinary talent, you confuse the issue with a hundred memories, you permit the bias of friendship. Let the man defend himself by proofs and witnesses, not by eloquence and sentiment.' Yet he did not add—perhaps he hardly knew—that the memories and friendship would but have balanced a direct enmity, and that witnesses and proofs would be denied. Again he used that argument of government—had not they saved France? were they not the head of the police? did not they know in the past what they were doing? He assured them that a little waiting would produce conviction in them also. It did not, but time was gained; already half the Convention doubted.

Legendre, bewildered, faltered a reply; he admitted error, and begged Robespierre not to misunderstand. He could have answered for Danton as for himself, but the tribunal was of course to be trusted. It was almost an apology.

On that changing, doubtful opinion came with the force of a steel mould the hard, high voice of St Just.

St Just spoke rarely. There has been mention in an earlier part of this book of the speech against the Girondins. There will be mention again of a vigorous and a nearly successful attempt to save Robespierre. That he should have been given the task of defending the Committee's action that day is a singular proof of the grip which they had of the circumstances. Barrère could never have convinced an unsympathetic public opinion. Robespierre could meet a rising enthusiasm with nothing but dry and accurate phrases. But St Just had the flame of his youth and of his energy, and his soul lived in his mouth.

The report, even as we read it, has eloquence. Coming from him then, with his extreme beauty, his upright and determined bearing, it turned the scale. The note of the argument was as ably chosen as could be; moreover it represented without question the attitude of his own mind: it was this. 'The last of the factions has to be destroyed; only one obstacle stands between you and the appreciation of the Republic.[1] Time and

---

[1] 'Quand les restes de la faction . . . ne seront plus . . . vous n'aurez plus d'exemples à donner . . . il ne restera que le peuple et vous, et le gouvernement dont vous êtes le centre inviolable.'

again we have acted suddenly, but time and again we have acted well and on sufficient reasons — so it is now. If you save Danton you save a personality—something you have known and admired; you pay respect to individual talent, but you ruin the attempt in which you have so nearly succeeded. For the sake of a man you will sacrifice all the new liberty which you are giving to the whole world.' There follows a passionate apostrophe in which he speaks to Danton as though he stood before him, as striking as the parallel passage in the fourth Catiline Oration.[1] Had Danton been present he would have been a man against a boy; a loud and strong voice, not violent in utterance, but powerful in phrase and in delivery, a character impressing itself by sheer force of self upon vacillating opinion. Had Danton spoken in reply, his hearers would have said with that moral conviction which is stronger than proof: 'This man is the chief lover of France.'

But such is rhetoric, its falsity and its success—the gaps of silence grew to a convincing power. The accusations met with no reply; they remained the echo of a living voice; the answers to them could be framed only in the silent minds of the audience. The living voice won.

And there was, as we have said, intense conviction to aid St Just. He was a man who would forget and would exaggerate with all the faults of passion, but he believed the facts he gave. Not so Robespierre. Robespierre had furnished the notes of St Just's report,[2] and Robespierre must have known that he had twisted all to one end. Robespierre was a man who was virtuous and true only to his ideal, not to his fellow-men. Robespierre had not deceived himself as he wrote, but he had deceived St Just, and therefore the young 'Archangel of Death' spoke with the added strength of faith, than which nothing leaps more readily from the lips to the ears. Can we doubt it? There is a phrase which convinces. When he ends by telling them what it is they save by sacrificing one idol, when he describes the Republic, he uses the phrase common to all apostolates, the superb 'les mots que nous avons dits ne seront jamais perdus sur la terre' —the things which they had said would never be lost on earth.

[1] 'Mauvais citoyen, tu as conspiré; faux ami, tu disais, il y a deux jours, du mal de Desmoulins que tu as perdu; méchant homme, tu as comparé l'opinion publique à une femme de mauvaise vie, tu as dit que l'honneur était ridicule . . . si Fabre est innocent, si Orléans, si Dumouriez furent innocents tu l'es sans doute. J'en ai trop dit—tu répondras à la justice.'
[2] Robespierre's notes for St Just's report were published by M. France in 1841 among the *Papiers trouvés chez Robespierre*.

It ended. No one voted; the demand of the Committee passed without a murmur. The Convention was never again its own mistress; it had silenced and condemned itself.[1]

Meanwhile at the Luxembourg the magistrate Dénizot was making the preparations for the trial. Each prisoner was asked the formal question of his guilt, and each replied in a single negative, but Danton added that he would die a Republican, and to the question of their defence replied that he would plead his own cause. Then, at half-past eleven, they were transferred to the Conciergerie.

From that moment his position becomes the attitude of the man fighting, as we have known it in the crisis of August 1792 and of the calling up of the armies. Ready as he had always been to see the real rather than the imaginary conditions, he recognized death with one chance only of escape. He knew far better than did poor Desmoulins the power of a State's machinery; he felt its grasp and doubted of any issue. The people, for Desmoulins, were the delegators of power; for Danton the people were those who should, but who did not rule. To live again and enter the arena and save the life of the Republic the people must hear his voice, or else the fact of government would be more strong than all the rights and written justice in the world.

He was like a man whose enemy stands before him, and who sees at his own side, passive and bewildered, a strong but foolish ally. His ally was the people, his enemy was Death.

Therefore we have of his words and actions for the next four days two kinds; those addressed to death and those to his ally. Where he desired to touch the spirit of the crowd—in what was for their ears—we have the just, practical, and eloquent man apologizing for over-vehemence, saying what should strike hardest home—an orator, but an orator who certainly uses legitimate weapons.

But there is another side. In much that he said in prison, in all that he said on his way to the scaffold, he is simply speaking to Death and defying him. The inmost thing in a man, the stock of the race, appears without restraint; he becomes the

---

[1] 'La Convention Nationale après avoir entendu les rapports des Comités de Sureté générale et du Salut Public, décrète d'accusation Camille Desmoulins, Hérault, Danton, Phillippeaux Lacroix . . . en conséquence elle declare leur mise en jugement.' These were the last words of St Just's speech, and formed his substantive motion.

'Ce décret est adopté à l'unanimité et au milieu des plus vifs applaudissements.'—*Moniteur*, 2nd April 1794 (13th Germinal, year II).

Gaul. That most un-northern habit of defiance, especially of defiance to the inevitable and to the strongest, the custom of his race and their salvation, grows on his lips.

He insults Death, he jests; his language, never chaste or self-conscious, takes on the laughter of the Rabelaisian, and (true Rabelaisian again) he wraps up in half a dozen words the whole of a situation.

Thus we see him leaning against the window of his prison and calling to Westermann in the next cell, 'Oh! if I could leave my legs to Couthon [1] and my virility to Robespierre, things might still go on.' And again when Lacroix said, 'I will cut my own hair at the neck, so that Sanson the executioner shall not meddle with it,' Danton replied: 'Yet will Sanson intermeddle with the vertebrae of your neck.' So he meets death with a broad torrent of words; and that a civilization accustomed rather to reticence should know what this meant in him, my readers must note his powerful asides to Desmoulins and to Hérault coinciding with the fearful pun in which he tried to raise the drooping courage of D'Eglantine.

Also in his prison this direct growth of the soil of France 'talked often of the fields and of rivers.' Shakespeare should have given us the death scenes of so much energy, defiance, coarseness, affection, and great courage.

In the Conciergerie they spent the rest of the day waiting for the trial, and this time Danton was next to Westermann, to whom and to Desmoulins he said: 'We must say nothing save before the Committees or at the trial.' It was his plan to move the people by a public defence, but his enemies in power had formed a counter-plan, and, as we shall see, forestalled him.

Desmoulins, 'the flower that grew on Danton,' was still bewildered. So he remained to the end; at the foot of the scaffold he could not understand. 'If I could only have written a No. VII I would have turned the tables.' [2] 'It is a duel of Commodus; they have the lance and I have not even a reed.' To that man, his equal in years, [3] but a boy compared with him in

---

[1] Couthon was a cripple. Once (later) in the Convention it was called out to him 'Triumvir,' and he glanced at his legs and said: 'How could I be a triumvir?' The logical connection between good legs and triumvirates was more apparent to himself than to those whom he caused to be guillotined.

[2] We have the fragments of this 'No. VII,' which was not published. See M. Claretie's C. Desmoulins, p. 274 of Mrs Cashel Hoey's translation.

[3] Danton would have been thirty-five in October. Desmoulins had been thirty-four in March—not thirty-three, as he said at the trial. I give this on the authority of M. Claretie, who in his book quotes the birth-certificate, which he himself had seen (2nd March 1760).

spirit, Danton had always shown, and now continued to show, a
peculiar affection.   He treated him like a younger brother, and
never made him suffer those violent truths with which all France
and most of his friends were familiar in his mouth.   So now,
and in the trial, and on the way to the scaffold, his one attempt
was to calm the bitter violence and outburst of Camille.

There are two phrases of Danton's which have been noted on
this first day passed at the Conciergerie, and which cannot be
omitted, though in form they have not his diction, yet in spirit
they might be his; they are recollections presumably of something of greater length called to Westermann.

The first: 'On such a day [1] I demanded the institution of the
Revolutionary tribunal.   I ask pardon of God and of man.'

The second: 'I am leaving everything at sixes and sevens; one
had better be a poor fisherman than meddle with the art of
governing men.'   There you have the real Danton—a reminiscence of some strong and passionate utterance put into this un-
dantonesque and proverbial form.   A real sentiment of his—
all of him; careless of life, intense upon the interests of life,
above all upon the future of the Revolution and of France,
knowing the helpless inferiority of the men he left behind.   And
in the close of the phrase it is also he; it is the spirit of great
weariness which had twice touched him, as sleep an athlete
after a day of games.   It was soon to take the form of a noble
sentence: 'Nous avons assez servi—allons dormir.'

On the 13th (2nd April 1794), about ten in the morning, they
were led before the tribunal.

The trial began.

It must not be imagined that the Dantonists alone came
before the tribunal to answer for their particular policy.   There
had originated under Robespierre (and later when he alone was
the master it was to be terribly abused) the practice of confusing
the issues.   Three groups at least were tried together, and the
Moderates sat between two thieves—for D'Eglantine on a charge
of embezzlement alone, Guzman, the Freys as common thieves
and spies to the Republic, were associated on the same bench.
Fourteen in all, they sat in the following order: Chabot, Bazire,
Fabre, Lacroix, Danton, Delaunay, Hérault, Desmoulins, Guzman, Diederichsen, Phillippeaux, D'Espagnac, and the two

---

[1] 10th March 1793.   Exception has been taken to the whole sentiment
by Dr Robinet, but great, or rather unique, as is his authority, I cannot
believe that an appeal—especially an exclamatory appeal of this nature
—was foreign to his impetuous and merciful temper.

Freys. D'Eglantine occupied 'the arm-chair,' and it will be seen that the *five*—the Moderates—were carefully scattered.

The policy was a deliberate one; it was undertaken with the object of prejudicing public opinion against the accused. Nor was it permitted to each group to be separate in accusation and in its method of defence. They were carefully linked to each other by men accused of two out of the three crimes.

Herman was president of the tribunal, and sat facing the prisoners; on either side of him were Masson-Denizot, Foucault, and Bravé, the assistant judges. They say that Voullaud and Vadier, of the lower committee, appeared behind the bench to watch the enemies whom they had caught in the net. Seven jurors were in the box to the judges' left, by name Renaudin (whom Desmoulins challenged in vain), Desboisseaux, Trinchard, Dix-Aout, Lumière, Ganney, Souberbielle,[1] and to these we must add Topino-Lebrun, whose notes form by far the most vivid fragment by which we may reconstruct the scene. The jury of course was packed.[2] It was part of the theory of the Revolutionary Government that no chance element should mar its absolute dictatorship. It was practically a court of judges, absolute, and without division of powers.

At a table between the President and the prisoners sat Fouquier-Tinville, the public prosecutor; and finally, on the judges' right was the open part of the court and the door to the witnesses' room.

Here was a new trial with a great and definite chance of acquittal, a scene the like of which had not been seen for a year, nor would be seen again in that room. The men on the prisoners' bench had been the masters, one of them the creator, of the court which tried them; they were evidently greater and more powerful than their judges, and had behind them an immense though informal weight of popularity. They were public men of the first rank; their judges and the public prosecutor were known to be merely the creatures of a small committee. More than this, it was common talk that the Convention might yet change its mind, and even among the jury it was certain that discussion would arise.

By the evidence of a curious relic we know that the Committee actually feared a decree or a coup-de-main which would have destroyed their power. This note remains in the archives, a

[1] Wallon, *Tribunal Révolutionnaire*, vol. iii, p. 156.
[2] It is known that Fleuriot and Fouquier were alone when the jury were 'chosen by lot.' This appeared at the trial of Fouquier.

memorandum of a decision arrived at in the Committee on the early morning of the 13th or late in the night of the 12th.

'*Henriot to be written to, to tell him to issue an order that the President and the Public Prosecutor of the Revolutionary Tribunal are not to be arrested.*'

Then in another hand:

'*Get four members to sign this.*'

Finally, the memorandum is endorsed in yet another hand: '*13th Germinal.—A policeman took this the same day.*' [1]

It will thus be seen that the Committee was by no means sure of its ground. It had indeed procured through St Just the decree preventing Danton from pleading at the bar of the Convention and permitting his trial, but it would require the most careful manœuvring upon their part to carry through such an affair. As we shall see, they just—and only just—succeeded.

The whole of the first day (the 13th Germinal, 2nd of April 1794) was passed in the formal questions and in the reading of accusations. Camille, on being asked his age and dwelling, made the blasphemous and striking answer which satisfied the dramatic sense, but was not a true reply to the main question.

Danton gave the reply so often quoted: 'I am Danton, not unknown among the revolutionaries. I shall be living nowhere soon, but you will find my name in Walhalla.' The other answers, save that of Hérault, attempted no phrases.

Yet Guzman would have made more point of his assertion if he had chosen that moment to say: 'I am Guzman, a grandee of Spain, who came to France to taste liberty, but was arrested for theft'; while the two Freys missed an historic occasion in not replying: 'We are Julius and Emanuel Frey, sometime nobles of the Empire under the title of Von Schönfeld, now plain Jews employed by the Emperor as spies.'

The public prosecutor read the indictment. First at great length Amar's report on the India Company. The details of the accusations which cost Fabre his life need not be entered into here. Suffice it to say that it was an indictment for corruption, for having suppressed or altered for money the decree of the Convention in the autumn before, and being accomplice in the extra gains which this had made possible—one of those wretched businesses with which Panama and South Africa have deluged modern France and England. It is an example of the methods of the tribunal that Fouquier managed to drag in Desmoulins's

[1] Wallon, *Tribunal Révolutionnaire*, vol. iii, p. 155.

name because he had once said: 'People complain of not being able to make money now, yet I make it easily enough.'

The second group, the Freys, Guzman, the unfrocked priest D'Espagnac, and Diederichsen the Dane, were accused of being foreigners working against the success of the French armies, and at the same time lining their pockets. In the case of three of them the accusation was probably true. It was the more readily believed from the foreign origins of the accused, for France was full of spies, while the name of a certain contumacious Baron de Bartz made this list sound the more probable.

Finally, the small group at which they were really aiming (whose members they had already mixed up with the thieves) was indicated on nothing more particular than the report of St Just—virtually, that is, on Robespierre's notes. Danton had served the King, had drawn the people into the place where they were massacred in July 1791, did not do his duty on the 10th of August, and so forth—a vapid useless summary of impossible things in which no one but perhaps St Just and a group of fanatics believed. With that the day ended, and they were taken back to prison.

On the next day, the 14th Germinal (3rd of April 1794) Westermann, who, though already arrested, had only been voted upon in Parliament the day before, appeared on the prisoners' bench, and sat at the end after Emanuel Frey. He was the last and not the least noble of the Dantonists, with his great stature, his clumsy intellect, and his loyal Teutonic blood.

'Who are you?' they said. 'I am Westermann. Show me to the people. I was a soldier at sixteen, and have been a councillor of Strasbourg. I have seven wounds in front, and I was never stabbed in the back till now.'

This was the man who had led the 10th of August, and who had dared, in his bluff nature, to parley with the Swiss who spoke his language.

It was after some little time passed in the interrogation of the prisoners who had been arrested for fraud, especially of D'Espagnac, that the judge turned to Danton.

In the debate and cross-questioning that followed we must depend mainly upon the notes of Lebrun,[1] for they are more living, although they are more disconnected, than the official report. We discover in them the passionate series of outbursts, but a series which one must believe to have had a definite

---

[1] The speeches which I have written here are reconstructed from these notes.

purpose. There was neither hope of convincing the tribunal nor of presenting a legal argument with effect. What Danton was trying to do in this court, which was not occupied with a trial, but merely in a process of condemnation, was to use it as a rostrum from which he could address the people, the general public, upon whose insurrection he depended. He perhaps depended also on the jury, for, carefully chosen as they were, they yet might be moved by a man who had never failed to convince by his extraordinary power of language. He carries himself exactly as though he were technically what he is in fact—a prisoner before an informal group of executioners, who appeals for justice to the crowd.

He pointed at Cambon, who had sat by him on the Committee, and said: 'Come now, Cambon, do you think we are conspirators? Look, he is laughing; he believes no such thing.' Then he turned, laughing himself, to the jury and said: 'Write down in your notes that he laughed.'

Again, he uses phrases like these: 'We are here for a form, but if we are to have full liberty to speak, and if the French people is what it should be, it will be my business later to ask their pardon for my accusers.' To which Camille answered, 'Oh, we shall be allowed to speak, and that is all we want,' and the group of Indulgents laughed heartily.

It was just after this that he began that great harangue in answer to the questions of the judge, an effort whose tone reaches to this day. It is, perhaps, the most striking example of a personal appeal that can be discovered. The opportunities for such are rare, for in the vast majority of historical cases where a man has pleaded for his life, it has either been before a well-organized court, or before a small number of determined enemies, or by the lips of one who was paid for his work and who ignored the art of political oratory. The unique conditions of the French Revolution made such a scene possible, perhaps for the only time in history.

The day, early as was the season, was warm, the windows of the court, that looked upon the Seine, were open, and through the wide doors pressed the head of a great crowd. This crowd stretched out along the corridor, along the quays, across the Pont Neuf, and even to the other side of the river. Every sentence that told was repeated from mouth to mouth, and the murmurs of the crowd proved how closely the great tribune was followed. In the attitude which had commanded the attention of his opponents when he presented the first deputation from

Paris three years before, and that had made him so striking a figure during the stormy months of 1793, he launched the phrases that were destined for Paris and not for his judges. His loud voice (the thing appears incredible, but it is true) vibrating through the hall and lifted to the tones that had made him the orator of the open spaces, rang out and was heard beyond the river.

'You say that I have been paid, but I tell you that men made as I am cannot be paid. And I put against your accusation—of which you cannot furnish a proof nor the hint of a proof, nor the shadow nor the beginning of a witness—the whole of my revolutionary career. It was I who from the Jacobins kept Mirabeau at Paris. I have served long enough, and my life is a burden to me, but I will defend myself by telling you what I have done. It was I who made the pikes rise suddenly on the 20th of June and prevented the King's voyage to St Cloud. The day after the massacre of the Champ de Mars a warrant was out for my arrest. Men were sent to kill me at Arcis, but my people came and defended me. I had to fly to London, and I came back, as you all know, the moment Garran was elected. Do you not remember me at the Jacobins, and how I asked for the Republic? It was I who knew that the court was eager for war. It was I, among others, who denounced the policy of the war.'

Here a sentence was heard: 'What did you do against the Brissotins?'

Now Danton had, as we know, done all in his power to save the men who hated him, but whom he admired. It was no time for him to defend himself by an explanation of this in the ears of the people who had never understood, as he had, the height of the men who followed Vergniaud; but he said what was quite true: 'I told them that they were going to the scaffold. When I was a minister I said it to Brissot before the whole cabinet.'

He might have added that he had said to Guadet in the November woods on the night before he left for the army: 'You are headstrong, and it will be your doom.'

Then he went back again to the list of his services. 'It was I who prepared the 10th of August. You say I went to Arcis. I admit it, and I am proud of it. I went there to pass three days, to say good-bye to my mother, and to arrange my affairs, because I was shortly to be in peril. I hardly slept that night. It was I that had Mandat killed, because he had given the order to fire on the people. . . . You are reproaching me with the friendship of Fabre d'Eglantine. He is still my friend, and I still say that he is a good citizen as he sits here with me. You have told me that my defence has been too violent, you have recalled to me the revolutionary names, and you have told me that Marat when he appeared before the tribunal might have served as my model. Well, with regard to those names who were once my friends, I will tell you this: Marat had a character on fire and unstable; Robespierre I have known as a man, above all, tenacious; but I—I have served in my own fashion, and I would embrace my worst enemy for the sake of the country, and I will give her my body if she needs the sacrifice.'

This short and violent speech, which I have attempted to reproduce from the short, disjointed, ill-spelt notes of Lebrun, hit the mark. The crowd, the unstable crowd, which he contemned as he passed to the guillotine, moved like water under a strong wind; and his second object also was reached, for the tribunal grew afraid. These phrases would soon be repeated in the Convention, and no means had been taken to silence that terrible voice. The President of the court said to him that it was the part of an accused man to defend himself with proofs and not with rhetoric. He parried that also with remarkable skill, saying in a much quieter tone which all his friends (they were now growing in number) immediately noted: 'That a man should be violent is wrong in him I know, unless it is for the public good, and such a violence has often been mine. If I exceeded now, it was because I found myself accused with such intolerable injustice.' He raised his voice somewhat again with the words, 'But as for you, St Just, you will have to answer to posterity,' and then was silent.

When the unhappy man who had taken upon his shoulders the vile duty of the political work that day, when Herman was himself upon his trial, he said, 'Remember that this affair was out of the ordinary, and was a political trial,' when a voice rose from the court, 'There are no political trials under a Republic.' He would have done well, obscure as he is before history, to have saved his own soul by refusing a task which he knew to involve injustice from beginning to end.

It was at the close of that day that three short notes passed between Herman and the public prosecutor, Fouquier-Tinville. Herman wrote: 'In half an hour I shall stop Danton's defence. You must spin out some of the rest in detail.' Tinville answered:

'I have something more to say to Danton about Belgium'; and Herman replied: 'Do not bring it in with regard to any of the others.' This little proof of villainy, which has survived by so curious an accident (it is in the Archives to-day),[1] closed the proceedings of that hearing.

The next day, the 15th of Germinal (4th April), Danton himself said little. It was given over mainly to the examination of Desmoulins; and as with Danton it had been rumours or opinions, so with Desmoulins only the vague sense of things he had written were brought in to serve as evidence in this tragic farce.

Fouquier, the distant cousin of Camille, to whom he owed the post in which he was earning his bread by crime,[2] tried to put something of complaint against the nation and of hatred to the Republic into his reading of the Old Cordelier. Even in his thin unpleasant voice there was only heard the noble phrase of Tacitus, and—it is a singular example of what the tribunal had become—they dared not continue the quotation because every word roused the people in the court. But Camille, so great with the pen, had nothing of the majesty or the strength of Danton. His defence was a weak, disconnected excuse, and, like all men who are insufficient to themselves, he was inconsistent.

Hérault made on that same day a far finer reply. Noble by birth, holding by his traditions and memories to that society which he himself had helped to destroy, and of which Talleyrand has said: 'Those who have not known it have not lived'; accustomed from his very first youth to prominence in his profession and to the favour of the court, he remained to the last full of contempt for so much squalor, and he veiled his eyes with pride.

'I understand nothing of this topsy-turvydom. I was a diplomat, and I made the neutrality of Switzerland, so saving 60,000 men to the Republic. As for the priest you talk about, who was guillotined in my absence at Troyes, I knew him well. He was a Canon, if I remember, and by no means a reactionary. You are probably joking about it. It is true he had not taken

---

[1] Wallon, *Tribunal Révolutionnaire*, vol. iii, p. 169, quotes *Archives*, W. 342, *Dossier* 641, 1st Part, No. 34.

[2] Fouquier had written a letter to his distant relative Desmoulins, begging for some employment, on 20th August 1792, just after the success of Danton's party, in which Desmoulins had of course shared. It is by no means dignified and almost servile. See Claretie, *Desmoulins*, English edition, p. 318.

the oath, but he was a good man; he helped me, and I am not ashamed of my friendship. I will tell you something more. On the 14th of July two men were killed, one on either side of me.' He might have added, 'I was the second man to scale the Towers.'

It was not until the day's proceedings had been drawn out for a considerable time that a sentence was spoken, the full import of which was not understood at the time, but which was, as a fact, the first step in those four months of irresponsibility and crime which are associated with the name of Robespierre, and which hang like a weight around the neck of the French nation. Lacroix had just said with a touch of legal phraseology, 'I must insist that the witnesses whom I have demanded should be subpoenaed, and if there is any difficulty about this, I formally demand that the Convention shall be consulted in the matter'; when the public prosecutor answered: 'It is high time that this part of the trial, which has become a mere struggle, and which is a public scandal, should cease. I am about to write to the Convention to hear what it has to say, and its advice shall be exactly followed.'

Both the public prosecutor and the judge signed the letter. The first draft which Fouquier had drawn up was thought too strong, and it appears that Herman revised it.[1] 'Citoyens Représentants,—There has been a storm in the hall since this day's proceedings began. The accused are calling for witnesses who are among your deputies. . . . They are appealing to the people, saying that they will be refused. In spite of the firmness of the president and of all the tribunal, they continue to protest that they will not be silent until their witnesses are heard, unless by your passing a special decree.' [This was false, and was the only part of the letter calculated to impress the Parliament.] 'We wish to hear your orders as to what we shall do in the face of this demand; the procedure gives us no way by which we can refuse them.'

But note the way in which the letter was presented to a Parliament in which there yet remained so much sympathy for the accused, and the way in which it was received. St Just appeared in the tribune with the letter in his hands, and, instead of reading it, held it up before them and made this speech:

---

[1] This is M. Wallon's opinion, who gives both versions, and from whom I take so much of this description. See *Tribunal Révolutionnaire*, vol. iii, p. 177.

'The public prosecutor of the Revolutionary Tribunal has sent
to tell you that the prisoners are in full revolt, and have interrupted the hearing, saying they will not allow it to continue until
the Convention has taken measures. You have barely escaped
from the greatest danger which has yet menaced our new liberty,
and this revolt in the very seat of justice, of men panic-stricken
by the law, shows what is in their minds. Their despair and
their fury are a plain proof of the hypocrisy which they showed
in keeping a good face before you. Innocent men do not revolt.
Dillon, who ordered his army to march on Paris, has told us that
Desmoulins's wife received money to help the plot. Our thanks
are due to you for having put us in the difficult and dangerous
post that we occupy. Your Committees will answer you by the
most careful watching,' and so forth. When the Convention
had had laid before them every argument and every flattery
which could falsify their point of view, he proposed the decree
that any prisoner who should attempt to interrupt the course of
justice by threats or revolt should be outlawed.

As they were about to vote, Billaud Varennes added his word,
'I beg the Convention to listen to a letter which the Committees
have received from the police concerning the conspirators, and
their connection with the prisoners.' The letter is not genuine.
Even if it were, it depends entirely upon the word of one obscure
and untrustworthy man (Laflotte), but it did the work. The
Committees, as we know, were names to conjure with. Their
secret debates, their evident success, the fact that their members
had been chosen for the very purpose of guarding the interests
of the Republic, all fatally told against the prisoners. The
decree passed without a vote. Robespierre asked that the
letter might be read in full court, and his demand was granted.
It was from that letter, from this obscure and uncertain origin,
that there dated the legend of the 'conspiracy in the prisons'
which was to cost the lives of so many hundreds.

It was at the very close of this day, the 4th of April, that the
decree of the Convention was brought back to the tribunal.
Amar brought it and gave it to Fouquier, saying: 'Here is
what you wanted.' Fouquier smiled and said, 'We were in
great need of it.' It was read in the tribunal. When Camille
heard the name of his wife mentioned in connection with
St Just's demand he cried out: 'Will they kill her too?' and
David, who was sitting behind the judges, said: 'We hold
them at last.' [1]

---

[1] All this appears in the trial of Fouquier.

The fourth day, the 16th Germinal (5th April), the court met at half-past eight in the morning, instead of at the ordinary hour of ten. Almost at once, before the accused had time to begin their tactics of the day before, the decree was read. The judge, relying on the law which had already been in operation against others, and which gave the jury the right to say after three days whether they were satisfied, turned to them, and they asked leave to deliberate.

Before the prisoners had passed into the prison Desmoulins had found time to tear the defence which he had written into small pieces, and to throw them at the feet of the judge. Danton cried out, and checked himself in the middle of his sentence. All save poor Camille had kept their self-control. He, however, clung to the dock, determined on making some appeal to the people, or to the judges, or to posterity. Danton, who calmed him a few hours later at the foot of the scaffold, could do nothing with him then, and it was in the midst of a terrible violence that the fifteen disappeared.

The prisoners were taken back to the Conciergerie, but in their absence occurred a scene which is among the most instructive of the close of the Revolution. One of the jury could not bring himself to declare the guilt of men whom he knew to be innocent. Another said to him: 'This is not a trial; it is a sacrifice. Danton and Robespierre cannot exist together; which do you think most necessary to the Republic?' The unhappy man, full of the infatuation of the time, stammered out: 'Why, Robespierre is necessary, of course, but——' 'It is enough; in saying that you have passed judgment.' And it came about in this way that the unanimous verdict condemned the Indulgents. Lhuillier alone was acquitted.

Of what passed in the prison we only know from the lips of an enemy,[1] but I can see Danton talking still courageously of a thousand things; sitting in his chair of green damask and drinking his bottle of Burgundy opposite the silver and the traps of D'Eglantine.[2] They were not taken back to hear their sentence; it was read to them, as a matter of form, in the Conciergerie itself. Ducray read it to them one by one as they were brought into his office. Danton refused to hear it in patience; he hated the technicality and the form, and he knew that he was condemned long ago. He committed himself to a last burst of passion before summoning his strength to meet the

---

[1] They are given in Claretie's *Desmoulins* in the Appendix.
[2] See the list of the prisoner's effects in Claretie's *Desmoulins*.

ordeal of the streets, and followed his anger by the insults which for days he had levelled at death. Then for a few hours they kept a silence not undignified, save only Camille, unfitted for such trials, and moaning to himself in a corner of the room, whom Danton continually tried to console, a task in which at the very end of their sad journey he succeeded. It was part of his broad mind to understand even a writer and an artist, he who had never written and had only done.

It was between half-past four and five o'clock in the evening of the same day, the 5th of April 1794, that the prisoners re-appeared. Two carts were waiting for them at the great gate in the court of the Palais—the gate which is the inner entrance to the Conciergerie to-day.[1] About the carts were a numerous escort mounted and with drawn swords, but the victims took their seats as they chose, and of the fifteen the Dantonists remained together. Hérault, Camille, Lacroix, Westermann, Fabre, Danton went up the last into the second cart, and the procession moved out of the courtyard and turned to the left under the shadow of the Palais, and then to the left again round the Tour de l'Horloge, and so on to the quay. They passed the window of the tribunal, the window from which Danton's loud voice had been heard across the river; they went creaking slowly past the old Mairie, past the rooms that had been Roland's lodgings, till they came to the corner of the Pont Neuf; and as the carts turned from the trees of the Place Dauphine on to the open bridge, they left the shade and passed into the full blaze of the westering sun within an hour of its setting.

Early as was the season, the air was warm and pleasant, the leaves and the buds were out on the few trees, the sky was un-clouded. All that fatal spring was summerlike, and this day was the calmest and most beautiful that it had known. The light, already tinged with evening, came flooding the houses of the north bank till their glass shone in the eyes. There it caught the Café de l'Ecole where Danton had sat a young lawyer seven years before, and had seen the beauty of his first wife in her father's house; to the right the corner of the old Hôtel de Ville caught the glow, to the left the Louvre flamed with a hundred windows.

Where the light poured up the river and came reflected from the Seine on to the bridge, it marked out the terrible column that was moving ponderously forward to death. A great crowd,

---

[1] This gate may be seen to-day just to the right of the great staircase in the court of the Palais de Justice. It has an iron grating before it.

foolish, unstable, varied, of whom some ran to catch a near sight
of the 'Indulgents,' some pitied, and a few understood and
despaired of the Republic—all these surging and jostling as a
crowd will that is forced to a slow pace and confined by the
narrowness of an old thoroughfare, stretched from one end of
the bridge to the other, and you would have seen them in the
sunlight, brilliant in the colours that men wore in those days,
while here and there a red cap of liberty marked the line of
heads.

But in the centre of this crowd and showing above it, could be
seen the group of men who were about to die.   The carts hidden
by the people, the horses' heads just showing above the mob,
surrounded by the sharp gleams that only come from swords,
there rose distinguished the figures of the Dantonists.   There
stood Hérault de Séchelles upright, his face contemptuous, his
colour high, 'as though he had just risen from a feast.'   There on
the far side of the cart sat Fabre d'Eglantine, bound, ill, col-
lapsed, his head resting on his chest, muttering and complaining.
There on the left side, opposite Fabre, is Camille, bound but still
frenzied, calling loudly to the people, raving, 'Peuple, pauvre
Peuple!'   He still kept in his poet's head the dream of the
People!   They had been deceived, but they were just, they
would save him.   He wrestled with his ropes and tore his shirt
open at the bosom, clenching his bound hands—clutched in his
fingers through all the struggle shone the bright hair of Lucille.
Danton stood up immense and quiet between them.   One of
those broad shoulders touched D'Eglantine, the other Desmoulins; their souls leant upon his body.   And such comfort as
there was or control in the central group came out like warmth
from the chief of these friends.

He had been their leader and their strength for five years; they
were round him now like younger brothers orphaned.   The
weakness of one, the vices of another, came leaning for support
on the great rock of his form.   For these were not the Girondins,
the admirable stoics, of whom each was a sufficient strength to
his own soul: they were the Dantonists, who had been moulded
and framed by the strength and genius of one man.   He did
not fail them a moment in the journey, and he died last to give
them courage.

As they passed on the left the river, they lost the light again
and plunged into shadow; the cool air was about them in the
deep narrow streets.   They could see the light far above them
only, as they turned into the gulf of the Rue St Honoré, down

which the lives of men poured like a stream to be lost and wasted in the Place de la Révolution. Up its steep sides echoed and re-echoed the noise of the mob like waves. They could see as they rolled slowly along the people at the windows, the men sitting in the cafés or standing up to watch them go by. One especially Danton saw suddenly and for a moment. He was standing with a drawing-book in his hand and sketching rapidly with short interrupted glances. It was David, an enemy.

Then there appeared upon their left another sight; it was the only one in that long hour which drove Danton out of his control: it was the house of Duplay. There, hidden somewhere behind the close shutters, was Robespierre. They all turned to it loudly, and the sentence was pronounced which some say God has executed—that it should disappear and not be known again, and be hidden by high walls and destroyed.

The house was silent, shut, blockaded. It was like a thing which is besieged and which turns its least sentient outer part to its enemies. It was beleaguered by the silent and unseen forces which we feel pressing everywhere upon the living. For it contained the man who had sent that cartload of his friends to death. Their fault had been to preach the permanent sentiments of mankind, to talk of mercy, and to recall in 1794 the great emotions of the early Revolution—the desire for the Republic where every kind of man could sit and laugh at the same table, the Republic of the Commensales. They were the true heirs of the spirit of the Federations, and it was for this that they were condemned. Even at this last moment there radiated from them the warmth of heart that proceeds from a group of friends and lovers till it blesses the whole of a nation with an equal affection. Theirs had been the instinct of and the faith in the happy life of the world. It was for this that the Puritan had struck them down; and yet it is the one spirit that runs through any enduring reform, the only spirit that can lead us at last to the Republic.

In a remote room, where the noise of the wheels could not reach him, sat the man who, by some fatal natural lack or some sin of ambition unrepented, had become the Inquisitor—the mad, narrow enemy of mercy and of all good things.

For a moment he and his error had the power to condemn, repeating a tragedy of which the world is never weary—the mean thing was killing the great.

Nevertheless, if you will consider the men in the tumbril, you will find them not to be pitied except for two things, that they were loved by women whom they could not see, and that they were dying in the best and latest time of their powerful youth. All these young men were loved, and in other things they should be counted fortunate. They had with their own persons already transformed the world. Here the writer knew that his talent, the words he had so carefully chosen and with such delight in his power, had not been wasted upon praise or fortune, but had achieved the very object. There the orator knew and could remember how his great voice had called up the armies and thrown back the kings.

But if the scene was a tragedy, it was a tragedy of the real that refused to follow the unities. All nature was at work, crowded into the Revolutionary time, and the element that Shakespeare knew came in of itself—the eternal comedy that seems to us, according to our mood, the irony, the madness, or the cruelty of things, was fatally present to make the day complete; and the grotesque, like a discordant note, contrasted with and emphasized the terrible.

Fabre, who had best known how omnipresent is this complexity—Fabre, who had said: 'Between the giving and taking of snuff there is a comedy'—furnished the example now. Danton hearing so much weakness and so many groans from the sick man said: 'What is your complaint?' He answered: 'I have written a play called *The Maltese Orange*, and I fear the police have taken it, and that someone will steal it and get the fame.' Poor Fabre! It is lost, and no one has the ridicule of his little folly. Danton answered him with a phrase to turn the blood: 'Tais toi! Dans une semaine tu feras assez de vers,' and imposed silence. Nor did this satisfy Fate; there were other points in the frame-work of the incongruous which she loves to throw round terror. A play was running in the opera called the *10th of August*; in this the Dantonists were represented on the stage. When the Dantonists were hardly buried it was played again that very night, and actors made up for Hérault and the rest passed before a public that ignored or had forgotten what the afternoon had seen. More than this, there was already set in type a verse which the street-hawkers cried and sold that very night. For the sake of its coincidence I will take the liberty of translating it into rhymed heroics:

> When Danton, Desmoulins, and D'Eglantine
> Were ferried over to the world unseen,
> Charon, that equitable citizen,

Handed their change to these distinguished men.
'Pray keep the change,' they cried; 'we pay the fare
For Couthon, and St Just, and Robespierre.' [1]

Danton spared only Camille, and as he did not stop appealing
to the people, told him gently to cease. 'Leave the rabble
there,' he said, 'leave them alone.' But for himself he kept
on throwing angry jests at death. 'May I sing?' he said to
the executioner. Sanson thought he might, for all he knew.
Then Danton said to him: 'I have made some verses, and
will sing them.' He sang loudly a verse of the fall of Robespierre, and then laughed as though he had been at the old
café with his friends.

There was a man (Arnault of the Academy) who lived afterwards to a great age, and who happened to be crossing the
Rue St Honoré as the carts went past. In a Paris that had all
its business to do, many such men came and went, almost forgetting that politics existed even then. But this batch of
prisoners haunted him. He had seen Danton standing singing
with laughter, he hurried on to the Rue de la Monnaie, had his
say with Michael, who was awaiting him, and then, full of the
scene, ran back across the Tuileries gardens, and pressing his
face to the railings looked over the great Place de la Révolution.
The convoy had arrived, the carts stood at the foot of the
guillotine, and his memory of the scene is the basis of its history.

It was close on six, and the sun was nearly set behind the
trees of the Etoile; it reddened the great plaster statue of
Liberty which stood in the middle of the Place, where the
obelisk is now, and to which Madame Roland delivered her last
phrase. It sent a level beam upon the vast crowd that filled
the square, and cast long shadows, sending behind the guillotine a dark lane over the people. The day had remained serene
and beautiful to the last, the sky was stainless, and the west
shone like a forge. Against it, one by one, appeared the figures

---

[1] The original of this I take from Claretie, who quotes P. A. Lecomte
Memorial sur la Révolution Française:

'Lorsqu'arrivés aux bords du Phlégéton
Camille Desmoulins, D'Eglantine et Danton,
Payèrent pour passer ce fleuve redoutable
Le nautonnier Charon (citoyen équitable)
A nos trois passagers voulait remettre en mains
L'excédent de la taxe imposée aux humains.
"Garde," lui dit Danton, "la somme toute entière;
Je paye pour Couthon, St Just et Robespierre."'

of the condemned. Hérault de Séchelles, straight and generous in his bearing, first showed against the light, standing on the high scaffold conspicuous. He looked at the Garde Meuble, and from one of its high windows a woman's hand found it possible to wave a farewell. Lacroix next, equally alone; Camille, grown easy and self-controlled, was the third. One by one they came up the few steps, stood clearly for a moment in the fierce light, black or framed in scarlet, and went down.

Danton was the last. He had stood unmoved at the foot of the steps as his friends died. Trying to embrace Hérault before he went up, roughly rebuking the executioner who tore them asunder, waiting his turn without passion, he heard the repeated fall of the knife in the silence of the crowd. His great figure, more majestic than in the days of his triumph, came against the sunset. The man who watched it from the Tuileries gate grew half afraid, and tells us that he understood for a moment what kind of things Dante himself had seen. By an accident he had to wait some seconds longer than the rest; the executioner heard him muttering, 'I shall never see her again . . no weakness,' but his only movement was to gaze over the crowd. They say that a face met his, and that a sacramental hand was raised in absolution.[1]

He stood thus conspicuous for a moment over the people whom he had so often swayed. In that attitude he remains for history. When death suddenly strikes a friend, the picture which we carry of him in our minds is that of vigorous life. His last laughter, his last tones of health, his rapid step, or his animated gesture reproduce his image for ever. So it is with Danton; there is no mask of Danton dead, nor can you complete his story with the sense of repose. We cannot see his face in the calm either of triumph or of sleep—the brows grown level, the lips satisfied, the eyelids closed. He will stand through whatever centuries the story of the Revolution may be told as he stood on the scaffold looking westward and transfigured by the red sun, still courageous, still powerful in his words, and still instinct with that peculiar energy, self-forming, self-governing, and whole. He has in his final moment the bearing of the tribune, the glance that had mastered the danger in Belgium, the force that had nailed Roland to his post in September, and that had commanded the first Committee. The Republic that

[1] It was Madame Gély who told this to Despoi's grandfather. Claretie has mentioned it. But Michelet must have heard from the family about this same priest (Kerénavant le Breton), for according to Madame Gély was he who married Danton for the second time.

he desired, and that will come, was proved in his carriage, and passed from him into the crowd.

When Sanson put a hand upon his shoulder the ghost of Mirabeau stood by his side and inspired him with the pride that had brightened the death-chamber of three years before. He said: 'Show my head to the people; it is well worth the while.' Then they did what they had to do, and without any kind of fear, his great soul went down the turning of the road.

They showed his head to the people, and the sun set. There rose at once the confused noise of a thousand voices that rejoiced or questioned, or despaired, and in the gathering darkness the Parisians returned through the narrow streets eastward to their homes.

A DESCRIPTION OF ROBESPIERRE

In height Robespierre was a little below the medium, but this feature, which would not in itself convey an impression of insignificance, went with a certain slightness of build that left him unnoticed unless, by the accident of the tribune, he were withdrawn from the crowd. His frame was of a delicate mould, his hands and feet small and well-shaped, his chest neither broad nor deep. He had not that vitality of action which proceeds from well-furnished lungs; neither the voice nor the gesture, the good humour, nor the sudden powers that belong to men whose fires have draught to them. Indeed his complexion, though clear, was of that pale cast which we often associate with a kind of morbidity, and he was throughout his youth and public life affected with the frequent approach, though never with the continuance, of ill-health. The recollection of his pallor and of the delicacy of his skin gave rise (when his living presence was no longer there to correct the error) to an impression of sourness and nervous bile which has vitiated most historical descriptions; for, as will be seen in much that follows, his temper was even beyond the common, his smile, though cold, was frequent, and his patience firm.

He had, in common with the whole of that French professional class from which he sprang, a pronounced habit of order, a regularity of demeanour, and a very remarkable capacity for prolonged mental work; but this last so tended to expend itself upon imaginaries and perpetual deductions that he lost the sustenance which it afforded in countless other cases to the more practical minds of the Revolution; nor did it produce in him that reaction towards common things which was so marked in Carnot, and which had at the end begun to appear in St Just. This appetite for arrangement evoked in his mind a character which must be mentioned later; in his outer life it gave him the neatness of dress which has so often been justly insisted upon by the historians of the Revolution. He pushed to some excess a amiable vice whereby the care of the person was made the special social duty of the old régime, and is still preserved in exaggerated reverence by the social class of which he formed a member. Moderate as was his expenditure at every period

of his life, he found the means for a careful wardrobe, an
devoted a regular portion of his time to its maintenance. I
the variety of colours which the age permitted he chose suc
as were best suited to his type and presence, and, partly from
a desire to avoid exaggeration, partly from taste, he preferre
the sober colours of the contemporary fashion of his rank,
warm brown or olive green for the colour of his coat.   Later h
ventured upon the brighter colours of '93, and especially upon
favourite light blue, which the accident of two dates has rendere
famous.   In the careful elegance of his silk stockings, in th
buckles which, even after the change of fashion in 1792, h
continued to wear upon his shoes, in his white stock and sma
lace wristbands, he displayed at every point the general tast
of his society, but that heightened by a far more scrupulou
attention and a somewhat greater choice than his neighbour
could show.   It is evident that with such a taste he woul
observe to a detail the conventions of the age in his barbering
His brown hair, carefully brushed back and standing fully ou
wards, was powdered with exact and daily regularity, and i
is related of him that in all the vigils and alarms of the las
years, even when those street battles joined up whole days an
made men forget sleeping and waking, he was never seen un
shaven till the awful watch that ended his life.

Such habits were necessarily accompanied by an erect figur
by a rapid though not decided step, and by a certain sligh
vivacity in the movements of the head, though he dealt a
rarely as any other northerner in the language of gesture, bein
restrained in every attitude and careful to preserve his pois

When you came to look at his face there was apparent
peculiar character which engravers and sculptors greatly exag
gerated after his death, but which a study of contemporar
painting reduces to juster proportions; it consisted in th
prominence of the facial bones and a lack of softness in th
contours.   This meagre hardness produced no very striking (
violent effect, but it was sufficiently emphatic to place him
when we call up the great gallery which the Revolution afford
in the group of over-keen, sharp-featured portraits wherein a
found also Sieyès, Jean-Bon, Camus, Couthon, and many oth
dissimilar men united only in a common appearance of emphas
and precision.

Such effects as this accident of leanness produced in h
expression were heightened by details that often accompan
its presence.   Thus the cheek-bones were high and formed th

broadest part of his face. His nose was short, delicate and quite without an arch, his lips compressed and thin; and there was an insufficient development of the jaw accompanied by a sharpness of the chin, which when his little constant smile was absent, lent a somewhat false appearance of bitterness to his appearance. The upper part of his face, that the hollowness of his cheeks thus threw into relief, was remarkable for a feature which the hair-dress of the eighteenth century tended indeed to exaggerate, but which yet was common to half the public men of the time; I mean the broad, high and retreating forehead which seems to promise grasp and rapid reason, but which ignores the mysteries and is unacquainted with doubt. You may find it in every profile of all the Bourbons, of Diderot, of Voltaire and even of Mirabeau. For the rest his head was regular though somewhat small, and such impressions as it might afford of intellectual power, or rather alacrity, were increased by an upward holding of it common to men of his inferior stature. His words thus reached the whole of an assembly, and the direction of his gaze, which was commonly above the horizon, added to his carriage an air of confidence that was hardly in keeping with the attitude of his mind.

His eyes, whence most of his self pierced outward, gave immediate evidence of the homogeneity, sincerity, and circumscription as they did also of the half-unquiet of his mind and of its unfittedness for reception. For the slight prominence of their brows made them seem deeper set and closer together than they really were, but this gave no special effect of energy or profundity since their colour and a physical weakness in their action modified or destroyed their impression. They were peculiarly pale and of a neutral greenish grey, not without light but quite bereft of brilliance; so far from possessing that command which is common to the vision of those who control parliaments, a nervous weakness that caused a recurrent trembling in their lids compelled him to the use of spectacles when he was at work or when (as was his universal habit) he read his speeches. The expression of these eyes of his was not unkindly, and it accentuated the slight, smiling tension which was the common contour of his lips; but an over-rapid glance that seemed to watch upon every occasion, gave evidence of what became in circumstances of danger an unbalancing habit of suspicion. Then, too, he would often raise his forehead in wrinkles when he spoke and play a little with his fingers. These nervous faults that took away so much from his physical capacity for

dominion were repeated also in certain slight movements of the
lower face that gained upon him in moments of irritation or of
concentrated attention; as though the slight tremor from which
his eyes suffered provoked a sympathetic action in the facial
muscles of the jaw.

But it would be very ridiculous to make of these symptoms a
principal matter in the picture of Robespierre. They were
generally absent from his later, as they were entirely from his
earlier life, and they serve but as indications of the manner in
which his temperament was affected by an extreme success and
a corresponding danger, for either of which it was utterly unsuited. In evidence of this it may be noted that his face was
free from the lines which constant anxiety or ceaseless assiduity
drew upon those of his contemporaries, nor had he any marked
development of such indications of character, save in the furrow
that flank the mouth and that stand commonly for some perception of irony and for a habit of self-control.

I will believe that his voice though somewhat weak and
possessing no wide range, yet had a power of very varied modu-
lation, was sympathetic and clear. It was pitched to such a
tenor that in the silence generally accorded to him it reached
with exact articulation to the furthest recesses of the galleries in
the Menus Plaisirs, or even in the vast oval of the Manège. But
whenever a hubbub arose he was quite unable to meet it, and
would either endure till it had passed or succumb to it as to a
physical oppression. In the open air, when there were no walls
to make a sounding-board, he could hardly be heard. In all
this he differed widely from those whom he supplanted, from
Mirabeau and Danton, whose deep, loud voices could fill an open
arena, and in any closed and silent debate could sound like
large bells above a gale. If there was any other thing to help
the success of his oratory beside the clarity of articulation and
the pitch to which I have alluded, it lay in the reputation that a
small surrounding of friends had made for his manner; a reputation inherited from his half-literary youth in college and at Arras
where it is indubitable that he had exercised a permanent if
exiguous charm, and one that Carnot, Le Bas, Desmoulins or the
Roberts would certainly remember.

Such in general, then, is the picture one must take with one in
following his adventure and tragedy. A figure slight but erect
and sufficiently well filled, a little dainty and always exquisitely
fitted, not disdainful of colour but contemptuous of ornament
he maintained to the end those externals which had been the

enamel of the old society; shaming, astonishing or irking the sick slipshod of a Marat, the casual rough negligence of a Danton, the dust of maps and floors that soiled a sleepless Carnot, the common tongue of a Hébert or the guard-room coarseness of a Henriot. We must see his small, set and pointed, but open and somewhat lifted face developing in the course of a stress for which he was not made and which a nascent ambition could alone compel him to suffer, some growing nervousness of manner. His pale complexion upon whose temples and forehead the veins would show, his blonde, grey-green, short-sighted, luminous but weakening eyes, his lips compressed and thin, but often set to an expression of advance or attention, his large retreating forehead, his reserve of gesture—all these form the expression of which a voice somewhat high and tenuous but not without attraction was the organ.

He passes up the Revolution as in his physical gait he passed up the gangway of the parliament: rapidly, but not over decidedly; lacking, apparently, the power of controlling others, but with the constancy of attitude that proceeds from strict limitations and with a singular fixity of carriage. A man, with all this, absorbed in the effort after form, possessed of a considerable literary ambition, pale, insufficient, exact, laborious, he does not seem much more than the successful and locally prominent county lawyer, a trifle pedantic but enjoying a sound connection of justly admiring and somewhat unimpressive friends; one that, entering politics, might draft or criticize, but that could hardly attract a general observation.

This he should have been, and such things he should have done. What did he?

He held first a group, then a great political machine, then a sovereign assembly, and at last a nation, attentive. He became the title and front of the republic: the kings regarded him; he put some fear into the priests; the armies converged upon his tenement; the general run of European society stood aghast at his supposed enormities; the most generous, the most practical, and the most violent of the great Reformers alike insisted upon his bearing their standard; he may become for the martyrs and prophets of complete democracy an idol, as he has already become their legend. Whence did this astonishing contrast between his native, probable career and his actual fate proceed? It proceeded from the fact that his character contained a something which the special nature of the time craved, which it insisted upon and would not abandon. That something was but one factor of his whole temperament, it might have lain dormant though it could never have been atrophied, but certainly it would have suffered neglect in ordinary times, and with that neglect he would himself, in ordinary times, have remained contented.

To discover this hidden and permanent part of him which the Revolution deified, it is necessary to examine what inner temper accompanied or gave rise to the externals I have described, and such a task I shall now undertake: to show the mind that made this body.

The character of Robespierre is contained in these two connected facts: First, that he was a man of the old régime—divining nothing outside of it, undisturbed by that germinating of the future which worked in and troubled the great minds around him, and threw an energy of travail into their splendid tragedy; secondly, that he had to an inhuman, or (if the word be preferred) to an heroic, degree the potentiality of intense conviction; for God had given him a kind of stone tabernacle within the soul where he could treasure absolute truths and this tabernacle remained impregnable.

THE LAST DAYS OF MARIE ANTOINETTE

MONDAY, the 14th of October:

The fate of the Queen and of the Republic had each come to a final and critical issue when the light broke, dully in either place, over Paris and over the pastures of the frontier. There the army lay to arms in the valley, with Coburg entrenched upon the ridge above them, and beyond him the last famine of Maubeuge: from dawn the French lines could hear, half a day's march to the northward, the regular boom of the bombardment. But Carnot was now come.

. . . .

In Paris, when it was broad day, the chief Court above the prison was prepared.

The populace had crammed the side galleries of the great room and were forming a further throng, standing in the space between the doors and the bar. The five Judges, Herman the chief, filed on to the Bench; a little below them and on their right a jury of fifteen men were empanelled. It was on the courage, the conviction or the fanaticism of these that the result would turn.

They presented, as they sat there awaiting the prisoner, a little model of the violent egalitarian mood which had now for a year and more driven the military fury of the Republic. Among them would be seen the refined and somewhat degraded face of a noble who had sat in the earlier Parliaments and who had drifted as Orleans had drifted—but further than had Orleans. There also were the unmistakable eyes of precision which were those of an optician, a maker of instruments. There were, resting on the rail of the box, the firm hands of a great surgeon (Souberbielle). A few of the common people were mingled with these: contractors also, prosperous men, and master-carpenters. There was a hatter there, and a barber, a man who had made violins, and another who painted pictures for the rich. Of such elements was the body comprised which had now to determine so much in the history of Europe. Above them a presiding figure, Herman the judge, with his dark aquiline face, controlled them all. They looked all of them towards the door that led from the cells below, where two warders came upward through it, leading between them the Queen.

She also as she entered saw new things. The silence and the darkness of her long imprisonment fell from her: the noise of the streets came in from the windows before her; she heard the rumour and she saw the movement of the populace which—save for that brief midnight drive two months ago—had been quite cut off from her since last she had shrunk from the mob on the evening when she had heard the gate of the Temple bolted behind her carriage. After that hush which had been so dreadfully divided by evil upon evil, she came out suddenly into the sound of the city and into the general air. In that interval the names of months and of days, the mutual salutations of men, religion, and the very habit of life had changed. In that interval also the nation had passed from the shock of arms to unimagined crimes, to a most unstable victory, to a vision of defeat and perhaps of annihilation. France was astrain upon the edge of a final deliverance or of a final and irretrievable disaster. Its last fortress was all but fallen, all its resources were called out, all its men were under arms, over the fate of the frontier hung a dreadful still silence. In the very crisis of this final doubt and terror the Queen stood arraigned.

The women lowered their knitting-needles and kept them still. The little knot of Commissioners sitting with Counsel for the State, the angry boys in the crowd who could remember wounds or the death of comrades, stretched forward to catch sight of her as she came up the stairs between her guards: they were eager to note if there had been any change.

She had preserved her carriage, which all who knew her had regarded since her childhood as the chief expression of her soul. She still moved with solemnity and with that exaggerated but unflinching poise of the head which, in the surroundings of Versailles, had seemed to some so queenly, to others so affected, which here, in her last hours, seemed to all, as she still preserved it, so defiant. For the rest she was not the same. Her glance seemed dull and full of weariness; the constant loss of blood which she had suffered during those many weeks spent below ground had paled her so that the artificial, painted red of her cheeks was awful in that grey morning and her still ample hair was ashen and touched with white, save where some traces of its old auburn could be perhaps distinguished.

She was in black. A little scarf of lace was laid with exacti-

tude about her shoulders and her breast, and on her head she
wore a great cap which a woman who loved her, the same who
had served her in her cell, put on her as she went to her passion.
The pure white of this ornament hung in great strings of lawn
on either side, and round it and beneath it she had wound the
crape of her widowhood. So dressed, and so standing at the
bar, so watched in silence by so many eyes, she heard once more
the new sound which yesterday she had first learned to hate:
the hard and nasal voice of Herman. He asked her formally
her name. She answered in a voice which was no longer strong,
but which was still clear and well heard in that complete silence:

'Marie Antoinette of Austria, some thirty-eight years old,
widow to Louis Capet the King of France.'

To the second formal question on the place of her first
arrest, that:

'It was in the place where the sittings of the National Assembly
were held.'

The clerk, a man of no great learning, wrote his heading:
'The 23rd day of the first month of the fourth year of Freedom,'
and when he had done this he noted her replies, and Herman's
short questions also: his bidding to the jury that they must be
firm, to the prisoner that she must be attentive.

Into the clerk's writing there crept, as there will into that of
poor men, certain grievous errors of grammar which in an
earlier (and a later) time would not have appeared in the record
of the meanest Court trying a tramp for hunger; but it was the
Revolution and they were trying a Queen, so everything was
strange; and this clerk called himself Fabricius, which had a
noble sound—but it was not his name.

This clerk read the list of witnesses and the indictment
out loud.

When these formalities were over they brought a chair. The
Queen sat down by leave of the Court and the trial began.
She saw rising upon her right a new figure of a kind which she
had not known in all her life up to the day when the door of the
prison had shut her out from the noise and change of the world.
It was a figure of the Terror, Fouquier-Tinville. His eyes were
steadfast, the skin of his face was brown, hard and strong; he
was a hired politician covered with the politician's outer mask
of firmness. Within he was full of the politician's hesitation and
nervous inconstancy. A genuine poverty and a politician's
hunger for a salary had been satisfied by the post of Public
Prosecutor. He earned that salary with zeal and with little

discernment, and therefore, when the time came, he also was condemned to die. It was he now in this forenoon who opened against the Queen.

His voice was harsh and mechanical: his speech was long, dull, and violent: rhetorical with that scenic and cardboard rhetoric which is the official commonplace of all tribunals. The Widow Capet was a Messalina; she was a leech; she was a Merovingian Tyrant; she was a Medicis. She had held relations with the 'Man called King' of Bohemia and Hungary; she had urged Capet on to all his crimes. She had sent millions to aid her family in their war against the French people. She had woven the horrid plot of the 10th of August, which nothing but incredible valour had defeated. She was the main enemy which the new and angry Freedom for which he spoke had had to meet and to conquer.

Apart from its wearisome declamation the accusation was true; save that—through no fault of her own, poor woman!—she had not aided the foreign cause with gold, all the story was evident and publicly known. She sat as near this orator as is a nurse to a bedside. She heard him with her suffering and disdainful face quite fixed and unmoved, save at one point: the mention of her son.

Fouquier-Tinville was sane: he saw the crass absurdity of Hébert's horrors, he barely touched upon them very hurriedly (and as the rapid and confused words escaped him, her lips twitched with pain), but even as he did so he knew he had given the defence a hold.

It is held on principle in French Courts that an impartial presentation of the truth cannot be obtained unless witnesses are heard in a chance sequence, not divided into friends and foes as with us, but each (such is the theory) telling what he believes to be the truth. Even in these political trials of the Terror (which were rather Courts-Martial or condemnations than trials) the rule was observed, and when Fouquier sat down the file of witnesses began.

The parade was futile. For plain political facts known to the whole world no list of witnesses were needed, nor could their evidence be of the least avail. Moreover, that evidence was lacking. The witnesses defiled one after the other, each vaguer than the last, to prove (and failing to prove) things that were commonplaces to all Europe. Long past midday the empty procession continued through the drowsy hours, past one o'clock and two: remembering trifles of her conduct true and false. To every assertion as the judge repeated it (true or false) she answered quietly by a denial: that denial was now false, now true.

Even if the Revolutionary Tribunal could have subpœnaed Mallet or the Emperor or Fersen, it would have meant little to the result. Her guilt, if it was guilt so to scheme against the nation, was certain: what yet remained in doubt was the political necessity of such a trial at such a moment, the limit of hardihood in her judges and the possible effect in a democracy of public sympathy at some critical phase of the pleadings: and much more potent than any of these three, because it included them all, was the news that might come at any moment from the frontier and from the hunger of Maubeuge—no news came.

Last of these witnesses Hébert, all neat and powdered, presented his documents and put forward his abominations, his fixed idea of incest. The public disgust might here have turned the trial. There was a stir all round: her friends began to hope. As for the officials, they could not stop Hébert's mouth, but Herman was careful to omit the customary repetition: he was hurrying on to the next witness when a juryman of less wit than his fellows and filled with the enormous aberrations of hate, pressed the charge.

The Queen would not reply. She half rose from her chair and cried in a high voice: 'I appeal to every mother here,' and then sank back again.

The crowd in the galleries began to move and murmur, the women raised their voices against the angry orders of the ushers and of the Bench demanding silence. Away, dining beyond the Seine, Robespierre, hearing of it, broke a plate at table in his anger, and thought Hébert's lunacy had saved her. A further witness, though he spoke of the flight to Varennes, could hardly be heard, and spoke quite unheeded; and when he had concluded, the Court abruptly rose in the midst of the commotion, hubbub and change.

The Queen was led to her cell, keeping as she left her place, in spite of her hopeless fatigue, the steady step wherewith she had entered; and as she passed she heard one woman in the press sneering at her pride.

It was three o'clock. The first act in that long agony had lasted, without food or breathing-time, for seven hours.

While the Republic thus held the old world prisoner in Paris and tortured it in the person of the Queen, out on the frontier in the water-meadows of Avesnes, the Republic lay in its chief peril from the old world free and armed. Coburg and every privilege held the crest of the hills invincibly, and Maubeuge was caught fast, unreachable beyond the entrenchments of that ridge.

Carnot, looking westward down the valley of the Helpe, saw the deep orchards laden with October, nourished by the small and very winding stream. He saw the last French frontier hamlets and their mills: St Hilaire, Dompierre, Tenieres, dwindling away to where, far off in its broad trench, ran the Sambre.

Before him also in this valley, as he looked westward down it, he saw stretched for some ten miles the encampment of his army: bivouac after bivouac, one beyond the other along the lines, and smoke rising from them. Tall hedges, not yet bare, divided the floor of the valley and the village grounds: here also Caesar had marched through against the Nervii: for this corner of Europe is a pack of battlefields. Malplaquet lay just before the army; within a march, Fleurus; within sound of cannon, Jemappes.

Up above them beyond that wood of Avesnes, the line of the heights along the sky, was the enemy. It had loomed so dark before the late, dull and rainy dawn, that they had seen the notches in that line which were the emplacement of guns. The early afternoon had shone upon the sides of the hills, and the French outposts had seen the outposts of the enemy busy in the little villages that mark the foot of the slopes: St Vaast, Dourlers, Foursies. And all day long boomed to the north behind the hills the sullen guns before Maubeuge. At any hour that dull repeated sound might cease, and it would mean that the last fortress had fallen.

All that day Carnot passed in silence. The troops, some last detachments of which had but just marched in, lay dully in such repose as soldiers can steal: a jumble of forty patchwork battalions, militia, regulars, loud volunteers, old stark gunners; they listened to the distant and regular thunder of the siege. In some stations the few horses were grooming: in others, fewer still, the rare guns were cleaned.

An hour before dusk the six generals were called to Carnot's tent, and here and there the bugles roused the troops called for reconnaissance. These few detachments crossed the woods, pierced gaps in the hedges [1] to prepare the advance of the morrow, noted and exchanged shots with the outposts of the evening, and at evening they retired. As they retired Carnot gave orders to the guns. Out of effective range, vague and careless of a target, they fired and proclaimed the presence of a relieving army to the besieged.

Maubeuge in that still evening, during a lull of the siege-pieces, heard those French guns, and Ferrant and the general officers with him counselled a sortie. Only Chancel stood out; but Chancel was in command of the camp of Maubeuge, and his authority was unassailable. He did not distinguish the French fire, he thought it Austrian; no instinct moved him. Therefore all the next day while the battle was engaged, the garrison of Maubeuge failed to move; and later, for this error, Chancel was tried and killed.[2]

When the guns had been thus fired, the reconnaissance ended. The troops fell back again through the wood of Avesnes and slept the last sleep before battle. In Paris during that same evening, the long trial of the Queen proceeded.

. . . . .

At five, just in that hour when Carnot was recalling his scouts and ordering that warning cannon, the Court gathered and the prisoner was recalled.

In her cell she had not been silent.

As a great actress in an interval between her hardest lines will refuse repose and will demand rather comment or praise, so had she filled this little respite of two hours with questions and with doubts professed. She had dwelt upon the forms of the trial, she had begged her counsel to reassure her. She had despised the evidence. She had said she feared but one witness —Manuel—and indeed all who could have spoken as eye-witnesses to a hundred notorious truths were now over the frontier or dead.

With her entry the trial was resumed and the file of witnesses continued. It was as monotonous and as vague as before. Even Manuel, whom she had feared, was vague, and the very servants of the prison (though they had been witnesses to con-spiracy) were uncertain and rambling. And this fatuity of the

[1] So on the same field had Caesar been compelled to clear the hedgerows. So little does the French peasantry change in a thousand years, and so tenacious is each French province of its customs.

[2] And the other version is that Chancel was for moving but that Ferrant would not. Choose.

witnesses who were so solemnly and so strictly examined did
not proceed from the turmoil of the time alone, nor even from
the certitude which all then had (and which history has now)
upon the past action of the Queen in cherishing the hope of
foreign domination and in procuring it: rather did it proceed
from the fact that these dreadful days were filled not with a
judicial but with a political action, and that the Court was met
not to establish truths at once unprovable and glaring, but to
see whether or no the Revolution could dare to condemn the
prisoner. It was an act of War and a challenge to What lay
entrenched up there before Maubeuge, training its guns on the
last hope, the ragged army in the valley of Avesnes below.

If all the witnesses which history possesses to-day, if Mole-
ville, Fersen, Mallet, could have been brought into that Court
and have had the Truth dragged from them, it would have
affected the issue very little. One thing alone could effect that
issue, the news of victory: and no news came. All reports from
the frontier had ceased.

The lights in the Court were lit, smoky and few. The air,
already foul from the large concourse, grew heavy even for the
free; for the sickened prisoner it became intolerable as the
night hours drew in—six dark interminable hours. She heard
the succeeding witnesses distantly, more distantly. Her head
was troubled and her injured eyesight failed her. It was very
late. The droning of the night was in her ears. She vaguely
knew at last that there was a movement around her and that
the Court was rising. She asked faintly for water. Busne, the
officer in guard of her, brought it to her and she drank. As he
supported her with some respect down the short passage to her
cell he heard her murmuring: 'I cannot see. . . . I cannot see.
. . . I have come to the end. . . .'

She lay down when her doors had received her, and just
before midnight she fell asleep. She slept deeply and for the
last time.

.   .   .   .   .   .

Tuesday, 15th October.

A little before dawn the French bugles upon the frontier
roused the troops of Avesnes; their calls ran down the line,
they passed from the Diane to the Générale, the woods before
them sent back echoes, and soon the army moved. Far off
upon the left Fromentin, upon the far right Duquesnoy, began
marching forwards and inwards, converging, but the main body

in the centre took the high road, which, if they could force its passage, would lead them straight to Maubeuge.

The sun was still level over the glinting wet fields when Carnot came to the summit of the long swell whence could be perceived, over an intervening hollow, the village of Dourlers, and above it the level fringe of trees which held the Austrian cannon; an impregnable crest upon whose security Coburg and the Allies founded the certitude of victory. The guns began.

Among the batteries of the French (too few for their task) two batteries, one of sixteen-pounders, the other of twelve, were the gift of the city of Paris. By some accident these, though ill manned, silenced the Austrian fire at one critical and central point above the Dourlers itself and close to the high road. Whether the French aptitude for this arm had helped to train the volunteers of the city, or whether these had such a leaven of trained men as sufficed to turn the scale, or whether (as is more probable) some error or difficulty upon the opposing slope or some chance shot had put the invaders out of action, cannot be known. Carnot seized upon the moment and ordered the charge. As his columns advanced to carry Dourlers he sent word at full speed to either wing that each must time itself by the centre, and forbade an advance upon the left or right until the high road should be forced and the centre of the Austrian position pierced or confused.

As he stood there looking down from the height where the road bifurcates, all the battle was plain to him, but his sapper's eye for a plan watched the wings much more anxiously than they watched the centre before him. The stunted spire of Wattignies a long way off to the east, the clump that hid St Remy to the west, marked strong bodies of the enemy, and, in the open plateau beyond, their numerous cavalry could crush either extremity of his line (which at either extremity was weak) should either be tempted forward before the centre had succeeded. The front was long—over five miles—he could not enforce sagacity nor even be certain of intelligence, and as he doubted and feared the action of his distant lieutenants, he saw the centre advancing beneath his eyes.

The Austrian cannon had abandoned the duel. The French line approached Dourlers, deployed, and began the ascent. A sudden and heavy fire of musketry from the hollow road and from the hedges met the sixteen thousand as they charged; they did not waver, they reached the garden walls, and closed until, to those watching from the hill, the attempt was confused and hidden by a rolling smoke and the clustered houses of the village. It was past mid-morning.

.　　　.　　　.　　　.　　　.

In Paris they had awakened the Queen, tardily. She wondered perhaps to see Busne not there. He had suffered arrest in the night; he was detained to see if he could tell the Court or the Committee some secret gathered from his prisoner. It was under another guard that she left her cell.

It was nearly nine before the Court assembled in the dull light, and later before the futile drag of evidence was renewed.

Whether sleep had revived her, or whether some remnant of her old energy had returned to her for such an occasion, no further weakness was perceived in the Queen. She sat, as she had sat all the day before until her faintness had come upon her, very ill, pale, and restrained, but erect and ready for every reply. Moreover, in that morning the weary monotony of such hours was broken by an incident which illuminated, though it made more bitter, the last of her sad days; for after D'Estaing, the Admiral, had been heard to no purpose, another noble, also a prisoner, was called; and as she saw his face she remembered better times, when the struggle was keen and not hopeless, and when this bewildering Beast that called itself now 'Freedom,' now 'The Nation,' had been tamed by the class which still governed Europe outside and which in that day controlled her kingdom also. It was La Tour du Pin, the soldier who had been responsible for the repression of the Mutiny at Nancy three years—three centuries—before.

He still lived. Against no man had '93 a better ground for hate, and indeed the time came when the Revolution sent him down also to meet his victims under the earth, but so far his commanding head was firm upon his shoulders. He enjoyed, as did all the prisoners of that time, the full use of his wealth. He was clothed and fed in the manner of his rank. He entered, therefore, with pride and with that mixture of gaiety and courage upon which, since the wars of religion, all his kind had justly plumed themselves: and as he entered he bowed with an excessive ceremony to the Queen.

The Judge asked him the formal question: Whether he recognized the prisoner? He bowed again and answered: 'Indeed I know this Lady very well'; and in a few moments of his examination he defended himself and her with a disdainful ease that brought Versailles vividly out of its tomb.

Revived or stung by such a memory, the Queen replied to
question after question exactly and even with some power:
upon her frivolities, her expenses, her Trianon—all the legends
of debauch which were based upon that very real and very
violent fugue of pleasure in which she had wasted her brilliant
years. The close of that dialogue alone has a strict interest
for history, when Herman came at last to the necklace. Trianon
had been on his lips a dozen times, and as he spoke the word
he remembered that other fatal thing:

'Was it not in Trianon that you first came to know the
woman La Motte?'

'I never saw her!'

'Was she not your victim in the affair of the necklace?'

'She could not be, for I had never known her!'

'You still deny it?'

'I have no plan to deny. It is the truth, and I shall
always say the same.'

It is a passage of great moment, for here indeed the prisoner
said precisely what was true and precisely what all, even those
who would befriend her, least believed to be true. She would
pretend a love for the French and a keen regard for their glory
—even for the success of their armies. She would pretend to
have obeyed the King and not to have led him; to have desired
nothing for her son, but only the welfare of the people. Trapped
and abandoned, she thought every answer, however false, legitimate; but in that one thing in which her very friends had
doubted her, another spirit possessed her and her words were
alive with truth.

After that episode no further movement followed. There
was opened before the Court (as the law compelled) her little
pocket and the trinkets taken from her on the day of her
imprisonment: the poor relics of her affection—the lock of hair,
the miniature—were laid before the Judges. They heard Simon,
the cobbler, in whose house her son was lodged—perhaps she
looked more curiously at his face than at others—but he had
nothing to say. They heard the porter of the Temple and
sundry others who had seen, or pretended to have seen, her
orders for the payments of sundry thousands—but all that
business was empty and all those hours were wasted: it was
not upon such vanities that the mind of Paris and of the crowded
Court was turned, but upon the line of Flemish hills a long way
off and upon the young men climbing up against the guns.

Paris and the mob in the street outside that Court of Justice and the hundreds crammed within it strained to hear, not Valazé, nor Tiset, nor any other useless witness, but some first breath of victory that might lift off them the oppression of those days; nay, some roaring news of defeat and of Coburg marching upon them: then at least, before their vision was scattered by the invader, they could tear this Austrian woman from her too lenient Judges for a full vengeance before they themselves and that which they had achieved should die. At the best or at the worst they panted for a clear knowledge of their fortune; but on through the day and well into the afternoon, when the Court rose for its brief interval, no hint or rumour even had come to Paris from before Maubeuge.

.   .   .   .   .   .

Carnot had come down the hill from the fork of the roads; he, and Jourdan beside him, followed behind the assault, bringing the headquarters of that general plan some half-mile forward. So they knew that the village of Dourlers was held. It was noon before the place was secured, and now all depended upon the action of the extreme wings.

It was certain that the struggle for this central village would be desperate: all depended upon the extreme wings. If these (and both of them) could hold hard and neither advance too far up the slope nor suffer (either of them) a beating-in, then the work at Dourlers would be decisive. And indeed the village was won, lost, and won and lost again: all the hard work was there. The French carried it, they went beyond, they were almost upon the ridge above it. In the upland field below the crest of wood the Austrian cavalry under Nuffling struck them in flank, and they were disordered. They were back in the village of Dourlers, and the fight for it was from house to house and from window to window. Twice it was cleared, twice lost. The French carry to an immortal memory a lad of fourteen who slipped forward in those attacks, got in behind the lines of the Hungarian Grenadiers who held the market-place, and, in lanes beyond, drummed the charge to make his comrades think that some were already so far forward and thus to urge them on. Many years after in digging up that ground his little bones were found buried side-long with the bones of the tall Hungarian men, and he has now his statue beating the charge and looking out towards the frontier from the gateways of Avesnes.

I have said that the horns of that crescent, the extreme wings, were ordered to be cautious, and warned that their

caution alone could save the fight; for if they went too far while
Dourlers in the centre was still doubtful, that centre would certainly be thrown back by such a general as Coburg, who knew
very well the breaking-point of a concave line. The fourth
attack upon Dourlers was prepared and would have succeeded
when Carnot heard that Fromentin, up on the far left, up on
the extreme tip of the horn of that crescent, had carried his
point of the ridge, and, having carried it, had had the folly to
pursue; he had found himself upon the plateau above (an open
plateau bare of trees and absolutely bare of cover) with his
irregulars all boiling, and even his regulars imagining success.
Weak in cavalry, commanding men untrained to any defensive,
he found opposed to him the cavalry reserve of the enemy—a
vast front of horse suddenly charging. That cavalry smashed
him all to pieces. His regulars here and there formed squares,
his irregulars tried to, they were sabred and galloped down.
They lost but four guns (though four counted in so under-
gunned an army), but, much worse, they lost their confidence
altogether. They got bunched into the combes and hollows,
the plateau was cleared. They in their turn were pursued, and
it would have been a rout but for two accidents: the first accident was the presence of a fresh reserve of French cavalry,
small indeed, but very well disciplined, strict and ready, certain
Hussars who in a red flash (their uniform was red) charged on
their little horses and for a moment stopped the flood of the
enemy. The check so given saved the lives though not the
position of the French left wing. It was beaten. It was
caved in.

The second accident was the early close of an October day.
The drizzling weather, the pall of clouds, curtained in an early
night, and the left thus failing were not wholly destroyed: but
their failure had ruined the value of the central charge upon
Dourlers. The final attack upon that central village was
countermanded; the Austrians did not indeed pursue the retreat
of the French centre from its walls and lanes, but the conception of the battle had failed.

   .   .   .   .   .

In the Court-room, in Paris, during those hours, while the
Judges raised the sitting, the Queen sat waiting for their return;
they brought her soup which she drank; the evening darkened,
the Judges reappeared, and the trial began anew.

The witnesses called upon that last evening, when the lights were lit and the long night had begun, were for the most part those who had come personally into the presence or into the service of the Queen. Michonis, especially, who was rightly under arrest for attempting her rescue, appeared; Brunier appeared, the doctor who had attended to the children in the Temple. The farce went on. The night grew deeper, the witnesses succeeded each other. All that they had to say was true. Nothing they said could be proved. One put forward that she had written some note asking if the Swiss could be relied upon to shoot down the people. She had said and written one hundred of such things. Her counsel, who were mere lawyers, worried about the presentation of the document —meanwhile night hastened onwards, and behind their veil of October cloud the stars continually turned.

.   .   .   .

Upon the frontier the damp evening and the closed night had succeeded one the other, and all along the valley of the little river it was foggy and dark. The dead lay twisted where they had fallen during that unwrought fight, and a tent pitched just behind the lines held the staff and Carnot. He did not sleep. There was brought to him in those midnight hours a little note, galloped in from the far south: he read it and crumpled it away. It is said to have been the news that the lines of Weissembourg were forced—and so they were. The Prussians were free to pass those gates between the Ardennes and the Vosges. Then Maubeuge was the last hold remaining: the very last of all.

Jourdan proposed, in that decisive Council of a few moments, held under that tent by lantern light in the foggy darkness while the day of their defeat was turning into the morrow, some plan for reinforcing the defeated left and the playing of some stalemate of check and countercheck against the enemy; but Carnot was big with new things. He conceived an adventure possible only from his knowledge of what he commanded; he dismissed the mere written traditions of war which Jourdan quoted, because he knew that now—and within twelve hours —all must certainly be lost or won. He took counsel with his own great soul, and called, from his knowledge of the French, upon the savagery and the laughter of the French service. He knew what abominable pain his scheme must determine. He knew by what wrench of discipline or rather of cruelty the thing must be done, but more profoundly did he know the temper of young French people under arms to whom the brutality of superiors is native and who meet it by some miraculous reserve of energy and of rebellious smiles.

Those young French people, many half-mutinous, most of them ill-clothed, so many wounded, so many more palsied by the approach of death—all drenched under the October drizzle, all by this time weary of any struggle whatsoever, were roused in that night before their sleep was deep upon them.

Carnot had determined to choose 7,000, to forbid them rest, to march them right along his positions and add them to the 8,000 on his right extreme wing, and then at morning, if men so treated could still charge, to charge with such overwhelming and unexpected forces on the right, where no such effort was imagined, and so turn the Austrian line.

There were no bugle-calls, no loud voice was permitted; but all the way down the line for five miles orders were given by patrols whose men had not slept for thirty hours. They roused the volunteers and the cursing regulars from the first beginnings of their sleep; they broke into the paltry comfort of chance bivouac fires; they routed men out of the straw in barns and stables; they kicked up the half-dead, half-sleeping boys who lay in the wet grass marshes of Tarsy; and during all that night, by the strength which only this service has found it possible to conceive (I mean a mixture of the degrading and the exalted, of servitude and of vision), from the centre and from the left—from the forces which had been shot down before Dourlers and from the men who had fled before the Austrian cavalry when Fromentin had failed—a corps was gathered together under the thick night, drawn up in column and bidden march through the darkness by the lane that led towards the right of the position. With what deep-rooted hatred of commandment simmering in them those fellows went after thirty hours of useless struggle to yet another unknown blind attempt, not historians but only men who have suffered such orders know. They were 7,000; the thick night, I say, was upon them; the mist lay heavy all over the wet land; and as they went through the brushwood and chance trees that separated the centre from the right of the French position, they heard the drip of water from the dead, hanging leaves. Their agony seemed to them quite wanton and purposeless. They were halted at last mechanically like sheep at various points under various sleeping farms in various deserted, tiny, lightless villages. The night was far spent; they could but squat despairing, each squadron at its halting-place waiting for the dawn and for new shambles. Meanwhile it was thick night.

. . . . .

It was nearing midnight in Paris, but none yet felt fatigue, neither the Judges nor their prisoner; nor did any in the straining audience that watched the slow determination of this business suffer the approach of sleep. The list of the witnesses was done and their tale was ended.

Herman leant forward, hawk-faced, and asked the Queen in the level judicial manner if she had anything to add to her defence before her advocates should plead. She answered complaining of the little time that had been afforded her to defend —and the last words she spoke to her Judges were still a vain repetition that she had acted only as the wife of the King and that she had but obeyed his will.

The Bench declared the examination of the witnesses closed. For something like an hour that bronzed and hollow-faced man next by her, Fouquier-Tinville, put forward the case for the Government; he was careful to avoid the mad evidence Hébert had supplied. When he sat down, the Defence spoke last— as has since Rome been the custom or rather the obvious justice of French procedure; so that the last words a Jury may hear shall be words for the prisoner at the bar—but this was not a trial, though all the forms of trial were observed. Chauveau Lagarde spoke first, his colleague next. When they had ceased they were arrested and forbidden to leave the building, lest certain words the Queen had whispered should mean some communication with the invader.

The summing up (for summing up was still permitted, and a century of Revolutionary effort was to pass before the pressure of the Bench upon the Jury should be gradually destroyed) was what the angers of that night expected and received. It was three o'clock in the morning before the four questions were put to the Jury. Four questions drawn indeed from the Indictment but avoiding its least proved or least provable clauses. Had there been relations between the Executive and the foreign enemies of the State, and promises of aid to facilitate the advance of their armies? If so, was Marie Antoinette of Austria proved to have been privy to that plan?

The Jury left the hall. A murmur of tongues loosened rose all around. The prisoner was led out beyond the doors of the chamber. For one long unexpected hour she was so detained while the Jury were still absent; then a signal was given to her guards and they led her in.

The cold violence of formal law still dominated the lawyers. Herman put forth the common exhortation of judges against applause or blame. He read to her the conclusions of the Jury: they were affirmative upon every point of the four. He asked her with that same cold violence of formality, after the Public Prosecutor had demanded the penalty of death set down for such actions as hers in the new Penal Code, whether she had anything to say against her sentence. She shook her head.

She was at the end of human things. She stood and saw the Judges upon the Bench conferring for a moment, she stood to hear her sentence read to her, and as she heard it she watched them in their strange new head-dress all plumes, and she fingered upon the rail before her with the gestures ladies learn in fingering the keys: she swept her fingers gently as though over the keys of an instrument, and soon the reading of the sentence was done and they led her away. It was past four o'clock in the morning.

On the terrace of his castle in Germany that night George of Hesse saw the White Lady pass, the Ghost without a face that is the warning of the Hapsburgs, and the hair of his head stood up.

.   .   .   .   .

The long dark hours of the morning still held the troops that had marched over from the left to the right of the French position before Maubeuge. The first arrivals had some moments in which to fall at full length on the damp earth in the extremity of their fatigue, but all the while the later contingents came marching in until, before it was yet day but when already the farms about knew that it was morning, and when the cocks had begun to crow in the steadings, all rose and stood to arms. The mist was deepening upon them, a complete silence interpenetrated the damp veil of it, nor through such weather were any lights perceptible upon the heights above which marked the end of the Austrian line.

.   .   .   .   .

The Queen went down the stone steps of the passage: she entered regally into the cell made ready. She called without interval for pen and paper, and she sat down to write. She felt, after the transition from the populous Court to the silence of those walls, an energy that was not natural and that could not endure, but that served her for an inspiration. She had tasted but a bowl of soup since the morning—nay, since the evening before, thirty hours—soon she must fail. Therefore she wrote quickly while her mood was still upon her.

She sat and wrote to her dead husband's sister the letter which, alone of all her acts, lends something permanently noble to her name. It is a run of words exalted, dignified, and yet tremendous, nor does any quality about that fourfold sheet of writing, yellow with years, more astound the reader than the quality of revelation: for here something strong and level in her soul, something hitherto quite undiscovered, the deepest part of all, stands and shines. The sheet is blurred—perhaps with tears: we do not know whether ever it was signed or ended; but before the morning came she laid herself upon her bed in her poor black dress, her head was raised somewhat upon her right hand, and so lying she began very bitterly to weep.

The priest of St Landry, the parish church of the prison, entered to minister to her: she spoke just such few words to him as might assure her that he had sworn the civic oath and was not in communion. When she knew this she would not hear him. But he heard her murmuring against the bitter cold, and bade her put a pillow upon her feet. She did so and was again silent.

The hours wore on, the scent of newly lighted fires came from the prison yard and the noise of men awakening. The dripping of the damp weather sounded less in the increase of movement, and on the pavement of the quays without began the tramp of marching and the chink of arms; from further off came the rumble of the drums: 30,000 were assembling to line her Way. The two candles showed paler in the wretched room. It was dawn.

.   .   .   .   .

The 16th of October broke upon the Flemish hills: the men who had endured that night-march along the front of the battlefield, the men who had received them among the positions of the extreme right, still drooped under the growing light and were invigorated by no sun. The mist of the evening and of the night from dripping and thin had grown dense and whitened with the morning, so that to every soldier a new despair and a new bewilderment were added from the very air, and the blind fog seemed to make yet more obscure the obscure designs of their commanders. The day of their unnatural vigil had dawned, and yet there came no orders nor any stirring of men. Before them slow schistous slopes went upwards and disappeared into the impenetrable weather which hid clogged ploughland and drenched brushwood of the rounded hill; hollow lanes led up through such a land to the summit of the little rise and the hamlet of Wattignies; this most humble and least of villages was waiting its turn for glory.

The downward slope which formed the eastern end of the Austrian line, the low rounded slope whose apex was the spire of the village, was but slightly defended, for it was but the extreme of a position, and who could imagine then—or who *now* —that march through the sleepless night, or that men so worn should yet be ready for new action with the morning? No reinforcement, Coburg knew, could come from behind that army: and how should he dream that Carnot had found the power to feed the fortunes of the French from their own vitals and to drag these shambling 7000, wrenched from west to east during the darkness: or how, if such a thing had been done, could any man believe that, such a torture suffered, the 7,000 could still charge?

Yet, had Coburg known the desperate attempt he would have met it, he would have covered that ultimate flank of his long ridge and reinforced it from his large reserve. But the deep mist and the dead silence harshly enforced during the night-march had hidden all the game, and in front of Wattignies, holding that round of sloping fields and the low semicircular end of the ridge before the village, there were but 3,000; the infantry of Klebek, of Hohenlohe, and of Stern; for their cavalry they had behind them and alongside of the village farms a few dragoons; certain Croatian battalions stood in a second line. These in that morning, expecting nothing but perhaps the few troops as they had met easily the day before, waited under the mist in formation and heard no sound. The morning broadened; the white vapour seemed lighter all around, but no voices could be heard, nor did there come up through its curtain any rumble of limber from the roads below.

. . . . .

As the Queen so lay disconsolate and weeping bitterly, stretched in her black gown upon the wretched bed and supporting her head upon her hand, there came in the humble girl who had served her faithfully and who was now almost distraught for what was to come. This child said:

'You have not eaten all these hours. . . . What will you take now that it is morning?'

The Queen answered, still crying: 'My child, I need nothing more: all is over now.'

But the girl added: 'Madam, I have kept warm upon the hob some soup and vermicelli. Let me bring it you.' The Queen, weeping yet more, assented.

She sat up a moment (but feebly—her mortal fatigue had come upon her—her loss of blood increased and was continued), she took one spoonful and another; soon she laid the nourishment aside, and the morning drew on to her death.

She must change for her last exit. So much did the Revolution fear to be cheated of its defiance to the Kings that the warders had orders not to lose sight of her for one moment: but she would change. She would go in white to her end.

The girl who had served her screened her a little, and in the space between the bed and the wall she crouched and put on fresh linen, and in place of her faded black a loose white muslin gown. Her widow's head-dress also, in which she had stood proudly before her Judges, she stripped of its weeds, and kept her hair covered by no more than the linen cap.

Her Judges came in and read to her her sentence.

The executioner, awkward and tall, came in. He must bind her hands. 'Why must you bind my hands? The King's hands were not bound.' Yet were her hands bound and the end of the rope left loose that her jailer might hold it: but she perhaps herself, before they bound her, cut off the poor locks of her hair.

They led her out past the door of the prison: she was 'delivered' and signed for; on the steps before the archway she went up into the cart, hearing the crowd howling beyond the great iron gates of the Law Courts, and seeing seated beside her that forsworn priest to whom she would not turn. . . . Nor were these the last humiliations: but I will not write them here.

Up and down the passages of the prison a little dog whom she had cherished in her loneliness ran whining and disconsolate.

The cart went lumbering on, past the quay, over the bridge under the murky drizzle. The windows beyond the river were full of heads and faces; the edges of the quays were black with the crowd. The river Seine ran swollen with the rains; its tide and rolling made in such weather no mark upon the water-walls of stone. The cart went lumbering on over the rough wet paving of the northern bank. It turned into the Rue St Honoré, where the narrow depth was full of noise. The long line of troops erect and close upon either side. The dense crowd still roared behind them: their prey sat upon the plank, diminished, as erect as the constraint of her bonds and her failing strength would allow. Her lips, for all their droop of agony, were still proud; her vesture was new; her delicate high shoes had been chosen with care for that journey—but her face might have satisfied them all. The painted red upon her cheeks was dreadful against her utter paleness: from beneath the linen of her cap a few whitened wisps of hair hung dank upon her hollowed temples: a Victim. Her eyes were sunken, and of these one dully watched her foes, one had lost its function in the damp half-darkness of the cells: it turned blank and blind upon the rabble that still followed the walking jolt of the two cart-horses and the broad wheels. At the head of those so following, an actor-fellow pranced upon a horse, thrusting at her by way of index a sword, and shouting to the people that they held the tigress here, the Austrian. In the midst of those so following, an American eager to see elbowed his way and would not lose his vantage. From the windows of the narrow gulf a continued noise of wonder, of jeers, and of imprecations reached her. She still sat motionless and without speech: the executioner standing behind her holding the loose end of the cord, the forsworn priest sitting on the plank beside her but hearing no words of hers.

It is said that as the tumbril passed certain masts whence limp tricolour pendants hung she glanced at them and murmured a word; it is to be believed that, a few yards further, at the turn into the Rue Royale, she gave way at the new sight of the Machine set up for her before the palace gardens.

This is known, that she went up the steps of the scaffold at liberty and stood for a bare moment seen by the great gathering in the square, a figure against the trees of what had been her gardens and the place where her child had played. It was but a moment, she was bound and thrown, and the steel fell.

.   .   .   .   .

On the low mud and slope of Wattignies the mist began to wreathe and thin as the hours approached high noon. Through gaps of it the three Austrian regiments could see trees now and then in the mid-distance, showing huge, and in a moment covered again by new whorls of vapour. But still there was no sound. In front of them towards Dimont, to their left round the corner of the slope in the valley of Glarges, with every lift of vapour the landscape became apparent, when suddenly, as the mist finally lifted, the wide plain showed below them rolling southwards, a vast space of wind and air, and at the same moment they heard first bugles, then the shouts of command, and lastly the rising of the *Marseillaise*: Gaul was upon them.

The sleepless men had been launched at last, the hollow lanes were full of them swarming upwards: the fields were ribbed with their open lines, and as they charged they sang.

Immortal song! The pen has no power over colour or over music, but though I cannot paint their lively fury or make heard their notes of triumph, yet I have heard them singing: I know the place, and I have seen their faces as they cleared the last hedges of the rise and struck the 3,000 upon every side.

These stood, wavered, fell back to re-form: then they saw new masses of the Republicans roaring up from Glarges behind their flank, broke and were scattered by the storm. The few heavy guns of the Austrians there emplaced were trained too late to check the onrush. The little pieces of the climbing and the surging men were dragged by laniards, unmasked behind gaps in the hurrying advance, crashed grape and were covered again for a moment by the living cover of the charge. The green at the hilltop was held, the poor yards and byres of Wattignies were scoured and thundered through, and Carnot, his hat upon his sword, and Duquesnoy, his face half blood, and all the host gloried to find before them in their halting midday sweat when the great thrust was over, the level fields of the summit, the Austrian line turned, and an open way between them and Maubeuge.

Two charges disputed their certain victory. First the Hungarian cavalry galloped and swerved and broke against the dense and ever denser bodies that still swarmed up three ways at once and converged upon the crested edge of the upland plain; then the Royal Bourbon, emigrants, nobles, swept upon the French, heads down, ready to spend themselves largely into death. They streamed with the huge white flag of the old Monarchy above them, and on it the faint silver lilies, and from either rank the cries that were shouted in defiance were of the same tongue which since Christendom began has so perpetually been heard along all the battle fronts of Christendom.

.   .   .   .

These also failed: a symbol in name and in flag and in valour of that great, once good, and very ancient thing which God now disapproved.

The strong line of Coburg was turned. It was turned and must roll back upon itself. Its strict discipline preserved it, as did the loose order of the Republican advance and the maddened fatigue of the young men who had just conquered: for these could work a miracle but not yet achieve a plan. The enemy fell back in order, sombre, massed and regular, unharassed, towards the Sambre. The straggling French soldiery, wondering that the fighting had ceased (but wisely judged incapable of pursuit), possessed the main road unhindered; next day they drank with their comrades in Maubeuge.

In this way was accomplished what a principal critic of the art of war [1] has called 'The chief feat of arms of the Republic.'

It was somewhat past noon.

. . . . .

Upon that scaffold before the gardens which had been the gardens of her home and in which her child had played, the Executioner showed at deliberation and great length, this way and that on every side, the Queen's head to the people.

[1] Napoleon Buonaparte.

THE COLD

WHENEVER men are passionate in the discussion of the past they will receive and establish falsehood upon either side of that discussion.

The Retreat from Moscow gave rise to a legend very firmly established in the European mind for a century, that the great and undefeated enemy of the Emperor was the Cold. Every picture of that disaster is a picture of blood-tracks in the snow, and of dull, frozen horizons, and of bare wastes sterile with Cold. The modern critic (whose chief offence it is that he does not understand tradition) has pretended to reverse this permanent and established legend; and more than one writer (concerned it would seem, only to belittle what is great, with no power himself to perceive or to enkindle) makes out that return to Europe to have been commonplace enough for weather. Such contradictions suit our times and their jaded itch for paradox.

Now the truth is here what the truth is in nearly every legend, in nearly every great tradition. Such legends represent whatever grew rooted in the minds of those who actually suffered, saw, and did the thing; but contemporary suffering and doing invariably falsifies the numerical proportion of things. Hence it is easy for the critic, following day by day the changes of that winter, to show how much of the efforts in which the last of the Grand Army dissolved were free from that chief terror which loomed up so very high in the recollection of the men that really met it—the Cold. Nevertheless, the legend is the truth and its criticism is the falsehood. The Cold *was* the abominable thing: the dreadful enemy against which men could not fight and which destroyed them.

The winter of 1812 came later than do most winters of Central Russia. One may even say that there was a sort of benignity in the air, lasting far longer than, in the short autumn of those plains, Napoleon had right to hope for. The season, I say, was late, propitiously as it seemed. But the gods mocked. When winter came it came not only with a suddenness and a severity, but also in such a juncture that all the remaining lifetime of one who survived the snow was haunted by it. It was at the end of the first week in November, just as the Retreat began to be pressed, confused, and most perilous, that the Cold struck. In what fashion it struck, and after what a sequence of days, I shall now proceed to describe.

.   .   .   .   .

When after Maloyaroslavetz the now ninety thousand or less turned backward and northward to make for the Smolensk road, they still had above and around them the lovely October weather which had blessed all the last days in Moscow and the initial vain attempt to slip past Kutusoff and carry the stores of Kaluga. My readers will remember how the hazy and quiet skies of that week had been broken by the one bad day of rain— a day that coincided with the Western movement by which Napoleon had slipped from the eastern to the western road, in the hope of eluding the vigilance of the Russian cavalry.

Now that the Retreat had begun in earnest, this fair weather continued, one might almost say, to *ensnare* the host. At any rate, it made possible the haste of the withdrawal. The sharp early mornings were hazy as were the evenings, in which great suns set through brume upon the wooded horizons of those empty, slightly rolling leagues of land. One day after another such suns set slowly in the west, to which the column was hurrying.

It was a march morally anxious, but not yet pressed, with the enemy hovering near, and now and then striking home; his main force some twenty miles away. We must imagine the Grand Army, in broad, irregular, parallel belts, darkening the open land for miles and miles: men, wagons, and guns, a convoy not yet exhausted, arms still borne by the most part, the as yet undiminished host came once more to the battlefield of Borodino. They had fought there seven weeks before.

Three years on, in the rout after Waterloo, the last army of Napoleon was to see a similar sight. The broken men, pouring in the moonlight down the Charleroi road, stumbled in panic past the naked corpses of Quatre-Bras. So here at Borodino, in full daylight, the miles of straggling broad columns hurried past, and contemporaries have recorded for us the odd silence in which all this great number of men pressed forward to be rid of that sight (and worse) with its memories: for the forty thousand dead lay many of them unburied and still packed in heaps—after nearly two months.

The fighting had been desperately close; there was the great redoubt, pestiferous; there were the southern fieldworks outlined in what was left of horses, of saddles, of sodden uniforms, and of what once were men. The metal had suffered least, but the swords also were rusted. Some sabres still, they say, lay clenched in the bones of the hands that had held them when Murat charged; the leather thong that holds the sword was caught corrupted about the corrupted wrist.

By the evening of the fourth day of the Retreat all that battlefield was passed, and wonderfully eased were those driven men to have passed it!

That evening also was an evening of fine weather still enduring, fresh but clear. The bivouacs were possible enough.

Three days later came the first bad pressure. A whole section of the army was cut off by the pursuers. It was compelled to fight its way back; and did so at last with loss but success. The French dignified that day by the name of a general action, and even, in the case of some regiments, I think, recorded that action upon the colours. But not this feat of self-preservation, nor even the now perpetual anxiety which the enemy had planted in the mind of Napoleon and of his men, nor anything that had as yet come to them in their backward march to the west, was comparable to that which fell in the night between 5th and 6th November: not the road, which the rearguard (now under the command of Grenet) found strewn with an odd trail of books, of vessels of gold and of silver, of pictures, of arms and all that was shed from the loot; not the surface which, traversed already for months by the upward march to Moscow and the innumerable train, was becoming with every mile more and more detestable; not the ominous serving out of horse flesh to the Guard and the threat of short rations; not even the snow which had already begun to fall abundantly, in advance of what was coming, and to impede the marching of the soldiers—none of these things, I say, counted, compared with what befell upon the 5th after darkness had fallen. This was the Cold.

The bivouacs were formed upon the snow, still tolerable enough. The rearguard stood outside the defile through the great forest of Viasma, protecting the passage of the army. A thick fog descended. The sentries felt for the first time no longer discomfort, even of that acute and gnawing sort which seems to those who read of it under civilian conditions to be a hell; what they felt as the night advanced was a thing new to them, and perfectly intolerable to humankind—a thing no Westerner among them had yet known—the winter advancing from out of Asia, from the Frozen Steppes.

It came through the thick fog like something sentient. It had come out of the east, striding. It had caught them up. In the silence, in the wrapping of dense cloud (so dense that the bivouac fires on the snow were not to be seen one from another) Cold caught the whole world, and killed men where they lay.

Men talk of having breathed that night an air itself freezing, and of having felt the rasp of that air, so that at last they could only breathe through the coverings of the mouth.

When, after such hours of agony and of death's beginnings, the fog, a little thinner, was dully mixed with a first light of morning, the intensity of that pain was lifted. The march of the next day (passing from fog to further driving snow in a high wind), though lamentable enough to men now disarmed by the hundred and the thousand, and to stragglers falling out continually as they stumbled through the drifts, is recorded to have been warmer. The first blow of that enemy had spent itself, being too hard; but the enemy had come, and though I have described him with violence, I have not exaggerated his power. With great pressure and less, now lifting his hand, now striking hard again, he felled the men of the Grand Army by packets and by groups until—more than the Cossack and much more than the formed bodies of Russians (who did not sufficiently press the Retreat)—Cold had destroyed the command of Napoleon altogether.

VENDÉMIAIRE

The army in the South knew the name of Buonaparte, but Paris hardly knew it as yet. It was he that had largely assured the triumph at Toulon; but there were others to be remembered besides him, and far more widely spoken of. Moreover the Parliament would be suspicious of new names. Within a few weeks of Toulon the remarkable youth—he was twenty-four—had been made a General Officer—as yet but a Brigadier; and immediately he had stumbled upon an accident. Though he had refused to come to Paris, his friendship with the younger Robespierre, when that Parliamentarian had been sent south to Toulon, linked his name with him whom the public at least believed (they were wrong) to be the head of the Terror. When the Terror ended in Thermidor, the high summer of the next year, 1794, the names of Buonaparte and the two Robespierres, just guillotined, were mixed. He was arrested in those days, imprisoned in the fort at Antibes, released, proposed for the inglorious work of fighting against the Royalist rebels in La Vendée, refused the task, and was taken off the list of generals on active service.

He was falling into obscurity; his name was now hardly heard; the Committee of Public Safety gave him some small salary in the geographical department of the Army; thereon he lived, but now with some few of his young companions, notably Junot—still apart, lodged in a poor hotel recalling those rooms of his first lonely poverty in Paris, near the Halles (the lodging-house still stands), for a few pence a day. (He recalled in after years how, ashamed of his poverty, he would push the payment for his meal across the table wrapped in a scrap of paper, so that no one from a neighbouring table should see how little he was spending.) So much at a loose end was he that he had thoughts of asking leave to take service with the Sultan, in the Near East, where an instructor from the French Artillery might be well paid. But in this period of early eclipse, in this same year '94, he did a thing which should have been immediately most famous, most renowned, but which passed for the moment quite unknown.

It was this:

Those were the days when the Republic must defend itself desperately against its chief enemy, the Empire, the Austrians; among other fronts (of which the Rhine was chief) it must at least hold, and if possible advance upon, the line of the Alps in Italy, where a portion of the Austrian forces, worked from their Milanese possessions in Lombardy, allied with Piedmont against France. The young General, from his seclusion, drew up a memorandum, a plan for that campaign, a scheme whereby the enemy in the Lombard Plain should be struck not directly from across the Alps of Mont Cénis and the Mont Genèvre, but from the south, in flank, over the Genoese Ligurian hills. The authorities (or perhaps only that one man who saw it) could make nothing of it, and set it aside at first for a folly. Later Carnot, the true military brain of those years, was to see it and remark it. It was the basis of all the coming marvels, the prophecy of Lodi, of Rivoli, of Arcole.

As he so lay, reaching the end of his resources and his patience, Fate again intervened.

It was nearly two years since Toulon. It was the beginning of October '95, Vendémiaire of the year IV of Liberty (and V of Equality), when to the Sections of Paris both the Equality and the Liberty allowed them seemed insufficient.

They were prepared to rise against the Governing Power, that Parliamentary Assembly called 'The Convention,' which had led the Revolution to its height and still ruled.

The discontent of the Sections of Paris with the Convention came about thus:

The Parliamentarians had to save themselves from a menacing future. They had put a King to death. They had made an economic as well as a political revolution, selling the goods of the emigrants and the clergy. Huge fortunes had arisen upon these sales as also upon speculations, upon furnishing the armies, and by all the avenues which, in times of civil and foreign wars, serve to enrich the worst—especially when political lawyers and orators rather than soldiers govern. By their theory, they, the members of the Convention, were but the voice of the nation and could be replaced by its vote—but if that vote were adverse they were doomed—and it might be adverse: men might grow tired of their enthusiasm.

After the execution of Robespierre, after the accidental upsetting of the Terror by those who most desired to continue the Terror, the reaction began in spite of them, and it might grow formidable.

On this account the Parliamentarians had framed an artificial constitution, belying their own principles, but safeguarding themselves. They had committed treason to the goddess whom they professed to worship, forbidding the popular voice to be fully heard, insisting that of their number two-thirds must remain and only one-third be re-elected—and this they did lest —now that the tide was ebbing out fully against the exaltation of the high revolutionary years—the popular voice should bring them to book for what they had done, but especially for the killing of the King.

The Jacobin fury was exhausted; a change in the mind of Paris was apparent, and the Sections or Districts of the Capital, forty-eight in number, each of which could put forward a battalion of a thousand bayonets, were, for the most part (more than two-thirds of them), prepared to march against the politicians. These had, to defend them, of regular forces hardly one-fifth of the bayonets which the insurgents could oppose; and as for the guns of the National Guard, they were parked two miles away on the sandy heights outside Paris to the west, near where the Trocadero now stands but somewhat upon the farther side; it was a district then unbuilt on and far from the city itself; it was called the 'Sablons.'

The day was the 12th Vendémiaire (4th October), and the attack menaced for the morrow. The Parliament, at its wits' end for a soldier, mistrusted Menou, the commander of its insufficient force; he had refused to fire upon 'The People,' he had parleyed with them, in particular with the armed section of the Filles-Saint-Thomas, where the Bourse now stands. And its position made it that one of the sections which the Parliament most dreaded, it stood, with one other, its neighbour, due north of the Tuileries where the Convention sat: on the other, south side, of the Palace was the obstacle of the river, but on this north side there was nothing. From those sections the narrow streets led everywhere directly down towards the Palace. No, the unpopular politicians could not trust Menou, they accused him of treason, and, whether it were from weakness or from a secret Royalism, he was clearly of worse than no service to them. The night fell, and there remained only the hours of that night—for, the next day, the thing would be decided.

There sat upon the benches of that Parliament one Barras whom we saw before Toulon, known to Buonaparte and Buonaparte to him; a man already of middle age, full-bodied, square-faced, firm-eyed, with presence; courageous enough, a noble of the old régime: like so many of them rotten with debts but perhaps also not insincere in his enthusiasm for the Revolution into which he had thrown himself. He had the manners, the luxury, the corrupt morals of his class and of the drawing-rooms before '89; but he had also decision, and still more, a strong determination to save his own neck, for he would have been the first victim if the Royalist insurrection—for it had become that—were to prove master of Paris.

This same Barras, now a wealthy man, had had the necessary daring to march upon the Town Hall fifteen months before in the critical hours of Thermidor, when Robespierre had been outlawed. His name could not but be on all their lips. They put him at the head of their few thousand bayonets, and bade him go to work.

Now Barras was a clear-headed because a cynical man.

He liked to swagger in a uniform but he had no illusions upon his capacity as a soldier nor any belief in his nominal rank of Brigadier-General. He *did* know of what military value the submerged young Buonaparte had proved, for already in the Committee of Public Safety Carnot had reiterated his name. Moreover they had met, for that morning Napoleon had seen Barras a few minutes and when, during that critical night, there was a question of joining a subsidiary to Barras, Carnot suggested certain names, Buonaparte's among them. Napoleon that evening was at the play, in the Théâtre Feydou, only a stone's throw from the place where Menou had been parleying with the insurgents. Barras sent for him and the young man, paler than ever, thinner than ever, suffering from that gunner's skin disease which he had caught at Toulon and which proved obstinate, his eyes now more fiery from disappointment than they were wont to be in the Toulon days, appeared before him. Buonaparte knew all that had passed, he had come—mixing with the public—to watch the debates in the Palace.

Barras asked him whether he would take command, and in doing so he put the dilemma: if Buonaparte would aid in suppressing the popular revolt and should succeed, it was a gate to promotion: if he failed it would mean death—for the insurrection would not spare its opponents. The two men, the younger and the older, the large one with already so much power, and the lesser frail, short, dark one standing in his presence with as yet no holding ground at all, faced each other. There was a silence of less than three minutes during which the young Napoleon weighed with a racing mind the balance of fortune either way. He decided for the risk. To him the parties were indifferent but not the task: he knew himself well fitted for the task. He saw at once what Thiers, in a similar crisis of the Commune a lifetime later, failed to see—the gunner saw that it was a question of guns. Now the guns far down the river on the Sablons hill, away outside the town, were as yet with neither party. Against the guns the bayonets of the sections would not be powerless. The guns might be rushed, and indeed, in what followed, pieces were taken and retaken; but the guns would at least restore even chances between the 30,000 bayonets of the revolt and the 6,000 or less of the Parliament; especially if the guns should be in the hands of men who knew them, pitted against civilians with muskets. If the guns were seized by the Insurgents they *must* succeed.

There was immediately at hand a tall fierce energetic young cavalry officer, Murat by name; he was sent off in the small hours for the guns with a sufficient force. The sections also had bethought them of the guns, but Murat and his men, galloping through the night, got to the Sablons a quarter of an hour ahead. Still in those very early hours the horses were harnessed, the drivers were mounted, and the sixty pieces were led back along the riverside towards the Palace gardens and the issues of the street bridges. The rumble and clatter of the artillery wheels over the stone pavements was loud enough but gave no warning —or if it did, what was there to set against the guns?

Before it was day the bridges were held and all the approaches to the Parliament: there was a battery at each bridge-head whereby any of the sections south of the river could arrive; there was a battery at the gate of the Palace park where it overlooked what is to-day the Place de la Concorde; there was a battery at each issue of the narrow streets coming from the most dangerous of the sections down on to the Tuileries from the north; notably was there a battery in what was then the Rue du Dauphin and what is now the Rue St Roch, between the Church and the Tuileries Gardens the most direct point for an assault on the Palace. During that day (5th October, 13th Vendémiaire) the Parliament still hesitated; the soldiers were not free to act. The politicians, in their bewilderment and lack of unity, even allowed deputations to come through the cordon and discuss with them some terms of settlement. But there was no arrangement. The armed men of the sections without grew exasperated with the delay and turbulent. Somewhere about half-past four in the afternoon the first shot was heard from down along the quay-side by the Louvre, and with that a general attack began.

Buonaparte himself was with the battery facing the Church of St Roch—that is immediately at the north end of the Palace, the approach from which attack would be most dangerous. Here also were the two sections best organized and best armed and politically most determined. Nor was the struggle settled by a mere discharge of grape against the citizens, for these fought hard, one of the young General's guns was taken under his eyes and had to be retaken as best might be; his horse was shot under him: but during the welter, while the day was fast failing, he manœuvred a couple of pieces round in the Rue St Honoré upon the flank of the fighting, and that was what broke the advancing tide of the rebellion in this narrow space. Canister did it.

It was the same at all other points, dispersed along the surroundings of the Palace by the riverside and the bridge-heads as well as along the north.

When the early dark was falling, between six and seven o'clock, the struggle had ceased; save here and there a further sound where fugitives were being pursued—men who had taken refuge in the buildings at hand. Before it was fully dark all was over and the Parliament was saved; those converging columns of the insurgent bayonets had been everywhere broken by the guns.

It was Napoleon who had seen to it; it was Napoleon who had inspired the guns; when Murat had gone off to bring them, galloping up to the Sablons and back through the darkness and setting them all in order before dawn across the bridges. Napoleon, till then second in command, took over the army of Paris—and now indeed he was known.

AUSTERLITZ

A MILE or two out of Boulogne, along the great highway to Paris, there stands at Pont de Briques, on the right, a charming little house, modest, classical, retired. Therein lay the Emperor during those summer days of 1805 when, after so long a peace in Europe, the coalition was forming which should once more challenge the Revolution and its captain.

It was yet dark, some time after four in the morning of 13th August, when news arrived: the French fleet, which was expected under Villeneuve in the Channel, had turned back to Ferrol. Of Napoleon's double plan, his alternatives, the invasion of England was in graver doubt than ever—Villeneuve had not understood the essential factor of Time. The Emperor was halted by the check. The coalition formed upon the other side, inland, grew stronger and threatened from the east: Russia and Austria would be upon him.

He sent for Daru, who found him in a flame of anger, with his hat pulled down hard to his brows and his eyes flashing and his lips, as he furiously paced the room, pouring imprecations upon Villeneuve. These exhausted, he made a sudden stop, and said abruptly: 'Sit down and write.'

Daru sat him down, pen in hand, at a desk laden with notes and papers, and then received and took down under the dawn an astonishing piece of dictation—no less than all the plan of the march against Austria, the advance which was to triumph at Austerlitz. Every stage of the vast enterprise, its halts and its separate roads, numbers, the dates of each arrival, poured out for hours, without notes to guide the memory, till the whole campaign was there, down on paper and concluded. Later, when this maze in one man's head, this idea, passed into reality and became things done, Daru marvelled as date after date fell due, was met, like a prophecy fulfilled.

.   .   .   .   .   .

It was the end of the first week of September 1805. The Grand Army had broken up from before the Channel. It had marched across Europe by its parallel roads at fifteen miles a day with the precision of a machine, all the map which Napoleon had held vividly before his mind during the spate of dictation in that charming little house by the highway out of Boulogne. Every march was effected as it had been planned, and the Grand Army was sweeping forward to the Danube; but the dance of its drums and bugles and the clatter of its horse and limbers had sent no sufficient echo before them. Mack, in Ulm, had been trapped by mid-October in the net so swiftly cast around him, and had surrendered; the fruit of this first almost silent and complete success was fifty thousand prisoners, disarmed.

But there remained to the east down the valley the hosts of Russia and the free Austrian contingents combined with them. Would not Prussia add her army to these? It was a power which every soldier in Europe still regarded as the model of soldiery, and the most formidable force in the world. Would not its present chief and King, Frederick William, arrive in arms side by side with the Czar?

A week after Ulm it already seemed that such united strength would be opposed to the conqueror, and the King of Prussia be found with all his men, coming down from the north to save Austria, the Emperor, and brother-in-arms with that young Emperor of Russia whose thousands were already in the field.

Prussia, the Queen of Prussia, had got them together on a November night—two days after the Day of the Dead, 4th November 1805. In the crypt of the army church, the garrison church of Potsdam, lies buried that great perverted captain, who for his talents in war is justly called the Great, Frederick—not so long dead. Here in that crypt, and before that tomb, the Queen of Prussia, beautiful and still young, had staged a scene worth playing. Under the Queen's arrangement Alexander the Czar and Frederick William swore firm friendship against that new portent or god who was threatening to destroy or to restore the world. Prussia should reinforce the two Emperors; her hardened steel of an army, the tradition of which was still so strong a thing throughout Europe, should be thrust forward 150,000 strong, as the spear-point of the Kings.

And a thing was to be done which should put stuff into the plan: Napoleon was to be summoned, and if he would not yield to be destroyed. Were there not several fortunes—the common fortune of the ancient world—to be defended? And in the vision of that woman this common cause would certainly prevail. Haugwitz was to be sent to present that summons, but to call it 'peace.'

Was it intended that the summons should succeed?

Had Napoleon yielded to it he was beaten in the conflict. Was it intended by Prussia that if Napoleon rejected it all the three Kings (Russia, Prussia, and Austria) should march shoulder to shoulder, and make certain of success? The Queen of Prussia thought so—but she was not Prussia, and Prussian steel is cold. Prussia, when confident of victory, will make war at once, and ruthlessly; it is her trade and her principle of being: but though she is of steel, that steel, I say, is cold, and this cold calculation lay below the surface: 'The two Emperors combined can do the work, and doubtless they will do it. But even victors lose blood and are exhausted. If we stand aside watching the struggle, the final settlement will be ours.'

It is a calculation often made, and is better fitted to wrestling than to earthquakes. Now it was an earthquake, and not a wrestling-match that was to come. Or again, a man that has lost blood in a duel may be succoured to the profit of the one that comes in aid; but what profit can there be in coming to the succour of one who has been stricken by a thunderbolt? And it was a thunderbolt that was about to fall.

.   .   .   .   .   .

Lightning that falls from heaven is a vivid thing, and its blinding flash, to one who has seen it strike and destroy, is memorable for ever.

The mechanics of the awful thing, an analysis of its action and causes is grey and unmoving, but it is of high interest, because, as Napoleon also said: '*Why* and *how*, are words so important that they cannot be too often used.'

Let us examine, before we look on the storm of Austerlitz, what plan of victory that was which underlay the triumph.

.   .   .   .   .   .

Every man devoted to some particular art, and having high skill therein, nourishes some model, some type, of its execution. It is so with painters and with poets. It may with any man, however gifted, degenerate into a repetition and a trick. But all creative men have it; and in Napoleon's mind there had floated for years the conception of a model battle, a master-piece of grand tactics.

We do not know this from any affirmation of his, from any essay; but it may be deduced from the way in which he wrote of past action, and from the form which his criticism of others would take.

In particular it is of the highest interest to see how after Marengo that action transformed itself in his imagination. It was the experience of Marengo that haunted him, and raised this image of a perfect action in his mind. He wrote and re-wrote, modifying and remodifying, his account of Marengo. With every recension of the account he thinks of it more and more, as though it had been planned—which it was not—on the lines of this ideal combination to which he returns throughout his wars. As we know, Marengo was not planned at all: victory there was a gift of fortune and a mighty hazard: yet Marengo inspired him through all the future. He, there, at Marengo galloping in his bright blue coat, and with loud voice rallying the hard-pressed, half-defeated, wavering lines, till Desaix came in at the last desperate hour and turned the tide— this was the picture ever before his mind, and the result from which he drew his lesson; his model of what a victory should be.

This model of his, formed from Marengo, was what may be called a 'Pivot Battle.'

Its essential was the swinging of a line back upon the hinge of some impregnable point at one extremity, while the other extremity (the marching wing) either fallen back under pressure or voluntarily retired should lead the enemy to stretch his line further and further on in an attempt to get round. This 'stretching' would necessarily and progressively weaken the enemy centre. When this situation had developed to the point where his own line was in peril of outflanking, there should fall upon the enemy, so pressing forward on one extremity, the surprise of an unexpected reserve left, detached from the general body and coming suddenly into action. The falling of that new, additional, weight at the critical point should determine the issue. The enemy would find himself entangled just where he most hoped for success; his strength would be still further drawn towards the threatened point, his centre would be still further weakened, and, by the choice of the right moment, might be pierced. This done, the enemy forces were broken into two fractions, each unable to support the other, and at the mercy of the still united army which had separated them. The Pivotal Battle would end as victory through dislocation.

To such a model Austerlitz came nearest of all the great Napoleonic fields. It was that one in which the enemy most did what Napoleon had hoped he would do, that one in which the surprise of the suddenly appearing reserve force was most fully calculated and most exactly brought into play, that one

THE MANŒUVRE OF AUSTERLITZ

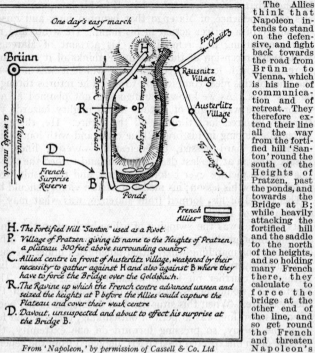

One day's easy march

Brünn

To Vienna — a week's march

From Olmütz

Rausnitz Village

Brook Goldbach

Plateau of Pratzen

H

P

R

C

Austerlitz Village

To Hungary

D

French Surprise Reserve

B

Ponds

French ▭
Allies ▬

H. The Fortified Hill "Santon" used as a Pivot.

P. Village of Pratzen : giving its name to the Heights of Pratzen, a plateau 300 feet above surrounding country.

C. Allied centre in front of Austerlitz village, weakened by their necessity to gather against H and also against B where they have to force the Bridge over the Goldbach.

R. The Ravine up which the French centre advanced unseen and seized the heights at P before the Allies could capture the Plateau and cover their weak centre

D. Davout, unsuspected and about to effect his surprise at the Bridge D.

From 'Napoleon,' by permission of Cassell & Co. Ltd

The Allies think that Napoleon intends to stand on the defensive, and fight back towards the road from Brünn to Vienna, which is his line of communication and of retreat. They therefore extend their line all the way from the fortified hill 'Santon' round the south of the Heights of Pratzen, past the ponds, and towards the Bridge at B; while heavily attacking the fortified hill and the saddle to the north of the heights, and so holding many French there, they calculate to force the bridge at the other end of the line, and so get round the French and threaten Napoleon's retreat.

Napoleon, however, does not mean to stand on the defensive, but to take the offensive. He sees that the Austrians have so drawn out their line that in spite of some superiority in number they will weaken its centre at C, and the centre will grow weaker as their effort on their extreme right towards the saddle, and their extreme left, eight miles off at the bridge, increases. When their centre is at its weakest, a rapid stroke from the French centre will be able to break it, and so decide the action.

But in order to do this, it is essential for Napoleon's own centre to get on to the Heights of Pratzen before the Allies bring up a sufficient force there to cover their weakened centre.

Soult gets up the Ravine at R, his movements hidden by the slope, and reaches the summit of the heights first.

The Allies, drawn on more and more towards B in their effort to force the bridge, are suddenly attacked from D by Davout, whose presence they had not suspected.

While the Allies are thus held in great numbers at the bridge, Soult comes down from the heights on to the weakened centre in front of Auster-litz village, breaks it, then swerves round to the south, and with his artillery directs a plunging fire upon the now isolated Allied left at the bridge and the ponds: having his guns on the southern edge of the plateau. This isolated Allied left is shattered; the right, to the north, similarly cut off by the breaking of the centre, gets away as best it can after their heavy losses.

in which the rupture of the enemy's centre was complete, and
that one in which the decision was most absolute. It was at
once the most sweeping and final of his victories, and the action
most closely conformed to that paradigm copy of a battle which
ever lay near the surface of his imagination.

The elements of the position will enable us to understand
that development and its conclusion.

The prime factor in the ground whereupon the great victory
was decided is the long broad lump of high land known from the
village on its summit as 'the heights of Pratzen.' It remains
at this day much what it then was—indeed the whole battlefield when it is revisited by the ghosts of those days must still
be familiar to them in all its details save in this, that a certain
chain of small and shallow meres, which will be spoken of in a
moment, has been drained, leaving behind to-day no more than
marshy meadows.

These heights of Pratzen, though not considerable (less than
three hundred feet above the surrounding country), are separate
and distinct enough. As you come out from modern Brünn,
its detestable industrial air, and pass south-westwards into the
open country beyond its main suburbs, you see that long lump
like a stranded whale lying bare against the eastern horizon
eight miles away. The heights which, thus looked at from far
off and from the side, seem like a ridge (but which are really,
as I have said, a plateau), end sharply and steeply upon the
south, where a slope, down which guns or cavalry can only
descend with caution, drops immediately upon the flats of the
ponds. But at the northern end the heights of Pratzen are not
isolated. There is here a saddle or depression between them,
and another more confused group to the north, across the edge
of which second piece of higher land runs the main road from
Brünn to Olmütz. It so happens that there stands amid these
somewhat confused rises one sharply defined hill, admirably
suited to serve the purpose of the 'pivot.'

Under the eastern edge of the heights of Pratzen runs a
small stream called the Goldbach. It runs south, from a mere
trickle where it springs, and growing to a still shallow and still
quite narrow brook at the end of the few miles where it gets
beyond the Pratzen heights and finds the open land. Nowhere
in its length would an untrained eye regard it as an obstacle.
Yet in its lower part at least it is something of that; there is
much mud about its banks; the bottom is often soft, and it is
even essential for the crossing of it by artillery in one capital

point—that on a level with the extreme south of the heights—
to obtain command of a village and its bridge: the bridge and
village of Sokolnitz.

Such are the elements of the ground; and to appreciate how
the enemies of Napoleon would upon that day deal with such
a ground we must seize the second main factor, which is the
direction of his communications with Vienna, of his opportunities
for retreat, and for retiring upon and holding the capital, from
which it would be the enemy's chief desire to exclude him.

The only road available for such retirement is the main highway which runs directly south from Brünn to Vienna, a week's
average marching. The enemy advancing from the east, with
Napoleon lying between him and Brünn, would necessarily have
it for his chief objective to reach, and to cut, this road. Therefore they would be led, as the Emperor saw, to get their left
round the French right, turning and outflanking the French,
and at the same time getting between them and that highway
the French communications and line of retreat. While they
attacked the pivot point, the saddle and the heights, H, with
all the northern or right half of their forces they would bend
the southern or left half round below the heights, force the
crossing of the brook Goldbach at Sokolnitz, B, and, having done
that, be round the Emperor's left flank, and between him and
the Vienna road.

If they could achieve such a manœuvre they would have the
French cut off and half encircled, their retreat closed—and,
what is more, the end of their advancing line would be in a
position to move northward upon the brook, and, if they were
completely successful, to roll Napoleon's line.

That they should so act, as Napoleon believed they would,
seemed almost necessary, from the nature of the position. In
so acting that long crescent of theirs would be dangerously
extended. Although they had over him an appreciable superiority of men—ten thousand, more than one-eighth of his own
force—yet, formed thus on a concave curve, they would be more
and more strained as they stretched out by their left; and while
they were thus pressing to curl round from the south weakness
should appear about C in the centre of their exaggerated length
of line, drawn further and further out as it would be, the more
the effort to cross the brook and turn the French flank proceeded. On that weak point at the centre Napoleon would
strike, when he, or the commander immediately upon the spot,
should judge that the opportunity had come.

With the driving home of that central shock the enemy's line would fall into two fractions; and its fragments would attempt in vain to recover cohesion, and would each be destroyed in their isolation and increasing confusion.

But to enhance the drawing out of their strength towards the left, and to make certain that the strain would be more than their forces could bear it would be necessary that the extreme left of the enemy should suffer the surprise of a sudden attack from new forces whose presence they did not suspect. A fresh body held in hand at D unperceived, and at some little distance while they were fighting for the crossing of the brook, must fall upon them in the midst of that struggle. Such an attack would necessarily draw them to increase their efforts upon this left of theirs; such increase of effort there would ensure the weakening of their crescent at its centre and the success of the blow to be delivered at that point.

Of course the enemy would be aware that their extension to the left weakened their centre. To protect it they would advance on to the heights of Pratzen and so cover the weak spot: and this they thought they could do at the outset of the battle because they believed the Emperor meant to act on the defensive. This was their cardinal error. Napoleon stood as though on the defensive but intending from the outset an offensive battle, and, while only holding at his two extremes, north and south, was to seize the height of Pratzen at once and throw back the enemy's advance thereon.

According to such a plan the Emperor knew throughout the action that his intention exactly conformed to the motions of the enemy; the enemy, misunderstanding his plan, and thinking that he stood on the defensive, nervous for his communications, would suffer the consequences of their own misconception, and it would be at the moment when they were most certain of having turned his line and being within striking distance of the main road that their dislocation would suddenly be affected by a blow at the centre and their destruction thereby achieved.

All this, which lay in Napoleon's mind in the two days which he devoted to the preparation of the battle, came about with an exactitude which has ever remained an exemplar. No other one of the great actions which make those few years unique in the history of Europe had the perfection, the simplicity and finality of this. And hence it is that the name Austerlitz stands for us all like a steadfast light, or like a summit high overtopping a range. And that word 'Austerlitz' sums up in itself the fullness of Napoleon's achievement. It is his symbol.

Therefore it is proper to such times as these in which we live that the name itself should have been found an offence. You will look in vain for that word 'Austerlitz' upon the maps drawn up since the Great War by the new authorities of Bohemia. It passes under a new title, and the little place which was perhaps more famous under its ancient title than any field of arms in Christendom must be known to the traveller to-day as 'Slavka.'

.   .   .   .   .   .

Kutasoff, commanding the army of the two Emperors, moved slowly. It has been well said that in dealing with Napoleon one should never dawdle, but his cautious advance had some method in it, for he desired to make all his plans solid, to establish his line securely, and to know his ground.

He was convinced, as we have seen, that Napoleon envisaged a defensive battle; that he would not risk the very existence of the Grand Army against superior numbers with his line of retirement upon Vienna for the moment abandoned and, in case of failure in a rash attack, his whole force cut off and lost. No, Napoleon, he could not but believe, for such seemed the common sense of the situation, would fight parallel, line against line, with, as his great object, the preservation of the road behind him so that if the pressure upon him became too great he could fall back in good order, saving himself from being outflanked and remaining master of the only way by which he might ultimately be compelled to retire southward towards Vienna.

In this conception the Russian Commander-in-Chief was the more confirmed by the Emperor's own actions on and after 29th November. For Napoleon drew in his outposts, recalled his most advanced force, the cavalry in Rausnitz under Murat, and seemed determined to stand upon the heights of Pratzen. These appeared to the Russian Commander so obvious a defensive position that he could not but believe they would be used for that defensive action which alone he thought possible to his opponent in the situation wherein he found himself. And when the Russians in their turn had come up to Rausnitz and occupied it (discovering Murat's retirement) their conception of the situation was confirmed. They did not know—but Napoleon knew —that one portion of his forces under Bernadotte was still far off and might not come up in time, but that another under

Davout could only be present upon the field if action could be postponed.

On the next day, the 30th, Kutasoff, holding with one extreme of his line the country between Rausnitz and the tableland, extended the rest more and more southward until his left was in the pond country, south of those Pratzen heights. They lay, therefore, in a shallow crescent some eight miles long, expecting on the morrow of that day to meet and press back the defensive upon the summit of the tableland. For there by this time the outposts of the Grand Army lay. Napoleon had bivouacked upon a hill northward of the depression, or saddle, which bounds the Pratzen heights, and afterwards had gone from behind these to headquarters established more centrally and further behind the line, just south of the main road from Brünn to Rausnitz and Olmütz. On that day, 30th November, Napoleon rode along the heights watching the enemy below, and the more was it borne in upon the command of the Austro-Russian army that the French would on the morrow or the next day stand to hold the heights and, if numbers were too much for them, fall back on Brünn and the Vienna road.

But Napoleon had long made up his mind between defending his communications and line of retirement, and staking his all upon his own quickness and his reliance thereon, his exactitude of judgment, the precision with which his subordinates would co-ordinate their movements. It was not a defensive battle at all which he was about to wage but a vigorous and shattering offensive, the central hammer-blow of which should be delivered in the critical hour.

On the next day, 1st December, he acted in a fashion which, though it puzzled the enemy's headquarters, made them still more certain that the defensive was in his mind: even perhaps a retreat. It seemed to them as though Napoleon were possibly refusing battle. He withdrew the mass of his forces still further till they lay upon the Goldbach brook, and no longer held the Pratzen tableland at all; but to the north of it he organized his pivot.

All round a dominating almost isolated hill which stands on the extreme north of the position above the Olmütz road he threw up strong entrenchments and garnished them with many heavy guns. The older soldiers nicknamed that hill 'Santon' in memory of a bluff in Egypt which had been so called. Davout was timed to arrive by the next morning, well behind the extreme right of the line and detached from it out of observation, about the Abbey of Raigern, ready to effect his surprise. That afternoon Napoleon dined with his marshals and gave his orders. He told them how he had seen the Russian line extended further and further to the left until, 'to his inexpressible joy' they had even come on beyond the ponds, and he repeated the phrase he had used during his ride of the day before upon the eight-mile crescent of men below the Pratzen heights, 'before to-morrow evening that army will be mine.'

He explained all. Soult, on the stream below the middle of the plateau at Kobelnitz, was to be ready to gain the heights the moment the order should reach him on the following morning. This column it was which was to strike at the centre from the summits of the tableland when the critical moment had come. Davout, who would be up by Raigern Abbey before morning, should form there a detached flying wing to attack the extreme Russian left just when it would be most easily engaged in attempting to force the brook below Soult, at Sokolnitz village and bridge, where the watercourse emerges on to the plain beyond the Pratzen heights.

While this would draw pressure to the extreme left he himself would see that the enemy should also be clustered on the extreme right, further weakening their centre; for they would attack Santon, though its defences were too strong for them; they could not leave the forces at Santon threatening their right flank, they must attack there, though they would have to be in great numbers to do so, and they would at the same time have to attack the saddle—the depression north of the Pratzen heights and south of Santon. And Santon having drawn their mass thus up northward and on to the saddle, Napoleon would counter-attack down the valley which falls eastward from that depression with all the strength he had there assembled: all this would ensure the Russian forces being drawn up northward here from the centre. There would thus be a double congestion of the Russians, one mass more and more heavily engaged to the north; the other far off as heavily engaged to the south, confused and rallying hard to meet the unexpected attack of Davout (which should just then have been launched). At the height of this, when the centre was at its weakest, Soult, from the Pratzen tableland which he had occupied, would fall upon that centre, and, having dislocated it, wheel to the right and attack in flank the isolated Russian left still engaged in a desperate effort to force the Sokolnitz crossing and turn the French line.

Napoleon was not, however, content to give his orders thus to his subordinates upon the eve of battle; he determined upon a novel experiment in the heartening and uplifting of his men. He sent orders that the battalions should be massed, each under its commander, and that to the rank and file so assembled there should be read out in a loud voice which all could hear, each unit from its chief, the nature of the battle they went to fight on the morrow. He made the least private soldier of those thousands a partner in his plan, indifferent as to whether such open news should reach the enemy or no, and confident, no doubt, that if it did they would conclude the thing to be a ruse and think his real plans were quite other than what he had divulged so simply and candidly to his men.

'The enemy' (those thousands each heard with their own ears from their colonels) 'think to outflank me by my right, so as to come between me and Vienna and cut my communications. They will thus weaken themselves by the over-extension of their line, and then we shall strike. We shall do with them what we will.'

That night was frosty, moonless and with many stars; no mist as yet had begun to rise: the air was clear and still.

In the darkness the Emperor rode through the lines, dismounting to visit the bivouacs on foot. There came a moment when he had reached again his headquarters upon the height (where a sort of hut had been made for him of straw for shelter) when Kutasoff and the two Emperors, Alexander and Francis, saw from afar across the saddle, looking westward, a long line of lights against the sky. They said: 'These are the bivouac fires of the French which they are leaving lit by a common ruse, meaning to retire still further in the darkness to cover the Vienna road.'

They were wrong. The glares were not those of bivouac fires, they were the Torches of Austerlitz.

The soldiers, as their Emperor passed, had taken bundles of straw from the bivouacs in which they lay, set fire to them, and brandishing the flames in his honour had shouted his praise. They remembered how the next day was the anniversary of his crowning, 2nd December; his glory filled them, and his glory was theirs, and those fires thus seen in the darkness were a salute to coming victory.

At the end of the night a mist arose, covering the hills and the plain. Through that mist no observation could be made from the heights on which the headquarters lay, just south of the road. Along the rivulet of the Goldbach the fog was densest, and with the slow approach of the winter morning all was in dead silence along the miles of the French line. The plateau was deserted, and round Santon—awaiting the role it had to play— the cold brume rolled about the guns. Before it was yet light, bread and soup and wine were served out to the troops and the marshals gathered round the Emperor on his bivouac height and heard the last details of the plan. With the first glimmerings of day the fog still held, there was still no movement and no sound, but by seven o'clock it suddenly dispersed and there shone over the great frozen field a brilliant sun which was remembered ever after as 'The Sun of Austerlitz.' The forces were joined and the thunder of the guns had begun.

At that moment Napoleon turned to Soult, as he was mounting to ride off to his command in the valley under the centre of the heights (a point where a combe led up to them steeply, within the sides of which all movement could be concealed) and 'Soult,' he asked, 'how long will it take your men to reach the summit of the plateau?' 'Twenty minutes,' said Soult as he rode away.

The whole line was engaged, and the morning opened with the noise before them of the Russians swarming up to force Santon hill, and pressing in dense columns upon the saddle below, while very far off to the south could be heard the booming of the artillery which was supporting that other vigorous attack upon the extreme Russian left against the extreme French right, the carrying of the bridge at Sokolnitz; the crossing of the Goldbach, the attaining of the open country beyond and then the advance up north beyond the brook to cut off the French from the Vienna road.

In the centre the two Emperors themselves were climbing the eastern ramp of the Pratzen heights, deserted and apparently open for the occupation of their men when these Allied columns should have reached the village and the flat of the plateau. But Soult had had his orders earlier; his massed command in that combe by the brook had gone forward with all speed and as the enemy, thinking to meet no resistance till much further on, none perhaps till the plateau should be crossed and the watercourse beyond should be reached, found themselves suddenly and unexpectedly faced with the rapidly deploying line of the French, Soult commanded an immediate attack with all the vigour of the forces at his disposal.

But there could be no reinforcement of those central troops of the Allies thus surprised and thrown backwards. Up to the

north the struggle raged more furiously than ever; battalion
after battalion was thrown in by Kutasoff; the undue massing
of men upon the extreme north was working as Napoleon saw it
would work, and it did seem at one moment as though that
enemy right would succeed, would force the saddle, would break
through between the pivot of Santon and the plateau of Pratzen
below. When the moment seemed ripe Kutasoff threw in a
heavy charge of cavalry which he might well believe would
decide the matter on his right at least and therefore perhaps the
battle. Napoleon had gone forward towards the threatened
spot and counter-attacked, summoning the cavalry of the Guard,
and those superb horsemen came thundering down in column
carrying all before them, pressing back the nearly successful
attack, thrusting it in confusion down the slope of the valley,
eastward, and, in the success of their fury, compelling more and
yet more of the Russian troops to be summoned hastily up to
the threatened spot, leaving the enemy centre, against which
Soult was victoriously at work, without reinforcement and its
diminished strength falling back already in confusion. The
breaking-point had been found and a gap was opening between
the right and the left of that far too stretched crescent, the
Austro-Russian line. In effect already Austerlitz was won.

For, to the south on that extreme left where the Russians were
desperately fighting hand to hand at the bridge and through
Sokolnitz village, determined to carry the watercourse and
already believing that victory, at this point at least, was theirs,
Davout effected a complete surprise.

He arrived from Raigern Abbey upon the field in the mid-
morning and with his fresh troops fell into the midst of the turmoil.

The enemy left at Sokolnitz fought on, still calling for reinforcement from behind, not knowing yet that the centre had
broken far behind them over their right shoulders upon the
eastern slopes of Pratzen Hill, and thinking that one more effort
might, even in spite of Davout and his new thousands, carry the
crossing of the stream and turn the French flank at last. But it
was far too late for such a hope. Soult on the plateau, the enemy
centre being no longer his concern (for that was gone), wheeled
round to the right, precisely as the order had been given the day
before, and was coming up on the southern edge of the Pratzen
tableland in force; his guns were already playing upon the road
below whereby the doomed and isolated left of the Russian force
could alone bring up its munitions and such reinforcement as
remained to it.

The men fighting in the village of Sokolnitz and the bridge heard that most fearful of sounds—gunfire from behind them—and knew that they were doomed. They began to surge back, at first in some order, then in greater and greater confusion. It was hoped, blindly, that they might break their way out by the road along which they had come, and in the great mass of their retirement (it was now almost a rout) thousands of them, horses, guns, and men, were moving, fleeing northward and eastward over the thin ice of the frozen meres. Down on that ice the shot from Soult's cannon above plunged, breaking it upon all sides, so that the struggling masses drowned in the mud and slush and the freezing shallow water; and the guns sank and were caught, and the plunging horses, and the wagons. Of all that great host, on the Russian left, more than 30,000, a remnant wildly got through eastwards and as individuals saved their lives: the rest were lost.

Napoleon, from the place in which he had seen the success of the counter-attack from the saddle on the north, galloped south along the bare plateau to find Soult, and as he passed he called to the soldiers that the day was won. The news swept through the army, all along the great line of it, as the firing to the north grew more and more desultory with the closing in of the short day; and as the noise of the guns crashing their fire down upon the ice of the ponds proclaimed the conclusion, every man knew that the greatest of decisions had been arrived at.

It was past four o'clock. The sun was sinking red in a now rising haze behind the battlefield upon the plains to the west, and the affair of Austerlitz was at an end.

But that night a cold fine rain fell upon the wounded.

.   .   .   .   .

Within ten days, upon 14th December, Haugwitz was at Schönbrunn, bowing obsequiously before Napoleon and loading the triumph of the Emperor with praise. But Napoleon said to him: 'You might to-day be paying compliments to others, save for what Fate has willed.' And immediately, as the other was taken aback, he followed up the shock by presenting terms. He would have alliance with Prussia; and he detailed the conditions. They were accepted.

THE MOTHER AND DEATH

It was the birthday of the Emperor, 15th August 1815, the anniversary of that Assumption, 46 years ago, when the young mother had been hastened from the Cathedral of Ajaccio to bear such a son. The *Northumberland* was in the midst of the seas, slowly surging southward towards St Helena.

All the bells of Rome were ringing for the feast, when there drove through the gates of the city a great travelling coach, its wheels clattering under the porch of the Falconieri Palace at eight in the morning. On the panels were the Imperial arms; the blinds were drawn to protect from the public gaze the travellers within.

These, when the door was opened, stepped down. They were a man and a woman, each aged, the woman somewhat prematurely so. Letizia Buonaparte, in her sixty-fifth year, fatigued by the journey and leaning on the arm of that half-brother, Cardinal Fesch, who as a little boy had held her hand in the High Mass at the Cathedral of Ajaccio all those years ago, thus entered into her place of exile and of refuge; for the Pope had offered her the hospitality of his States.

. . . . . .

It was nightfall on Sunday, 29th April 1821. Napoleon lay dying. The little iron camp-bed with the silver eagles on its four corners and its green curtains was placed in the middle of the low petty room, its head to the light between the two windows, its foot towards the simple fireplace, on the mantelpiece of which, in front of a large square looking-glass, stood the bust of his little son.

Wretched as the room was, it was the best in that shanty of a house—a place that was soon to be turned into common stables and was most suitable perhaps for that. It had been worse when first the Emperor and the few who followed him came into that exile. They had found the shreds of the wallpaper turned mouldy and rotten with moisture and the ragged carpet on the floor gnawed into holes by rats. So much had been set right; muslin had been stretched over the walls and fluted round, the ceiling white-washed, and the place made reasonably clean.

It stood not far from the summit of a sort of very wide shallow cup sloping down easterly towards the sea from one of the ridges of that volcanic island, the floors of the long low place being somewhat less than two thousand feet above the sea, the noise of which could be heard coming up the funnel from the mouth of the depression below. And up that broad cup of the valley and from the ocean below too frequently blew the south-east gales—which the failing Emperor dreaded, finding that they suited him ill.

To the right of the bed as he lay in such extremity he looked through an open door at the chapel which had been set up as best might be in the next room of the suite, the dining-room. He gazed to the wooden altar which the Chinese workmen (serfs of the East India Company) had set up; and his eyes could rest there on one of the last monuments of his name; the four golden letters 'N' embroidered on either corner of the green velvet cloth which covered the two steps. Through this door that morning he had heard the Sunday Mass which Bertrand's young son had served. There also was the Tabernacle, rough, amateur, cardboard-covered, but ornamented as best might be with gilt paper and the white of it gleaming against the red satin behind, while above stood a great Crucifix in ebony, too large it seemed for the altar-piece. Its great silver figure of Christ dominated the scene. He had given orders that when his last agony should be upon him the Blessed Sacrament should be exposed and the Prayers for the Dead recited; also, said he, he desired to fulfil all the duties of the Catholic Faith.

Now as he had said these words Antommarchi, the surgeon attendant upon him, who was atheist from the spirit of his time as also from the boast of science that he had, could not restrain a smile; whereat Napoleon, with some remnant of strength, flamed up at him and cried: 'Be off! Stupidity fatigues me, but I can forgive shallow wits or even bad manners. I cannot forgive dullness of heart.'

It being long after dark, Montholon had already taken up his watch at nine o'clock, which he changed alternately with the valet Marchand, and it ran till two o'clock in the morning. But on that day he had occasion to leave the Emperor alone, for this reason, that the priest Vignali was to attend. For Napoleon had said long before, when first he discovered what awaited him in his exile: 'I must have a priest about me: I would not die like a dog.'

The Emperor had not feared death. He had seen it coming

for now long past, ever since the beginning of the year. For when, on New Year's Day, Marchand had pulled the curtains in the morning, Napoleon—who loved a joking converse with a familiar and was devoted to those about him—had said: 'Well, and what present have you for me this New Year?'

Marchand had answered: 'Sire, the hope of seeing Your Majesty soon set to rights and leaving this air which does you only ill.'

But to such words Napoleon, no longer smiling, had gravely replied: 'It will not last long, my son. My end is on me; I cannot carry on much more.'

Said Marchand: 'As I see things it is not so.'

And then Napoleon had ended all this by the few words: 'It shall be as God wills.'

As his illness had increased upon him he had known more and more that certainly it was death.

There came a time when he could no longer walk or ride out of doors, and when he attempted to do so turned faint. In March his blood had chilled and they needed to put warm cloths about his feet, and by the middle of the month he said to a doctor who begged him to take the remedies prescribed: 'Well, sir! I am at your orders! But do you not see that death will be to me a gift from Heaven? I do not dread it. I will do nothing to hasten it but I would try no sortilege to make my life the longer.' And at another time he said: 'Death has now been for some weeks beside me upon my pillow,' meaning that he had become familiar with that Visitor.

He had told them also, with more instinctive knowledge than their science possessed, that he was dying of what his father had died of; and so he was—with a cancer in the stomach which was certain soon to make an end; so that he could also say, when his English doctor asked him how he felt upon a certain day: 'I shall soon give back to the earth the remnant of that life which it is of such import to the Kings to seize.'

He had asked, while still he could attend to reading, that they should read him Homer for a while; and that same day, Sunday the 29th, he had dictated, as he had dictated upon the day before, what he termed, 'A Reverie'—would that we possessed it! But now, when the night had come, greater things were at hand. The priest was with him alone.

Napoleon Buonaparte confessed, and was absolved; his peace with the Faith was made; the Last Sacraments were administered—save for this, that he might not receive the Viaticum since he could retain no food. They therefore dared not give him the Eucharist. But he was at peace, while yet his reason remained to him.

It remained to him still for a brief four days. Upon the next day, the last of April, the Monday, his thoughts being still clear but his weakness very great and the sickness upon him very grievous, he kept his eyes still fixed upon the bust of his little son showing there against the glass at the foot of the bed upon the mantel. His sleep had left him, but he lingered on through 2nd May and until the 3rd. Upon the 3rd, the last flicker of his great will being, as he thought, still at his service, he attempted to rise for a moment, but fell back. They gave him wine, and as he tasted it he murmured: 'How good is wine!'

With that night of the 3rd, however, all around knew that the end was upon him, and all watched. With the morning, before noon (the morning of Friday the 4th) his delirium began, in the frenzy of which at one moment he attempted to seize on Montholon at his side; and in that fever he muttered continually words the whispered confusion of which suggested now this, now that. It is said that the last of them which any mortal could distinguish were: 'Army . . . army . . .' and 'Head of the Army. . . .' But there can be no certain record of such things.

All that day long, all the afternoon, right on through the night till four in the morning of the Saturday, the 5th, that final unconscious communion with the last flicker of this life continued. Drowning the slight murmurs of it, came violent rain for hours against the window-panes at either side of the bed's head, and mixed with that noise the saying of the Prayers before the Altar. Out of the sea a great wind arose and blew furiously up the valley, shaking the frail and miserable tenement with its gusts and rattling the casements and driving more furiously still the waters of the tempest against the glass.

But as that afternoon grew louder in the heavens without the Emperor at last lay still, and even the faint whisperings from his lips were no longer heard; but they still moved almost imperceptibly in breathing. The household were assembled. It was near six in the evening. At nine minutes to the hour the sunset gun was heard far off down the wind; and as the rush of the tropical twilight fell under the hurrying clouds and that now lessening gale all those silent about him saw the change: the mouth half fell, the eyes opened; but they saw nothing of this world any more: Napoleon was dead.

They covered him with the cloak he had worn at Marengo, a Crucifix upon it, and by his side they laid his sword.

.   .   .   .   .   .

On the same evening, but while it was still just daylight, a stranger came to the great doors of the Falconieri Palace in Rome, wherein Letizia Buonaparte kept her secluded state. He asked to be allowed to see Her Highness. The porter answered that unless an audience had been granted to him he certainly could not be admitted. To which the stranger replied in his turn, in a solemn fashion, that he had made no request for an audience but that it was a strict duty for him to see the mother of the Emperor in order to give her a message of the first importance.

Why the porter gave way to the stranger we are not told, save in the phrase that 'there was some authority about him' which seemed to constrain obedience, so that he was at last shown into the outer hall, where the domestics of the household were, and one of them was bidden tell the footman of Her Highness that an unknown stranger demanded the honour of seeing her. The footman asked the visitor's name, who answered that it could be told only to the Lady of the House in person —but told it never was.

In her room Letizia Buonaparte had at her side her chamberlain, Colonna, and Rosa Mellini, her companion. She chose to receive the man who thus so strangely claimed admittance, and Colonna, going out to him, found him pacing up and down— nervous, impatient, as another had been when immediate action was halted—as another had been on the misty slope above Jena when Soult delayed.

Colonna bade the stranger enter; but even within the room he made another request—what he had to say must be said to Letizia Buonaparte alone. To this request also she yielded, waiting to hear what he should have to say. Whereat, when they were alone together, he spoke to her a moment of the Emperor, in the tone and manner of a man who had just left Napoleon; and then, putting his hand upon his breast, where he had concealed a Crucifix, he said to her these words: 'At the moment in which I speak Napoleon is freed from his sufferings, and is at peace.' The mother heard him in a daze, wherein she still sat when, immediately he had ceased speaking, he passed through the door and was gone.

IV. TRAVEL AND THE SEA

THE CRUISE OF THE 'NONA'

IT was late in May, near midnight, the air being very warm and still, and the sky not covered but somewhat dim, with no moon, when I took the *Nona* out from Holyhead harbour, having on board one companion to help me work the boat, and a local man who could speak Welsh for me in whatever places I might make along the coast.

The very slight breeze, which had barely moved us through the water after we had got up the anchor, died away long before we reached the end of the breakwater, and it was necessary to pull her out with the dinghy in order to fetch round the end of the stonework and get to sea. There was at that time of the tide a little current running towards the Stack, which would slightly help us on our way once we were outside, and with this we drifted a full hour and more, aided now and then by faint breaths of air, which rose and died again like memories. So came we, with the turn of the night, under the glare of the lighthouse at last, and then put the nose of the little ship round for the point of Carnarvonshire and the strait between the mainland and Bardsey Island, which is called Bardsey Sound.

It was a course of about thirty-three miles, with no chance, apparently, of covering it in all that night, nor perhaps in all the coming day as well; for we had struck, as it seemed, that hot, steady, summer weather in which one may play at a drifting match for days on end.

While it was still dark the distant mountains could barely be seen as something a little blacker than the sky. They looked astonishingly low, as mountains always do on a moonless night, when there is nothing to distinguish their details, and nothing against which to compare them, or by which to tell their distance. Already—it being now nearer two than one o'clock —a little wind had arisen, settling down, as it seemed, into somewhat east of north, and blowing over the Anglesey flats. It gave us perhaps no more than a couple of knots an hour, but it was heartening after the long calm, and as we had all sail set she pulled to it steadily enough. I was at the helm, my companion was still awake, sitting in the cock-pit and talking

to me, and the hand who was to be with us till we next lande
smoked beside us on deck.

The wind had freshened somewhat, we were making perhap
four or five knots, when the dawn began to show beyon
Snowdon, and those great hills at once looked higher agains
the glimmer of grey light. Soon the whole coast was apparent
and the Yreifles with their triple peaks (clearer than I ha
expected; indeed, too clear for fine weather) lay right ahea
and Bardsey Island beyond them and the narrow sound i
between. The wind seemed steady, as though it would hold
I reckoned that the tide would turn against us anywhere betwee
six and seven in the morning, that it would turn back throug
the Sound about noon or one o'clock, and I calculated that w
should be running into Cardigan Bay, past Bardsey, on th
middle of the ebb, an hour or two later than that time.

But what happened was something wholly unexpected; it i
always so at sea, and that is why it is said that the sea bring
all adventures. Indeed, I think that as we go on piling measure
ments upon measurements, and making one instrument afte
another more and more perfect to extend our knowledge c
material things, the sea will always continue to escape us
For there is a Living Spirit who rules the sea and many attendan
spirits about him.

But on that brightening morning there was nothing to war
us. The glass was high and, if I remember right, still rising
The sky uncovered and clearer than it had been by night; th
wind slight, but holding steady, and all was soldier's weathe
so that any one could have taken that little ship through suc
weather where he would. It was weather, one would say, mad
for the instruction of the young in the art of sailing.

By the time it was fully light, we were making between si
and seven knots, for the wind had sharply risen. As it was a
off-shore wind, there was as yet no sea raised, but little tumblin
white caps, very pleasant to look at, and all the movemen
coming on our quarter from over the land. With the rising c
the sun it blew hard. We were yielding to it too much; we ha
taken down the topsail an hour before, and now I thought i
wise to take in a reef as well, which we did in the headsail an
the mainsail, but leaving the jib as it was, for that sail was no
a large one.

I have sailed a great deal off and on in boats of this siz
(that is, somewhat more than thirty feet over all, with eigh
or nine feet beam, and drawing from five to six feet of water

utter rigged), and I know it is an illusion; yet I can never get
over the idea that a reef makes no difference. Two reefs—
yes—but one reef I cannot 'feel.' It is an obtuseness in me;
but so it is.

However, it seemed wiser to take in a reef of some sort, and
two reefs would have reduced the sail quite unnecessarily, for
t was not yet blowing so hard as all that.

We slipped down the coast smartly, nearing it all the time
upon our slantwise course, and as we did so, the sun being now
fully risen, it blew harder and harder every minute. A sea
rose, a good following sea, but higher than one would have
expected so nearly off the land from a land wind; and, as this
boat has very little freeboard (it is her only defect, for she rises
magnificently to the water, and bears herself better the worse
the weather may be), I watched the swirl of the foam under her
low counter as each wave slightly broke under the now fierce
wind.

We shortened down to three reefs, but even so the helm was
pulling hard, and when we changed jibs and put up the smallest
we had, it griped more than I liked, straining my arm after so
long a spell at the tiller. I handed it over to the man who was
with us, and went forward to see that everything was clear, for
t was now blowing really hard, and anything like a tangle if
we got into difficulties would be dangerous. The gale rose
higher and the sea with it; but, tearing through the water as
we now were under three reefs, we should soon make the Sound
and get round the point of Carnarvonshire into easier water
right under the lee of the land.

There was only one thing that troubled me, which was this
question: Should we make the Sound before the tide turned?
It was an important question, because, although I have never
been in those parts before, off-shore, in a boat of my own, yet
I could judge that in such a piece of water, with all the Bay
pouring through a channel barely two miles wide with a deep
of barely one, the tide against such a gale would raise an
impossible sea. If we could just make it on the tail of the tide,
on the very last of the ebb, we should have nothing to bear
but a strong following sea, such as that before which we were
running at the moment: for the southerly stream was still
strong under us. But if the water turned before we got into
the Sound, we should have a time to remember; and so we did.

For I had done something or other to annoy the Earth
Shaker, and he pursued me viciously, making the tide turn just

before we reached the mouth of the Sound. In a time much shorter than I had expected, with no lull in between, the steady run of sea which had been combing behind us, towering above the counter, but regular and normal to deal with, turned into a confusion of huge tumbling pyramidical waves, leaping up, twisting, turning and boiling in such a confusion as I had never seen, not even in Alderney Race, which I had gone through many years before when I was a boy. The painter which held the dinghy to the stern parted, and that boat, a good and serviceable one, was lost. There was no question of turning in such a sea and under such a wind; the dinghy had to be abandoned. The tide against us was so fierce that even under that gale we hardly moved; and it was strange to see, from the leaping and struggling of the *Nona*, as the foam rushed by in a millrace, how steady remained the points on the Carnarvonshire shore, and how slowly we opened the Sound. The pace was irregular. There were moments when we advanced at perhaps a knot or a knot and a half against that fierce tide. There were others when we even slipped back. All the while the wind howled and the sea continued to rise and to boil in a cauldron more violent as the gale on the one hand and the tide against it on the other grew in strength, and in the fierceness of their struggle. In seas like this one never knows when some great tumbling lump of water may not break upon one's decks, for there is no run and follow, it is all confusion; and I remember thinking as I took the helm again in the midst of the turmoil of something I had seen written once of Portland Race: 'The sea jumps up and glares at you'—a sound phrase.

We had thus (in some peril, but still able to keep a course, and, on the whole, advancing) got at last between the point and the Island, that is, to the heart of the Sound; and a very few more yards would have brought us round out of the cauldron into smooth water and a run for some quiet anchorage right under the protection of the coast when (since at sea bad luck always goes gathering impetus) the jib blew out with a noise like a gun. A few rags hung on to its fastenings; the rest of the canvas went away out to sea like a great wounded bird, and then sailed down and flopped into the seething of the water.

You may guess what that did to a boat in our straits! It made the helm almost impossible to hold with the violent gripe of the mainsail, half our head canvas being gone; and at the same time it stopped our way. We drifted back again into the worst of the water, and lost in five minutes what it had taken

us more than an hour to make. The danger was real and
serious. The man that was with us expressed his fears aloud;
my companion, though new to the sea, took it all with great
calm. As to what happened to myself, I will record it though
it is a little detailed and personal: I will record it for the sake
of the experience, of which others may make what they will.

I looked at the Carnarvonshire coast there close at hand,
the sinking lines of the mountains as they fell into the sea, and
I discovered myself to be for the first time in my life entirely
indifferent to my fate. It was a very odd sensation indeed,
like the sensation I fancy a man must have to find he is para-
lysed. Once, under the influence of a drug during an illness
some such indifference had pervaded me, but here it was in the
broad daylight and the sun well up above the mountains, with
a clear sky, in the grip of a tremendous gale and of an angry
countering sea, ravening like a pack of hounds. Yet I could
only look with indifference on the sea and at the land. The
sensation was about as much like courage as lying in a hammock
is like a hundred yards race. It had no relation to courage,
nor, oddly enough, had it any relation to religion, or to a right
depreciation of this detestable little world which can be so
beautiful when it likes.

Such as it was, there it was. I had always particularly
disliked the idea of death by drowning, and I had never believed
a word of the stories which say that at the end it is a pleasant
death. Indeed, as a boy I was caught under the steps of a
swimming bath and held there a little too long before I could
get myself out, and pleasant it was not at all. But here in
Bardsey Sound, I was indifferent, even to death by drowning.
All I was really interested in was to watch what way we lost
and what chance we had of getting through.

Indeed, the whole question of fear is beyond analysis, and
there is only one rule, which is, that a man must try to be so
much the master of himself that he shall be able to compel
himself to do whatever is needful, fear or no fear. Whether
there be merit or not in the absence of fear, which sentiment
we commonly call courage when it is allied to action, may be,
and has been, discussed without conclusion since men were men.
The absence of fear makes an admirable show, and excites our
respect in any man; but it is not dependent upon the will.
Here was I in very great peril indeed off Bardsey, and utterly
careless whether the boat should sink or swim; yet was I the
same man who, in a little freshness of breeze that arose off the

Owers a year or two ago, was as frightened as could well be—
and with no cause. And if this be true of change of mood in
one man, it must be true of the differences of mood in different
men.

I had occasion during the War, when I had been sent to write
upon the Italian front, to be swung to the high isolated rock of
a mountain peak in the Dolomites by one of those dizzy wires
which the Italian engineers slung over the gulfs of the Alps for
the manning and provisioning of small high posts. It was an
experience I shall ever remember, a vivid, hardly tolerable
nightmare; but the man I was with, an Italian officer of great
and deserved fame, earned during that campaign, not only felt
nothing, but could not understand what my terror was. We
sat, or rather lay, in one of those shallow trays which travel
slowly along these wires over infinite deeps of air; and during
the endless crawling through nothingness he told me, by way of
recreation, the story of a private soldier who had been coming
down from the isolated post some weeks before. The machinery
had gone wrong, and the tray remained suspended over the
gulf, half-way across, for some twenty minutes. When it worked
again and they hauled it in they found that the man had gone
mad.

When the time came for the return journey, I very well
remember asking myself whether I had the control to face that
second ordeal or no. It was an obscure crisis, unknown to
others, but as real and as great within as any of those which
stand out in fiction or history. I would rather have gone down
by the path which clung to the steep, the precipitous mountain-
side. This was forbidden because it was under direct Austrian
fire; I knew that I should not be allowed. So I faced the
return—and it was worse than the going.

Also in my life I have known two men who have hunted lions,
and each of them has told me that fear in the presence of peril
from the beast was wholly capricious, and that sometimes when
an exceedingly unpleasant death seemed certain, the man who
had just missed his shot felt indifferent. I can believe it.

Anyhow, here I was in Bardsey Sound, with many deaths
moving over the howling fury of the sea, and not one of them
affecting me so much as a shadow passing over a field.

The end of that adventure was odd and unreasonable—as
things will be at sea. It was perhaps because we had been
buffeted and pushed into some edge of the conflict between
wind and water where the tide runs slacker; or it was perhaps

because the wind had risen still higher. But, at any rate, after three separate raids forward (in the second of which we were very nearly out of our peril and into smooth water), and as many set-backs (one of which got us into the worst violence we had yet suffered) the *Nona*, in a fourth attempt (it was her own, not ours—we could do nothing but keep her, as best we might, to her course), slipped out and reached an eddy beyond the tide. For a moment it was very difficult to keep her to it, she slewed round; but then again she got her head southerly, and we found ourselves running past the great Black Rock which stands there—the Carrig Dhu—and marks the smooth water beyond the edge of the tide.

We breathed again; and as I took her on through an easy sea, close under the land with not too much strain upon the helm (for the high shore now broke the gale), I was free to look over my right shoulder and watch, passing away behind us, further and further, the hell of white water and noise, through which we had barely come to safety.

Danger keeps men awake and makes them forget necessity, but with this relief, our fatigue came upon us. My friend and I had now been awake for some twenty-five or twenty-six hours, and it was time for sleep.

We got the poor *Nona*, which had behaved so well, up into a lonely little bay where was an old abandoned mine working, but no other sign of man. The Welshman with us told us it was good holding ground; we let go the anchor and stowed sail. I remember how I fell half asleep as I stretched the cover over the mainsail boom and yard and tied it down at the after end. The gale still blew, yet, as it seemed, more steadily and less fiercely. There was no danger of dragging. We were well under the lee of the land. I gave one look, under the violent but clear morning sky, to seaward before I went below; and there I saw how, at a certain distance from the land, in a long line, the white water began. It was like being in a lagoon, like being protected by a bank from the sea outside; but really it was only the effect of the lee of the land making a belt of smooth water along shore. Then we all lay down to sleep and slept till evening.

.   .   .   .   .   .

One of the saddest things I know about the beach near Bideford River is the deadly hatred with which the Dons have persecuted poor, dear Kenwith. Kenwith is a place where a few boatloads of Danes landed in the Dark Ages, and were defeated by the English. The name is quite clear, the tradition is equally clear, and the description of the position is unmistakable. Therefore have the learned, as is their wont, insisted with the utmost virulence that the tradition, the name, the description, are all a popular error, and that the place where the little scrimmage really came off was miles away.

It is interesting to analyse the motives of this sort of thing. We are all familiar with it. The universities of all countries, but especially of our own, are a regular hothouse for breeding it; but when one first comes across it, one is puzzled why it should come into being at all. Whence springs this lust for saying that the Gospel of St John was not written by St John? That Homer was not written by Homer? That the Battle of Hastings was not called the Battle of Hastings—although all the people who fought there called it the Battle of Hastings? That William the Conqueror only had a handful of men there —though his secretary, who saw them, and read all the documents connected with them, gives us fifty thousand? That Julius Caesar's *Gallic War* was written by his tutor—and all the rest of the nonsense?

The powerful force urging Dons to make fools of themselves in this way seems to me to come from a convergence of three currents. First of all there is the vanity of the learned man, who has all the better opportunities for action because few have any knowledge at all of the matter, and he is fairly safe from criticism—or thinks himself so. His fellows will not give him away. It is clearly a flattering thing to think that one is right where all the world has been wrong, and, in a time like ours, when there has been accumulated such a mass of special technical knowledge, people are ready to swallow almost any assertion, because they know not what new evidence may have appeared.

The second source is that very human thing, the love of the marvellous—though it is the love of the marvellous appearing in a very degraded form. Your pedant says: 'All the apparent evidence, all tradition, all that you would call common sense, would make out Little Muddipool to be that same Little Muddipool where the treaty of Little Muddipool was signed. It is called in plain words "The Treaty of Little Muddipool," and its last words are "Made by us at Little Muddipool." But *I* tell you that it was not Little Muddipool at all, but a place a hundred miles away with a different name.' The spirit at work there is

xactly the same spirit as that which says: 'Common sense and
your own experience will tell you that the bishop must have
crossed the river either by a bridge or by a boat. *I* tell you that
he holy man sailed across it on his coat. What do you think
of that?'

And the third cause is a negative one. The perpetual substi-
ution of hypothesis for fact (which is the great mark of Dons
to-day) ends by getting men into a state of mind where they can
no longer weigh the proportions of evidence; they can no longer
distinguish between the certain, the probable, and the absurd.
Thus, it was but a little time ago that an Oxford Don came out
with a miracle. He said he had discovered any number of
classical passages containing concealed anagrams, furnishing the
most astonishing information; for instance, that Euripides, when
he was a little boy, wrote the plays of Æschylus. A stopper was
put on him, however, by a man, who wrote to the *Spectator* (of
all papers), proving that the said Don's name was but thinly
concealed in an anagram of the opening lines of the *Iliad*, so
that he must have written that excellent poem, not when he was
a little boy, but long before he was born—and so much for that.

.   .   .   .   .   .

It is a heavenly piece of coast, all this southern bulge of
Devon, with its little secret rivers and untainted towns. The
people are good and the land. So, with reservations, is its sea
even beyond the Sound. Though once, indeed, I did suffer off
Bolt Head one of the two most abominable spills of wind I ever
suffered—and the first was off Beachy Head by Birling Gap on
Whit-Tuesday, 1902, a day ever to be remembered.

For the air fell off Birling Gap just like water out of a bucket,
and nearly blew the *Nona* flat upon her beam. I let go the sheet
with a run, but as it was she dipped, perhaps, a third of her mainsail, and nearly broke her lover's heart with fear. It is so sometimes with these high lands. The wind does not run true. It
blows over them, and curls through a depression upon their
edges, and curves, splashing down solid, in a bolt, on to the deep
below. For, on that day by Beachy, all those years ago, the
true wind was but just enough northerly to let me keep a course
for Newhaven, hauled very close and saving every inch. But
that gust came suddenly right on the weather beam, from far
east of north, and nearly settled my then young craft and him
that cherished and still cherishes her.

As for the spill off Bolt Head, it fell after a clear midnight,

since the War, and it was more than a spill; for it blew steadily
for the best part of an hour and then ceased. But, like its
younger brother off Beachy, it was peculiar to the high land;
for it came due northerly, whereas the main wind had east in it.
I was watching the morning star burning like a sacred furnace on
the edges of the black hills when Satan sent that wind and tried
to drown three men. But we reefed in time—there were three
of us, one for the helm and two to reef; and when dawn broke,
and the blessed colours of the east renewed the day, strange!—
one end of the boom had three reefs down, and the other only
two!

    .   .   .

Upon this piece of coast, setting out once from Plymouth,
there came to me an experience of no particular moment as
history, but of powerful effect upon my mind. It marked, in a
sort of mysterious omen way, or, perhaps, I should say in a sort
of visionary way, the unleashing of the Great War.

It so happened that in that summer of 1914 I had had occasion
to go from Hampshire to one of the western ports, where I was
to pick up my boat, and take her ultimately into Plymouth
Sound, and thence, when I should have the leisure, I proposed to
take her out again, and stand eastward up the coast.

I was staying in Hampshire with a friend who had a house in
the New Forest. It was on a Sunday I set out thence. He sent
me in his motor to Salisbury, where I wished to get Mass before
going on by train. During the Mass, the priest, after his an-
nouncements, asked the congregation to pray for the soul of the
Archduke Heir-Apparent of Austria, who had been murdered
at a place called Sarajevo. I had never heard the name, and I
had but a vague idea of who this archduke was, of his relationship to the Emperor, and of his heirship to the throne of Haps-
burg-Lorraine. I came to the *Nona*, where she lay, and sailed
out with her into the sea for some days. I had no conception
that anything could be brewing.

When I came to land again, and went up to London, I found
the air to be filled with all the possibilities of that time. The
Austrian Government had sent to the Servian Government a
note, the like of which had not been heard in the history of
Christendom. It made demands which no government claiming
to sovereignty could accept. For my part, when I read the
terms of the note, I was in no doubt it was of Prussian dictation.
I am in no doubt to this day that it was of Prussian dictation.

There are two ways of ascertaining the origin of such a thing. One is the material way, the consultation of the only available documents, and the only certified direct human evidence. The other is the moral way, when one says: 'This can only have been written by so and so,' or, at the very least, 'Can only have been inspired by so and so.' Thus, if I find upon the table of a doubtful, weak kind of a man—and a courteous one at that—a letter framed in the very terms and manner of a bully, constantly his associate, then, though the letter be in the handwriting of the former, and on his own paper, even if there were convincing proof that when the actual writing was done the man was alone, I should yet say that the real author was the bully, and not the gentleman. He may have learnt it by heart at dictation. He may have copied it from the other's draft. At any rate, it is morally certain that the one man, and not the other, is the true author of the thing launched—is the one responsible.

Now, in the case of this note to Servia, the whole thing is Prussian from beginning to end: the extreme arrogance, the deliberate provocation, the exactitude, the aridity and, above all, the unintelligence. And as for proof upon the other side, we have none, except what the various culprits chose themselves to give us.

As I went about London getting all men's views, as is my custom when grave things threaten, I heard many judgments passed upon the probable consequences of the note. The man whose judgment in European affairs I trusted most, one who had been largely employed in the foreign business of this country, and who also had a deep and solid knowledge of history, told me that there would not be war, even between Austria and Servia, let alone an extension of the peril.

The reason he gave for this was curious. He said that a document of that extreme violence would not have been issued if war were the object. The object was to make bargaining acutely necessary, and to get a further hold over Balkan land as a result of a long haggling. For very violent actions—of which this was the most extreme case yet known to Europe—the excess of offensive and inhuman brutality could only, he said, be used as a blind.

Though I then knew very much less of the European situation, I hesitated to agree with him as to the motive; but, on the other hand, I certainly did not think there would be war. I thought Servia would yield in all save the very worst and most humiliating points, and that these would at last be waived.

Many other opinions of various colours did I gather in that interval, but only one foreseeing a war; and to that one I paid no attention, because it was very foolishly expressed, and for the wrong reason. It was given me by a man who had travelled widely, and who was an expert in many languages, as well as a man of great knowledge in certain forms of mechanical construction. He had also a high scientific training. He had no public post. This man said to me there would be war, because Austria was known to be in a rotten condition, because upon the outbreak of war the various sections of her tessellated dominion would break apart, and the Servians, knowing this, and having the Russians behind them, would take up the challenge. The Prussian power, or 'Reich,' would be so alarmed at the prospect that it would attempt to stave off hostilities, or, failing that, to leave the Austrian Crown to its fate. Such was the folly and ill-judgment of the only man who thought that war was coming, among all those whom I consulted. It was a good example of hitting a mark by firing wide: like the duellist in the dark room who in mercy shot up the chimney, yet brought down his opponent.

For, note you, that though a great many men up and down Europe had said that Prussia was making for war, and that a conflict must come about in some near future, and though I myself had written it over my own signature (if I remember rightly), when, in 1911, Prussia raised her special war tax, and the French were compelled to reintroduce the three years' service; yet *this* did not seem to be the occasion—for it was too abrupt. There seemed to be no plot or plan; and the season was already late.

I did not know what we know now, that Prussia firmly calculated on two things: first, the neutrality of England, and, secondly, a very complete and very rapid victory over the French, a decisive victory, destroying the whole of the French Army within a month of the frontier crossing; a battle beginning as did Charleroi, but ending very differently from the Marne.

When I next had occasion to leave London, in order to find again my boat at Plymouth, and to take her out, nothing was decided. One might almost say that the suspense, such as it was, seemed less burdensome, and the sense of peril less acute. I came down by night; I saw no morning papers; I got aboard with my companion, and spent the whole forenoon before the slight tide would serve in putting things to right for the cruise.

We dropped out under a soft air, which soon died away. We

spent the whole mortal day drifting down to the Mewstone, and then, in that exasperating calm, the turn of the tide took us up again towards the breakwater. It was not till the fall of day that a breeze arose; I cannot remember from what quarter, but I think it was off the land—that is, from the north-east—but, at any rate, it served us; we could go eastward without having to beat, and we made out down the Sound. It was still light when we passed the Mewstone again. Through the last of evening and through all the darkness we ran along the coast to Devon for the Start.

I knew that the times were perilous, but I knew no more than any other man, in that odd week's lull before the storm, exactly how perilous they were. It was nearly a month, I think, since I had heard the priest read out, from those altar steps of Salisbury, prayers for the Archduke who had been murdered at Sarajevo.

When I had set out from Plymouth there was nothing but rumour, nothing certain. The Fleet had dispersed already some days past from the great review at Spithead, and was, as we were told, in the Atlantic at manœuvres. A night, a day, and now another night had passed; I had heard no news.

Nothing was further from my mind than war and armament as the sun rose on that glorious July morning, right out of a clean horizon, towards which the wind blew fresh and cool. It was a light but steady wind of morning that filled my sails as I sat at the tiller with a blanket about me, and laying her head to the north.

We had just rounded the Start at dawn. My companion went below to sleep. I watched, over the quarter, the Start Light flashing pale and white in the broadening day, and at last extinguished. Then the sun rose, as I have said. Immediately after its rising a sort of light haze filled the air to eastward. It was denser than it seemed to be, for it did not obscure the low disc of the sun, nor redden it, but, as you will read in a moment, it performed a mystery. The little ship slipped on, up past the Skerries Bank, and I could see far off the headland which bounds Dart Bay. There was no sail in sight. I was alone upon the sea; and the breeze neither freshening nor lowering, but giving a hearty line of course (along which we slipped, perhaps, five knots or six) made the water speak merrily upon the bows and along the run of our low sides. In this loneliness and content, as I sailed northward, I chanced to look, after an hour's steering or so, eastward again towards the open sea—and then it was that there passed me the vision I shall remember for ever, or for so long as the longest life may last.

Like ghosts, like things themselves made of mist, there passed between me and the newly risen sun, a procession of great forms, all in line, hastening eastward. It was the Fleet recalled.

The slight haze along that distant water had thickened, perhaps, imperceptibly; or perhaps the great speed of the men-of-war buried them too quickly in the distance. But, from whatever cause, this marvel was of short duration. It was seen for a moment, and in a moment it was gone.

Then I knew that war would come, and my mind was changed.

The bright air was the same around me and the heartening morning wind; the happy course of the *Nona*, making for a known port with all in her favour and something of youth in her and all round. What that war would bring, its magnitude, its character, was veiled from us all; but the advent of it, the mass of it coming, put a new face on everything I saw and felt and heard; on the steady breeze, on the little lapping of the salt sea-water, on the strong headlands of England. So went I northward alone as the day grew, until by mid-morning the breeze having dropped somewhat and the boat running more sluggishly, we lay abeam of the rock called the Druid's Mare, and began to run up the coast for Torbay. My companion wakened and came on deck. I told him what I had seen.

*   *   *   *   *

I remember sitting up to a very late and clear sunset of a Whit-Monday, gazing, under the sharp north-east breeze (the *Nona* moored at last to the wooden quay), at the pyramid of red roofs, and the highly successful walls and battlements of Rye, and considering within my mind many things.

First I considered within my own dear mind how marvellously this place had been preserved, seeing what modern England is, and what modern travel is. It is, of course, a Stage Scenery town, such as I have heard that Rothenburg is in Germany, and, therefore, there is an interest in preserving it; but I never heard that any such pains were taken to prevent its destruction by increase or rebuilding, or by any of those courses which bring death to beauty, such as a good train service, clubs, large and torturing hotels. Rye manages to live on. I suppose there is a spell. At any moment it may be broken, and the flood will pour in.

Being what it is, you cannot begin thinking about Rye without finding yourself dragged on to consider preciosity, and from that to the business of letters is but half a step.

Here at Rye did I meet and speak with Henry James, who was in the very heart of letters. Here also did I meet his brother, William James, whose business in life it was to write about philosophy, but whose conversation when I met him turned principally upon the subtle diplomatic genius of the King of England then reigning; upon the stability of English institutions; the excellence of the English police, and the singular faculty shown by our institutions of permitting differences without conflict. Also the piercing wit of the paper, *Punch*, and the profound wisdom of *The Times*. I had just come back with a companion from foreign parts; I had been sleeping rough, and I was in no condition to take part in polite conversation, so I did all the listening, and, as I listened, I still considered how literary was Rye. And so now, years after, looking at Rye from my boat, was I led on to consider the trade or business of letters.

When a writing man approaches that subject, he feels—at least I feel—like a man before a jumbled heap of material of all kinds—one of those refuse heaps in which you may pick up stray bits of machinery, or salve a little fuel, or find what you will. Or again, it is like being in one of those shops—there are few of them left, alas!—where an old half-wit has collected all manner of things, so that one knows not whether to begin by the furniture, or the glass, or the pictures, or the second-hand telescopes, or the books. For there is an indefinite number of ways of considering letters.

To those who have had to pursue letters as a trade (and to this I have been condemned all my life since my twenty-fifth year) it certainly is the hardest and the most capricious, and, indeed, the most abominable of trades, for the simple reason that it was never meant to be a trade.

A man is no more meant to live by writing than he is meant to live by conversation, or by dressing, or by walking about and seeing the world. For there is no relation between the function of letters and the economic effect of letters; there is no relation between the goodness and the badness of the work, or the usefulness of the work, or the magnitude of the work, and the sums paid for the work. It would not be natural that there should be such a relation, and, in fact, there is none.

This truth is missed by people who say that good writing has no market. That is not the point. Good writing sometimes has a market, and very bad writing sometimes has a market. Useful writing sometimes has a market, and writing of no use whatsoever, even as recreation, sometimes has a market. Writing important truths sometimes has a market. Writing the most ridiculous errors and false judgments sometimes has a market. The point is that the market has nothing to do with the qualities attached to writing. It never had and it never will. There is no injustice about it, any more than there is an injustice in the survival of beauty or ugliness in human beings, or the early death of the beautiful or the ugly. There is no more injustice about it than there is in a dry year hurting a root crop, and a wet harvest hurting a corn crop. The relationship between the excellence or the usefulness of a piece of literature, and the number of those who will buy it in a particular form, is not a causal relationship, it is a purely capricious one; and I, for my part, have never complained of the absence of a market, nor flattered myself upon the presence of one when a market turned up, though I have certainly been astonished at the way the market would behave.

For some few months thousands upon thousands—at one moment sixty thousand a week—of the articles I wrote upon the war were demanded by the public. Some months later the same articles, of the same value, or lack of value, were no longer demanded. There was no particular reason, the articles were clear, and based upon such insufficient knowledge as I shared with all my fellow-citizens. I had no private information save upon the point of numbers, and that was the very point upon which the public grew most easily fatigued, and were at last most sceptical.

Mr Hutchinson, for whose work I personally have (though I am afraid my judgment is not worth much in these things) a great liking, wrote among other books a book called *Once Aboard the Lugger*. It was exceedingly amusing, fresh, and, as I should have said, well worth anybody's buying. I do not know how many copies he sold of it, but I should imagine nothing very astonishing. A little while after he wrote a book called *If Winter Comes*, and it sold by the stack, and by the ton. One could see it piled up man-high upon the counters of shops in America, and it sold, and it sold, and it sold.

Mr Wells wrote a book which is most remarkable, and will probably make a mark in English literature. It was called *The Time Machine*. When Henley (I think it was) was bringing it out by instalments, the appearance of each was, for me at least, and for very many others, the chief event of the month. I do not know how many copies he sold, but there again I will swear nothing comparable to the numbers he has sold of later books which certainly will not stand out in English literature. That one which I hear has sold most largely has always seemed to me to be a mere repetition of what his audience already thought they knew, and of a philosophy which they already held: I mean his *Outline of History*. It was mainly a repetition of the popular mythology of to-day, of antiquated scientific jargon, full of the popular errors, but it was clear, well-proportioned and vivacious, showing a rare economy in the use and placing of words. It was also (and that is high minor praise for any book purporting to deal with history) astonishingly accurate in details. The names were properly spelt; south was never written for north, nor east for west; the dates were all right. Any one who has attempted the writing of history will not belittle such a feat: I, least of all, because I am constitutionally inaccurate in such things, and I will write left for right and north for south as a matter of course, and the word 'Tyre' for the word 'Acre,' and so on. At any rate, the book, with all its good and bad qualities, is obviously not of the first class, and equally obviously is not destined to endure, while *The Time Machine* is quite certainly of the first class, and is quite likely to endure. But I believe that the huge ephemeral demand for the *Outline of History* created no special, certainly no very great, demand for the more permanent *The Time Machine*. In general, I am assured by publishers, that when there is a sudden boom in a writer's work, they hardly ever manage to float on that boom a resale of earlier works; while if these earlier works are unknown, it is almost impossible to give them a popular fame on the strength of the later works. Witness the late Mr Hudson's *Crystal Age*. I came across it as a young man in a book shop in the Euston Road on a winter evening. I took it up and began reading it, and I read it so long that the bookseller told me I must buy it, which I did. Now, towards the end of Mr Hudson's life, he became deservedly famous as a writer upon the things of the natural world, and especially upon animals. But what made him famous was not his subject, though he was both accurate and learned; it was his manner of writing. One would have expected, therefore, that the *Crystal Age* would, upon his fame tardily arising, have a quiet and equal fame. It did not. I say that there are no laws governing these movements. They are capricious and incalculable.

Sometimes one hears that a great demand for a book, or for a set of newspaper articles, is due to something touching a common feeling in a particular fashion, something which great bodies of men necessarily feel together. There is a sense, of course, in which that is a mere truism, for it is clear that obscure stuff, or stuff dealing with matters that could not interest great numbers, will never sell. Why should it? But if the statement is intended to mean (as it usually is) that whatever sells in great numbers does so through this quality of a common appeal, that anything having this quality will always sell in great numbers, and that this quality is in some way a rare thing discoverable only in 'best sellers,' then the statement is manifestly false. A great deal of matter which possesses this appeal —enormously the greater part of such matter—remains unknown, and that which is best known is often rather weak in such an appeal. There are a great many factors entering into the result of a great popular demand which people forget because they are irrational: fashion is one, routine is another, inertia is a third. I know one man whose name, for the honour I bear it (he is now dead), I would not publish, since what I am about to say of his work is not flattering. He wrote a great number of stories, all of them with exactly the same plot and exactly the same characters. There was a beautiful chocolate-box girl, there was a villain, there was a hero who became rich after being poor, there were parents who objected to the match, and there was a racehorse. Had he departed from the formula, he would not have sold. As it was, he sold by the million. He was not only as modest a man as you could find, but exceedingly generous. He put on no airs; he made no error as to the nature of his success; he is already forgotten. Nothing shall persuade me that any one of many thousand men could not have written exactly the same; but a certain vast public got used to that particular insipid food, and wanted it unchanged, just as you and I get used to a particular kind of breakfast, and eat it every day of our lives.

Of course, there is a different set of factors operating in different phases of society. The popular best-seller of to-day depends upon the existence of our great towns with their machine-made citizens, all working blindly in little grooves, lacking any common direction—a dust of individuals. He depends also on that new-fangled, mechanical, and, let us hope ephemeral, institution called 'popular education.' If you tell millions of boys and girls (nearly all the citizens of the State), at the age when they receive unquestioning any dogmatic teaching, that their ancestors were repulsive savages, first actually bestial, later exceedingly vile, and that these ancestors passed through certain stages, and were 'Cavemen,' and men of the 'Stone Age,' and of the 'Bronze Age,' and so forth; then, obviously, writers using such terms, and taking for granted such a mythology, will fit in with the popular market. The demand for books, or of writing in any form, is created by minds already moulded, and any kind of writing which tends to break the mould is resented and left on one side. In older phases of society, judgment upon writing was passed by a few well-trained and leisured people, who handed down their judgments to a larger class, but still a small class compared with the whole State; and it is clear that in such a condition of society—which was that of England from the last third of the eighteenth century to the last third of the nineteenth—there would be no best sellers in our modern sense, and that there would be a nearer approach between the demand for a book and its excellence. But there also the mould had to be considered. Macaulay's false rhetoric sold well, because it agreed with the religion of his day. No historical work telling the truth about James II would have sold in his day, nor for that matter would any such matter sell in ours.

For religion is here, as elsewhere, at the root of effect. Robert Louis Stevenson was an excellent writer, but his popularity reposed not upon his excellence alone, but also upon the consonance of his religion with that of his readers. A man who was perpetually telling you that it was your duty to be cheerful, that you must take pleasure in God's creation, that you had a 'task of happiness' would cut no ice with the Irish, or with the Italians, or, in general, with the Catholic culture of Europe, but he rings true in the ears of the Protestant culture. Conversely, what the French powerfully call the 'bitter taste of reality' has very little chance with the crowd of the North. It is a spur and a relish to the crowd of the South. You could not sell Barrie in Arles nor Baudelaire in Pudsey.

The truth remains that the relation, or the lack of relation, between the economic result of a literary effort, and its success as a piece of craft, is of very much less importance than the consideration of the Canon, the attempt to achieve a standard. To get a Canon is the first requirement of letters. For though it is said that time will test literature for us in any case, this is not universally true; and, even in so far as it is true, it is better to have the good things to our hand than to wait for time to establish them. Such a Canon requires not only intelligent analysis, but a common philosophy into which our rules must fit. It is, therefore, with great difficulty arrived at, or perhaps not to be arrived at at all, in a period of confusion like ours. But the attempt to arrive at it never loses interest—no, not even to-day.

One of the things which always seem to me best worth saying in connection with letters is that prose should be distinguished, not only from verse, but also from rhetoric; and that prose in itself, mere lucid, economic, unornamented prose, is the foundation of good letters.

If the national prose is sound, the rest of national expression will come of itself. But this matter of prose has to-day been nearly forgotten. For most of us perhaps the phrase 'good prose,' or 'fine prose,' really means rhetoric. It means a passage in which the soul is stirred by a choice of rhythm and sound, and a mystical connotation of words in some passage not definitely reduced to versification. Thus, all the great passages from the Jacobean translation of the Hebrew scriptures, which are familiar as examples to our generation, are essentially rhetoric; so are the excerpts quoted from Bunyan, such as the fine closing passage of the *Pilgrim's Progress*; so is every single passage quoted from Carlyle; so are even those quoted from Newman and (I am sorry to say) those quoted from the greatest of our modern prose writers, Huxley.

But prose is rightly to be distinguished from anything of that kind. The excellence of prose lies in its adaptation to the function of intelligent expression or of narration. It is a statement; the end of it is not the exciting of emotion but the clear presentation, whether of a record (in fiction or fact) or of an idea, which the writer desires to communicate to his fellows.

He that succeeds in presenting the idea lucidly, so that no modification of subsidiary idea confuses the process; he that succeeds in presenting as vividly to the reader an image of particular fact, or of imagined fiction, vividly arisen in his own mind, is a writer of good prose; and the better he succeeds in this faculty of mere exposition, the more he excels in the supreme character of lucidity, the better his prose. Prose which is redundant is worse than prose which is economic in the use of words, simply because economic prose is the better statement. Exactitude of word and idea makes better prose than the use of many synonyms and of vague terms, simply because it ministers to lucidity. A mass of adjectives or adverbs is usually (not always) ill in prose, because usually (not always) the idea which the writer has to express does not involve all these modifications; they only slip from his pen through laziness or through having heard them before. It is obviously better prose to say 'I was tired out,' than to say 'I was wholly tired out,' unless for any particular reason you wish to express complete exhaustion. It is obviously better prose to say 'The sky,' than 'The blue sky,' unless for any particular reason you are concerned in your description with the colour of the sky.

But the worst enemy of prose to-day is the snobbishness of rules and forms, the mumbo-jumbo of hieratic prescription. The influence of these is a very good example of that excellent rule laid down by St Thomas Aquinas that all evil exists in mistaking, or misusing, the means for the end. This plague of pedantry does not rage quite as severely as it did when I was young, but it is still pretty severe. You are told that it is good prose, for instance, to have as few adjectives as possible. That is nonsense. It is good prose to have as many adjectives as you need, and *no more*. You are told, as a sort of eleventh commandment, never to split an infinitive; the rule is that of an excellent master of English, the late Professor Ker, who adds, 'except when euphony demands it.' I would go further; I would say that when the spoken language has arrived, as ours has to-day, at the universal use of the split infinitive, the written language may follow at some little distance behind. We are told that prose must never be emphatic, or excited, or this, or that, or the other. All that is nonsense. Prose must be emphatic when special emphasis is to be expressed, excited when excitement is to be expressed, and so forth. But certainly the character of good prose is the subordination of everything in it to the end, which is expression of what you have to say; and that is the distinction between good prose and rhetoric and verse. For in rhetoric and in verse the end is the emotion you desire, non-rationally, to excite; but in prose the end is rational, presentation, narration or statement of thesis: nothing more.

Judged by such standards, the two best prose writers in English are, I think, Dean Inge and Mr Gosse; for they, each of them, write on subjects where they have much to say, with the use of no words other than those needed for such expression, and they put those words invariably in the right order. Cecil Chesterton is dead.

I had almost written that there is no such thing as 'great'

prose, in the sense in which there is 'great' rhetoric or 'great' verse. The very best prose may be dull if the subject expressed is dull to the reader. You will get no better prose, for instance, than Newman's *Arians of the Fourth Century*. It is not dull to me, because I happen to be interested in that bit of history, but it would be fiercely dull to any reader who was not. Nevertheless it is first-rate prose. Newman having to write about a particular thing upon which he had made himself immensely learned; having to tell a certain number of facts, and to express a certain number of ideas, does so with the best choice of words in the best order—and that is prose.

The very fact that any sound definition of prose involves many negatives and only one positive (to wit, the positive need for lucid expression) makes it true that good prose is a common art. Excellence in prose is not common to all: far from it; but the faculties whereby excellence is reached are common to all. A man who is a first-rate walker, who carries his body with an exact poise, who can walk far without fatigue, and at a good pace, is a rare man; but we can all walk, and we all approach in various degrees, the standard that man has reached. So it is with prose. Those who think that good prose must have something odd about it—a few archaic words, little eighteenth-century tricks here and there, subjunctives popped in, like currants into a cake—these resemble men who in walking every now and then in high spirits do a little dance for fun. They are free to do so; we are not displeased. We cannot help noticing them (which is, perhaps, their object), and no one is the worse for the *gambado*. But in so far as they indulge in the fantasy, they are not walking; and if they do it the least bit too much, they are playing the fool. A wise man said to me once: 'Don't go and get your words from the artist colourman's.' Would that I had remembered his words in youth as I now humbly acknowledge them in age.

But the rhetorician wisely indulges in extravagance, and as for the poet, he may use what words he likes, and go to any extreme, or to any excess, so long only as he hits the mark. For it is with poetry as with love and with singing in tune. It is with poetry as with the sense of reality. It is with poetry as with the toothache. Either you have it, or you have it not.

There is no getting near Poetry; and though there are degrees in it, the boundary between its being and its not being is as sharp as a razor: on the one side is It, and on the other is nothingness. By which I do not mean to say that poetry is only found in certain violent stabs of emotion such as Shakespeare and Keats can launch, for it often inhabits page upon page, as throughout (I will maintain) all the Fourth Book of *Paradise Lost*, and countless other great achievements of the past in every tongue. But I mean that in a long flight or a short one, immediate or continuous—poetry is poetry, and not to be mistaken for anything else. Charles Kingsley (I ought to have dragged this in at Appledore, and not have waited for Rye) said to a woman, 'Madame, there is poetry and there is verse; and verse is divided into two kinds—good verse and bad verse. What you have here shown me is not poetry, it is verse. It is not good verse, it is bad verse.'

But, really, if I go on in this endless way of discussing the difficult trade of letters, I shall never get her nose round for the sea again. I had almost forgot I was sailing. What! Of two such occupations, the benediction of dealing with the sea and the degradation of scribbling, you can forget the better for the worse? I can. I am of a fallen race. I follow downwards.

But I am aboard the *Nona* again, and must put her out down Channel. This will I now do, and sail out of Rye by the first of the ebb under too strong a north-east wind at two o'clock in the morning with the waning moon just rising, the sky clear, two reefs in my mainsail, the second jib and a reef in my foresail, knowing well that I must watch all night, and that I shall get no sleep till morning. For it is one of the glories of sailing that you are under the authority of the heavens, and must submit to the whole world of water and of air, of which you are a part, not making laws to yourself capriciously, but acting as servant or brother of universal things.

THE PATH TO ROME

I SCRAMBLED down the mountain, for here, on the south side of the pass, there was no snow or ice, and it was quite easy to leave the road and take the old path cutting off the zigzags. As the air got heavier, I became hungry, and at the very end of my descent, two hundred feet or so above the young Rhône, I saw a great hotel. I went round to their front door and asked them whether I could eat, and at what price. 'Four francs,' they said.

'What!' said I, 'four francs for a meal! Come, let me eat in the kitchen, and charge me one.' But they became rude and obstinate, being used only to deal with rich people, so I cursed them, and went down the road. But I was very hungry.

The road falls quite steeply, and the Rhône, which it accompanies in that valley, leaps in little falls. On the bridge I passed a sad Englishman reading a book, and a little lower down, two American women in a carriage, and after that a priest (it was lucky I did not see him first. Anyhow, I touched iron at once, to wit, a key in my pocket), and after that a child minding a goat. Altogether, I felt myself in the world again, and as I was on a good road, all down hill, I thought myself capable of pushing on to the next village. But my hunger was really excessive, my right boot almost gone, and my left boot nothing to exhibit or boast of, when I came to a point where at last one looked down the Rhône valley for miles. It is like a straight trench, and at intervals there are little villages, built of most filthy chalets, the said chalets raised on great stones. There are pine trees up, up on either slope, into the clouds, and beyond the clouds I could not see. I left on my left a village called 'Between the Waters.' I passed through another called 'Ehringen,' but it has no inn. At last, two miles farther, faint from lack of food, I got into Ulrichen, a village a little larger than the rest, and the place where I believed one should start to go either over the Gries or Nufenen Pass. In Ulrichen was a warm, wooden, deep-eaved, frousty, comfortable, ramshackle, dark, anyhow kind of a little inn called 'The Bear.' And entering, I saw one of the women whom God loves.

She was of middle age, very honest and simple in the face,

kindly and good. She was messing about with cooking and stuff, and she came up to me stooping a little, her eyes wide and innocent, and a great spoon in her hand. Her face was extremely broad and flat, and I had never seen eyes set so far apart. Her whole gait, manner, and accent proved her to be extremely good, and on the straight road to heaven. I saluted her in the French tongue. She answered me in the same, but very broken and rustic, for her natural speech was a kind of mountain German. She spoke very slowly, and had a nice soft voice, and she did what only good people do, I mean, looked you in the eyes as she spoke to you.

.   .   .   .   .   .

Beware of shifty-eyed people. It is not only nervousness, it is also a kind of wickedness. Such people come to no good. I have three of them now in my mind as I write. One is a Professor.

And, by the way, would you like to know why universities suffer from this curse of nervous disease? Why the greatest personages stammer or have St Vitus' dance, or jabber at the lips, or hop in their walk, or have their heads screwed round, or tremble in the fingers, or go through life with great goggles like a motor car? Eh? I will tell you. It is the punishment of their *intellectual pride*, than which no sin is more offensive to the angels.

What! here are we with the jolly world of God all round us, able to sing, to draw, to paint, to hammer and build, to sail, to ride horses, to run, to leap; having for our splendid inheritance love in youth and memory in old age, and we are to take one miserable little faculty, our one-legged, knock-kneed, gimcrack, purblind, rough-skinned, underfed, and perpetually irritated and grumpy intellect, or analytical curiosity rather (a diseased appetite), and let it swell till it eats up every other function? Away with such foolery.

LECTOR. When shall we get on to . . .

AUCTOR. Wait a moment. I say, away with such foolery. Note that pedants lose all proportion. They never can keep sane in a discussion. They will go wild on matters they are wholly unable to judge, such as Armenian Religion or the Politics of Paris or what not. Never do they use one of those three phrases which keep a man steady and balance his mind, I mean the words: (1) *After all it is not my business*. (2) *Tut! tut! You don't say so!* and (3) *Credo in Unum Deum Patrem Omnipotentem,*

Factorem omnium visibilium atque invisibilium; in which last there is a power of synthesis that can jam all their analytical dust-heap into such a fine, tight, and compact body as would make them stare to see. I understand that they need six months' holiday a year. Had I my way they should take twelve, and an extra day on leap years.

LECTOR. Pray, pray return to the woman at the inn.

AUCTOR. I will, and by this road: to say that on the day of Judgment, when St Michael weighs souls in his scales, and the wicked are led off by the Devil with a great rope, as you may see them over the main porch of Notre Dame (I will heave a stone after them myself I hope), all the souls of the pedants together will not weigh as heavy and sound as the one soul of this good woman at the inn.

. . . .

She put food before me and wine. The wine was good, but in the food was some fearful herb or other I had never tasted before—a pure spice or scent, and a nasty one. One could taste nothing else, and it was revolting; but I ate it for her sake.

Then, very much refreshed, I rose, seized my great staff, shook myself and said: 'Now it is about noon, and I am off for the frontier.'

At this she made a most fearful clamour, saying that it was madness, and imploring me not to think of it, and running out fetched from the stable a tall, sad, pale-eyed man who saluted me profoundly and told me that he knew more of the mountains than any one for miles. And this by asking many afterwards I found out to be true. He said that he had crossed the Nufenen and the Gries whenever they could be crossed since he was a child, and that if I attempted it that day I should sleep that night in Paradise. The clouds on the mountain, the soft snow recently fallen, the rain that now occupied the valleys, the glacier on the Gries, and the pathless snow in the mist of the Nufenen would make it sheer suicide for him, an experienced guide, and for me a worse madness. Also he spoke of my boots and wondered at my poor cotton coat and trousers, and threatened me with intolerable cold.

It seems that the books I had read at home, when they said that the Nufenen had no snow on it, spoke of a later season of the year; it was all snow now, and soft snow, and hidden by a full mist in such a day from the first third of the ascent. As for the Gries, there was a glacier on the top which needed some kind of clearness in the weather. Hearing all this I said I would remain—but it was with a heavy heart. Already I felt a shadow of defeat over me. The loss of time was a thorn. I was already short of cash, and my next money was at Milan. My return to England was fixed for a certain date, and stronger than either of these motives against delay was a burning restlessness that always takes men when they are on the way to great adventures.

I made him promise to wake me next morning at three o'clock, and, short of a tempest, to try and get me across the Gries. As for the Nufenen and Crystalline passes which I had desired to attempt, and which were (as I have said) the straight line to Rome, he said (and he was right), that let alone the impassability of the Nufenen just then, to climb the Crystal Mountain in that season would be as easy as flying to the moon. Now, to cross the Nufenen alone, would simply land me in the upper valley of the Ticino, and take me a great bend out of my way by Bellinzona. Hence my bargain that at least he should show me over the Gries Pass, and this he said, if man could do it, he would do the next day; and I, sending my boots to be cobbled (and thereby breaking another vow), crept up to bed, and all afternoon read the school-books of the children. They were in French, from lower down the valley, and very Genevese and heretical for so devout a household. But the Genevese civilization is the standard for these people, and they combat the Calvinism of it with missions, and have statues in their rooms, not to speak of holy water stoups.

The rain beat on my window, the clouds came lower still down the mountain. Then (as is finely written in the Song of Roland), 'the day passed and the night came, and I slept.' But with the coming of the small hours, and with my waking, prepare yourselves for the most extraordinary and terrible adventure that befel me out of all the marvels and perils of this pilgrimage, the most momentous and the most worthy of perpetual record, I think, of all that has ever happened since the beginning of the world.

.   .   .   .

At three o'clock the guide knocked at my door, and I rose and came out to him. We drank coffee and ate bread. We put into our sacks ham and bread, and he white wine and I brandy. Then we set out. The rain had dropped to a drizzle, and there was no wind. The sky was obscured for the most part, but here and there was a star. The hills hung awfully above us in the night as we crossed the spongy valley. A little wooden bridge took us over the young Rhône, here only a stream, and we followed a path up into the tributary ravine which leads to the Nufenen and the Gries. In a mile or two it was a little lighter, and this was as well, for some weeks before a great avalanche had fallen, and we had to cross it gingerly. Beneath the wide cap of frozen snow ran a torrent roaring. I remembered Colorado, and how I had crossed the Arkansaw on such a bridge as a boy. We went on in the uneasy dawn. The woods began to show, and there was a cross where a man had slipped from above that very April and been killed. Then, most ominous and disturbing, the drizzle changed to a rain, and the guide shook his head and said it would be snowing higher up. We went on, and it grew lighter. Before it was really day (or else the weather confused and darkened the sky), we crossed a good bridge, built long ago, and we halted at a shed where the cattle lie in the late summer when the snow is melted. There we rested a moment.

But on leaving its shelter we noticed many disquieting things. The place was a hollow, the end of the ravine—a bowl, as it were; one way out of which is the Nufenen, and the other the Gries.

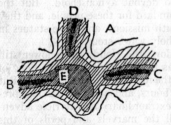

Here it is in a sketch map. The heights are marked lighter and lighter, from black in the valleys to white in the impassable mountains. E is where we stood, in a great cup or basin, having just come up the ravine B. C is the Italian valley of the Tosa, and the neck between it and E is the Gries. D is the valley of the Ticino, and the neck between E and it is the Nufenen. A is the Crystal Mountain. You may take the necks or passes to be about 8,000, and the mountains 10,000 or 11,000 feet above the sea.

We noticed, I say, many disquieting things. First, all that bowl or cup below the passes was a carpet of snow, save where patches of black water showed, and all the passes and mountains, from top to bottom, were covered with very thick snow; the deep surface of it soft and fresh fallen. Secondly, the rain had turned into snow. It was falling thickly all around. Nowhere have I more perceived the immediate presence of great

Death. Thirdly, it was far colder, and we felt the beginning
of a wind. Fourthly, the clouds had come quite low down.

The guide said it could not be done, but I said we must
attempt it. I was eager, and had not yet felt the awful grip
of the cold. We left the Nufenen on our left, a hopeless steep
of new snow buried in fog, and we attacked the Gries. For
half an hour we plunged on through snow above our knees, and
my thin cotton clothes were soaked. So far the guide knew
we were more or less on the path, and he went on and I panted
after him. Neither of us spoke, but occasionally he looked back
to make sure I had not dropped out.

The snow began to fall more thickly, and the wind had risen
somewhat. I was afraid of another protest from the guide, but
he stuck to it well, and I after him, continually plunging through
soft snow and making yard after yard upwards. The snow
fell more thickly and the wind still rose.

We came to a place which is, in the warm season, an alp;
that is, a slope of grass, very steep but not terrifying; having
here and there sharp little precipices of rock breaking it into
steps, but by no means (in summer) a matter to make one
draw back. Now, however, when everything was still Arctic
it was a very different matter. A sheer steep of snow whose
downward plunge ran into the driving storm and was lost, whose
head was lost in the same mass of thick cloud above, a slope
somewhat hollowed and bent inwards, had to be crossed if we
were to go any further; and I was terrified, for I knew nothing
of climbing. The guide said there was little danger, only if
one slipped one might slide down to safety, or one might (much
less probably) get over rocks and be killed. I was chattering
a little with cold; but as he did not propose a return, I followed
him. The surface was alternately slabs of frozen snow and
patches of soft new snow. In the first he cut steps, in the second
we plunged, and once I went right in and a mass of snow broke
off beneath me and went careering down the slope. He showed
me how to hold my staff backwards as he did his alpenstock,
and use it as a kind of brake in case I slipped.

We had been about twenty minutes crawling over that wall
of snow and ice; and it was more and more apparent that we
were in for danger. Before we had quite reached the far side,
the wind was blowing a very full gale and roared past our ears.
The surface snow was whirring furiously like dust before it:
past our faces and against them drove the snow-flakes, cutting
the air: not falling, but making straight darts and streaks.

They seemed like the form of the whistling wind; they blinded us. The rocks on the far side of the slope, rocks which had been our goal when we set out to cross it, had long ago disappeared in the increasing rush of the blizzard. Suddenly as we were still painfully moving on, stooping against the mad wind, these rocks loomed up over as large as houses, and we saw them through the swarming snow-flakes as great hulls are seen through a fog at sea. The guide crouched under the lee of the nearest; I came up close to him and he put his hands to my ear and shouted to me that nothing further could be done—he had so to shout because in among the rocks the hurricane made a roaring sound, swamping the voice.

I asked how far we were from the summit. He said he did not know where we were exactly, but that we could not be more than eight hundred feet from it. I was but that from Italy and I would not admit defeat. I offered him all I had in money to go on, but it was folly in me, because if I had had enough to tempt him and if he had yielded we should both have died. Luckily it was but a little sum. He shook his head. He would not go on, he broke out, for all the money there was in the world. He shouted me to eat and drink, and so we both did.

Then I understood his wisdom, for in a little while the cold began to seize me in my thin clothes. My hands were numb, my face already gave me intolerable pain, and my legs suffered and felt heavy. I learnt another thing (which had I been used to mountains I should have known), that it was not a simple thing to return. The guide was hesitating whether to stay in this rough shelter, or to face the chances of the descent. This terror had not crossed my mind, and I thought as little of it as I could, needing my courage, and being near to breaking down from the intensity of the cold.

It seems that in a *tourmente* (for by that excellent name do the mountain people call such a storm) it is always a matter of doubt whether to halt or to go back. If you go back through it and lose your way, you are done for. If you halt in some shelter, it may go on for two or three days, and then there is an end of you.

After a little he decided for a return, but he told me honestly what the chances were, and my suffering from cold mercifully mitigated my fear. But even in that moment, I felt in a confused but very conscious way that I was defeated. I had crossed so many great hills and rivers, and pressed so well on my undeviating arrow-line to Rome, and I had charged this

one great barrier manfully where the straight path of my
pilgrimage crossed the Alps—and I had failed! Even in that
fearful cold I felt it, and it ran through my doubt of return like
another and deeper current of pain. Italy was there, just above,
right to my hand. A lifting of a cloud, a little respite, and every
downward step would have been towards the sunlight. As it
was, I was being driven back northward, in retreat and ashamed.
The Alps had conquered me.

Let us always after this combat their immensity and their
will, and always hate the inhuman guards that hold the gates
of Italy, and the powers that lie in wait for men on those high
places. But now I know that Italy will always stand apart.
She is cut off by no ordinary wall, and Death has all his army
on her frontiers.

Well, we returned. Twice the guide rubbed my hands with
brandy, and once I had to halt and recover for a moment,
failing and losing my hold. Believe it or not, the deep footsteps of our ascent were already quite lost and covered by the
new snow since our halt, and even had they been visible, the
guide would not have retraced them. He did what I did not
at first understand, but what I soon saw to be wise. He took
a steep slant downward over the face of the snow-slope, and
though such a pitch of descent a little unnerved me, it was well
in the end. For when we had gone down perhaps nine hundred
feet, or a thousand, in perpendicular distance, even I, half numb
and fainting, could feel that the storm was less violent. Another two hundred, and the flakes could be seen not driving in
flashes past, but separately falling. Then in some few minutes
we could see the slope for a very long way downwards quite
clearly; then, soon after, we saw far below us the place where
the mountain-side merged easily into the plain of that cup or
basin whence we had started.

When we saw this, the guide said to me: 'Hold your stick
thus, if you are strong enough, and let yourself slide.' I could
just hold it, in spite of the cold. Life was returning to me with
intolerable pain. We shot down the slope almost as quickly as
falling, but it was evidently safe to do so, as the end was clearly
visible, and had no break or rock in it.

So we reached the plain below, and entered the little shed,
and thence looking up, we saw the storm above us; but no one
could have told it for what it was. Here, below, was silence,
and the terror and raging above seemed only a great trembling
cloud occupying the mountain. Then we set our faces down

the ravine by which we had come up, and so came down to where the snow changed to rain. When we got right down into the valley of the Rhône, we found it all roofed with cloud, and the higher trees were white with snow, making a line like a tide mark on the slopes of the hills.

I re-entered 'The Bear,' silent and angered, and not accepting the humiliation of that failure. Then, having eaten, I determined in equal silence to take the road like any other fool; to cross the Furka by a fine high road, like any tourist, and to cross the St Gothard by another fine high road, as millions had done before me, and not to look heaven in the face again till I was back after my long detour, on the straight road again for Rome.

But to think of it! I who had all that planned out, and had so nearly done it! I who had cut a path across Europe like a shaft, and seen so many strange places!—now to have to recite all the litany of the vulgar; Bellinzona, Lugano, and this and that, which any railway travelling fellow can tell you. Not till Como should I feel a man again. . . .

Indeed it is a bitter thing to have to give up one's sword.

.   .   .   .   .

At the foot of the hill I prepared to enter the city, and I lifted up my heart.

There was an open space; a tramway; a tram upon it about to be drawn by two lean and tired horses whom in the heat many flies disturbed. There was dust on everything around.

A bridge was immediately in front. It was adorned with statues in soft stone, half-eaten away, but still gesticulating in corruption, after the manner of the seventeenth century. Beneath the bridge there tumbled and swelled and ran fast a great confusion of yellow water: it was the Tiber. Far on the right were white barracks of huge and of hideous appearance; over these the Dome of St Peter's rose and looked like something newly built. It was of a delicate blue, but made a metallic contrast against the sky.

Then (along a road perfectly straight and bounded by factories, mean houses and distempered walls: a road littered with many scraps of paper, bones, dirt, and refuse) I went on for several hundred yards, having the old wall of Rome before me all the time, till I came right under it at last; and with the hesitation that befits all great actions I entered, putting the right foot first lest I should bring further misfortune upon that capital of all our fortunes.

And so the journey ended.

.   .   .   .   .   .

It was the Gate of the Poplar—not of the People. (Ho, Pedant! Did you think I missed you, hiding and lurking there?) Many churches were to hand; I took the most immediate, which stood just within the wall and was called Our Lady of the People—(not 'of the Poplar.' Another fall for the learned! Professor, things go ill with you to-day!). Inside were many fine pictures, not in the niminy-piminy manner, but strong, full-coloured, and just.

To my chagrin, Mass was ending. I approached a priest and said to him:

'Pater, quando vel a quella hora e la prossimma Missa?'

'Ad nonas,' said he.

'Pol! Hercle!' (thought I), 'I have yet twenty minutes to wait! Well, as a pilgrimage cannot be said to be over till the first Mass is heard in Rome, I have twenty minutes to add to my book.'

So, passing an Egyptian obelisk which the great Augustus had nobly dedicated to the Sun, I entered. . . .

LECTOR. But do you intend to tell us nothing of Rome?

AUCTOR. Nothing, dear Lector.

LECTOR. Tell me at least one thing; did you see the Coliseum?

AUCTOR. . . . I entered a café at the right hand of a very long, straight street, called for bread, coffee, and brandy, and contemplating my boots and worshipping my staff that had been friends of mine so long, and friends like all true friends inanimate, I spent the few minutes remaining to my happy, common, unshriven, exterior, and natural life, in writing down this

DITHYRAMBIC
EPITHALAMIUM OR THRENODY

In these boots, and with this staff
Two hundred leaguers and a half—

(That means, two and a half hundred leagues. You follow? Not two hundred and one half league. . . . Well—)

Two hundred leaguers and a half
Walked I, went I, paced I, tripped I,
Marched I, held I, skelped I, slipped I,
Pushed I, panted, swung and dashed I;

Picked I, forded, swam and splashed I,
Strolled I, climbed I, crawled and scrambled,
Dropped and dipped I, ranged and rambled ;
Plodded I, hobbled I, trudged and tramped I,
And in lonely spinnies camped I,
And in haunted pinewoods slept I,
Lingered, loitered, limped and crept I,
Clambered, halted, stepped and leapt I ;
Slowly sauntered, roundly strode I,
And . . .   (Oh! Patron saints and Angels
           That protect the four evangels!
           And you Prophets vel majores
           Vel incerti, vel minores,
           Virgines ac confessores
           Chief of whose peculiar glories
           Est in Aula Regis stare
           Atque orare et exorare
           Et clamare et conclamare
           Clamantes cum clamoribus
           Pro nobis peccatoribus).

Let me not conceal it . . . . Rode I..
(For who but critics could complain
Of 'riding' in a railway train?)
Across the valleys and the high-land,
With all the world on either hand,
Drinking when I had a mind to,
Singing when I felt inclined to ;
Nor ever turned my face to home
Till I had slaked my heart at Rome.

LECTOR. But this is dogg——
AUCTOR. Not a word!

LONDON RIVER

THROUGH the flats that bound the North Sea and shelve into it imperceptibly, merging at last with the shallow flood, and re-emerging in distant sandbanks and less conspicuous shoals, run facing each other two waterways far inland, which are funnels and entries, as it were, scoured by the tide.

Each has at the end of the tideway a narrow, placid, inland stream, from whence the broader, noisier sea part also takes its name. Each has been and will always be famous in the arms and in the commerce of Europe. Each forms a sort of long great street of ships crowded in a traffic to and fro. For each has its great port. The one Antwerp, the other London. The Scheldt is the name of the first, which leads to Antwerp, and makes the opportunity for that great market of the world. But the second is the River of London, much older in its destinies, and probably more destined to endure in its functions of commerce.

I know not how to convey that picture in the mind, which the eyes do not see, and yet by which a man is haunted if he has read enough of books and seen the maps, when he comes up through the Narrows of Dover Straits from the wide, empty seas three days behind and knows that there lies before his owner a choice between the eastern and the western gate. That choice is in the case of every ship determined long before. She has the dull duty to do of turning to the right or to the left, and her orders bind her to the river of the Netherlands or of England as it may be. But if you will consider many centuries and the changing adventures of business you will still— as you pass northward between the two shores of Flanders and of Britain, and as you see their recession upon either side of the northern way which opens before you—understand that doubt upon the future and the rivalry of the two rivers which is soon to be so deeply impressed upon the politics of our time.

I could think of the Scheldt and of the Thames as two antagonists facing each other before conflict across a marked arena, which is that of the shallow, tumbling, and yellow water of the North Sea; or as two forces pitted one against the other, streams each of which would force the other back if it could find the strength; or as two Courts in a perpetual jealousy one of the other, intriguing and making and losing point after point in a game of polity.

When the statisticians have done their talk—and very brainless it is—of resources and of metals, two opposing *lives* are left standing behind either of the great towns, and either of the great sea rivers. The one is the experiment of the modern Germanies; the other is the founded tradition of England; and the more closely a man considers each of these the greater contrast does he discover between the causes of either's energy of come and go.

A third great tidal river is also concerned with these seas, also helps to determine their commerce, also supports its great inland town. That river is the Seine, and I shall, in the pages which follow, use the Seine also for the example it affords in the analogies and contrasts and parallels which I propose to draw. But it is the Scheldt and the Thames which still remain the greater opponents. The united political life of Gaul, which was inherited and transformed by the French Monarchy, forbade the growth of a great commerce to the north. Paris became not only the political centre of France but its main market as well, and to-day the water carriage of Paris—that is, the traffic of its port—is greater than that of any maritime town in the country. Only if Normandy had developed as an independent state would Rouen have become what Antwerp and London have become. Rouen would then have been, without doubt, the point of transhipment between the inland and the maritime waterways, and the distance of the town from coal would hardly have affected it more than does the distance of London. Its situation as a political junction would have determined its greatness. As it is the Lower Seine may be set beside the Scheldt and the Thames for an illustration in their topography and in the origins of their human settlements, but it does not afford a true commercial parallel to-day, and Rouen is no third rival to the two great ports which are before our eyes and in this generation struggling for primacy.

It is the custom of sailors to speak of that water by which they approach a great town under the name of the town. Men coming up from Yarmouth Roads inland do not speak of the Yare, but of Norwich River. For to the sailor the river is but a continuation of, or an access to, his port, and the Lower Thames is thus universally known from the sea as London River. The term is an accidental one, but it contains the true history of the connection between the stream and the town.

The Thames made London. London is a function of the Thames, and it is in such a connection that I propose to regard it in this essay: London as the great crossing place of the Thames, and as the custodian and fruit of what early may have been the chief ferry, but has for nearly two thousand years been the chief bridge; London as the market of which the Thames is the approach and the port; London as a habitation of which the great street is the Thames, a street for centuries the main highway of its people, lost for a time and now recovering its ancient use; London as the civil and religious head of revenues which were drawn from the Thames Valley; and London as the determinant, through its position upon the Thames, of English military history.

This intimate connection between the city and the river we all instinctively feel, and the two are connected together as no other waterway with its capital can be connected throughout Europe. For the Thames is all that every other river is to every other capital wherever some great stream is connected with a chief city. But whereas in every other case it is but one or another of the functions of such a stream that history can remark, in the case of London it can remark them all. Little sea-borne traffic reaches Paris by the Seine; the Tiber could never be a street for Rome; Vienna neglects the Danube; Antwerp protects no great crossing, nor has ever been the nucleus of a State; Rouen—the nearest parallel—was not the strategical pivot of Normandy, nor ever formed, as London forms, a chief fraction in the economic power of its province. The two rivers which are sacred to Lyons never fed that town; the Rhône watered but did not lead to Arles. The towns of Lombardy depend upon the fertility of the Po Valley, but the stream is nothing to their commerce or to their political eminence, and Milan, and Venice, and Turin are independent of it. Saragossa was the mistress of Aragon, but the Ebro did not make Saragossa, and as for Madrid, the trickle which runs below Madrid is best described in the story of the Spanish patriot who was dying of thirst after battle, but upon being offered a cup of water, said: 'Give it to the poor Manzanares.' Lisbon and Cadiz are maritime, not fluvial, and look where you will throughout the civilization of Europe you will not find, save in the case of London, this complete interdependence between a great town and its river.

In tracing or establishing this intimate bond between London and the Thames one must guard against an error which the modern reader rightly suspects and is justly ready to criticize or to deny when it appears in any piece of historical writing. That error is the error of materialism.

A generation ago it was universal, and there was no phenomenon in the story of England or of Europe from the emplacement of a city to the growth of the Church which was not traced to inanimate causes superior to, and independent of, any action of the Will. This philosophy narrowed, distorted, and dried up every department of knowledge, and while the area or learning increased with a rapidity hitherto unknown, the spirit inhabiting that conquest was starved. It was as though the time could not contain at once the energy to discover and the energy to know, and as though the covering of so vast a field in so short a period was achieved inevitably at a cost of profundity. That a bias towards the mechanical and the necessary should be present in the physical sciences—in chemistry for instance—is to be expected, that it should have invaded biology was less excusable, but that it should have been permitted to affect (as it did) the business native to man—his building, his institutions, his very dreams—was an excessive blunder, and the spirit of all the younger men to-day is running if anything too strongly in reaction against that ebb-tide of the soul. They reject the dogmas of their fathers which would bend everything man has done to material circumstance, which would talk of man as the slave rather than the master of his instruments, and which, in an argument absurdly circular, 'interpreted history in the terms of Economics': and they are right.

Even in the sphere of topography, where the physical limitations of human action are the main subject of the writer, they expect a full admission of the soul of man and even—which is very wise—some recognition of that mysterious genius which inhabits every place and is perhaps its vital part.

They are right. No one can see the marriage between London and its river without wondering in what degree things other than ponderable and measurable things may enter into the habitation of man. There is nothing man does, of course, which has not in it the soul. But it may be also true that there is nothing done to man wherein some soul is not also. Now the homes of man and the air and the water and the wind and the earth, against which in part and with which in part those homes arise, are so woven in with his fate—which is a spiritual fate—that we must properly lend to these insensate things some controlling motive; and we may rightly say, though only by the use of metaphor, that all these things have a spirit within them. I cannot get away from it that the Thames may be alive, and London most certainly is.

But all these things, though one may put them in the form of statements, are really questions; and questions to which no sort of answer has yet been discovered.

BARBARY

WHEN a man first sees Africa, if it is just before the rising of the sun, he perceives, right up against a clean horizon, what appear to be islands standing out distinct and sharp above the sea.

At this hour a wind is often blowing from the eastward, and awakens the Mediterranean as though it came purposely at dawn to make the world ready for the morning. The little waves leap up beneath it, steep towards their shadows, and the bows of the ship that had surged all night through a rolling calm begin, as sailors say, to 'speak': the broken water claps and babbles along the side. In this way, if he has good fortune, the traveller comes upon a new land. It is that land, shut off from all the rest between the desert and the sea, which the Arabs call the Island of the West, the Maghreb, but to which we in Europe for many hundred years have given the name of Barbary: as it says in the song about freedom:

> . . . as large as a Lion reclined
> By the rivers of Barbary.

It is the shore that runs, all built upon a single plan, from Tunis and the Gulf of Carthage to Tangier; that was snatched from Europe in one great cavalry charge twelve hundred years ago, and is now at last again in the grasp of Europe.

For many hours the traveller will sail towards it until at last he comes to a belt of smooth water which, in such weather, fringes all that coast, and then he finds that what he saw at morning was not a line of islands, but the tops of high hills standing in a range along the sea: they show darker against a stronger light and a more southerly sun as he draws nearer, and beyond them he sees far off inland the first buttress mountains which hold up the plateaux of Atlas.

The country which he thus approaches differs in its fortune and history from all others in the world. The soil and the relief of the Maghreb, coupled with its story, have made it peculiar and, as it were, a symbol of the adventures of Europe. Ever since our Western race began its own life and entered into its ceaseless struggle against the East, this great bastion has been held and lost again; occupied by our enemies and then taken back as our power re-arose. The Phoenician ruled it; Rome wrested it back; it fell for the last time when the Roman Empire declined; its reconquest has been the latest fruit of our recovery.

It is thoroughly our own. The race that has inhabited it from its origin and still inhabits it is our race; its climate and situation are ours; it is at the furthest limit from Asia; it is an opposing shore of our inland sea; it links Sicily to Spain; it retains in every part of it the Menhirs and the Dolmens, the great stones at which our people sacrificed when they began to be men: yet even in the few centuries of written history foreign gods have twice been worshipped there and foreign rulers have twice held it for such long spaces of time that twice its nature has been forgotten. Even to-day, when our reoccupation seems assured, we speak of it as though it were by some right originally Oriental, and by some destiny certain to remain so. During the many centuries of our decline and of our slow resurrection, these countries were first cut off so suddenly and so clean from Christendom, next steeped so long and so thoroughly in an alien religion and habit of law, that their very dress and language changed; and until a man has recognized at last the faces beneath the turbans, and has seen and grown familiar with the great buildings which Rome nowhere founded more solidly than in these provinces, he is deceived by the tradition of an immediate past and by the externals of things: he sees nothing but Arabs around him, and feels himself an intruder from a foreign world.

Of this Eastern spirit, which is still by far the strongest to be found in the states of Barbary, an influence meets one long before one has made land. The little ships all up and down the Mediterranean, and especially as one nears the African coast, are in their rig and their whole manner Arabian.

There is a sort of sail which may be called the original of all sails. It is the sail with which antiquity was familiar. It brought the ships to Tenedos and the Argo carried it. The Norwegians had it when they were pirates a thousand years ago. They have it still. It is nearer a lug-sail than anything else, and indeed our Deal luggers carry something very near it. It is almost a square sail, but the yard has a slight rake and there is a bit of a peak to it. It is the kind of sail which seems to come first into the mind of any man when he sets out to use the wind. It is to be seen continually to-day hoisted above small boats in the north of Europe.

But this sail is too simple. It will not go close to the wind, and in those light and variable airs which somehow have no force along the deck, it hangs empty and makes no way because it has no height.

Now when during that great renaissance of theirs in the seventh century the Arabs left their deserts and took to the sea, they became for a short time in sailing, as in philosophy, the teachers of their new subjects. They took this sail which they had found in all the ports they had conquered along this coast—in Alexandria, in Cyrene, in Carthage, in Caesarea—they lightened and lengthened the yard, they lifted the peak up high, they clewed down the foot, and very soon they had that triangular *lateen* sail which will, perhaps, remain when every other evidence of their early conquering energy has disappeared. With such a sail they drove those first fleets of theirs which gave them at once the islands and the commerce of the Mediterranean. It was the sail which permitted their invasion of the northern shores and the unhappy subjection of Spain.

We Europeans have for now some seven hundred years, from at least the Third Crusade, so constantly used this gift of Islam that we half forget its origin. You may see it in all the Christian harbours of the Mediterranean to-day, in every port of the Portuguese coast, and here and there as far north as the Channel. It is not to be seen beyond Cherbourg, but in Cherbourg it is quite common. The harbour-boats that run between the fleet and the shore hoist these lateens. Yet it is not of our own making, and, indeed, it bears a foreign mark which is very distinct, and which puzzles every northerner when first he comes across this sail: it reefs along the yard. Why it should do so neither history nor the men that handle it can explain, since single sails are manifestly made to reef from the foot to the leach, where a man can best get at them. Not so the lateen. If you carry too much canvas and the wind is pressing her you must take it in from aloft, or, it must be supposed, lower the whole on deck. And this foreign, quaint, unusual thing which stamps the lateen everywhere is best seen when the sail is put away in harbour. It does not lie down along the deck as do ours in the north, but right up along the yard, and the yard itself is kept high at the masthead, making a great bow across the sky, and (one would say) tempting Providence to send a gale and wreck it. Save for this mark—which may have its uses, but seems to have none and to be merely barbaric—the lateen is perfect in its kind, and might be taken with advantage throughout the world (as it is throughout all this united sea) for the uniform sail. For this kind of sail is, for small craft, the neatest and the swiftest in the world, and, in a general way, will lie closer to the wind than any other. Our own fore-and-aft rig is nothing else but a lateen cut up into mainsail, foresail, and jib, for the convenience of handling.

The little ships, so rigged, come out like heralds far from the coast to announce the old dominion of the East and of the religion that made them: of the united civilization that has launched them over all its seas, from east of India to south of Zanzibar and right out here in the western place which we are so painfully recovering. They are the only made thing, the only *form* we accepted from the Arab: and we did well to accept it. The little ships are a delight.

You see them everywhere. They belong to the sea and they animate it. They are similar as waves are similar: they are different as waves are different. They come into a hundred positions against the light. They heel and run with every mode of energy.

There is nothing makes a man's heart so buoyant as to see one of the little ships bowling along breast-high towards him, with the wind and the clouds behind it, careering over the sea. It seems to have borrowed something of the air and something of the water, and to unite them both and to be their offspring and also their bond. When they are middle-way over the sea towards one under a good breeze, the little ships are things to remember.

So it is when they carry double sail and go, as we say of our schooners, 'wing and wing.' For they can carry two sails when the wind is moderate, and especially when the vessel is running before it, but these two sails are not carried upon two masts, but both upon the same mast. The one is the common or working sail, carried in all weathers. The other is a sort of spinnaker, of which you may see the yard lying along decks in harbour or triced up a little by the halyard, so as to swing clear of the hands.

When the little ships come up like this with either sail well out and square and their course laid straight before the general run of a fresh sea, rolling as they go, it is as though the wind had a friend and companion of its own, understanding all its moods, so easily and rapidly do they arrive towards the shore.

A little jib (along this coast at least) is bent along the forestay, and the dark line of it marks the swing and movement of the whole. So also when you stand and look from along their wake and see them leaving for the horizon along a slant of the Levantine, with the breeze just on their quarter and their laden hulls careening a trifle to leeward, you would say they were great birds, born of the sea, and sailing down the current from which they were bred. The peaks of their tall sails have a turn to them like the wing-tips of birds, especially of those darting birds which come up to us from the south after winter and shoot along their way.

Moreover, the sails of these little ships never seem to lose the memory of power. Their curves and fullness always suggest a movement of the hull. Very often at sunset when the dead calm reflects things unbroken like an inland pond, the topmost angle of these lateens catches some hesitating air that stirs above, and leads it down the sail, so that a little ripple trembles round the bows of the boat, though all the water beside them is quite smooth, and you see her gliding in without oars. She comes along in front of the twilight, as gradual and as silent as the evening, and seems to be impelled by nothing more substantial than the advance of darkness.

It is with such companions to proclaim the title of the land that one comes round under a point of hills and enters harbour.

CONSTANTINE

CONSTANTINE is, perhaps, the most deeply stamped city of the West. It is certainly the one which, in site and relief, stands out most strongly of all those that I have seen between the Russian plains and the Atlantic.

Many towns have one great hill or rock to mark them, for most towns have risen round the nucleus of a stronghold; and an isolated rock, if only it has water, is the best choice for early defence. Many towns are peninsular in shape; built on a loop of river and only to be approached by a narrow neck of land. Such are Angoulême, Luxemburg, Poitiers; and many of these peninsular towns have something of a cliff or steep bank defending them for some part of their circuit.

But Constantine is like nothing else on earth that ever I saw. And from the first moment that I saw it, it has stood vividly fixed in my mind, as, I suppose, it will stand in the mind of any man who comes upon it from any side.

For the note of Constantine is this: that it is a considerable city, standing quite alone, upon a platform wholly isolated save for the narrowest isthmus-neck of approach. On every side beyond that very narrow neck of approach there fall away from its walls not steep or common cliffs, but tremendous precipices. It is, as it were, one rock as big as a mountain; but a mountain sufficiently levelled upon its upper side against the sky to give foundation for a large town. Fifty or sixty thousand human beings may have lived crowded upon that strange table. Upon the one side the prodigious overhanging rocks look down on a broad valley, I know not how many hundred feet below; upon the other, they plunge into, and equally overhang, a gorge so deep that when you look down into it you think you have seen the river bed at the bottom, when really you have only caught sight of a ledge and a track running half-way between the height and the stream. That stream is the tumbling, yellow torrent which has been called since the Mohammedan conquest 'El Rhummel,' that is, 'The Tawny'; and I think it will give some conception of the gorge and of its depth when I say that the noise of its waters, even in spate, are hardly heard in the night by a man upon the city walls so high above them.

Segovia is of this character—a town on a rock, and so is Castro Giovanni. But neither of them can compare for magnitude of impression with Constantine.

The neck, or isthmus, by which the plateau of Constantine is reached, is much narrower than in the parallel instances of the other similar towns. The rocks which bound Constantine's almost isolated plateau are everywhere more precipitous and the plunge to the water-level more profound; and the approach also rises steeply, and the keep of the stronghold, the Kasbah, the Castle, is on the frontier point of it. The prow of that ship rises in a high forecastle, the poop is low.

Enemies storming Constantine have not only had for so many centuries to approach by a very narrow pass; but having once mastered that unique neck of land, they had the task imposed upon them of still fighting uphill all the way, till they came to the last fortification—the heart of the place—at the very extreme of the lifting plateau.

Nevertheless, Constantine (like nearly all these seemingly impregnable places) has been stormed time after time. Indeed, the cities that have boasted many centuries of immunity, or even complete immunity, from conquest, have never been cities apparently inexpugnable. Cities which seem made for eternal defence, these, by the very fact of their challenge, lure armies on: and Constantine, which still looks to the eye all but impregnable has fallen with every new conquest of Barbary; the last not a century ago; the next to be we know not when.

The city was originally called Cirta—a word which some men think means 'the Rock' in a Punic dialect. And it remained up to the conversion of the West from paganism 1600 years ago, and in popular speech long after that. But the official name was changed by the great Constantine when he had conquered the world with his French and English forces against the Southern and Levantine troops of his pagan rivals; and the new name had so far taken root when the Mohammedan desert men came swarming over all this land that they kept it in a corrupted form, and that its inhabitants call it 'Ksantina' to this day. Nevertheless, I know not why, it is always as Cirta that it returns to my mind; perhaps because one sees the word so often in modern works upon ancient North Africa; perhaps because that which most profoundly moved me when I first saw the place, the old tombs, have that name upon them—coming as they do long before the final revolution which established the Catholic faith upon the ruins of the Roman world. Of those old inscriptions above the dead, one still haunts me. I put it into my writing upon North Africa many years ago. It is upon the tomb of a woodland priestess who died young, and for whom her friends thus wrote upon the stone: 'The Dryads wept.'

It will never be Cirta again officially, for the Punic language is dead. And even the Berber language, from which, perhaps, the name derived, still older than the Syrian merchants of Carthage, only carries on a painful life, and will not here oust again (one may surely say) the Semitic or the Latin speech. But it was to Cirta that the Kings of the Berbers returned from before the beginning of history to triumph after victory, or to stand a siege after defeat. It was in Cirta that the great tragedy of Jugurtha was accomplished. It was back to Cirta that the host of native cavalry retired, when Caesar threatened to achieve, and achieved, his final victory, near the Tunisian shore.

If there is one place in which I could regret the recovery to Roman land and the return of Europe to North Africa (which is justly but a province to Europe) that place is Cirta: Constantine. For it seems to have a sort of savage right to independence, and its tremendous cliffs challenge order and the domination of universal government. It is a great chieftain's town.

The birds of the air are not yet accustomed to think that Constantine is a human capital, though it has been so now for longer than any man can remember. The vultures love to poise in mid-heaven above the abysses around the city, flying on a level with its highest roofs; and I have known days when, the mist covering the lower ground of the broad valleys to the left and of the gorge to the right, all Constantine seemed like a thing of the air; a city setting out to navigate between earth and sky.

The French have done with such a site what might be predicted of their energy, their bureaucracy, their order; also their itch for change. Upon that narrow neck of approach which the Roman, the Arab, the Turk, the Vandal, the Byzantine generals had forced in turn, they have put up their monument to the great Lamoricière—but I very much prefer his noble tomb in Nantes, although it be but a translation from the Italian. Upon the pedestal of this statue they have the words of the trooper who shouted to his general through the dusk after the first repulse, on the eve of victory: 'To-morrow the town will be yours, or I shall be dead.' The French have also put up a statue of Constantine himself, the August, the Victorious. He is just outside the railway station on the far side of the town, on the edge of the gorge whence you look across the deep to the ramparts of the city. But the most characteristic thing they have done is to emphasize this unique isolation and dominance and height in two ways: first by building flying bridges which span the gulf and show its dizziness, next by driving a road of the most fantastic sort all round the circuit of those unclimbable rocks. It should not be so, perhaps, but so it is, that this new highway, cut into the precipice (in some places driven in tunnels and arches through huge boulders, and in other places so poised that from its parapet you look sheer down into the gorge) does not detract from the fearfulness of the place, nor even from its majesty. It enhances both.

I have, in speaking of other parts of Barbary, asked the question: What will happen? Can it endure? But of Constantine, on the rock of Cirta, I have little doubt. These things are greater than man, and even should man abandon them, it will stand as mighty as ever. What a stone!

THE GREAT HOUSE OF DURTAL

I KNOW not why it is, but there are many places which, through the mechanical accidents of our time, become overknown, and others which one might call underknown. Too many people know Assisi; not nearly enough people know Loretto. Too many people know Rabat and Fez, even to-day. Too many people know Montserrat, and not enough know the Chimneys of Riglos, which are among the wonders of the world.

Durtal, the Great House of Durtal, is one of the lesser known things. Perhaps I ought to be glad of that, for I can easily imagine it ruined by crowds. But, at any rate, if it has pride in itself, or if its ghostly owners could feel human pride in whatever place they now may be, it seems unfair that such a thing should not be as famous to-day as it most assuredly is splendid.

The Great House of Durtal is a lesser example of the spirit which, when it had all the wealth of the kingship behind it, set up those neighbouring castles of the Loire which are certainly among the much too well-known things. Durtal had no such wealth behind it; it was the great house of a big private gentleman. But Lord, what an effect he got for his money! You will look in vain, I think, for any other private house in Europe, in the countrysides, at least—for I do not know whether one should call the Barberini House a palace or not—which gives you such an impression of nobility, of magnificence: in the old sense of the term magnificence: 'A great doing—a making of something worthy.'

The builder played every trick—and legitimately—to give this effect of magnificence. When first the place had been set up as a stronghold, in the Dark Ages when all such strongholds were founded, a knoll above the quiet river had been castellated. It was the castle of Durtal; but when greater wealth and less power came to the descendants of that house, the falling ground was fronted with a projecting three sides of Renaissance work which makes to-day the Great House of Durtal, three piled-up stories high above the low-lying ground to the south; but on the north, at the top of the steep hill the ground on a level with its second story. The builder spread out the stone basement

347

of that cliff of a façade at an angle, after the fashion of the Egyptians, to give a look of support and strength to the weight above; and in the eastern corner he married the high Renaissance roof to the last battlements of the Middle Ages, just as the builders of the Medicean Louvre in Paris joined the Middle Ages to sixteenth-century Italy.

One would have thought that Durtal would have been famous if through Rabelais alone, for all the glorious episode of Picrochole turns upon Durtal; he was Lord of Durtal, if you remember, when he was struck with that sudden burst of imperialism of his and determined to conquer the whole world 'without fear of being turned upon his flank by the Muscovites.'

But Rabelais has brought no fame to this, and for a hundred who see the master in bronze upon the public place of Chinon, scarcely one, I suppose, has ever seen Durtal.

Perhaps the choice of travellers is wise, for Durtal is dead, in spite of all its beauty and strength. These things were intended for human habitations and for lordships. They went with personal powers and personal prides. They have now no functions to fulfil, because the builders of them have departed and their descendants inhabit them no more. You may go through the halls of that old place and find no ornament; the promise of the great façade is not fulfilled within; one wing at the back which closed the courtyard has disappeared; and as for using the place, it has been turned into a hospital. Durtal is no longer Durtal, because it is no longer alive. But it is worth seeing, all the same, and if a man wants a series in which the history of all our vivid developments between the Crusades and the Reformation may stand before him, let him visit Durtal after Angers—an hour in the local train and less in a motor. He will see at Angers—and he will be wise to approach from the river—a castle of stark bastions, wholly devoid of any grace at all, a great quadrilateral of half-round towers, not very high, gigantically thick and strong, with hardly a slit for light or for arrows round the wall, built, too early for battlements, of a dark and forbidding stone which you can hardly distinguish from the rock out of which it springs and into which it is dovetailed. Angers, though it is the Plantagenet castle in which first were heard the songs of the Arthurian cycle, within the gaunt naked walls of which arose the beginnings of the Middle Ages, is built wholly for use, and for one use—the use of war; and of war when war meant the rumbling of mangonel engines attempting to batter down walls almost as strong as the walls of nature. Angers is sheerly for defence, the stronghold of a man who was a king. Then came the great four hundred years of development, and at the end of them, Durtal, no longer a castle in the old sense at all, not built for defence nor suggesting it, yet still suggesting strength and, above all, power of tradition.

I sometimes wonder, when I see the way in which the rich build nowadays, failing nearly always to reach the effect they desire, that they do not merely copy. Why had not some one of our modern rich set to work to reproduce Durtal? He would certainly have a house better than anything they have built in Europe for two hundred years. But I suppose when he had done it some other revolution like that which has taken the soul out of Durtal would nullify his efforts, and that the palace which he had raised for the satisfaction of his vanity or of his legitimate pride in blood would be debased to false uses in its turn.

At any rate, there is Durtal, as good a thing in death as I know. Perhaps some rich man with a kind heart will buy it back from the governors of the hospital, destroy in it the devices of the religious who tend the sick, turn its chapel into a dancing-hall, re-erect the fallen north wing, complete the courtyard again, and fill Durtal once more with a false life. And if that happens I know not whether I shall be glad or sorry.

V. CRITICISM

RONSARD

IF it be true that words create for themselves a special atmosphere, and that their mere sound calls up vague outer things beyond their strict meaning, so it is true that the names of the great poets by their mere sound, by something more than the recollection of their work, produce an atmosphere corresponding to the quality of each; and the name of Ronsard throws about itself like an aureole the characters of fecundity, of leadership, and of fame.

A group of men to which allusion will be made in connection with Du Bellay set out with a programme, developed a determined school, and fixed the literary renaissance of France at its highest point. They steeped themselves in antiquity, and they put to the greatest value it has ever received the name of poet; they demanded that the poet should be a kind of king, or seer. Half seriously, half as a product of mere scholarship, the pagan conception of the muse and of inspiration filled them.

More than that; in their earnest, and, as it seemed at first, artificial work, they formed the French language. Some of its most famous and most familiar words proceed from them—for instance, the word *Patrie*. Some few of their exotic Greek and Latin adaptations were dropped; the greater part remained. They have excluded from French—as some think to the impoverishment of that language—most elements of the Gothic—the inversion of the adjective, the frequent suppression of the relative, the irregularity of form, which had survived from the Middle Ages, and which make the older French poetry so much more sympathetic to the Englishman than is the new—all these were destroyed by the group of men of whom I speak. They were called by their contemporaries the Pleiade, for they were seven stars.

Now, of these, Ronsard was easily the master. He had that power which our anæmic age can hardly comprehend, of writing, writing, writing, without fear of exhaustion, without irritability or self-criticism, without danger of comparing the better with the worse. Five great volumes of small print, all good—men of that facility never write the really paltry things—all good, and most of it glorious; some of it on the level which only the great poets reach here and there. It is in reading this man who rhymed unceasingly for forty years, who made of poetry an occupation as well as a glory, and who let it fill the whole of his life, that one feels how much such creative power has to do with the value of verse. There is a kind of good humility about it, the humility of a man who does not look too closely at himself, and the health of a soul at full stride, going forward. You may open Ronsard at any page, and find a beauty; you may open any one of the sonnets at random, and in translating it discover that you are compelled to a fine English, because he is saying, plainly, great things. And of these sonnets, note you, he would write thirty at a stretch, and then twenty, and then a second book, with seventy more. So that as one reads one cannot help understanding that Italian who said a man was no poet unless he could rap out a century of sonnets from time to time; and one is reminded of the general vigour of the age and of the way in which art of all sorts was mingled up together, when one remembers the tags of verses, just such verses as these, which are yet to be seen in our galleries set down doubtfully on the margin of their sketches by the great artists of Italy.

Ronsard, with these qualities of a leader, unconscious, as all true leaders are, of the causes of his leadership, and caring, as all true leaders do, for nothing in leadership save the glory it brings with it, had also, as have all leaders, chiefly the power of drawing in a multitude of friends. The peculiar head of his own group, he very soon became the head of all the movement of his day. He had made letters really great in the minds of his contemporaries, and having so made them, appeared before them as a master of those letters. Certainly, as I shall quote him in a moment when I come to his dying speech, he was 'satiated with glory.'

Yet this man did not in his personality convey that largeness which was his principal mark. His face was narrow, long, and aquiline; his health uneven. It was evidently his soul which made men quickly forget the ill-matched ease which bore it; for almost alone of the great poets he was consistently happy, and there poured out from him not only this unceasing torrent of verse, but also advice, sustenance, and a kind of secondary inspiration for others.

In yet another matter he was a leader, and a leader of the utmost weight, not the cause, perhaps, but certainly the principal example of the trend which the mind of the nation was taking as the sixteenth century drew to a close. I mean in the matter

of religion, upon whose colour every society depends, which is
the note even of a national language, and which seems to be the
ultimate influence beyond which no historical analysis can
carry a thinking man.

But even those who will not admit the truth of this should
watch the theory closely, for with the religious trend of France
is certainly bound up, and, as I would maintain, on such an
influence is dependent, that ultimate setting of the French
classic, that winding up of the Renaissance. . . . .

The stream of Catholicism was running true. The nation
was tumbling back after a high and turbulent flood into the
channel it had scoured for itself by the unbroken energies of
a thousand years. It is no accident that Ronsard, that Du
Bellay, were churchmen. It is a type. It is a type of the truth
that the cloth admitted poets; of the truth that in the great
battle whose results yet trouble Europe, here, on the soil where
the great questions are fought out, Puritanism was already
killed. The epicurean in them both, glad and ready in Ronsard,
sombre and Lucretian in Du Bellay, jarred indeed in youth
against their vows; but that it should have been tolerated, that
it should have led to no excess or angry revolt, was typical of
their moment. It was typical, finally, of their generation that
all this mixture of the Renaissance with the Church matured at
last into its natural fruit, for in the case of Ronsard we have a
noble expression of perfect Christianity at the end.

In the November of 1585 he felt death upon him; he had
himself borne to his home as soon as the Huguenot bands had
left it, ravaged and devastated as it was. He found it burnt
and looted, but it reminded him of childhood and of the first
springs of his great river of verse. A profound sadness took
him. He was but in his sixty-second year, his mind had not
felt any chill of age. He could not sleep; poppies and soporifics
failed him. He went now in his coach, now on a litter from
place to place in that countryside which he had rendered famous,
and saw the Vendomois for the last time; its cornfields all
stubble under a cold and dreary sky. And in each place he
waited for a while.

But death troubled him, and he could not remain. Within a
fortnight he ordered that they should carry him southward to
the Loire, to that priory of which—by a custom of privilege,
nobility and royal favour—he was the nominal head, the priory
which is 'the eye and delight of Touraine'—the Isle of St Cosmo.
He sickened as he went. The thirty miles or so took him three

painful days; twice, all his strength failed him, and he lay half-fainting in his carriage; to so much energy and to so much power of creation these episodes were an awful introduction of death.

It was upon the 17th of November that he reached the walls wherein he was Superior; six weeks later, on the second day after Christmas, he died.

Were I to describe that scene to which he called the monks, all men of his own birth and training, were I to dwell upon the appearance and the character of the oldest and the wisest, who was also the most famous there, I should extend this essay beyond its true limit, as I should also do were I to write down, even briefly, the account of his just, resigned, and holy death. It must suffice that I transcribe the chief of his last deeds; I mean, that declaration wherein he made his last profession of faith.

The old monk had said to him: 'In what resolution do you die?'

He answered, somewhat angrily: 'In what did you think? In the religion which was my father's and his father's, and his father's and his father's before him—for I am of that kind.'

Then he called all the community round him, as though the monastic simplicity had returned (so vital is the Faith, so simple its primal energies), and as though he had been the true prior of some early and fervent house, he told them these things which I will faithfully translate on account of their beauty. They are printed here, I think, for the first time in English, and must stand for the end of this essay:

He said: 'That he had sinned like other men, and, perhaps, more than most; that his senses had led him away by their charm, and that he had not repressed or constrained them as he should; but none the less, he had always held that Faith which the men of his line had left him, he had always clasped close the creed and the unity of the Catholic Church; that, in fine, he had laid a sure foundation, but he had built thereon with wood, with hay, with straw. As for that foundation, he was sure it would stand; as for the light and worthless things he had built upon it he had trust in the mercy of the Saviour that they would be burnt in the fire of His love. And now he begged them all to believe hard, as he had believed; but not to live as he had lived; they must understand that he had never attempted or plotted against the life or goods of another, nor ever against any man's honour, but, after all, there was nothing therein wherewith to glorify one's self before God.'

When he had wept a little, he continued, saying, 'that the world was a ceaseless turmoil and torment, and shipwreck after shipwreck all the while, and a whirlpool of sins, and tears and pain, and that to all these misfortunes there was but one port, and this port was Death. But, as for him, he carried with him into that port no desire and no regret for life. That he had tried every one of its pretended joys, that he had left nothing undone which could give him the least shadow of pleasure or content, but that at the end he had found everywhere the oracle of Wisdom, vanity of vanities.'

He ended with this magnificent thing, which is, perhaps, the last his human power conceived, and I will put it down in his own words:

'Of all those vanities, the loveliest and most praiseworthy is glory—fame. No one of my time has been so filled with it as I; I have lived in it, and loved and triumphed in it through time past, and now I leave it to my country to garner and possess if after I shall die. So do I go away from my own place as satiated with the glory of this world as I am hungry and all longing for that of God.'

ON *RASSELAS*

THE other day I saw, I held in my hands, a first edition of *Rasselas*. I bowed down and adored.

I had known the book in every form all the days of my life, for those from whom I come have worshipped it before me and have possessed it I suppose, in one edition and another, all those years since first it came from the press. They must have had the first edition in their time, but it has not come down to me.

I do not agree with those who pretend that first editions are a vanity. Great wealth will divert them from their proper function and place, as it will divert anything in these days. It will add something precious, ridiculous, and vain to the idea of first editions as it will add folly and pretence and false luxury to such admirable things as the sailing of a boat and hunting.

But the first edition of a great book is a thing to be revered. It carries with it (I know not why) something of immediate contact with the author, and of the air in which it was written. Any one who has been brought up on the first edition of a great work will never feel the same when he reads it in another form. As a child I read *The Rose and the Ring* in the first edition, which our family had had from Thackeray, and I cannot feel the same of any other. I learned my Dasent's *Tales of the Norse* in a first edition, and all others seem to me degraded. I read my *Masterman Ready* in a first edition, and when I gave it to my own children I was at pains to get hold of a similar copy. I could not bear that they should feast upon that admirable story without the proper furniture of the good square English type, the solid rag paper, and the charming woodcuts, which all went together in my mind with the tale told, and without which the old sailor was not himself.

But to go back to *Rasselas*—every man ought to read *Rasselas*, and every wise man will read it half a dozen times in his life. Indeed, a man would do well to read it once a year at least; for never was wisdom better put, or more enduringly; and if it be true that the test of a book is the mood in which we lay it down, then this book must have as high marks as anything ever written in English and, therefore, the highest marks of anything ever written in the world.

It came out a few days before *Candide,* and men customarily contrast the one against the other; giving, of course, by far the higher place to Voltaire. But here, in my judgment, they err; for I will stoutly maintain the commonplace that a work of art is not to be judged wholly nor even generally by its effect as a work of art, but is rather to be judged by its whole social effect upon man. If it be a piece of writing and that writing fiction, and that fiction fabular, then one great part of our praise must attach to the attraction of the fiction, the fable, the style. But these are not all. There is also the prime question whether the book be noble or ignoble, moral or immoral, whether it does us good or harm; and our most general judgment must depend upon the old test imposed upon us by the ancients, the mood in which we lay it down.

Now a man laying down *Candide* is in a mood of delight in its wit and of satisfaction with its style—polished jade. He may even obtain some moral advantage from the ridicule of much that is worthy of ridicule. But upon the whole, he will have found good things to be so much hated by the author and the best things to be so poisonously attacked, that either his mood will have something of bitterness and disgust, or, if he takes satisfaction in this attack on decency and good, it will be because his mind was already tainted before he took up the volume. No good man is the better for having read *Candide,* but every man is the better for having read *Rasselas.*

I will even confess (but this I know to be personal and not generally defensible) that I am much better fed by the style of Johnson than by the style of Voltaire. The second is like the blows of a hammer chiselling out a marble statue of great perfection, but the first is like a rhythmical swell of deep water; and I prefer that movement; it suits me better. Moreover, while Voltaire is lapidary and will pack a sentence tight with meaning leaving it still quite clear, Johnson, nearly always, and especially in *Rasselas,* puts all there is to say of a considered judgment—and a true one—into the antithetical form, than which no better medium has ever been discovered for condensing and preserving a conclusion. Voltaire's economy is like a sphere: the maximum content for its surface. Johnson's is like strong soup: a concentration of nourishment:

'Some are the slaves of servants whom they have trusted with their affairs. Some are kept in continual anxiety by the caprice of rich relations, whom they cannot please and dare not offend. Some husbands are imperious, and some wives perverse; and, as it is always more easy to do evil than good, though the wisdom or virtue of one can very rarely make many happy, the folly or vice of one may often make many miserable.'

'If such be the general effect of marriages,' said the Prince, 'I shall, for the future, think it dangerous to connect my interest with that of another, lest I should be unhappy by my partner's fault.'

'I have met,' said the Princess, 'with many who live single for that reason; but I never found that their prudence ought to raise envy. They dream away their time without friendship, without fondness, and are driven to rid themselves of the day for which they have no use, by childish amusements, or vicious delights. They act as beings under the constant sense of some known inferiority, that fills their minds with rancour, and their tongues with censure. They are peevish at home, and male-volent abroad; and, as the outlaws of human nature, make it their business and their pleasure to disturb that society which debars them from its privileges. To live without feeling or exciting sympathy, to be fortunate without adding to the felicity of others, or afflicted without tasting the balm of pity, is a state more gloomy than solitude; it is not retreat, but exclusion from mankind. Marriage has many pains, but celi-bacy has no pleasures.'

I would maintain upon this long extract (and I could pick you out a dozen as good in the short work) that it has these four qualities: What it says is (1) true, (2) important, (3) of good moral effect, and (4) packed.

There are some men who think that concision is a matter of short sentences and short words. It is not so. Concision is a matter of giving what you have to give in the least compass compatible with lucidity; and Johnson pulls it off.

There are whole stacks of novels giving one criticism and another of marriage; half of them strained in epigram, and not one of them clamping down the truth in its frame as it is done here in *Rasselas*.

I am glad to say that Johnson was well paid for *Rasselas*. And I am also glad to say that he took very little trouble over it. I am a humble colleague of that great man, being myself a hack writer, and I know how much any of my brothers in slavery is to be congratulated upon good payment for an easy job.

He promised to write it in five days; he did write it in under seven. He used only a few of the later hours of each day at the task, and he was paid what would correspond to about £400 to-day; that is, he was paid a sum which would keep a man in a very quiet middle-class way for a year. He was paid one hundred pounds; and one hundred pounds in the middle of the eighteenth century would do that, just as four hundred pounds will barely do it to-day. He had even better luck, for though he sold his copyright (which is always a mistake—but I do not know how the laws stood in that time; they are still offensively unjust to the sons of Apollo) his bookseller voluntarily gave him, I believe, another £25 when he saw the thing selling. That has never happened to me. I sold a book once out and out for a tiny sum in my youth. It has gone through thirteen editions and I have seen none of that further money it has earned. But, after all, if you sell a thing you sell it, and you have no right to complain.

So much for *Rasselas*; or rather, so little. It is a book round about which a man might write for ever; solid stuff; beef; good roast beef with Yorkshire pudding; real roast beef, not your modern baked stuff, but beef roasted from a jack in front of a great coal fire.

. . . . . .

After so writing of *Rasselas*, my American friend Colonel Isham (who has perhaps the best collection of Dr Johnson's work, and of everything around it) showed me another copy of that great book and one to be treasured, in my judgment, more even than that first edition which moved me so greatly.

It is Mrs Piozzi's own copy—the one she had in old age; and upon page after page it is annotated in her own clear and beautiful writing, more than a hundred years ago.

Now here is an amazing thing! Here is something in which all the elements of historical value arise—the living contemporary witness, the intimate witness, the original document: all combined.

It is nearly certain that this woman, upon whom the great Englishman's affection centred so strongly during all those last years when he was increasingly lonely with the hubbub of fame about him, was born in 1740. She was thirty years younger than he, she outlived him by half a lifetime, for she did not die till she was eighty-one years of age. She died the same year as Napoleon.

It is curious to note that this copy, in which she has made

so many annotations, is as late as the year 1818. It is Sharpe's Edition. That writing of hers, therefore, which we here see so small and so clear in the margin of page after page, was set down in the very last moments of her life, when she had approached, or had passed her eightieth year, and when the book itself had been in the hands of all Europe, and famous, for just on sixty years.

Here was this vivacious, energetic, admired old lady, living on into a world over which the storm of the French Revolution had passed and steeping herself in the memories of a youth more than half a century dead. She had been a girl of nineteen, perhaps barely that, when *Rasselas* first issued from the press. She returned to it in the very extreme of life when death was before her, who had lived life so fully, and when she could write as younger people cannot write.

In the margin on the corner of page 8 she has written:

Man feels from home in this Life but rests and expatiates in the World to come.

She writes thus, in age, as an annotation to Johnson's phrase:

Man surely has some latent sense for which this place affords no gratification, or he has some desires distinct from sense, which must be satisfied before he can be happy.

The book is of small size, about eight inches by five inches, and has perhaps a dozen of those very careful little steel engravings which are so characteristic of the day.

It is a lady's book altogether, and it is a lady's mind commenting perpetually on as manly a piece of work as was ever set down by a man. Also sometimes (but rarely) she dares to underline at the risk of defacing the page; and, herein again, she was a lady of her day.

I find underlined four words upon page 99 at the end of Chapter XXVII, at the end of the Princess Nekayah's discourse upon 'Whether perfect happiness would be procured by perfect goodness'—that admirable speech which begins: 'Whether perfect happiness would be procured by perfect goodness this world will never afford an opportunity of deciding' (I wish I could write like that!), and again, 'All that virtue can afford is quietness of conscience, a steady prospect of happier state: this may enable us to endure calamity with patience: but remember that patience must suppose pain.'

Johnson's vivacious, active young friend, now grown so old,

underlines in this last phrase the words 'enable,' 'endure,' 'patience' and 'suppose.'

I would argue with the Doctor (if he were alive and before me now, and promised not to roar too loud) upon that matter of a quiet conscience. I do not believe that good men have quiet consciences. I hold that an uneasy conscience—at any rate nowadays—is the first requisite for Heaven, and that an inflamed, red, feverish, angry conscience is a true mark of increasing virtue. I have met many men with quiet consciences, not all of them wholly unintelligent, but nearly all of them scoundrels.

Mrs Piozzi (for I must not leave the lady alone any longer) has further added: 'Some diseases are caused by virtue as some are by vice.' Yes, Madam! And many more by virtue than by vice! I know of no disease striking down a swindler or one of those rich beasts who are for ever thinking of their body's health, or the vile fellow who would rather drink water than wine: I do not say who is ordered water by a doctor, him I can forgive, but who drinks it of his own accord and glories in it.

The oppression of the poor brings no disease to a man. But generosity embarrasses his finances and brings him to loss of sleep and sometimes to madness. Indignant virtue has even worse effects. Patriotism, if it be too active, will land him in the tortures of a jail; and of nervous indigestion there is no more common cause than deep affection withdrawn or gone awry.

But to go back to Mrs Piozzi and her *Rasselas*.

There is not in all this monument of Johnson a truer or a more profound phrase than that which I find annotated a little earlier in the same chapter:

'Discontent,' answered Rasselas, 'will not always be without reason under the most just and vigilant administration of public affairs.'

Which is as much as to say that complaint against government is a permanent and essential necessity, even where that government is exceptionally good. It is an imperative duty in common times; in times of plutocratic corruption, such as our own, it is a crying and immediate necessity if the State is not to die of the poison.

Mrs Piozzi writes by the side of this: 'Well observed and to me new; except having once read it in Italy.' She quotes the name of an Italian author or subject, which I cannot decipher, and then a translation of his words: 'Men in Power are no Gods.'

How excellent also is the following. She finds Johnson saying through the mouth of the Princess: 'He does nothing who endeavours to do more than is allowed to humanity.' Mrs Piozzi puts by the side: 'True, true, make your Decision and be content,' and then, 'Quod sis, esse velis.'

I could write all day upon this singular treasure of a book. Let me find room for two last citations. The first is from words written fairly early, I think, in the course of this marginal work of hers, for they were written while her hand was still quite steady.

On the last page, page 184, below the final line of the text and the words: 'The end,' followed by a full stop, Mrs Piozzi has cut out the full stop with a dash, and has added in her own handwriting 'of a Book unrivalled in Excellency of Intention, in Elegance of Diction: in minute knowledge of human life—and sublime Expression of Oriental Imagery.'

But the most touching, the most arresting sentence, is what may have been, I think was, the last of all her pen work on the paper of this volume; for it is written in a larger and trembling hand, surely a little before she died. It is in connection with the passage in Chapter XXXVI upon the progress of sorrow. Here again the Princess is speaking and says: 'What is to be expected from our pursuit of happiness, when we find the state of life to be such that happiness itself is the cause of misery?' and to this the old woman's shaking fingers add: '*Oh melancholy Truth, to which my heart bears witness.*' And after that comes only a long quavering line.

REVIEWING

THE ancient and honourable art of Reviewing is, without question, the most important branch of the great calling which we term the 'Career of Letters.'

As it is the most important, so also it is the first which a man of letters should learn. It is at once his shield and his weapon. A thorough knowledge of Reviewing, both theoretical and applied, will give a man more popularity of power than he could have attained by the expenditure of a corresponding energy in any one of the liberal professions, with the possible exception of Municipal politics.

It forms, moreover, the foundation upon which all other literary work may be said to repose. Involving, as it does, the reading of a vast number of volumes, and the thorough mastery of a hundred wholly different subjects; training one to rapid, conclusive judgment, and to the exercise of a kind of immediate power of survey, it vies with cricket in forming the character of an Englishman. It is interesting to know that Charles Hawbuck was for some years principally occupied in Reviewing; and to this day some of our most important men will write, nay, and sign, reviews, as the press of the country testifies upon every side.

It is true that the sums paid for this species of literary activity are not large, and it is this fact which has dissuaded some of our most famous novelists and poets of recent years from undertaking Reviewing of any kind. But the beginner will not be deterred by such a consideration, and he may look forward, by way of compensation, to the ultimate possession of a large and extremely varied library, the accumulation of the books which have been given him to review. I have myself been presented with books of which individual volumes were sometimes worth as much as forty-two shillings to buy.

Having said so much of the advantages of this initial and fundamental kind of writing, I will proceed to a more exact account of its dangers and difficulties, and of the processes inherent to its manufacture.

It is clear, in the first place, that the Reviewer must regard herself as the servant of the public, and of her employer; and service, as I need hardly remind her (or him), has nothing in it dishonourable. We were all made to work, and often the highest in the land are the hardest workers of all. This character of service, of which Mr Ruskin has written such noble things, will often lay the Reviewer under the necessity of a sharp change of opinion, and nowhere is the art a better training in morals and application than in the habit it inculcates of rapid and exact obedience, coupled with the power of seeing every aspect of a thing, and of insisting upon that particular aspect which will give most satisfaction to the commonwealth.

It may not be uninstructive if I quote here the adventures of one of the truest of the many stout-hearted men I have known, one indeed who recently died in harness reviewing Mr Garcke's article on Electrical Traction in the supplementary volumes of the *Encyclopædia Britannica*. This gentleman was once sent a book to review; the subject, as he had received no special training in it, might have deterred one less bound by the sense of duty. This book was called *The Snail: Its Habitat, Food, Customs, Virtues, Vices, and Future*. It was, as its title would imply, a monograph upon snails, and there were many fine coloured prints, showing various snails occupied in feeding on the leaves proper to each species. It also contained a large number of process blocks, showing sections, plans, elevations, and portraits of snails, as well as detailed descriptions (with diagrams) of the ears, tongues, eyes, hair, and nerves of snails. It was a comprehensive and remarkable work.

My friend (whose name I suppress for family reasons) would not naturally have cared to review this book. He saw that it involved the assumption of a knowledge which he did not possess, and that some part of the book might require very close reading. It numbered in all 1,532 pages, but this was including the index and the preface.

He put his inclinations to one side, and took the book with him to the office of the newspaper from which he had received it, where he was relieved to hear the Editor inform him that it was not necessary to review the work in any great detail. 'Moreover,' he added, 'I don't think you need praise it too much.'

On hearing this, the Reviewer, having noted down the price of the book and the name of the publisher, wrote the following words—which, by the way, the student will do well to cut out and pin upon his wall, as an excellent example of what a 'short notice' should be:

The Snail : Its Habitat, etc. Adam Charles. Pschuffer. 21s. 6d.
This is a book that will hardly add to the reputation of its author. There is evidence of detailed work, and even of conscientious research

in several places, but the author has ignored or misunderstood the whole teaching of   and the special discoveries of   and what is even more remarkable in a man of Mr Charles's standing, he advances views which were already exploded in the days of   .

He then took an Encyclopedia and filled up the blanks with the names of three great men who appeared, according to that work, to be the leaders in this branch of natural history.   His duty thus thoroughly accomplished and his mind at rest, he posted his review, and applied himself to lighter occupations.

Next day, however, the Editor telephoned to him, to the effect that the notice upon which he had spent so much labour could not be used.

'We have just received,' said the Editor, 'a page advertisement from Pschuffer.   I would like a really good article, and you might use the book as a kind of peg on which to hang it. You might begin on the subject of snails, and make it something more like your "*Oh! my lost friend*," which has had such a success.'

On occasions such as these the beginner must remember to keep full possession of himself.

Nothing in this mortal life is permanent, and the changes that are native to the journalistic career are perhaps the most startling and frequent of all those which threaten humanity.

The Reviewer of whom I speak was as wise as he was honourable.   He saw at once what was needed.   He wrote another and much longer article, beginning:

The Snail : Its Habitat, etc.   Adam Charles.   Pschuffer.   21s. 6d.
There are tender days just before the spring dares the adventure of the Channel, when our Kentish woods are prescient, as it were, of the south.   It is calm . . .

and so forth, leading gradually up to snails, and bringing in the book here and there about every twentieth line.

When this long article was done, he took it back to the office, and there found the Editor in yet a third mood.   He was talking into the telephone, and begged his visitor to wait until he had done.   My friend, therefore, took up a copy of the *Spectator*, and attempted to distract his attention with the masterful irony and hard crystalline prose of that paper.

Soon the Editor turned to him and said that Pschuffers had just let him know by telephone that they would not advertise after all.

It was now necessary to delete all that there might be upon

snails in his article, to head the remainder 'My Kentish Home,' and to send it immediately to *Life in the Open*. This done, he sat down and wrote upon a scrap of paper in the office the following revised notice, which the Editor glanced at and approved:

The Snail : Its Habitat, etc. Adam Charles. Pschuffer. 21s. 6d.
This work will, perhaps, appeal to specialists. This journal does not profess any capacity of dealing with it, but a glance at its pages is sufficient to show that it would be very ill-suited to ordinary readers. The illustrations are not without merit.

Next morning he was somewhat perturbed to be called up again upon the telephone by the editor, who spoke to him as follows:

'I am very sorry, but I have just learnt a most important fact. Adam Charles is standing in our interests at Biggleton. Lord Bailey will be on the platform. You must write a long and favourable review of the book before twelve to-day, and do try and say a little about the author.'

He somewhat wearily took up a sheet of paper and wrote what follows: a passage which I must again recommend to the student as a very admirable specimen of work upon these lines.

The Snail : Its Habitat, etc. Adam Charles. Pschuffer. 21s. 6d.
This book comes at a most opportune moment. It is not generally known that Professor Charles was the first to point out the very great importance of the training of the mind in the education of children. It was in May 1875 that he made this point in the presence of Mr Gladstone, who was so impressed by the mingled enlightenment and novelty of the view, that he wrote a long and interesting post card upon the author to a friend of the present writer. Professor Charles may be styled—nay, he styles himself —a 'self-made man.' Born in Huddersfield of parents who were weavers in that charming northern city, he was early fascinated by the study of natural science, and was admitted to the Alexandrovna University. . . .

(And so on, and so on, out of *Who's Who*.)

But this would not suffice for his growing genius.

(And so on, and so on, out of the *Series of Contemporary Agnostics*.)

. . . It is sometimes remarkable to men of less wide experience how such spirits find the mere time to achieve their prodigious results. Take, for example, this book on the Snail. . . .

And he continued in a fine spirit of praise, such as should be given to books of this weight and importance, and to men such as he who had written it. He sent it by boy-messenger to the office.

The messenger had but just left the house when the telephone rang again, and once more it was the Editor, who asked whether the review had been sent off. Knowing how dilatory are the run of journalists, my friend felt some natural pride in replying that he had indeed just dispatched the article. The Editor, as luck would have it, was somewhat annoyed by this, and the reason soon appeared when he proceeded to say that the author was another Charles after all, and not the Mr Charles who was standing for Parliament. He asked whether the original review could still be retained, in which the book, it will be remembered, had been treated with some severity.

My friend permitted himself to give a deep sigh, but was courteous enough to answer as follows:

'I am afraid it has been destroyed, but I shall be very happy to write another, and I will make it really scathing. You shall have it by twelve.'

It was under these circumstances that the review (which many of you must have read) took this final form, which I recommend even more heartily than any of the others to those who may peruse these pages for their profit, as well as for their instruction.

The Snail : Its Habitat, etc. Adam Charles. Pschuffer. 21s. 6d.
We desire to have as little to do with this book as possible, and we should recommend some similar attitude to our readers. It professes to be scientific, but the harm books of this kind do is incalculable. It is certainly unfit for ordinary reading, and for our part we will confess that we have not read more than the first few words. They were quite sufficient to confirm the judgment which we have put before our readers, and they would have formed sufficient material for a lengthier treatment had we thought it our duty as Englishmen to dwell further upon the subject.

Let me now turn from the light parenthesis of illuminating anecdote to the sterner part of my task.

We will begin at the beginning, taking the simplest form of review, and tracing the process of production through its various stages.

It is necessary first to procure a few forms, such as are sold by Messrs Chatsworthy in Chancery Lane, and Messrs Goldman, of the Haymarket, in which all the skeleton of a review is provided, with blanks left for those portions which must, with the best will in the world, vary according to the book and the author under consideration. There are a large number of these forms, and I would recommend the student who is as yet quite a novice in the trade to select some forty of the most conventional, such as these on page 7 of the catalogue:

Mr —— has hardly seized the pure beauty of
We cannot agree with Mr —— in his estimate of
Again, how admirable is the following:

At the same establishments can be procured very complete lists of startling words, which lend individuality and force to the judgment of the Reviewer. Indeed I believe that Mr Goldman was himself the original patentee of these useful little aids, and among many before me at this moment I would recommend the following to the student:

There is somewhat of the	Absolute Immediate Creative Bestial Intense Authoritative Ampitheatrical Lapsed Miggerlish Japhetic Accidental Alkaline Zenotic	in Mr ——'s style Mrs ——'s Miss ——'s

Messrs Malling, of Duke Street, Soho, sell a particular kind of cartridge paper and some special pins, gum, and a knife, called 'The Reviewer's Outfit.' I do not know that these are necessary, but they cost only a few pence, and are certainly of advantage in the final process. To wit: Seizing firmly the book to be reviewed, write down the title, price, publisher, and (in books other than anonymous) the author's name, at the *top* of the sheet of paper you have chosen. The book should then be taken in both hands and opened sharply, with a gesture not easily described, but acquired with very little practice. The test of success is that the book should give a loud crack and lie open of itself upon the table before one. This initial process is technically called 'breaking the back' of a book, but we need not trouble ourselves yet with technical terms. One of the pages so disclosed should next be torn out and the word 'extract' written in the corner, though not before such sentences have been deleted as will leave the remainder a coherent paragraph. In the case of historical and scientific work, the preface must be torn out bodily, the name of the Reviewer substituted for the word 'I,' and the whole used as a description of the work in question. What remains is very simple. The forms, extracts, etc., are trimmed, pinned, and gummed in order upon the cartridge paper (in some offices brown paper), and the whole is sent to press.

I need hardly say that only the most elementary form of review can be constructed upon this model, but the simplest notice contains all the factors which enter into the most complicated and most serious of literary criticism and pronouncements.

In this, as in every other practical trade, an ounce of example is worth a ton of precept, and I have much pleasure in laying before the student one of the best examples that has ever appeared in the weekly press of how a careful, subtle, just, and yet tender review, may be written. The complexity of the situation which called it forth, and the lightness of touch required for its successful completion, may be gauged by the fact that Mr Mayhem was the nephew of my employer, had quarrelled with him at the moment when the notice was written, but will almost certainly be on good terms with him again; he was also, as I privately knew, engaged to the daughter of a publisher who had shares in the works where the review was printed.

A YOUNG POET IN DANGER

MR MAYHEM'S 'PEREANT QUI NOSTRA'

WE fear that in *Pereant qui Nostra*, Mr Mayhem has hardly added to his reputation, and we might even doubt whether he was well advised to publish it at all. *Tufts in an Orchard* gave such promise that the author of the exquisite lyrics it contained might easily have rested on the immediate fame that first effort procured him.

'Lord, look to England; England looks to you,'

and—

'Great unaffected vampires and the moon,'

are lines the Anglo-Saxon race will not readily let die.

In *Pereant qui Nostra*, Mr Mayhem preserves and even increases his old facility of expression, but there is a terrible falling-off in verbal aptitude.

What are we to think of 'The greatest general the world has seen' applied as a poetic description to Lord Kitchener? Mr Mayhem will excuse us if we say that the whole expression is commonplace.

Commonplace thought is bad enough, though it is difficult to avoid when one tackles a great national subject, and thinks what all good patriots and men of sense think also. 'Pour être poëte,' as M. Yves Guyot proudly said in his receptional address to the French

Academy, 'Pour être poëte on n'est pas forcément aliéné.' But commonplace *language* should always be avoidable, and it is a fault which we cannot but admit we have found throughout Mr Mayhem's new volume. Thus in *Laura* he compares a young goat to a 'tender flower,' and in *Billings* he calls some little children 'the younglings of the flock.' Again, he says of the waves at Dover in a gale that they are 'horses all in rank, with manes of snow,' and tells us in *Eton College* that the Thames 'runs like a silver thread amid the green.'

All these similes verge upon the commonplace, even when they do not touch it. However, there is very genuine feeling in the description of his old school, and we have no doubt that the bulk of Etonians will see more in the poem than outsiders can possibly do.

It cannot be denied that Mr Mayhem has a powerful source of inspiration in his strong patriotism, and the sonnets addressed to Mr Kruger, Mr O'Brien, Dr Clark, and General Mercier are full of vigorous denunciation. It is the more regrettable that he has missed true poetic diction and lost his subtlety in a misapprehension of planes and values.

'Vile, vile old man, and yet more vile again,'

is a line that we are sure Mr Mayhem would reconsider in his better moments: 'more vile' than what? Than himself? The expression is far too vague.

'Proud Prelate,' addressed to General Mercier, must be a misprint, and it is a pity it should have slipped in. What Mr Mayhem probably meant was 'Proud Caesar' or 'soldier,' or some other dissyllabic title. The word *prelate* can properly only be applied to a bishop, a mitred abbot, or a vicar apostolic.

'Babbler of Hell, importunate mad fiend, dead canker, crested worm,' are vigorous and original, but do not save the sonnet. And as to the last two lines,

'Nor seek to pierce the viewless shield of years,
    For that you certainly could never do,'

Mr Mayhem must excuse us if we say that the order of the lines make a sheer bathos.

Perhaps the faults and the excellences of Mr Mayhem, his fruitful limitations, and his energetic inspirations, can be best appreciated if we quote the following sonnet; the exercise will also afford us the opportunity (which we are sure Mr Mayhem will not resent in such an old friend) of pointing out the dangers into which his new tendencies may lead him.

'England, if ever it should be thy fate
    By fortune's turn or accident of chance
To fall from craven fears of being great,
    And in the tourney with dishevelled lance
To topple headlong, and incur the Hate
    Of Spain, America, Germany, and France,
What will you find upon that dreadful date
    To check the backward move of your advance?

A little Glory; purchased not with gold
    Nor yet with Frankincense (the island blood
Is incommensurate, neither bought nor sold),
    But on the poops where Drake and Nelson stood
An iron hand, a stern unflinching eye
To meet the large assaults of Destiny.'

Now, here is a composition that not every one could have written.
It is inspired by a vigorous patriotism, it strikes the right note
(Mr Mayhem is a Past Seneschal of the Navy League), and it
breathes throughout the motive spirit of our greatest lyrics.

It is the execution that is defective, and it is to execution that
Mr Mayhem must direct himself if he would rise to the level of his
own great conceptions.

We will take the sonnet line by line, and make our meaning clear,
and we do this earnestly for the sake of a young poet to whom the
Anglo-Saxon race owes much, and whom it would be deplorable to
see failing, as Kipling appears to be failing, and as Ganzer has failed.

Line 1 is not very striking, but might pass as an introduction;
line 2 is sheer pleonasm—after using the word 'fate,' you cannot
use 'fortune,' 'accident,' 'chance,' as though they were amplifications
of your first thought. Moreover, the phrase 'by *fortune's turn*' has
a familiar sound. It is rather an echo than a creation.

In line 3, 'craven fears of being great' is taken from Tennyson.
The action is legitimate enough. Thus, in Wordsworth's *Excursion*
are three lines taken bodily from *Paradise Lost*, in Kipling's *Stow It*
are whole phrases taken from the *Police Gazette*, and in Mr Austin's
verses you may frequently find portions of a *Standard* leader.
Nevertheless, it is a licence which a young poet should be chary of.
All these others were men of an established reputation before they
permitted themselves this liberty.

In line 4, 'dishevelled' is a false epithet for 'lance'; a lance has
no hair; the adjective can only properly be used of a woman, a wild
beast, or domestic animal.

In line 5, 'incur the hate' is a thoroughly unpoetic phrase—we
say so unreservedly. In line 6, we have one of those daring experi-
ments in metre common to our younger poets; therefore we hesitate
to pronounce upon it, but (if we may presume to advise) we should
give Mr Mayhem the suggestion made by *The Times* to Tennyson—
that he should stick to an exact metre until he felt sure of his
style; and in line 8, 'the backward move of your advance' seems a
little strained.

It is, however, in the sextet that the chief slips of the sonnet
appear, and they are so characteristic of the author's later errors,
that we cannot but note them; thus, 'purchased not with gold or
Frankincense' is a grievous error. It is indeed a good habit to
quote Biblical phrases (a habit which has been the making of half
our poets), but not to confuse them: frankincense was never used as
coin—even by the Hittites. 'Incommensurate' is simply meaningless. How can blood be 'incommensurate'? We fear Mr Mayhem
has fallen into the error of polysyllabic effect, a modern pitfall.
'Island blood' will, however, stir many a responsive thrill.

The close of the sonnet is a terrible falling off. When you say a thing is purchased, 'not with this but——' the reader naturally expects an alternative, instead of which Mr Mayhem goes right off to another subject! Also (though the allusion to Nelson and Drake is magnificent) the mention of an iron hand and an eye by themselves on a poop seems to us a very violent metaphor.

The last line is bad.

We do not write in this vein to gain any reputation for preciosity and still less to offend. Mr Mayhem has many qualities. He has a rare handling of penultimates, much potentiality, large framing; he has a very definite chiaroscuro, and the tones are full and objective; so are the values. We would not restrain a production in which (as a partner in a publishing firm) the present writer is directly interested. But we wish to recall Mr Mayhem to his earlier and simpler style—to the *Cassowary*, and the superb interrupted seventh of *The Altar Ghoul*.

England cannot afford to lose that talent.

TALKING OF BAD VERSE

William, you vary greatly in your verse;
Some 's none too good, but all the rest is worse.

IT has always astonished me that my colleagues, friends, enemies, and butts, the critics, do not review verse as it ought to be reviewed: I might say, 'as *only* it can be reviewed.' I am no critic myself; I can say with justice that no living man I ever heard of or met was less capable of criticism than I; but just as a man who cannot skate may very well judge the antics of people who crash on the ice and go through it, so can I judge the errors of my contemporary critics in the matter of verse.

Surely it is quite clear that there is present, at any moment, either a little very good verse or none.

Poetry is perhaps another matter. I can understand the man who calls poetry so rare that it could only be spotted every half lifetime or so. But good verse, though rare, is not so rare as all that; and, I say again, I marvel that it should not be dealt with as it deserves.

In the first place, there is no necessity for mentioning bad verse at all. Every man and woman who has reached a certain age has written verse. I know of no exception to this rule, save in the case of one woman who has been the occasion of verse in others. Normally, every man or woman writes verse at some time or another. Thirty years ago most of the stuff so written was not published. A certain small proportion was published in the provincial journals of the country, and in the lesser magazines. The tiny remnant that did pretend to be something appeared usually in book form, or, if the author or authoress were in debt, it would first be sold to some important review. Out of this very small number of pieces one could pick the two or three in a year which were good verse. That was the normal way of going on. Occasionally, indeed, good verse was found hidden away among the provincial or magazine stuff and dragged out to light. But as a rule it was hardly worth looking for.

The great mass of bad verse thus turned out—thousands of pieces in a year—went quite unnoticed save by the poetess and her friends. But there arose a little later a new kind of publication imported from America, which is now universal.

375

In this, verse was used to stop a gap, much as dirty old cloths are used on shipboard to stop a leak, or as any old book will be picked up to make a hoist for the baby's chair at meals. The editor would ask his sub-editor (I have seen him do it): 'I want four and a half inches of verse.' He was an efficient man and knew what he was talking about. He did not guess the space; he measured it with a little steel rule which he kept for the purpose. Then the sub-editor would answer (also measuring with a little steel rule): 'You couldn't space it out, could you? . . . Here's one just over four.' This he would answer, referring to a great quantity of verse already put up in type and waiting the moment when it could be so used. Then the editor would say: 'All right; tell 'em to lead it.'

And so the Muse came to her own.

When this new kind of Americanized magazine had taken firm root in England, the result was a great mass of verse appearing regularly before metropolitan eyes, educated eyes, gentle eyes, traditional eyes, liberalized eyes, trained eyes, generous eyes—upon my soul, I know not what adjective exactly fits; I fear there is not one in the English language, but let us say, 'your eyes and mine'; for my eyes are certainly of this kind, and no doubt it will flatter you to hear that yours are.

The next step was the printing of verse in bulk everywhere, and particularly in the high-brow journals peculiar to the literary herd.

At last England was filled with a steady and rising flood of verse, both free and servile; multitudinous; expansive; of a cubic capacity beyond experience.

The tide turned a little before the War; it is still running very strong; it has not yet reached its height.

Nearly all this stuff gets put into books. Even before it gets put into books, notices appear of it in the short reviews dedicated to the periodicals. When it is between covers it receives regular review through a commercial tradition now established in this country that everything which appears between covers must be criticized in print, in order to get advertisement.

With what result? Why, this: that nobody is so infamously bad that she gets some sort of faint praise somewhere, and that the better stuff is lumped in with the worse, and the best with the worst.

I only know of one writer who is consistently ignored, and she is the best of the lot, being in the great Elizabethan line.

I may be told that this way of going on does no great harm,

because good verse will pierce at last. I am not so sure. Probably poetry will pierce at last, sooner or later; but on good verse I have my doubts. Poetry is like lightning; you get the flash though the curtains are drawn and the shutters shut; but good verse is only like a strong lamp, and if it is not given its due access it will not be discovered. The reviewers (who are very tired men, having to race round so large a field day after day) have an odd habit of quoting what they think excellent. That gives away, not the reviewers indeed, but the people whom they quote; and as they nearly always quote the quite rotten stuff, one is left none the wiser.

To the jaded mind thus occupied, two qualities seem particularly to appeal; very emphatic rhythm, and subject. When the verse written is patriotic, or sporting, or public school, or sob-stuff (I say nothing of comic verse, for that is an irritant and left aside) or descriptive of panic or cruelty, or of any other general emotion, one half of the effect is achieved; and if to that there be added the kind of lilt which you get from an engine wheel with a flat in it bumping down an incline, then the other half is added, and the thing is complete. As, for instance:

> Ah, years ago, but I once was there
> And I wish I were there again;
> By Tumty River and Tumty Weir
> Along with the Tumty men.

(I put in Tumty so as not to offend any school or river, for I would rather die than offend the meanest stream that crawls; but you can fill it in at will, anyhow.)

This is praised; and it ought not to be praised.

By the way, I forgot to add the religious motive, and when I say religious, I mean the vague, the conventional, the pantheistic, and suburban—curse it!

It is responsible for wagon-loads of bad verse; and if it is mixed up with patriotism it becomes intolerable.

The best way out of the trouble is not to review verse at all. Since it must be printed by the haystack and the square mile, why, let it be printed, but let the reviewers leave it free to find its level. As it is, they do nothing but disturb the slow and natural stratification of the muddy waters.

THE GOOD POET AND THE BAD POET

ONCE there was a poet who wrote such beautiful poetry that he became immensely rich and built a large house of red brick in Fitzjohn's Avenue, Hampstead; where he lived surrounded by his friends, the Good Architect, the Good Painter and a few others of the same sort who had, like himself, made gigantic fortunes by their excellence in their respective arts.

One night about Christmas time, this Good Poet was coming home in his Rolls-Royce from dining with the Lord Mayor of London. It was nearly midnight, there was no moon and there had been a deep fall of snow. Just as the motor was turning into the gate of his Splendid Mansion, he felt the wheels bump over something and was much annoyed to conjecture that a log must have been left lying in the fairway, but the Second Chauffeur (for he always had two men to drive him) jumped down and told him in respectful tones that they had had to pull up because they had run over a man.

The Good Poet's first impulse was to bid them drive on and disregard the obstacle, but his better nature and a fear of paragraphs prompted him to give orders that the fellow should be picked up and taken into the house.

Luckily for him who had thus impertinently lain in the gateway of the Good Poet, the snow had already covered him so deeply that he was not very badly hurt. He had fallen inanimate from lack of food some hours before, and his chief danger seemed to be the catching of a chill from his exposed position. When they had thawed him in front of the great kitchen fire, and given him a basin of skilly, some stale bread crusts and a glass of pure cold water from the tap, he revived sufficiently to murmur a few words; and the Good Poet, having heard the state of affairs from his Groom of the Chambers (to whom the Butler had made report upon the evidence of the First Footman), was so charitable as to order that the fellow should be allowed to lie all night in the garage, with a few rugs to keep him from freezing to death; he even added that he might be given some sort of breakfast the next morning. Further, he was not to go away until the Good Poet had seen him, in order that he might make sure that there should be no trouble about Third Party Claims. For it had been the unfortunate experience of the Good Poet (as of all wealthy men, alas!) that even the humblest of the poor may be driven to some dirty act of ingratitude at the solicitation of a base lawyer who shares the swag.

It so happened that next day the Good Poet gave one of his accustomed great luncheon parties, at which were present all manner of famous men: Generals and Politicians, Judges, Men who Promoted Companies, Owners of Newspapers which printed news of murders and other exciting things and put in pictures of people under sentence of death, famous Divines and even Bankers. Indeed, not a few of the Guests were Peers.

The luncheon was over, and they had all retired to the Good Poet's library, where they were drinking bitter coffee with Armagnac, Cointreau, Grand Marnier, Arquebuse, Izzarra of the Basques, Strega, Calvados, and other commoner liqueurs such as Brandy, Kümmel, Curaçao, Benedictine and Crême de Menthe itself, when the Good Poet, whose brain was always more active under the influence of conversation and its accompaniments, suddenly remembered the poor fellow who was still thawing down below. He therefore desired a Bishop among his Guests to touch the electric bell at his side and, when a liveried servant had answered the summons, he asked for a report upon the stranger. The Domestic bowed low and returned in a brief time with the account that the man was now fairly restored, his clothes were nearly dry and he had been given some more skilly and bread for his midday meal.

'You must know,' said the Good Poet, 'that this unfortunate man had fallen from exhaustion before my gate, and I thought it only decent to have him taken in and looked after.' At which the assembled Guests murmured their appreciation of so much goodness, and the Bishop said, 'For my part, I thank you personally from my heart for your Christian Deed.'

'Let us have him brought up here,' said the Good Poet, 'it is quite possible he may have something interesting to tell us; for these tramps often have odd adventures.'

The man was therefore brought up and came in among all these great people very shamefacedly and awkwardly. And, indeed, it was a difficult moment, because his clothes were hardly decent and had obviously been ready-made, even when they were new; while his boots were burst and presented a very disgusting appearance.

But the Good Poet, who was a Man of the World, affected not

to notice all this, and asked the stranger (who stood before them nervously twiddling an offensive and greasy cap) who he might be.

'Sir,' said he, in a low, despairing and feeble voice, interrupted by a dreadful cough, 'I am a Poet.   Alas, my dear mother often warned me to take to some more solid profession, but I was young and would not heed, and now she lies in the quiet churchyard of——'

'Yes! Yes! We will take all that as read,' said the Good Poet who could not bear *longueurs*.   'But surely you must have been singularly bad at your trade to have reached the position in which we now find you?'

The unfortunate man (whom we will now call the Bad Poet) hung his head and suffered severely the indignant and reproachful glances of the seated company.

'It may be so,' he admitted unhappily, 'no man is a judge of his own work; and certainly I have had not fame, no have I even been able to sell my verses, so I suppose they cannot be good, any of them; and yet I have been proud enough of some, even when they were sent back to me by American and other editors.   And though I may not have done anything really good yet, perhaps, if I keep plodding away, I shall be able to achieve something of value before I die.   But the trouble is that I get exceedingly weak from lack of food and from the inclemency of our climate, especially in the winter months.'

The Good Poet, who knew from long experience the signs of mendicancy, stopped him short at this point and changed the direction which his talk was taking.

'Suppose you recite us some of your stuff.   Have you anything that you retain in mind?'

'Yes, sir'—('Charles,' interrupted the Good Poet, 'Sir Charles, if you please').   'Yes, Sir Charles, I am even now composing an Heroic Poem upon Wine.   I have been at it four years, but alas, it is not yet completed, for I fear I am a very slow composer.'

'Never mind that,' said the Good Poet, 'let's have it, or bits of it at any rate.'   And they all settled back in their chairs, while the Bad Poet, after a terrible fit of coughing and leaning with one hand upon an inlaid table, because he felt very weak after standing so long, began as follows:

> 'To praise, revere, establish and defend;
> To welcome home mankind's mysterious friend;
> Wine, true begetter of all arts that be;
> Wine, privilege of the completely free;

> Wine, the foundation, wine the sagely strong;
> Wine, bright avenger of sly-dealing wrong—
> Awake! Ausonian Muse and sing the vineyard song!
> Sing how the Charioteer from Asia came
> And on his front the little dancing flame
> Which marked the godhead. Sing the panther team
> The cymbal and the thyrsus and the gleam
> Of bronze among the torches. . . .'

'Come! come! come!' said the Good Poet, 'we can't go on like this for ever!' To which all his Guests nodded assent. 'Give us a patch out of the middle, but spare us.'

The Bad Poet, after yet another fit of coughing, hesitated for a word and began:

> '. . . Where
> Upturned to Heaven, the large Hipponian Plain
> Extends luxuriant and invites the main;
> Or where, festooned about the tall elm-trees,
> Etrurian grapes regard Tyrrhenian seas;
> The . . .'

'This will never do,' said the Good Poet impatiently. 'Give us the very end and let's have done with it.'

The Bad Poet, his voice now failing from exhaustion, looked plaintively at them a moment and then murmured:

> 'When from the void of such waste labours done
> I too must leave the grape-ennobling sun,
> Turn to the home-lit plain my grateful sight
> And leave the mountain to the advancing night;
> When the poor end of such attempt is near,
> Just and benignant let my youth appear,
> Bearing a chalice, shallow, golden, wide,
> With benediction graven on its side.
> So touch my dying lip, so bridge that deep,
> So pledge my waking from the gift of sleep
> And sacramental raise me the Divine:
> Strong Brother in God and last Companion: Wine.'

'Is that the end?' said the Good Poet. 'Yes,' whispered the reciter, miserably, and then again began to cough in a really exasperating manner.

'It is very bad,' said the Good Poet, 'very bad indeed. Now if you want to know why you have failed and the difference between your stuff and the kind of thing I write, listen to this, for I also have written a poem on Wine—it is much shorter than yours and much better.'

With that he lifted himself out of his easy chair, all his Guests rising at the same time, out of respect. He took from a shelf a magnificently bound book, which was very thin, and, indeed, consisted of only four pages, on one of which only was there any printed matter. This the Good Poet opened and read:

> 'Wine exercises a peculiar charm.
> But, taken in excess, does grievous harm.'

He then reverently kissed the page and replaced the volume, while his guests broke into a buzz of applause.

After that supreme experience, there was nothing more to be done.

The Bad Poet was dismissed—and it only shows how true it is that good deeds bring misfortune in their train, that the Bad Poet died on his way downstairs, giving infinite trouble to his benefactor, whose party was spoilt by the wretched accident and who had to send for the Poorhouse Authorities to get the corpse out of the way.

The moral of this is, if you can't write good verse, don't write any at all.

A PLEA FOR THE SIMPLER DRAMA

IT is with the drama as with plastic art and many other things: the plain man feels that he has a right to put in his word, but he is rather afraid that the art is beyond him, and he is frightened by technicalities.

After all, these things are made for the plain man; his applause, in the long run and duly tested by time, is the main reward of the dramatist as of the painter or the sculptor. But if he is sensible he knows that his immediate judgment will be crude. However, here goes.

The plain man sees that the drama of his time has gradually passed from one phase to another of complexity in thought coupled with simplicity of incident, and it occurs to him that just one further step is needed to make something final in British art. We seem to be just on the threshold of something which would give Englishmen in the twentieth century something of the fullness that characterized the Elizabethans: but somehow or other our dramatists hesitate **to** cross that threshold. It cannot be that their powers are lacking: it can only be some timidity of self-torture which it is the business of the plain man to exorcize.

If I may make a suggestion in this essay to the masters of the craft it is that the goal of the completely modern thing can best be reached by taking the very simplest themes of daily life—things within the experience of the ordinary citizen—and presenting them in the majestic traditional cadence of that peculiarly English medium, blank verse.

As to the themes taken from the everyday life of middle-class men and women like ourselves, it is true that the lives of the wealthy afford more incident, and that there is a sort of glamour about them which it is difficult to resist. But with a sufficient subtlety the whole poignancy of the lives led by those who suffer neither the tragedies of the poor nor the exaltation of the rich can be exactly etched. The life of the professional middle-class, of the business man, the dentist, the money-lender, the publisher, the spiritual pastor, nay of the playwright himself, might be put upon the stage—and what a vital change would be here!. Here would be a kind of literary drama of which the interest would lie in the struggle, the pain, the danger, and the triumph which we all so intimately know, and next in the satisfaction (which we now do not have) of the mimetic sense— the satisfaction of seeing a mirror held up to a whole audience composed of the very class represented upon the stage.

I have seen men of wealth and position absorbed in plays concerning gambling, cruelty, cheating, drunkenness, and other sports, and so absorbed chiefly because they saw *themselves* depicted upon the stage; and I ask, Would not my fellows and myself largely remunerate a similar opportunity? For though the rich go repeatedly to the play, yet the middle class are so much more numerous that the difference is amply compensated.

I think we may take it, then, that an experiment in the depicting of professional life would, even from the financial standpoint, be workable; and I would even go so far as to suggest that a play could be written in which there did not appear one single lord, general, Member of Parliament, baronet, professional beauty, usurer (upon a large scale at least), or Cabinet Minister.

The thing is possible: and I can modestly say that in the little effort appended as an example to these lines it has been done successfully; but here must be mentioned the second point in my thesis—I could never have achieved what I have here achieved in dramatic art had I not harked back to the great tradition of the English heroic decasyllable such as our Shakespeare has handled with so felicitous an effect.

The play—which I have called *The Crisis*, and which I design to be the model of the school founded by these present advices —is specially designed for acting with the sumptuous accessories at the disposal of a great manager, such as Mr (now Sir Henry) Beerbohm Tree, or for the narrower circumstances of the suburban drawing-room.

There is perhaps but one character which needs any long rehearsal, that of the dog Fido, and luckily this is one which can easily be supplied by mechanical means, as by the use of a toy dog of sufficient size which barks upon the pressure of a pneumatic attachment.

In connection with this character I would have the student note that I have introduced into the dog's part just before the curtain a whole line of *dactyls*. I hope the hint will not be wasted. Such exceptions relieve the monotony of our English *trochees*. But, saving in this instance, I have confined myself throughout to the example of William Shakespeare, surely the best master for those who, as I fondly hope, will follow me in the regeneration of the British Stage.

THE CRISIS

Place : The study at the Vicarage.   Time, 9.15 p.m.

DRAMATIS PERSONAE

THE REV. ARCHIBALD HAVERTON: The Vicar.
MRS HAVERTON: His Wife.
MISS GROSVENOR: A Governess.
MATILDA: A Maid.
FIDO: A Dog.
HERMIONE COBLEY: Daughter of a cottager who takes in washing.
MISS HARVEY: A guest, cousin to Mrs Haverton, a Unitarian.

The Rev. Archibald Haverton is reading the 'Standard' by a lamp with a green shade.   Mrs Haverton is hemming a towel. Fido is asleep on the rug.   On the walls are three engravings from Landseer, a portrait of Her late Majesty Queen Victoria, a bookcase with books in it, and a looking-glass.

MRS HAVERTON. My dear—I hope I do not interrupt you— Helen has given notice.
REV. A. HAVERTON. [*Looking up suddenly.*]   Given notice? Who? Helen? Given notice? Bless my soul! [*A pause.*] I never thought that she would give us notice. [*Ponders and frowns.*]
MRS HAVERTON. Well, but she has, and now the question is, What shall we do to find another cook?
Servants are very difficult to get.   [*Sighs.*
Especially to come into the country
To such a place as this. [*Sighs.*] No wonder, either!
Oh! Mercy! When one comes to think of it,
One cannot blame them. [*Sighs.*] Heaven only knows
I try to do my duty!   [*Sighs profoundly.*
REV. A. HAVERTON. [*Uneasily.*] Well, my dear, I cannot *make* preferment.   [*Front door-bell rings.*
FIDO.   Bow! wow! wow!
REV. A. HAVERTON. [*Patting him to soothe him.*] There, Fido, there!

FIDO.   Wow! wow!

REV. A. HAVERTON. Good dog, there!

FIDO.   Wow, wow, wow!

REV. A. HAVERTON. [*Very nervous.*] There!

FIDO.   Wow! wow!

REV. A. HAVERTON. [*In an agony.*] Good dog!

FIDO.   Bow! wow! wow!

   Wow, wow! Wow!! WOW!!!

MRS HAVERTON. [*Very excited.*] Oh, Lord, he'll wake the
   children!

REV. A. HAVERTON. [*Exploding.*] How often have I told you,
   Dorothy,

   Not to exclaim 'Good Lord!' . . . Apart from manners—

   Which have their own importance—blasphemy

   (And I regard the phrase as blasphemous)

   Cannot——

MRS HAVERTON. [*Uneasily.*] Oh, very well! . . . Oh, very well!

                              [*Exploding in her turn.*

   Upon my soul, you are intolerable!

     [*She jumps up and makes for the door. Before she gets to
     it there is a knock and Matilda enters.*

MATILDA. Please, m'm, it's only Mrs Cobley's daughter

   To say the washing shall be sent to-morrow,

   And would you check the list again and see,

   Because she thinks she never had two collars

   Of what you sent, but only five, because

   You marked it seven; and Mrs Cobley says

   There must be some mistake.

REV. A. HAVERTON. [*Pompously.*] I will attend to it.

MRS HAVERTON. [*Whispering angrily.*] How can you, Archibald!

   You haven't got

   The ghost of an idea about the washing!

   Sit down. [*He does so.*] [*To Matilda.*] Send the girl in here.

                       [*Mrs Haverton sits down in a fume.*

REV. A. HAVERTON. I think . . .

MRS HAVERTON. [*Snapping.*] I don't care what you think!

   [*Groans.*] Oh, dear!

   I'm nearly off my head!

            Enter Miss Cobley. She bobs.

MISS COBLEY. Good evening, m'm.

MRS HAVERTON. [*By way of reply.*] Now, then! What's all
   this fuss about the washing?

MISS COBLEY. Please, m'm, the seven collars, what you sent—

I mean the seven what was marked—was wrong,
And mother says as you 'd have had the washing
Only there weren't but five, and would you mind . . .

Mrs Haverton. [*Sharply.*] I cannot understand a word you
say.
Go back and tell your mother there were *seven*.
And if she sends home *five* she pays for *two*.
So there! [*Snorts.*]

Miss Cobley. [*Sobbing.*] I 'm sure I . . .

Mrs Haverton. [*Savagely.*] Don't stand snuffling there!
Go back and tell your mother what I say . . .
Impudent hussy! . . . [*Exit Miss Cobley sobbing. A pause.*

Rev. A. Haverton. [*With assumed authority.*] To return to
Helen.
Tell me concisely and without complaints,
Why did she give you notice?
[*A hand-bell rings in the passage.*

Fido. Bow-wow-wow!

Rev. A. Haverton. [*Giving him a smart kick.*] Shurrup!

Fido. [*Howling.*] Pen-an'-ink! Pen-an'-ink! Pen-an'-ink!
Pen-an'-ink!

Rev. A. Haverton. [*Controlling himself as well as he can, goes
to the door and calls into the passage.*] Miss Grosvenor!
[*Louder.*] . . . Miss Grosvenor! . . . Was that the bell for
prayers?
Was that the bell for prayers? . . . [*Louder.*] Miss Grosvenor.
[*Louder.*] Miss Gros-ve-nor! [*Tapping with his foot.*] Oh! . . .

Miss Grosvenor. [*Sweetly and far off.*] Is that Mr Haverton?

Rev. A. Haverton. Yes! yes! yes! yes! . . .
Was that the bell for prayers?

Miss Grosvenor. [*Again.*] Yes? Is that Mr Haverton? Oh!
Yes!
I think it is. . . . I 'll see—I 'll ask Matilda.
[*A pause, during which the Rev. A. Haverton is in a qualm.*

Miss Grosvenor. [*Rustling back.*] Matilda says it *is* the bell
for prayers.
[*They all come filing into the study and arranging the chairs.
As they enter Miss Harvey, the guest, treads heavily on
Matilda's foot.*

Miss Harvey. Matilda? Was that you? I *beg* your pardon.

Matilda. [*Limping.*] Granted, I 'm sure, miss!

Mrs Haverton. [*Whispering to the Rev. A. Haverton.*] Do
not read the Creed!

Miss Harvey is a Unitarian.
I should suggest some simple form of prayer,
Some heartfelt word of charity and peace
Common to every Christian.
REV. A. HAVERTON. [*In a deep voice.*] Let us pray.

CURTAIN

VI. SONNETS AND VERSE

SONNETS

I

Lift up your hearts in Gumber, laugh the Weald
And you my mother the Valley of Arun sing.
Here am I homeward from my wandering,
Here am I homeward and my heart is healed.
You my companions whom the World has tired
Come out to greet me. I have found a face
More beautiful than Gardens; more desired
Than boys in exile love their native place.

Lift up your hearts in Gumber, laugh the Weald
And you most ancient Valley of Arun sing.
Here am I homeward from my wandering,
Here am I homeward and my heart is healed.
If I was thirsty, I have heard a spring.
If I was dusty, I have found a field.

II

I was like one that keeps the deck by night
    Bearing the tiller up against his breast;
I was like one whose soul is centred quite
    In holding course although so hardly prest,
And veers with veering shock now left now right,
    And strains his foothold still and still makes play
Of bending beams until the sacred light
    Shows him high lands and heralds up the day.

But now such busy work of battle past
I am like one whose barque at bar at last
Comes hardly heeling down the adventurous breeze;
And entering calmer seas,
I am like one that brings his merchandise
To Californian skies.

III

THE Winter Moon has such a quiet car
That all the winter nights are dumb with rest.
She drives the gradual dark with drooping crest
And dreams go wandering from her drowsy star
Because the nights are silent do not wake
But there shall tremble through the general earth,
And over you, a quickening and a birth.
The Sun is near the hill-tops for your sake.

The latest born of all the days shall creep
To kiss the tender eyelids of the year;
And you shall wake, grown young with perfect sleep,
And smile at the new world and make it dear
    With living murmurs more than dreams are deep;
    Silence is dead, my dawn, the morning 's here.

IV

IT freezes: all across a soundless sky
The birds go home. The governing dark 's begun.
The steadfast dark that waits not for a sun;
The ultimate dark wherein the race shall die.
Death with his evil finger to his lip
Leers in at human windows, turning spy
To learn the country where his rule shall lie
When he assumes perpetual generalship.

The undefeated enemy, the chill
That shall benumb the voiceful earth at last,
Is master of our moment, and has bound
The viewless wind itself. There is no sound.
It freezes. Every friendly stream is fast.
It freezes, and the graven twigs are still.

STANZAS WRITTEN ON BATTERSEA BRIDGE DURING A SOUTH-WESTERLY GALE

THE woods and downs have caught the mid-December,
  The noisy woods and high sea-downs of home;
The wind has found me and I do remember
  The strong scent of the foam.

Woods, darlings of my wandering feet, another
  Possesses you, another treads the Down;
The South West Wind that was my elder brother
  Has come to me in town.

The wind is shouting from the hills of morning,
  I do remember and I will not stay.
I 'll take the Hampton road without a warning
  And get me clean away.

The Channel is up, the little seas are leaping,
  The tide is making over Arun Bar;
And there 's my boat, where all the rest are sleeping
  And my companions are.

I 'll board her, and apparel her, and I 'll mount her,
  My boat, that was the strongest friend to me—
That brought my boyhood to its first encounter
  And taught me the wide sea.

Now shall I drive her, roaring hard a' weather,
  Right for the salt and leave them all behind;
We 'll quite forget the treacherous streets together
  And find—or shall we find?

There is no Pilotry my soul relies on
  Whereby to catch beneath my bended hand,
Faint and beloved along the extreme horizon
  That unforgotten land.

We shall not round the granite piers and paven
　To lie to wharves we know with canvas furled.
My little Boat, we shall not make the haven—
　It is not of the world.

Somewhere of English forelands grandly guarded
　It stands, but not for exiles, marked and clean;
Oh! not for us.　A mist has risen and marred it:
　My youth lies in between.

So in this snare that holds me and appals me,
　Where honour hardly lives nor loves remain,
The Sea compels me and my County calls me,
　But stronger things restrain.

.　　.　　.　　.　　.　　.

England, to me that never have malingered,
　Nor spoken falsely, nor your flattery used,
Nor even in my rightful garden lingered:
　What have you not refused?

THE SOUTH COUNTRY

When I am living in the Midlands
    That are sodden and unkind,
I light my lamp in the evening:
    My work is left behind;
And the great hills of the South Country
    Come back into my mind.

The great hills of the South Country
    They stand along the sea;
And it's there walking in the high woods
    That I could wish to be,
And the men that were boys when I was a boy
    Walking along with me.

The men that live in North England
    I saw them for a day:
Their hearts are set upon the waste fells,
    Their skies are fast and grey;
From their castle-walls a man may see
    The mountains far away.

The men that live in West England
    They see the Severn strong,
A-rolling on rough water brown
    Light aspen leaves along.
They have the secret of the Rocks,
    And the oldest kind of song.

But the men that live in the South Country
    Are the kindest and most wise,
They get their laughter from the loud surf,
    And the faith in their happy eyes
Comes surely from our Sister the Spring
    When over the sea she flies;
The violets suddenly bloom at her feet,
    She blesses us with surprise.

I never get between the pines
  But I smell the Sussex air;
Nor I never come on a belt of sand
  But my home is there.
And along the sky the line of the Downs
  So noble and so bare.

A lost thing could I never find,
  Nor a broken thing mend:
And I fear I shall be all alone
  When I get towards the end.
Who will there be to comfort me
  Or who will be my friend?

I will gather and carefully make my friends
  Of the men of the Sussex Weald,
They watch the stars from silent folds,
  They stiffly plough the field.
By them and the God of the South Country
  My poor soul shall be healed.

If I ever become a rich man,
  Or if ever I grow to be old,
I will build a house with deep thatch
  To shelter me from the cold,
And there shall the Sussex songs be sung
  And the story of Sussex told.

I will hold my house in the high wood
  Within a walk of the sea,
And the men that were boys when I was a boy
  Shall sit and drink with me.

COURTESY

Of Courtesy, it is much less
Than Courage of Heart or Holiness,
Yet in my Walks it seems to me
That the Grace of God is in Courtesy.

On Monks I did in Storrington fall,
They took me straight into their Hall;
I saw Three Pictures on a wall,
And Courtesy was in them all.

The first the Annunciation;
The second the Visitation;
The third the Consolation,
Of God that was Our Lady's Son.

The first was of Saint Gabriel;
On Wings a-flame from Heaven he fell;
And as he went upon one knee
He shone with Heavenly Courtesy.

Our Lady out of Nazareth rode—
It was Her month of heavy load;
Yet was Her face both great and kind,
For Courtesy was in Her Mind.

The third it was our Little Lord,
Whom all the Kings in arms adored;
He was so small you could not see
His large intent of Courtesy.

Our Lord, that was Our Lady's Son,
Go bless you, People, one by one;
My Rhyme is written, my work is done.

THE DEATH AND LAST CONFESSION OF
WANDERING PETER

WHEN Peter Wanderwide was young
    He wandered everywhere he would:
And all that he approved was sung,
    And most of what he saw was good.

When Peter Wanderwide was thrown
    By Death himself beyond Auxerre,
He chanted in heroic tone
    To priests and people gathered there:

'If all that I have loved and seen
    Be with me on the Judgment Day,
I shall be saved the crowd between
    From Satan and his foul array.

'Almighty God will surely cry,
    "St Michael! Who is this that stands
With Ireland in his dubious eye,
    And Perigord between his hands,

'"And on his arm the stirrup-thongs,
    And in his gait the narrow seas,
And in his mouth Burgundian songs,
    But in his heart the Pyrenees?"

'St Michael then will answer right
    (And not without angelic shame),
"I seem to know his face by sight:
    I cannot recollect his name . . . ?"

'St Peter will befriend me then,
   Because my name is Peter too:
"I know him for the best of men
   That ever wallopped barley brew.

'"And though I did not know him well
   And though his soul were clogged with sin,
I hold the keys of Heaven and Hell.
   Be welcome, noble Peterkin."

'Then shall I spread my native wings
   And tread secure the heavenly floor,
And tell the Blessed doubtful things
   Of Val d'Aran and Perigord.'

This was the last and solemn jest
   Of weary Peter Wanderwide.
He spoke it with a failing zest,
   And having spoken it, he died.

AUVERGNAT

THERE was a man was half a clown
  (It's so my father tells of it).
He saw the church in Clermont town
And laughed to hear the bells of it.

He laughed to hear the bells that ring
In Clermont Church and round of it;
He heard the verger's daughter sing,
And loved her for the sound of it.

The verger's daughter said him nay;
She had the right of choice in it.
He left the town at break of day:
He hadn't had a voice in it.

The road went up, the road went down,
And there the matter ended it.
He broke his heart in Clermont town,
At Pontgibaud they mended it.

DRINKING SONG

ON THE EXCELLENCE OF BURGUNDY WINE

MY jolly fat host with your face all a-grin,
Come, open the door to us, let us come in.
A score of stout fellows who think it no sin
If they toast till they're hoarse, and they drink till they spin,
    Hoofed it amain,
    Rain or no rain,
  To crack your old jokes, and your bottle to drain.

Such a warmth in the belly that nectar begets
As soon as his guts with its humour he wets,
The miser his gold, and the student his debts,

And the beggar his rags and his hunger forgets.
>   For there's never a wine
>   Like this tipple of thine
From the great hill of Nuits to the River of Rhine.

Outside you may hear the great gusts as they go
By Foy, by Duerne, and the hills of Lerraulx,
But the rain he may rain, and the wind he may blow,
If the Devil's above there's good liquor below.
>   So it abound,
>   Pass it around,
Burgundy's Burgundy all the year round.

HA'NACKER MILL

>   SALLY is gone that was so kindly
>   Sally is gone from Ha'nacker Hill.
>   And the Briar grows ever since then so blindly
>   And ever since then the clapper is still,
>   And the sweeps have fallen from Ha'nacker Mill.

>   Ha'nacker Hill is in Desolation:
>   Ruin a-top and a field unploughed.
>   And Spirits that call on a fallen nation
>   Spirits that loved her calling aloud:
>   Spirits abroad in a windy cloud.

>   Spirits that call and no one answers;
>   Ha'nacker's down and England's done.
>   Wind and Thistle for pipe and dancers
>   And never a ploughman under the Sun.
>   Never a ploughman. Never a one.

TARANTELLA

Do you remember an Inn,
Miranda?
Do you remember an Inn?
And the tedding and the spreading
Of the straw for a bedding,

And the fleas that tease in the High Pyrenees,
And the wine that tasted of the tar?
And the cheers and the jeers of the young muleteers
(Under the vine of the dark veranda)?
Do you remember an Inn, Miranda,
Do you remember an Inn?
And the cheers and the jeers of the young muleteers
Who hadn't got a penny,
And who weren't paying any,
And the hammer at the doors and the Din?
And the Hip! Hop! Hap!
Of the clap
Of the hands to the twirl and the swirl
Of the girl gone chancing,
Glancing,
Dancing,
Backing and advancing,
Snapping of a clapper to the spin
Out and in——
And the Ting, Tong, Tang of the Guitar!
Do you remember an Inn,
Miranda?
Do you remember an Inn?

Never more;
Miranda,
Never more.
Only the high peaks hoar:
And Aragon a torrent at the door.
No sound
In the walls of the Halls where falls
The tread
Of the feet of the dead to the ground
No sound:
But the boom
Of the far Waterfall like Doom.

BALLADE TO OUR LADY OF CZESTOCHOWA

I

LADY and Queen and Mystery manifold
  And very Regent of the untroubled sky,
Whom in a dream St Hilda did behold
  And heard a woodland music passing by:
  You shall receive me when the clouds are high
With evening and the sheep attain the fold.
This is the faith that I have held and hold,
  And this is that in which I mean to die.

II

Steep are the seas and savaging and cold
  In broken waters terrible to try;
And vast against the winter night the wold,
  And harbourless for any sail to lie.
  But you shall lead me to the lights, and I
Shall hymn you in a harbour story told.
This is the faith that I have held and hold,
  And this is that in which I mean to die.

III

Help of the half-defeated, House of gold,
  Shrine of the Sword, and Tower of Ivory;
Splendour apart, supreme and aureoled,
  The Battler's vision and the World's reply.
  You shall restore me, O my last Ally,
To vengeance and the glories of the bold.
This is the faith that I have held and hold,
  And this is that in which I mean to die.

Envoi

Prince of the degradations, bought and sold,
  These verses, written in your crumbling sty,
Proclaim the faith that I have held and hold
  And publish that in which I mean to die.

BALLADE OF UNSUCCESSFUL MEN

I

THE cause of all the poor in '93:
   The cause of all the world at Waterloo:
The shouts of what was terrible and free
   Behind the guns of *Vengeance* and her crew:
The Maid that rode so straightly and so true
   And broke the line to pieces in her pride—
They had to chuck it up; it wouldn't do;
   The Devil didn't like them, and they died.

II

Caesar and Alexander shall agree
   That right athwart the world their bugles blew:
And all the lads that marched in Lombardy
   Behind the young Napoleon charging through:
All that were easy swordsmen, all that slew
   The Monsters, and that served our God and tried
The temper of this world—they lost the clue.
   The Devil didn't like them, and they died.

III

You, the strong sons of anger and the sea,
   What darkness on the wings of battle flew?
Then the great dead made answer: 'Also we
   With Nelson found oblivion: Nelson, who
When cheering out of Portsmouth harbour grew
   To make one purpose with the wind and tide—
Our nameless hulks are sunk and rotted through:
   The Devil didn't like us and we died.'

Envoi

Prince, may I venture (since it's only you)
   To speak discreetly of The Crucified?
He was extremely unsuccessful too:
   The Devil didn't like Him, and He died.

EPIGRAMS

I

On His Books

WHEN I am dead, I hope it may be said:
'His sins were scarlet, but his books were read.'

II

On Noman, a Guest

Dear Mr Noman, does it ever strike you,
The more we see of you, the less we like you?

III

A Trinity

Of three in One and One in three
My narrow mind would doubting be
Till Beauty, Grace, and Kindness met
And all at once were Juliet.

IV

On Torture, a Public Singer

Torture will give a dozen pence or more
To keep a drab from bawling at his door.
The public taste is quite a different thing—
Torture is positively paid to sing.

V

On Paunch, a Parasite

Paunch talks against good liquor to excess,
And then about his raving Patroness;
And then he talks about himself. And then
We turn the conversation on to men.

VI

On Hygiene

Of old when folk lay sick and sorely tried
The doctors gave them physic, and they died.
But here's a happier age: for now we know
Both how to make men sick and keep them so.

VII

On Lady Poltagrue, a Public Peril

The Devil, having nothing else to do,
Went off to tempt My Lady Poltagrue.
My Lady, tempted by a private whim,
To his extreme annoyance, tempted him.

VIII

Fatigue

I'm tired of Love: I'm still more tired of Rhyme.
But Money gives me pleasure all the time.

IX

On Mundane Acquaintances

Good morning, Algernon: Good morning, Percy.
Good morning, Mrs Roebeck. Christ have mercy!

X

The Statue

When we are dead, some Hunting-boy will pass
And find a stone half-hidden in tall grass
And grey with age: but having seen that stone
(Which was your image), ride more slowly on.

DEDICATION

Child ! do not throw this book about ;
  Refrain from the unholy pleasure
Of cutting all the pictures out !
  Preserve it as your chiefest treasure.

Child, have you never heard it said
  That you are heir to all the ages ?
Why, then, your hands were never made
  To tear these beautiful thick pages !

Your little hands were made to take
  The better things and leave the worse ones.
They also may be used to shake
  The Massive Paws of Elder Persons.

And when your prayers complete the day,
  Darling, your little tiny hands
Were also made, I think, to pray
  For men that lose their fairylands.

THE YAK

As a friend to the children commend me the Yak.
  You will find it exactly the thing:
It will carry and fetch, you can ride on its back,
  Or lead it about with a string.
The Tartar who dwells on the plains of Thibet
  (A desolate region of snow)
Has for centuries made it a nursery pet,
  And surely the Tartar should know!
Then tell your papa where the Yak can be got,
  And if he is awfully rich
He will buy you the creature—or else he will *not*.
  (I cannot be positive which.)

THE WHALE

THE Whale that wanders round the Pole
  Is not a table fish.
You cannot bake or boil him whole
  Nor serve him in a dish;
But you may cut his blubber up
  And melt it down for oil.
And so replace the colza bean
  (A product of the soil).
These facts should all be noted down
  And ruminated on,
By every boy in Oxford town
  Who wants to be a Don.

THE ELEPHANT

WHEN people call this beast to mind,
  They marvel more and more
At such a LITTLE tail behind,
  So LARGE a trunk before.

THE PYTHON

A PYTHON I should not advise,—
It needs a doctor for its eyes,
And has the measles yearly.
However, if you feel inclined
To get one (to improve your mind,
And not from fashion merely),
Allow no music near its cage;
And when it flies into a rage
Chastise it, most severely.
I had an aunt in Yucatan
Who bought a Python from a man
And kept it for a pet.
She died, because she never knew
These simple little rules and few;—
The Snake is living yet.

THE LLAMA

THE Llama is a woolly sort of fleecy hairy goat,
With an indolent expression and an undulating throat
Like an unsuccessful literary man.
And I know the place he lives in (or at least—I think I do)
It is Ecuador, Brazil, or Chili—possibly Peru;
You must find it in the Atlas if you can.
The Llama of the Pampasses you never should confound
(In spite of a deceptive similarity of sound)
With the Lhama who is Lord of Turkestan.
For the former is a beautiful and valuable beast,
But the latter is not lovable nor useful in the least;
And the Ruminant is preferable surely to the Priest
Who battens on the woeful superstitions of the East,
The Mongol of the Monastery of Shan.

A

stands for Archibald who told no lies,
And got this lovely volume for a prize.
The Upper School had combed and oiled their hair,
And all the Parents of the Boys were there.
In words that ring like thunder through the Hall,
Draw tears from some and loud applause from all,—
The Pedagogue, with Pardonable Joy,
Bestows the Gift upon the Radiant Boy:—
'Accept the Noblest Work produced as yet'
(Says he) 'upon the English Alphabet;
Next term I shall examine you, to find
If you have read it thoroughly. So mind!'
And while the Boys and Parents cheered so loud,
That out of doors a large and anxious crowd
Had gathered and was blocking up the street,
The admirable child resumed his seat.

MORAL

Learn from this justly irritating Youth
To brush your Hair and Teeth and tell the Truth.

C

stands for Cobra; when the Cobra bites
An Indian Judge, the Judge spends restless nights.

MORAL

This creature, though disgusting and appalling,
Conveys no kind of Moral worth recalling.

G

stands for Gnu, whose weapons of Defence
Are long, sharp, curling Horns, and Common-sense.
To these he adds a Name so short and strong,
That even Hardy Boers pronounce it wrong.
How often on a bright Autumnal day
The Pious people of Pretoria say,
'Come, let us hunt the ——'   Then no more is heard
But sounds of Strong Men struggling with a word.
Meanwhile, the distant Gnu with grateful eyes
Observes his opportunity, and flies.

MORAL

Child, if you have a rummy kind of name,
Remember to be thankful for the same.

O

stands for Oxford.   Hail! salubrious seat
Of learning!   Academical Retreat!
Home of my Middle Age!   Malarial Spot
Which People call Medeeval (though it's not).
The marshes in the neighbourhood can vie
With Cambridge, but the town itself is dry,
And serves to make a kind of Fold or Pen
Wherein to herd a lot of Learned Men.
Were I to write but half of what they know,
It would exhaust the space reserved for 'O';
And, as my book must not be over big,
I turn at once to 'P,' which stands for Pig.

MORAL

Be taught by this to speak with moderation
Of places where, with decent application,
One gets a good, sound, middle-class education.

P

stands for Pig, as I remarked before,
A second cousin to the Huge Wild Boar.
But Pigs are civilized, while Huge Wild Boars
Live savagely, at random, out of doors,
And, in their coarse contempt for dainty foods,
Subsist on Truffles, which they find in woods.
Not so the cultivated Pig, who feels
The need of several courses at his meals,
But wrongly thinks it does not matter whether
He takes them one by one or all together.
Hence, Pigs devour, from lack of self-respect,
What Epicures would certainly eject.

MORAL

Learn from the Pig to take whatever Fate
Or Elder Persons heap upon your plate.

JIM,

Who ran away from his Nurse, and was eaten by a Lion

THERE was a Boy whose name was Jim;
His Friends were very good to him.
They gave him Tea, and Cakes, and Jam,
And slices of delicious Ham,
And Chocolate with pink inside,
And little Tricycles to ride,
And read him stories through and through,
And even took him to the Zoo—
But there it was the dreadful Fate
Befel him, which I now relate.

You know—at least you *ought* to know,
For I have often told you so—
That Children never are allowed
To leave their Nurses in a Crowd;
Now this was Jim's especial Foible,
He ran away when he was able,
And on this inauspicious day
He slipped his hand and ran away!
He hadn't gone a yard when—Bang!
With open Jaws, a Lion sprang,
And hungrily began to eat
The Boy: beginning at his feet.
Now, just imagine how it feels
When first your toes and then your heels,
And then by gradual degrees,
Your shins and ankles, calves and knees,
Are slowly eaten, bit by bit.
No wonder Jim detested it!
No wonder that he shouted 'Hi!'
The Honest Keeper heard his cry,
Though very fat he almost ran
To help the little gentleman.
'Ponto!' he ordered as he came
(For Ponto was the Lion's name),
'Ponto!' he cried, with angry Frown.
'Let go, Sir! Down, Sir! Put it down!'

The Lion made a sudden Stop,
He let the Dainty Morsel drop,
And slunk reluctant to his Cage,
Snarling with Disappointed Rage.
But when he bent him over Jim,
The Honest Keeper's Eyes were dim.
The Lion having reached his Head,
The Miserable Boy was dead!

When Nurse informed his Parents, they
Were more Concerned than I can say:—
His Mother, as She dried her eyes,
Said, 'Well—it gives me no surprise,
He would not do as he was told!'
His Father, who was self-controlled,
Bade all the children round attend
To James' miserable end,
And always keep a-hold of Nurse
For fear of finding something worse.

HENRY KING,

Who chewed bits of String, and was early cut off in Dreadful Agonies

The Chief Defect of Henry King
Was chewing little bits of String.
At last he swallowed some which tied
Itself in ugly Knots inside.
Physicians of the Utmost Fame
Were called at once; but when they came
They answered, as they took their Fees,
'There is no cure for this Disease.
Henry will very soon be dead.'
His Parents stood about his Bed
Lamenting his Untimely Death,
When Henry, with his Latest Breath
Cried—'Oh, my friends, be warned by me,
That Breakfast, Dinner, Lunch, and Tea
Are all the Human Frame requires. . . . .'
With that, the Wretched Child expires.

MATILDA

Who told Lies, and was Burned to Death

MATILDA told such Dreadful Lies,
It made one Gasp and Stretch one's Eyes;
Her Aunt, who, from her Earliest Youth,
Had kept a Strict Regard for Truth,
Attempted to Believe Matilda:
The effort very nearly killed her,
And would have done so, had not She
Discovered this Infirmity.
For once, towards the Close of Day,
Matilda, growing tired of play,
And finding she was left alone,
Went tiptoe to the Telephone
And summoned the Immediate Aid
Of London's Noble Fire-Brigade.
Within an hour the Gallant Band
Were pouring in on every hand,
From Putney, Hackney Downs, and Bow
With Courage high and Hearts a-glow
They galloped, roaring through the Town,
'Matilda's House is Burning Down!'
Inspired by British Cheers and Loud
Proceeding from the Frenzied Crowd,
They ran their ladders through a score
Of windows on the Ball Room Floor;
And took Peculiar Pains to Souse
The Pictures up and down the House,
Until Matilda's Aunt succeeded
In showing them they were not needed
And even then she had to pay
To get the Men to go away!

．　　．　　．　　．　　．

It happened that a few Weeks later
Her Aunt was off to the Theatre
To see that Interesting Play
The Second Mrs Tanqueray.
She had refused to take her Niece
To hear this entertaining Piece:
A Deprivation Just and Wise

To Punish her for Telling Lies.
That Night a Fire *did* break out—
You should have heard Matilda Shout!
You should have heard her Scream and Bawl,
And throw the window up and call
To People passing in the Street—
(The rapidly increasing Heat
Encouraging her to obtain
Their confidence)—but all in vain!
For every time She shouted 'Fire!'
They only answered 'Little Liar!'
And therefore when her Aunt returned,
Matilda and the House were burned.

A REPROOF OF GLUTTONY

The Elephant will eat of hay
Some four and twenty tons a day,
And in his little eyes express
His unaffected thankfulness
That Providence should deign to find
Him food of this delicious kind.
While they that pay for all the hay
Will frequently be heard to say
How highly privileged they feel
To help him make so large a meal.
The Boa Constrictor dotes on goats;
The Horse is quite content with oats,
Or will alternatively pass
A happy morning munching grass.
The great Ant Eater of Taluz
Consumes—or people say he does—
Not only what his name implies
But even ordinary flies:
And Marmosets and Chimpanzees
Are happy on the nuts of trees.
The Lion from the burning slopes
Of Atlas lives on Antelopes,
And only adds the flesh of men
By way of relish now and then:
As Cheetahs—yes, and Tigers, too

And Jaguars of the Andes—do.
The Lobster, I have heard it said,
Eats nobody till he is dead;
And Cobras, though they have the sense
To poison you in self-defence,
Restrict their food to birds and hares:
Which also may be true of Bears.
Indeed wherever we survey
Our Humble Friends we find that they
Confine their appetites to what
May happen to be on the spot.
Simplicity and moderation
Distinguish all the Brute Creation.
But Man—proud man! (as Dryden sings)
Though wolfing quantities of things—
Smoked salmon in transparent slices,
And Turbot à la Reine, and Ices,
And truffled Pies and Caviare,
And Chinese Ginger from the Jar;
And Oysters; and a kind of stuff
Called Cassouletto (good enough!)
And Mutton duly steeped in claret
(Or jumped with young shallot and carrot),
And Chicken Livers done with rice,
And Quails (which, I am told, are Mice),
And Peaches from a sunny wall,
And—Lord! I don't know what and all!—
Oh! Yes! And Sausages—is not
Contented with his Prandial lot.

MORAL

The Moral is (I think, at least)
That Man is an UNGRATEFUL BEAST.

ABOUT JOHN

Who lost a fortune by Throwing Stones

JOHN VAVASSOUR DE QUENTIN JONES
Was very fond of throwing stones
At Horses, People, Passing Trains,
But 'specially at Window-panes.

Like many of the Upper Class
He liked the Sound of Broken Glass [1]
It bucked him up and made him gay:
It was his favourite form of Play.
But the Amusement cost him dear,
My children, as you now shall hear.

JOHN VAVASSOUR DE QUENTIN had
An uncle, who adored the lad:
And often chuckled; 'Wait until
You see what's left you in my will!'
Nor were the words without import,
Because this uncle did a sort
Of something in the City, which
Had made him fabulously rich.
(Although his brother, John's papa,
Was poor, as many fathers are.)

He had a lot of stocks and shares
And half a street in Buenos Aires, [2]
A bank in Rio, and a line
Of Steamers to the Argentine.
And options more than I can tell,
And bits of Canada as well;
He even had a mortgage on
The house inhabited by John.
His will, the cause of all the fuss,
Was carefully indited thus:

'This is the last and solemn Will
Of Uncle William—known as Bill.
I do bequeath, devise and give
By Execution Mandative
The whole amount of what I've got
(It comes to a tremendous lot!)
In seizin to devolve upon
My well-beloved nephew John.
(And here the witnesses will sign
Their names upon the dotted line.)'

---

[1] A line I stole with subtle daring
From Wing-Commander Maurice Baring.

[2] But this pronunciation varies;
Some people call it Bu-enos Airés.

Such was the Legal Instrument
Expressing Uncle Bill's intent.

As time went on declining Health
Transmogrified this Man of Wealth;
And it was excellently clear
That Uncle Bill's demise was near.
At last his sole idea of fun
Was sitting snoozling in the sun.
So once, when he would take the air,
They wheeled him in his Patent Chair
(By 'They,' I mean his Nurse, who came
From Dorchester upon the Thame:
Miss Charming was the Nurse's name).
To where beside a little wood
A long abandoned green-house stood,
And there he sank into a doze
Of senile and inept repose.
But not for long his drowsy ease!
A stone came whizzing through the trees,
And caught him smartly in the eye.
He woke with an appalling cry,
And shrieked in agonizing tones:
'Oh! Lord! Whoever's throwing stones!'
Miss Charming, who was standing near,
Said: 'That was Master John, I fear!'
'Go get my Ink-pot and my Quill,
My Blotter and my Famous Will.'
Miss Charming flew as though on wings
To fetch these necessary things,
And Uncle William ran his pen
Through 'well-beloved John,' and then
Proceeded, in the place of same,
To substitute Miss Charming's name:
Who now resides in Portman Square
And is accepted everywhere.

ON FOOD

Alas! What various tastes in food,
Divide the human brotherhood!

Birds in their little nests agree
With Chinamen, but not with me.
Colonials like their oysters hot,
Their omelettes heavy—I do not.
The French are fond of slugs and frogs,
The Siamese eat puppy-dogs.
The nobles at the brilliant Court
Of Muscovy, consumed a sort
Of candles held and eaten thus
As though they were asparagus.
The Spaniard, I have heard it said,
Eats garlic, by itself, on bread:
Now just suppose a friend or dun
Dropped in to lunch at half-past one
And you were jovially to say,
'Here's bread and garlic! Peg away!'
I doubt if you would gain your end
Or soothe the dun, or please the friend.
In Italy the traveller notes
With great disgust the flesh of goats
Appearing on the table d'hôtes;
And even this the natives spoil
By frying it in rancid oil.
In Maryland they charge like sin
For nasty stuff called terrapin;
And when they ask you out to dine
At Washington, instead of wine,
They give you water from the spring
With lumps of ice for flavouring,
That sometimes kill and always freeze
The high plenipotentiaries.
In Massachusetts all the way
From Boston down to Buzzards Bay
They feed you till you want to die
On rhubarb pie and pumpkin pie,
And horrible huckleberry pie,
And when you summon strength to cry,
'What is there else that I can try?'

They stare at you in mild surprise
And serve you other kinds of pies.
And I with these mine eyes have seen
A dreadful stuff called Margarine
Consumed by men in Bethnal Green.
But I myself that here complain
Confess restriction quite in vain.
I feel my native courage fail
To see a Gascon eat a snail;
I dare not ask abroad for tea;
No cannibal can dine with me;
And all the world is torn and rent
By varying views on nutriment.
And yet upon the other hand,
De gustibus non disputand

       —Um.

THE MODERN TRAVELLER

I

The *Daily Menace*, I presume?
Forgive the litter in the room.
I can't explain to you
How out of place a man like me
Would be without the things you see—
The Shields and Assegais and odds
And ends of little savage gods.
Be seated; take a pew.
(Excuse the phrase. I'm rather rough,
And—pardon me!—but have you got
A pencil? I've another here:
The one that you have brought, I fear,
Will not be long enough.)
And so the Public want to hear
About the expedition
From which I recently returned:
Of how the Fetish Tree was burned;
Of how we struggled to the coast,
And lost our ammunition;
How we retreated, side by side;
And how, like Englishmen, we died.
Well, as you know, I hate to boast,
And, what is more, I can't abide
A popular position.
I told the Duke the other day
The way I felt about it.
He answered courteously—'Oh!'
An Editor (who had an air
Of what the Dutch call *savoir faire*)
Said, 'Mr Rooter, you are right,
And nobody can doubt it.'
The Duchess murmured, 'Very true.'
Her comments may be brief and true,
But very seldom trite.
Still, representing as you do
A public and a point of view,
I'll give you leave to jot
A few remarks—a very few—
But understand that this is not

A formal interview.
And first of all, I will begin
By talking of Commander Sin.

II

Poor Henry Sin from quite a child,
I fear, was always rather wild;
    But all his faults were due
To something free and unrestrained,
That partly pleased and partly pained
    The people whom he knew.
Untaught (for what our times require),
Lazy, and something of a liar,
    He had a foolish way
Of always swearing (more or less);
    And, lastly, let us say
A little slovenly in dress,
A trifle prone to drunkenness;
A gambler also to excess,
    And never known to pay.
As for his clubs in London, he
Was pilled at ten, expelled from three.
A man Bohemian as could be—
    But really vicious? Oh, no!
When these are mentioned, all is said.
And then—Commander Sin is dead:
    De Mortuis cui bono?

Of course, the Public know I mean
To publish in the winter.
I mention the intention in
Connection with Commander Sin;
    The book is with the Printer.
And here, among the proofs, I find
The very thing I had in mind—
The portrait upon page thirteen.[1]
Pray pause awhile, and mark
The wiry limbs, the vigorous mien,

---

[1] [All illustrations omitted in this edition.]

The tangled hair and dark;
The glance imperative and hot,
    That takes a world by storm:
All these are in the plate, but what
You chiefly should observe is
The—Did you say his uniform
Betrayed a foreign service?

Of course, it does! He was not born
In little England! No!
Beyond the Cape, beyond the Horn,
Beyond Fernando Po,
In some far Isle he saw the light
That burns the torrid zone,
But where it lay was never quite
Indubitably known.
Himself inclined to Martinique,
His friends to Farralone.
But why of this discussion speak?
The Globe was all his own!
Oh! surely upon such a birth
No petty flag unfurled!
He was a citizen of earth,
A subject of the world!

As for the uniform he bore,
He won it in the recent war
Between Peru and Ecuador,
    And thoroughly he earned it.
Alone of all who at the time
Were serving sentences for crime,
Sin, during his incarceration
Had studied works on navigation;
And when the people learned it,
They promptly let him out of jail,
But on condition he should sail.

It marked an epoch, and you may
Recall the action in
A place called Quaxipotle bay?
Yes, both the navies ran away;
And yet, if Ecuador can say
That on the whole she won the day,
The fact is due to Sin.

The Fleet was hardly ten weeks out,
When somebody descried
The enemy. Sin gave a shout,
The Helmsmen put the ship about;
For, upon either side,
Tactics demanded a retreat.
Due west retired the foreign fleet,
But Sin he steered due east;
He muttered, 'They shall never meet.'
And when, towards the close of day,
The foemen were at least
Fifteen or twenty miles away,
He called his cabin-steward aft,
The boldest of his men;
He grasped them by the hand; he laughed
A fearless laugh, and then,
'Heaven help the right! Full steam a-head,
Fighting for fighting's sake,' he said.

Due west the foe—due east he steered.
Ah, me! the very stokers cheered,
And faces black with coal
And fuzzy with a five days' beard
Popped up, and yelled, and disappeared
Each in its little hole.
Long after they were out of sight,
Long after dark, throughout the night,
Throughout the following day,
He went on fighting all the time!
Not war, perhaps, but how sublime!

Just as he would have stepped ashore,
The President of Ecuador
Came on his quarter-deck;
Embraced him twenty times or more,
And gave him stripes and things galore,
Crosses and medals by the score,
And handed him a cheque—
And then a little speech he read.

Of twenty years, your sentence said,
That you should serve—another week
(Alas! it shames me as I speak)

Was owing when you quitted.
In recognition of your nerve,
It gives me pleasure to observe
The time you still had got to serve
Is totally remitted.

'Instead of which these friends of mine'—
(And here he pointed to a line
Of Colonels on the Quay)—
Have changed your sentence to a fine
Made payable to me.
No—do not thank me—not a word!
I am very glad to say
This little cheque is quite a third
Of what you have to pay.'

The crew they cheered and cheered again,
The simple-loyal-hearted men!

Such deeds could never fail to be
Renowned throughout the west.
It was our cousins over sea
That loved the Sailor best,—
Our Anglo-Saxon kith and kin,
They doted on Commander Sin,
And gave him a tremendous feast
The week before we started.
O'Hooligan, and Vonderbeast,
And Nicolazzi, and the rest,
Were simply broken-hearted.

They came and ate and cried, 'God speed!'
The Bill was very large indeed,
And paid for by an Anglo-Saxon
Who bore the sterling name of Jackson.
On this occasion Sin was seen
Toasting McKinley and the Queen.
The speech was dull, but not an eye,
Not even the champagne was dry.

III

Now William Blood, or, as I still
Affectionately call him, Bill,
Was of a different stamp;
One who, in other ages born
Had turned to strengthen and adorn
The Senate or the Camp.
But Fortune, jealous and austere,
Had marked him for a great career
Of more congenial kind—
A sort of modern Buccaneer,
Commercial and refined.
Like all great men, his chief affairs
Were buying stocks and selling shares.
He occupied his mind
In buying them by day from men
Who needed ready cash, and then
At evening selling them again
To those with whom he dined.

But such a task could never fill
His masterful ambition
That rapid glance, that iron will,
Disdained (and rightfully) to make
A profit here and there, or take
His two per cent commission.
His soul with nobler stuff was fraught;
The love of country, as it ought,
Haunted his every act and thought.
To that he lent his mighty powers,
To that he gave his waking hours,
Of that he dreamed in troubled sleep,
Till, after many years, the deep
        Imperial emotion,
That moves us like a martial strain,
Turned his Napoleonic brain
        To company promotion.

He failed, and it was better so:
        It made our expedition.
One day (it was a year ago)
He came on foot across the town,

And said his luck was rather down,
And would I lend him half-a-crown?
    I did, but on condition
(Drawn up in proper legal shape,
Witnessed and sealed, and tied with tape,
And costing two pound two),
That, 'If within the current year
He made a hundred thousand clear,'
He should accompany me in
A Project I had formed with Sin
    To go to Timbuctoo.
Later, we had a tiff because
I introduced another clause,
    Of which the general sense is,
That Blood, in the unlikely case
Of this adventure taking place,
    Should pay the whole expenses.
Blood swore that he had never read
Or seen the clause. But Blood is dead.

Well, through a curious stroke of luck,
That very afternoon he struck
    A new concern, in which,
By industry and honest ways,
He grew (to his eternal praise!)
In something less than sixty days
    Inordinately rich.

Let me describe what he became
    The day that he succeeded,—
Though, in the searching light that Fame
Has cast on that immortal name,
    The task is hardly needed.

The world has very rarely seen
A deeper gulf than stood between
    The men who were my friends.
And, speaking frankly, I confess
They never cared to meet, unless
It served their private ends.

Sin loved the bottle, William gold;
'Twas Blood that bought and Sin that sold,
    In all their mutual dealings.
Blood never broke the penal laws;
Sin did it all the while, because
    He had the finer feelings.

Blood had his dreams, but Sin was mad:
While Sin was foolish, Blood was bad,
Sin, though I say it, was a cad.
    (And if the word arouses
Some criticism, pray reflect
How twisted was his intellect,
And what a past he had!)
But Blood was exquisitely bred,
    And always in the swim,
And people were extremely glad
    To ask him to their houses.
Be not too eager to condemn:
It was not he that hunted them,
    But they that hunted him.

In this fair world of culture made
For men of his peculiar trade,
Of all the many parts he played,
The part he grew to like the best
Was called 'the self-respecting guest.'
    And for that very reason
He found himself in great request
    At parties in the season,
Wherever gentlemen invest,
    From Chelsea to Mayfair.
From Lath and Stucco Gate, S.W.,
    To 90, Berkeley Square.
The little statesmen in the bud,
    The big provincial mayor,
    The man that owns a magazine,
    The authoress who might have been;
They always sent a card to Blood,
    And Blood was always there.
At every dinner, crush or rout,
A little whirlpool turned about

The form immovable and stout,
    That marked the Millionaire.
Sin (you remember) could not stay
In any club for half a day,
    When once his name was listed;
But Blood belonged to ninety-four,
And would have joined as many more
    Had any more existed.
Sin at a single game would lose
A little host of I.O.U's,
And often took the oath absurd
To break the punters or his word
    Before it was completed.
Blood was another pair of shoes:
A man of iron, cold and hard,
He very rarely touched a card,
But when he did he cheated.
Again the origin of Sin,
    Was doubtful and obscure;
Whereas, the Captain's origin
    Was absolutely sure.

A document affirms that he
Was born in 1853
Upon a German ship at sea,
    Just off the Grand Canary.
And though the log is rather free
And written too compactly,
We know the weather to a T,
The longitude to a degree,
The latitude exactly,
    And every detail is the same;
    We even know his Mother's name.
As to his father's occupation,
Creed, colour, character or nation,
    (On which the rumours vary);
He said himself concerning it,
With admirably caustic wit,
    'I think the Public would much rather
    Be sure of me than of my father.'

The contrast curiously keen
    Their characters could yield

Was most conspicuously seen
    Upon the Tented Field.
Was there by chance a native tribe
To cheat, cajole, corrupt, or bribe?—
In such conditions Sin would burn
    To plunge into the fray,
While Blood would run the whole concern
    From fifty miles away.

He had, wherever honours vain
Were weighed against material gain
A judgment, practical and sane,
    Peculiarly his own.
In this connection let me quote
An interesting anecdote
    Not generally known.
Before he sailed he might have been
    (If he had thought it paid him)
A military man of note.
Her gracious Majesty the Queen
    Would certainly have made him,
In spite of his advancing years,
A Captain of the Volunteers.
A certain Person of the Sort
That has great influence at Court,
    Assured him it was so;
And said, 'It simply lies with you
To get this little matter through.
You pay a set of trifling fees
To me—at any time you please——'
Blood stopped him with a 'No!'
'This signal favour of the Queen's
Is very burdensome. It means
A smart Review (for all I know),
In which I am supposed to show
    Strategical ability:
And after that tremendous fights
And sleeping out on rainy nights,
    And much responsibility.
Thank you: I have my own position,
I need no parchment or commission,
And every one who knows my name
Will call me "Captain" just the same.'

There was our leader in a phrase:
A man of strong decisive ways,
    But reticent[1] and grim.
Though not an Englishman, I own,
Perhaps it never will be known
    What England lost in him!

IV

The ship was dropping down the stream,
The Isle of Dogs was just abeam,
    And Sin and Blood and I
Saw Greenwich Hospital go past,
And gave a look—(for them the last)—
    Towards the London sky!
Ah! nowhere have I ever seen
A sky so pure and so serene!

Did we at length, perhaps, regret
    Our strange adventurous lot?
And were our eyes a trifle wet
With tears that we repressed, and yet
    Which started blinding hot?
Perhaps—and yet, I do not know,
For when we came to go below,
    We cheerfully admitted
That though there was a smell of paint
(And though a very just complaint
Had to be lodged against the food),
The cabin furniture was good
    And comfortably fitted.
And even out beyond the Nore
We did not ask to go ashore.

To turn to more congenial topics,
    I said a little while ago
    The food was very much below
The standard needed to prepare
Explorers for the special fare

---

[1] This reticence, which some have called hypocrisy
Was but the sign of nature's aristocracy.

Which all authorities declare
    Is needful in the tropics.
A Frenchman sitting next to us
Rejected the asparagus;
The turtle soup was often cold,
The ices hot, the omelettes old,
The coffee worse than I can tell;
And Sin (who had a happy knack
Of rhyming rapidly and well
Like Cyrano de Bergerac)
    Said 'Quant à moi, je n'aime pas
    Du tout ce pâté de foie gras!'
But this fastidious taste
Succeeded in a startling way;
At Dinner on the following day
    They gave us Bloater Paste.
Well—hearty Pioneers and rough
    Should not be over nice;
I think these lines are quite enough,
    And hope they will suffice
To make the Caterers observe
The kind of person whom they serve.——

   .   .   .   .   .

And yet I really must complain
About the Company's Champagne!
    This most expensive kind of wine
In England is a matter
Of pride or habit when we dine
    (Presumably the latter).
Beneath an equatorial sky
You *must* consume it or you die;
And stern indomitable men
Have told me, time and time again,
'The nuisance of the tropics is
The sheer necessity of fizz.'
Consider then the carelessness—
The lack of polish and address,
    The villainy in short,
Of serving what explorers think
To be a necessary drink
In bottles holding something less
    Than one Imperial quart,

And costing quite a shilling more
Than many grocers charge ashore.

.   .   .   .   .   .

At sea the days go slipping past.
Monotonous from first to last—
A trip like any other one
In vessels going south. The sun
    Grew higher and more fiery.

We lay and drank, and swore, and played
At Trick-my-neighbour in the shade;
And you may guess how every sight,
However trivial or slight,
    Was noted in my diary.
I have it here—the usual things—
A serpent (not the sort with wings)
    Came rising from the sea:
In length (as far as we could guess)
A quarter of a mile or less.
The weather was extremely clear
The creature dangerously near
    And plain as it would be.
It had a bifurcated tail,
And in its mouth it held a whale.
Just north, I find, of Cape de Verd
We caught a very curious bird
    With horns upon its head;
And—not, as one might well suppose,
Web-footed or with jointed toes—
    But having hoofs instead.
As no one present seemed to know
Its use or name, I let it go.

On June the 7th after dark
A young and very hungry shark
    Came climbing up the side.
It ate the Chaplain and the Mate—
But why these incidents relate?
    The public must decide,
That nothing in the voyage out
Was worth their bothering about.
Until we saw the coast, which looks
Exactly as it does in books.

V

Oh! Africa, mysterious Land!
Surrounded by a lot of sand
    And full of grass and trees,
And elephants and Afrikanders,
And politics and Salamanders,
And Germans seeking to annoy,
And horrible rhinoceroi,
And native rum in little kegs,
And savages called Touaregs
    (A kind of Soudanese).
And tons of diamonds, and lots
Of nasty, dirty Hottentots,
And coolies coming from the East;
And serpents, seven yards long at least
    And lions, that retain
Their vigour, appetites and rage
Intact to an extreme old age,
    And never lose their mane.

Far Land of Ophir! Mined for gold
By lordly Solomon of old,
Who sailing northward to Perim
Took all the gold away with him,
    And left a lot of holes;
Vacuities that bring despair
    To those confiding souls
Who find that they have bought a share
In marvellous horizons, where
The Desert terrible and bare
    Interminably rolls.

Great Island! Made to be the bane
Of Mr Joseph Chamberlain.
Peninsula! Whose smouldering fights
Keep Salisbury awake at nights;
And furnished for a year or so
Such sport to M. Hanotaux.

Vast Continent! Whose cumbrous shape
Runs from Bizerta to the Cape
(Bizerta on the northern shore,

Concerning which, the French, they swore
It never should be fortified,
Wherein that cheerful people lied).

Thou nest of Sultans full of guile,
Embracing Zanzibar the vile
And Egypt, watered by the Nile
(Egypt, which is, as I believe,
The property of the Khedive):
Containing in thy many states
Two independent potentates,
 And one I may not name.
(Look carefully at number three,
Not independent quite, but he
Is more than what he used to be.)
To thee, dear goal, so long deferred
Like old Æneas—in a word
 To Africa we came.

We beached upon a rising tide
At Sasstown on the western side;
 And as we touched the strand
I thought—(I may have been mistook)—
I thought the earth in terror shook
 To feel its Conquerors land.

VI

In getting up our Caravan
We met a most obliging man,
The Lord Chief Justice of Liberia,
And Minister of the Interior;
Cain Abolition Beecher Boz,
Worked like a Nigger—which he was—
 And in a single day
Procured us Porters, Guides, and kit,
And would not take a sou for it
 Until we went away.[1]
We wondered how this fellow made
Himself so readily obeyed,

 [1] But when we went away, we found
  A deficit of several pound.

And why the natives were so meek;
Until by chance we heard him speak,
And then we clearly understood
How great a Power for Social Good
  The African can be.
He said with a determined air:
'You are not what your fathers were;
Liberians, you are Free!
Of course, if you refuse to go—'
And here he made a gesture
He also gave us good advice
Concerning Labour and its Price.
'In dealing wid de Native Scum,
Yo' cannot pick an' choose;
Yo' hab to promise um a sum
Ob wages, paid in Cloth and Rum.
But, Lordy! that's a ruse!
Yo' get yo' well on de Adventure,
And change de wages to Indenture.'

We did the thing that he projected,
The Caravan grew disaffected,
  And Sin and I consulted;
Blood understood the Native mind.
He said: 'We must be firm but kind.'
  A Mutiny resulted.
I never shall forget the way
That Blood upon this awful day
Preserved us all from death.
He stood upon a little mound,
Cast his lethargic eyes around,
And said beneath his breath:
'Whatever happens we have got
The Maxim Gun, and they have not.'

He marked them in their rude advance,
He hushed their rebel cheers;
With one extremely vulgar glance
He broke the Mutineers.
(I have a picture in my book
Of how he quelled them with a look.)
We shot and hanged a few, and then
The rest became devoted men.

And here I wish to say a word
Upon the way my heart was stirred
   By those pathetic faces.
Surely our simple duty here
Is both imperative and clear;
While they support us, we should lend
Our every effort to defend,
And from a higher point of view
To give the full direction due
   To all the native races.
And I, throughout the expedition,
Insisted upon this position.

VII

Well, after that we toiled away
At drawing maps, and day by day
Blood made an acurate survey
   Of all that seemed to lend
A chance, no matter how remote,
Of letting our financier float
That triumph of Imagination,
'The Libyan Association.'
   In this the 'Negroes' friend'
Was much concerned to show the way
Of making Missionaries pay.

At night our leader and our friend
   Would deal in long discourses
Upon this meritorious end,
And how he would arrange it.
'The present way is an abuse
   Of Economic Forces;
They Preach, but they do not Produce.
Observe how I would change it.
I'd have the Missionary lent,
Upon a plot of land,
A sum at twenty-five per cent;
And (if I understand
The kind of people I should get)
An ever-present fear of debt
Would make them work like horses,

And form the spur, or motive spring,
In what I call "developing
    The Natural resources";
While people who subscribe will find
Profit and Piety combined.'

Imagine how the Mighty Scheme,
The Goal, the Vision, and the Dream
Developed in his hands!
With such a purpose, such a mind
Could easily become inclined
To use the worst of lands!
Thus once we found him standing still,
Enraptured, on a rocky hill;
Beneath his feet there stank
A swamp immeasurably wide,
Wherein a kind of fœtid tide
Rose rhythmical and sank,
Brackish and pestilent with weeds
And absolutely useless reeds,
It lay; but nothing daunted
At seeing how it heaved and steamed
He stood triumphant, and he seemed
Like one possessed or haunted.

With arms that welcome and rejoice,
We heard him gasping, in a voice
By strong emotion rendered harsh:
'That Marsh—that Admirable Marsh!'
The Tears of Avarice that rise
In purely visionary eyes,
Were rolling down his nose.
He was no longer Blood and Bold,
The Terror of his foes;
But Blood inflamed with greed of gold.

He saw us, and at once became
The Blood we knew, the very same
Whom we had loved so long.
He looked affectionately sly,
And said, 'perhaps you wonder why
My feelings are so strong?
You only see a swamp, but I——
My friends, I will explain it.

I know some gentlemen in town
Will give me fifty thousand down,
Merely for leave to drain it.'

A little later on we found
A piece of gently rolling ground
That showed above the flat.
Such a protuberance or rise
As wearies European eyes.
To common men, like Sin and me
The Eminence appeared to be
As purposeless as that.
Blood saw another meaning there,
He turned with a portentous glare,
And shouted for the Native Name.
The Black interpreter in shame
Replied: 'The native name I fear
Is something signifying Mud.'
    Then, with the gay bravado
That suits your jolly Pioneer,
In his prospectus Captain Blood
    Baptized it 'Eldorado.'
He also said the Summit rose
Majestic with Eternal Snows.

VIII

Now it behoves me (or behooves)
To give a retrospect that proves
    What foresight can achieve,
The kind of thing that (by the way)
Men in our cold agnostic day
Must come from Africa to say,
    From England to believe.

Blood had, while yet we were in town,
Said with his intellectual frown:
'Suppose a Rhino knocks you down
And walks upon you like a mat,
Think of the public irritation.
If with an incident like that,
We cannot give an illustration.'

Seeing we should be at a loss
To reproduce the scene,
We bought a stuffed rhinoceros,
A Kodak, and a screen.
We fixed a picture. William pressed
A button, and I did the rest.

To those Carnivora that make
An ordinary Person quake
    We did not give a care.
The Lion never will attack
A White, if he can get a Black.
And there were such a lot of these
We could afford with perfect ease
    To spare one here and there.
It made us more compact—and then—
It 's right to spare one's fellow men.

Of far more consequence to us,
And much more worthy to detain us,
    The very creature that we feared
(I mean the white Rhinoceros,
'*Siste Viator Africanus*')
    In all its majesty appeared.

This large, but peevish pachyderm
(To use a scientific term),
Though commonly herbivorous,
Is eminently dangerous.
It may be just the creature's play;
But people who have felt it say
That when he prods you with his horn
You wish you never had been born.

As I was dozing in the sun,
Without a cartridge to my gun,
    Upon a sultry day,
Absorbed in somnolescent bliss,
Just such an animal as this
    Came charging where I lay.
My only refuge was to fly,
But flight is not for me![1]

[1] Besides, I found my foot was caught
In twisted roots that held it taut.

Blood happened to be standing by,
He darted up a tree
And shouted, 'Do your best to try
And fix him with the Human Eye.'

Between a person and a beast
(But for the Human Eye at least)
The issue must be clear.
The tension of my nerves increased,
And yet I felt no fear.
Nay, do not praise me—not at all—
Courage is merely physical,
And several people I could name
Would probably have done the same.

I kept my glance extremely firm,
I saw the wretched creature squirm;
A look of terror over-spread
Its features, and it dropped down dead.
At least, I thought it did,
And foolishly withdrew my gaze,
When (finding it was rid
Of those mysterious piercing rays)
     It came to life again.
It jumped into the air, and came
With all its might upon my frame.

(Observe the posture of the hoof.
The wire and black support that look
So artificial in the proof
Will be deleted in the book.)

It did it thirty separate times;
When, luckily for all these rhymes,
Blood shot the brute—that is to say,
Blood shot, and then it ran away.

IX

We journeyed on in single file;
The march proceeded mile on mile
     Monotonous and lonely,
We saw (if I remember right)
The friendly features of a white
     On two occasions only.

The first was when our expedition
Came suddenly on a commission,
        Appointed to determine
Whether the thirteenth parallel
Ran right across a certain well,
Or touched a closely neighbouring tree;
And whether elephants should be
Exterminated all as 'game,'
Or, what is not at all the same,
        Destroyed as common vermin.

To this commission had been sent
Great bigwigs from the Continent,
        And on the English side
Men of such ancient pedigree
As filled the soul of Blood with glee;
        He started up and cried:
'I'll go to them at once, and make
These young adventurous spirits take
        A proof of my desire
To use in this concern of ours
Their unsuspected business powers.
The bearers of historic names
        Shall rise to something higher
Than haggling over frontier claims,
        And they shall find their last estate
        Enshrined in my directorate.'

In twenty minutes he returned,
His face with righteous anger burned,
And when we asked him what he'd done,
        He answered, 'They reject us,
I couldn't get a single one.
        To come on the prospectus.
Their leader (though he was a Lord)
Stoutly refused to join the board,
And made a silly foreign speech
Which sounded like No Bless Ableech.
I'm used to many kinds of men,
And bore it very well; but, when
        It came to being twitted
On my historic Sporting Shirt,

I own I felt a trifle hurt;
   I took my leave and quitted.'

There is another side to this;
With no desire to prejudice
   The version of our leader,
I think I ought to drop a hint
Of what I shall be bound to print,
   In justice to the reader.
I followed, keeping out of sight;
And took in this ingenious way
A sketch that throws a certain light
On *why* the master went away.
No doubt he felt a trifle hurt,
It even may be true to say
They twitted him upon his shirt.
But isn't it a trifle thick
To talk of twitting with a stick?
Well, let it pass. He acted well
This species of official swell,
   Especially the peer,
Who stoops to a delimitation
With any European nation
   Is doomed to disappear.
Blood said, 'They pass into the night.'
And men like Blood are always right.

THE SECOND shows the full effect
Of ministerial neglect;
Sin, walking out alone in quest
Of Boa-constrictors that infest
   The Lagos Hinterland,
Got separated from the rest,
   And ran against a band
Of native soldiers led by three—
A Frenchman, an official Prussian,
And what we took to be a Russian—
   The very coalition
Who threaten England's power at sea,
And, but for men like Blood and me,
Would drive her navies from the sea,
   And hurl her to perdition.

But did my comrade think to flee?
To use his very words—Not he!
He turned with a contemptuous laugh.
Observe him in the photograph.[1]
But still these bureaucrats pursued,
Until they reached the Captain's tent.
They grew astonishingly rude;
The Russian simply insolent,
Announcing that he had been sent
    Upon a holy mission,
To call for the disarmament
    Of all our expedition.
He said 'the miseries of war
Had touched his master to the core';
    It was extremely vexing
To hear him add, 'he couldn't stand
This passion for absorbing land;
    He hoped we weren't annexing.'
The German asked with some brutality
To have our names and nationality.
    I had an inspiration,
In words methodical and slow
I gave him this decisive blow:
    'I haven't got a nation.'
Perhaps the dodge was rather low,
And yet I wasn't wrong to
Escape the consequences so;
For, on my soul, I did not know
What nation to belong to.

The German gave a searching look,
And marked me in his little book:
'The features are a trifle Dutch—
    Perhaps he is a Fenian;
He may be a Maltese, but much
    More probably Armenian.'

Blood gave us each a trifling sum
To say that he was deaf and dumb,
    And backed the affirmation
By gestures so extremely rum,
They marked him on the writing pad;

[1] [All illustrations omitted in this edition.]

'Not only deaf and dumb, but mad.'
    It saved the situation.
'If such as man as *that*' (said they)
'Is Leader, they can go their way.'

X

Thus, greatly to our ease of mind,
Our foreign foes we left behind;
But dangers even greater
Were menacing our path instead.
In every book I ever read
Of travels on the Equator,
A plague, mysterious and dread,
Imperils the narrator;
He always very nearly dies,
But doesn't, which is calm and wise.
Said Sin, the indolent and vague,
'D' you think that we shall get the plague?'
It followed tragically soon;
In fording an immense lagoon,
We let our feet get damp.
Next morning I began to sneeze,
The awful enemy, Disease,
Had fallen on the camp!
With Blood the malady would take,
An allotropic form
Of intermittent stomach ache,
While Sin grew over warm;
Complained of weakness in the knees,
An inability to think,
A strong desire to dose and drink,
    And lie upon his back.
For many a long delirious day,
Each in his individual way,
    Succumbed to the attack.

XI

Our litters lay upon the ground
With heavy curtains shaded round;
    The Plague had passed away.

We could not hear a single sound,
 And wondered as we lay—
'Perhaps the Forest Belt is passed,
And Timbuctoo is reached at last,
The while our faithful porters keep
So still to let their masters sleep.'

Poor Blood and I were far too weak
To raise ourselves, or even speak;
 We lay, content to languish.
When Sin, to make the matter certain,
Put out his head beyond the curtain.
 And cried in utter anguish:
'This is not Timbuctoo at all,
But just a native Kraal or Crawl;
And, what is more, our Caravan
Has all deserted to a man.'

. . . . .

At evening they returned to bring
Us prisoners to their savage king,
 Who seemed upon the whole
A man urbane and well inclined;
He said, 'You shall not be confined,
 But left upon parole.'
Blood, when he found us both alone,
Lectured in a pedantic tone,
 And yet with quaint perfection,
On 'Prison Systems I have known.'
 He said in this connection:

'The primal process is to lug
A Johnny to the cells—or jug.
Dear Henry will not think me rude,
If—just in passing—I allude
To Quod or Penal Servitude.
Of every form, Parole I take
To be the easiest to break.'

On hearing this we ran
To get the guns, and then we laid
An admirable ambuscade,
In which to catch our man.

We hid behind a little knoll,
    And waited for our prey
To take his usual morning stroll
    Along the fatal way.
All unsuspecting and alone
He came into the danger zone,
    The range of which we knew
To be one furlong and a third,
And then—an incident occurred
Which, I will pledge my sacred word,
    Is absolutely true.

Blood took a very careful aim,
And Sin and I did just the same;
Yet by some strange and potent charm
The King received no kind of harm!
    He wore, as it appears,
A little fetich on a thread,
A mumbo-jumbo, painted red,
Gross and repulsive in the head,
    Especially the ears.

Last year I should have laughed at it,
But now with reverence I admit
That nothing in the world is commoner
Than Andrew Lang's Occult Phenomena.

On getting back to England, I
Described the matter to the Psy-
    Chological Committee.

Of course they thanked me very much;
But said, 'We have a thousand such,
    And it would be a pity
To break our standing resolution,
And pay for any contribution.'

XII

The King was terribly put out;
To hear him call the guard and shout,
    And stamp, and curse, and rave

Was (as the Missionaries say)
A lesson in the Godless way
    The heathen will behave.
He sent us to a Prison, made
Of pointed stakes in palisade,
    And there for several hours
Our Leader was a mark for bricks,
And eggs and coconuts and sticks,
    And pussy-cats in showers.
Our former porters seemed to bear
A grudge against the millionaire.

And yet the thing I minded most
    Was not the ceaseless teasing
(With which the Captain was engrossed),
Nor being fastened to a post
    (Though that was far from pleasing);
But hearing them remark that they
'Looked forward to the following day.'

XIII

At length, when we were left alone,
Sin twisted with a hollow groan,
    And bade the Master save
His comrades by some bold device,
    From the impending grave.

Said Blood: 'I never take advice,
But every man has got his price;
We must maintain the open door,
Yes, even at the cost of war!'
    He shifted his position,
And drafted in a little while
A note in diplomatic style
    Containing a condition.

'If them that wishes to be told
As how there is a bag of gold,
    And where a party hid it;

Mayhap as other parties knows
A thing or two, and there be those
    As seen the man wot hid it.'
The Monarch read it through, and wrote
A little sentence most emphatical:
'I think the language of the note
Is strictly speaking not grammatical.'
On seeing our acute distress,
The King—I really must confess—
    Behaved uncommon handsome;
He said he would release the three
If only Captain Blood and he
    Could settle on a ransom.
And it would clear the situation
To hear his private valuation.

'My value,' William Blood began,
'Is ludicrously small.
I think I am the vilest man
That treads this earthly ball;
My head is weak, my heart is cold,
I 'm ugly, vicious, vulgar, old,
Unhealthy, short and fat.
I cannot speak, I cannot work,
I have the temper of a Turk,
    And cowardly at that.
Retaining, with your kind permission,
The usual five per cent. commission,
I think that I could do the job
For seventeen or sixteen bob.'

The King was irritated, frowned,
And cut him short with, 'Goodness Gracious!
Your economics *are* fallacious!
I quite believe you are a wretch,
But things are worth what they will fetch.
I 'll put your price at something round,
Say, six-and-thirty thousand pound?'
But just as Blood began with zest,
To bargain, argue, and protest,
    Commander Sin and I
Broke in: 'Your Majesty was told
About a certain bag of gold;

If you will let us try,
We'll find the treasure, for we know
    The place to half a yard or so.'

Poor William! The suspense and pain
Had touched the fibre of his brain;
    So far from showing gratitude,
He cried in his delirium: 'Oh!
For Heaven's sake don't let them go.'
    Only a lunatic would take
        So singular an attitude,
    When loyal comrades for his sake
    Had put their very lives at stake.

    .   .   .   .

The King was perfectly content
To let us find it;—and we went.
But as we left we heard him say,
    'If there is half an hour's delay
    The Captain will have passed away.'

XIV

Alas! within a single week
The Messengers despatched to seek
    Our hiding-place had found us,
We made an excellent defence
(I use the word in legal sense),
        But none the less they bound us.
        (Not in the legal sense at all
        But with a heavy chain and ball)
With barbarism past belief
They flaunted in our faces
The relics of our noble chief;
With insolent grimaces,
Raised the historic shirt before
Our eyes, and pointed on the floor
To dog-eared cards and loaded dice;
If seems they sold him by the slice.
Well, every man has got his price.

The horrors followed thick and fast,
I turned my head to give a last

Farewell to Sin; but, ah! too late,
I only saw his horrid fate—
Some savages around a pot
That seemed uncomfortably hot;
And in the centre of the group
My dear companion making soup.

Then I was pleased to recognize
Two thumbscrews suited to my size,
And I was very glad to see
That they were going to torture me.
I find the torture pays me best,
It simply teems with interest.

They hung me up above the floor
Head downwards by a rope;
They thrashed me half an hour or more,
They filled my mouth with soap;
They jobbed me with a pointed pole
To make me lose my self-control,
　　But they did not succeed.
Till (if it's not too coarse to state)
There happened what I simply hate,
　　My nose began to bleed.
Then, I admit, I said a word
Which luckily they never heard;
But in a very little while
My calm and my contemptuous smile
　　Compelled them to proceed.
They filed my canine teeth to points
　　And made me bite my tongue.
They racked me till they burst my joints,
　　And after that they hung
A stone upon my neck that weighed
At least a hundred pounds, and made
Me run like mad for twenty miles,
And climb a lot of lofty stiles.
They tried a dodge that rarely fails,
The tub of Regulus with nails—
The cask is rather rude and flat,
But native casks are all like that—
The nails stuck in for quite an inch,
But did I flinch? I did not flinch.

In tones determined, loud, and strong
I sang a patriotic song,
Thank Heaven it did not last for long!
    My misery was past;
My superhuman courage rose
Superior to my savage foes;
    They worshipped me at last.
With many heartfelt compliments,
They sent me back at their expense,
And here I am returned to find
The pleasures I had left behind.

To go the London rounds!
To note the quiet peculiar air
Of courtesy, and everywhere
The same unfailing public trust
In manuscript that fetches just
A thousand! not of thin Rupees,
Nor Reis (which are Portuguese),
Nor Rubles; but a thousand clear
Of heavy, round, impressive, dear,
Familiar English pounds!

Oh! England, who would leave thy shores—
Excuse me, but I see it bores
A busy journalist
To hear a rhapsody which he
Could write without detaining me,
So I will not insist.
Only permit me once again
    To make it clearly understood
That both those honourable men,
    Commander Sin and Captain Blood,
Would swear to all that I have said,
Were they alive;
    but they are dead!

MADE AT THE
TEMPLE PRESS
LETCHWORTH
IN
GREAT BRITAIN

EVERYMAN'S LIBRARY

A LIST OF THE 947 VOLUMES
ARRANGED UNDER AUTHORS

Anonymous works are given under titles.
Anthologies, Dictionaries, etc. are arranged at the end of the list.

NOTE—The following numbers are at present out of print:

89, 109, 110, 111, 146, 147, 228, 244, 275, 346–350, 376, 390, 418, 432, 480, 493, 540, 541, 574, 597, 641–52, 664, 679

LONDON: J. M. DENT & SONS LTD.
NEW YORK: E. P. DUTTON & CO. INC.